# The Cult of Dismembered Limbs

The Cult of Dismembered Limbs

# The Cult of Dismembered Limbs

## *Jewish Rites of Death at the Scene of Palestinian Suicide Terrorism*

GIDEON ARAN

*Translated by*
JEFFREY GREEN

OXFORD
UNIVERSITY PRESS

Oxford University Press is a department of the University of Oxford. It furthers
the University's objective of excellence in research, scholarship, and education
by publishing worldwide. Oxford is a registered trade mark of Oxford University
Press in the UK and certain other countries.

Published in the United States of America by Oxford University Press
198 Madison Avenue, New York, NY 10016, United States of America.



CIP data is on file at the Library of Congress
ISBN 978–0–19–768915–8 (pbk.)
ISBN 978–0–19–768914–1 (hbk.)

DOI: 10.1093/oso/9780197689141.001.0001

Paperback printed by Marquis Book Printing, Canada
Hardback printed by Bridgeport National Bindery, Inc., United States of America

# Contents

## PART II:  THEMES IN THE ANTHROPOLOGY AND SOCIOLOGY OF ZAKA

# Preface

## ZAKA in Brief

The icon of Middle Eastern suicide terrorism is a masked Palestinian youth brandishing an assault rifle in one hand and grasping the Koran in the other. Around his chest is an explosive vest, and in the background is the golden Dome of the Rock. Another icon of Middle Eastern suicide terrorism is parallel to the first and complements it: a Jew, displaying a yarmulka, long beard and earlocks, wearing white coveralls, rubber gloves, and a dayglo yellow vest. He bends over the remains of the dead in the aftermath of an explosion, surrounded by puddles of blood and shards of glass, in the still smoldering, twisted body of a bus. The former is the human bomb, born in the territories occupied by Israel, sent by Hamas, the Islamic Jihad, or Fatah, the subject of my earlier book.[1] The latter, a ZAKA volunteer, is the main protagonist of the present study. Suicide terrorism was central to my earlier book, and ZAKA served as a medium for understanding it. In the present book, the opposite is the case.

ZAKA is an Israeli religious organization dedicated to dealing with the mutilated and scorched bodies and the severed limbs of the victims of violent death, mainly those killed by Palestinian terrorism. ZAKA arose, reached its peak, and gained fame during the two waves of suicide terrorism that characterized the intensification of the Israeli-Palestinian conflict in the last decade of the twentieth century and the first five years of the twenty-first century. ZAKA has a few hundred all-male activists, typically volunteers, exclusively Haredi, that is ultra-Orthodox Jews. Well trained and equipped, they are the first to arrive at the sites of unnatural death, especially the arenas of mass mortality, joining the emergency and rescue teams, and there they perform a scrupulous procedure, laden with symbolism. This involves collecting the corpses and body parts, sorting them, identifying them, and reassembling them while diligently preserving respect for the dead and for body parts, and preparing them for burial according to the strictures of Jewish law. In recent years ZAKA has become institutionalized and obtained a monopoly on many aspects of the treatment of extraordinary fatality in general.

Between 1989 and 2006 the Palestinian organizations of armed resistance committed thousands of murderous terrorist acts in Israel, including about two hundred suicide attacks, most of them during the second Intifada (2000–2005), claiming 734 victims (not including the terrorists themselves).[2] All the victims were dealt with by the death specialists of ZAKA. The following work is an ethnographical study of the cult that the pious volunteers maintained in the arena of violent death, a description and analysis of the roots of this cult, its meaning, and its consequences.

## Subject Matter

Researching ZAKA is highly relevant to research on suicide terrorism. There is a lacuna in the scientific literature on suicide terrorism, which, with the study of ZAKA, we attempt to fill. Present studies revolve either around the background and causes of this type of terrorism (e.g., the motivation of the perpetrator and the ideology of the organization) or on its results and implications (e.g., its success in changing the adversary's policy). Discussion of the terrorist event itself is conspicuously absent. Moreover, the literature deals with either the attacker or the victim, each separately, and barely says anything about the connection between them, about the place and time when they meet. In other words: description and analysis of the arena of the explosion is lacking. ZAKA is almost synonymous with this arena. Hence it is an indispensable vehicle by means of which the researcher can come as close as possible to the arena of terrorism. ZAKA is not just a witness and commentator on the scene of terrorist attacks, it is also a vital protagonist in it. ZAKA is an integral part of the arena of terrorism, a resourceful agent with an essential input on the nature of the arena. ZAKA does not merely respond to terrorist attacks. Together with the suicide bomber it sacralizes them.

The horrifying arena of terrorism has stood as the focus of my academic interests in the past years. In my earlier book I examined closely the very last moments before the explosion. In the present book I examine the very first minutes immediately *after* the explosion.

Interesting in its own right, ZAKA is at the same time a useful methodological vehicle and a creative heuristic medium for enriching discussion of several other phenomena in addition to terrorism: first, death in general and violent death in particular; second, religion, Judaism, and contemporary radical Jewish religiosity. Moreover, research into ZAKA offers a reservoir of unexpected insights into the human body, the Middle Eastern conflict, armed Palestinian resistance, Israeli society, and the Haredi community.

## Readership

This is an ethnography of a singular group of people in an extreme condition, a phenomenon whose various aspects touch upon many facets of life, and several fields of expertise are germane to its study. Accordingly, the chapters of the book treat several thematic focuses that are connected naturally and partially overlap. The book thus addresses potential readers whose curiosity is aroused by odd phenomena in their human surroundings, but it is especially intended for eight specific audiences:

Readers interested in terrorism, especially suicide terrorism. Ordinarily this topic is discussed from the viewpoint of political science and international and strategic studies. Here, for a change, the discussion is from the social and cultural perspective and sheds light on aspects of the phenomenon that are neglected in the literature.

Readers interested in the sociology and anthropology of death. In this book emphasis is placed on the management of unnatural and violent death. The chapters dealing with mortuary ritualism are written in the intellectual tradition of the fathers of the ethnography of death, James Frazer and Robert Hertz.

Readers interested in the human body, especially the religious and ethno-national body. We discuss the symbolic dimensions and behavioral implications of blood, flesh, limbs, wounds, mutilation, and sexuality.

Readers interested in religion, religious militancy, religious eccentricity, religious schisms, religious innovation, and fundamental manifestations of religious belief and ritual, life, sacrifice, and redemption. The adaptation of traditional forms of religious devotion to circumstances of advanced modernity is examined.

Readers interested in the Jewish heritage and Jewish history, and the transformations undergone by traditional Judaism in our times, especially the response of religious Judaism to the violent intercommunal clash.

Readers interested in the undercurrent dynamics of the Middle Eastern conflict, including the ethos of Palestinian movements of armed resistance.

Readers interested in Israeli society, relations within it between religion and Zionism and religion and the state, against the background of idiosyncratic initiatives for coping with crises in local and regional politics.

Finally, readers interested in Haredi society, especially recent trends and paradoxical development of ultra-Orthodoxy in response to the challenges of democracy, civil society, affluence, advanced technology, and threats to security.

The order in which the foregoing themes were listed does not reflect their relative importance or centrality in the discussion, nor are they treated separately in the book, but related to each other and largely intermingled. Other topics are also treated, such as savagery, practical uses of the Talmud and Kabbalah, vengeance, invention of tradition, black humor, boundaries and taboo violation, morbidity and sanctity, Hasidism, victimhood, current reverberations of ancient myths, masculinity, and action seeking.

The research underlying the present book required me to read extensively in the literature about the body and death, two subjects with which I was only partially acquainted. I will mention just two of these sources, which inspired me by their imaginative research, although they deal with the body and death in historical and cultural contexts quite different and alien from those of ZAKA, and they employ methodological and conceptual tools different from my own. The first of these books is *Death in Banaras*, by Jonathan Parry.[3] I followed his example in the effort to examine the practices of deathwork in our time in the light of motives inherited from primeval lore. In the case he researched, as in the case studied here, a local type of shaman turns a bad death into a good one by manipulating corpses. The second book is *This Republic of Suffering: Death and the American Civil War*, by Drew Gilpin Faust.[4] This work discusses the consequences of the dominant presence of violent death for nation building. I took particular interest in the role played by the procedures for locating bodies and body parts and their collection and identification, during and immediately after the war, in changing norms and establishing social institutions in the United States. I found that aspects of death in the violent conflict between the North and the South were analogous to aspects of death in Middle Eastern terrorism. For example, the dread of believers—both pious Christians and pious Jews—lest, on the day of judgment, dead people whose bodies were mutilated could not rise to new life. This reading convinced me that maimed bodies and disfigurement inflicted by violent acts could be a meaningful and engrossing subject. Both books taught me that unidentifiable severed limbs have long haunted civilization, and that writing about them is a proper and intriguing subject of research.

## The Structure of the Book

In lieu of an introduction, Chapter 1 offers a thick description of the arena of Palestinian suicide terrorism in Israel, emphasizing the operations of the ZAKA volunteers. The point of view alternates between that of the social scientist closely observing, but still from the outside, and that of the actors themselves, from within.

The following chapters of the book are arranged in two parts. Part I (Chapters 2 to 5) provides basic information about ZAKA: the background of the organization's appearance, the circumstances of its development, its religious and political surroundings, its goals and worldview, its subculture, and the profile of its members. This part is mainly ethnographic. Part II (Chapters 6 to 9) is mainly analytic. It covers selected aspects of the organization in different theoretical contexts, mainly those connected with death, body, religion, and Judaism.

Chapter 2 surveys the history of ZAKA and the structure and dynamics of the organization, while Chapter 3 acquaints the reader with the distinctive lifestyle of ZAKA, along with the typical personality and biography of its volunteers. Chapter 4 relates to ZAKA in the context of ultra-Orthodox Judaism and situates it in the context of Israeli society. The first half of the chapter discusses the status of the organization in the Haredi community, and the connections between its members and Haredim who do not belong to it. The second half of the chapter discusses the reciprocal relations between the organization and secular modern Jews, as well as the role it plays in relation to the institutions of the nation-state. Chapter 5 closes the first part by discussing ZAKA's religious Jewish canopy, the doctrine and rabbinical norms that guide the ritual behavior of the organization in the arena of terrorism, and the old-new theology that infuses the organization.

Chapter 6 opens the second part by considering the curious linkage between the ZAKA volunteer and the suicide terrorist and the place they each occupy in the other's imagination. Chapter 7 analyzes ZAKA's goal as mastery of Jewish devotion, bringing almost to absurdity the dialectical tension between stringent obedience and conservative defense of boundaries of the religion and deviation that expands those boundaries and smacks of transgression. Chapter 8 concentrates on lessons gained from research on the dead body and their application to the case of ZAKA in the arena of terrorism. A theoretical model is offered as the basis for developing of further insight, and several hypotheses are proposed both about the body and about death. Chapter 9 analyzes ZAKA as an active protagonist in the campaign against suicide terrorism. Thus, it sheds light on unfamiliar aspects of this violent phenomenon which casts a shadow on the entire world.

The epilogue is a mini–case study that stands on its own, viewing the horror of the holy work of ZAKA in the arena of the explosion from an anthropological perspective.

## Strategy and Research Methods

This book is based on a field study, mainly as a participant observer. In the later stages of the Intifada and slightly after it, in 2003–2007, I had a few opportunities to be present and active along with the ZAKA volunteers in the arenas of violent death, including instances of the horrific killing of Israeli citizens by Palestinian terrorists.

I forged relations of mutual trust with key figures in the organization. These, along with goodwill on the part of security agents and stratagems of my own, enabled me to enter the arena in the immediate aftermath of the lethal event, though I was taking a risk and breaking the law. ZAKA informants connected me to their emergency call network, and on occasion I was called from home to events that they knew would interest me. Sometimes I joined them in the frantic drive to the arena in their emergency vehicle, and sometimes I arrived there by my own means. They introduced me as one of their own in the arena. Once they shoved a roll of absorbent paper and plastic bags in my hands to get me past the police barrier and overcome suspicion, since my appearance betrays my obviously non-Haredi identity. Amid the feverish activity of the various rescue teams and ZAKA, I found opportunities to register my impressions, while struggling to cope with feelings of confusion, fear, sorrow, as well as revulsion that struck me. Now and then I offered or was asked to lend a hand to the volunteers in some technical capacity.

I also spent time with the ZAKA volunteers outside the arena: I observed a whole range of non-sensational activities of the organization, as well as routines of the members' private life. I spent long days in the ZAKA headquarters; I took part with them in briefings and professional training courses; in prayers and Torah lessons; and I danced and sang with them on their holidays. I was also invited to meals in their homes, to the wedding and barmitzvah celebrations of their relatives; I went shopping with them, I met their friends, I roamed through the alleys of their neighborhoods. I visited them in the places where they worked for a living and played games with their children.

At the sites of my research, I introduced myself straightaway as having the intention of writing a book about ZAKA. Most of the volunteers did not bother to try to understand what scientific research was, and every so often I got the feeling that they disparaged my project. However, they almost always cooperated with me, cordially accepting me among them.

Naturally access to the arena is restricted while it is still teeming with emergency activity. Observation of a catastrophic event entails obvious difficulties. My field notebooks contain only two cases of violent death in which I participated in dealing with the mutilated bodies of the victims from the beginning to the end, and was able to document the process closely and fully. I compensated for deficit in unmediated experience by reconstructing the arena with the assistance of briefings of witnesses and experts. To re-create the scene of horror I also conducted indirect observation by means of inspecting a rich collection of rare photographs documenting the immediate aftermath of the explosion. First, I viewed sixty-seven unedited, close-up video clips shot by ZAKA aides at the arena in real time, which I was clandestinely enabled to copy. Second, a famous newspaper photographer generously shared with me an uncensored reservoir of raw material that had piled up on the desk: dozens of still photographs before any were selected for publication.[5] These were pictures that he took at a half-dozen arenas of suicide terrorism in Tel Aviv and its surroundings. To take these pictures he intercepted messages about terrorist attacks on the police network and, frantically speeding on his motorcycle, was among the first to arrive after the explosion. With courage and fine lenses, he captured immediate images of the suicide bomber's target: the bus, the café, or the market. Third, several ZAKA volunteers allowed me to look briefly at the pictures they had surreptitiously taken while treating the victims and stored on their cell phones. By means of the pictures of the arena from these three sources, I could virtually touch the bodies of the victims of the attacks while they were still warm, so to speak.

For researching ZAKA I also made content analysis of hundreds of official and personal documents, some of them exclusive. These included the biweekly internal newsletter of the organization; public relations pamphlets; technical, spiritual, and halakhic instruction manuals; the rulings of the ZAKA rabbis; minutes of meetings of the leadership; all the items kept in the organization's offices, including correspondence with institutions and personages in the government and the community; the private archive of the founder of ZAKA and its first chairman; portions of the personal diaries and letters of the volunteers and their families; recordings of a psychotherapy session following a traumatic event; and, in addition to all these, newspaper reports and documentary films about ZAKA.[6]

To complement my observations, I held two series of in-depth interviews, both in parallel to my fieldwork during the Intifada and about ten years later. I interviewed six men whom I identified as key figures in ZAKA. Each of them devoted long hours to the interview, entire nights, and more nights, over coffee or during various activities at the arenas. An intermittent dialogue extending over several years developed with all of them. In addition, I held another fourteen interviews with a representative sample of titleholders, functionaries and rank-and-file ZAKA volunteers, old hands and initiates, members of different religious and ethnic groups, living in various places in Israel, with different levels of education and professions. My connection with some of them lasted throughout the research period and continues to this day. I also met a broad gallery of people who have professional or personal relations with ZAKA volunteers for shorter, focused interviews. Some of these subjects were partners or witnesses to the activity in the arena. Among them were the wives and neighbors of the volunteers, members of their communities—both sympathetic and critical—police officers, ISA agents, psychologists, physicians, forensic experts, undertakers, rabbis, journalists, local politicians and officials, men who had resigned from the organization, survivors of terrorist attacks, and a limited number of Palestinians related to the organizations of resistance to Israeli occupation.

Except for one important activist, they all accepted my request for interviews and found in them opportunities to glorify the organization and themselves, to gain public legitimation, and to free themselves from psychological burdens. The interviews apparently had therapeutic value for them. Perhaps they had an exhibitionist dimension. In some of the advanced interviews with volunteers whom I discerned as being reflective, I presented specific hypotheses that I wanted to test and shared my tentative conclusions with them. I also let two of the subjects read the drafts of certain relevant subchapters from my research. Their responses were valuable.

Two of my informants became close companions. Moreover, by virtue of their sophistication and introspection, and also perhaps because of their cynicism, which was partially connected to their somewhat problematic image in the community (e.g., one of them was divorced, God forbid, and another one's wife refused to submit to the severe dress code of the religious group), they gave me confidential data as well as intelligent insights.

In several places in the book I obscured a person's identity or blurred the description of an incident to avoid embarrassing the subjects, to defend them against the law, or against damage to their status in the community. Furthermore, as in any unbiased ethnographic study, in this one as well it is sometimes possible to find discrepancy among the various accounts. After all, social and psychological reality is laden with inner tension and contradictions. No version is more correct than any other, and both are real to the same degree. I tried to avoid creating the false impression that my subjects inhabit a seamlessly systematic experiential and exegetic universe by ironing out variety and inconsistency.[7]

In isolated instances, I presented certain anecdotes although I was unable to authenticate them definitively. Even though they seemed somewhat improbable, and even if there were those who claimed they were untrue, I felt that when similar variants of the same story appeared again and again in a variety of testimonies, over time, it indicates the existence of a significant element of psycho-social reality, sometimes only potential or unacknowledged. In other words, when a story flourishes in the heart of a folklore, it is because in one way or another it expresses an aspect of the "spirit of the group."[8] Here is an example: while ZAKA volunteers were dealing with the carnage in the aftermath of a suicide attack that claimed many victims, they came upon the body of a Jew from which a limb had been severed, and they could not find it.[9] In order to bury the body whole, they used the corpse of the suicide terrorist as a reservoir of available limbs and "borrowed" the missing limb. The majority among the interviewees swore that the story narrates historical fact. However a few others insisted that the story was apocryphal. Did it happen or not? In my fieldwork I encountered other instances, no less far-fetched, and no less shocking.

### Personal Note: Ethics and Aesthetics

Horror—in plain English, an intense feeling of fear, shock and disgust, or circumstances that produce such extremely unpleasant and disagreeable feelings—is intrinsically associated with injury to the body and death. The arena of suicide bombing, which lies at the focus of this book, is the epitome of horror. Consequently, the following pages contain dreadful descriptions.

Indeed, the masterpieces of world literature are replete with gruesome and macabre scenes, full of blood, mutilated bodies, and severed limbs. From the Bible through Shakespeare to contemporary American fiction, there are lines that could be used for a reliable and accurate presentation of the brutal and ghastly arena after the explosion during the Intifada.

Scholarly discussion of horror raises questions of ethics and aesthetics that might be used to challenge this book. My study will most probably arouse familiar arguments that relate to the methodical, scientific treatment of the violence of broken bones and spilled guts. The very focusing on the arena that allegedly betrays fascination with brutal death might be seen as disgusting morbidity, moral relativism, and kitsch.[10] Much has been written about the erotic attraction of horror, which is beyond good and evil. Horror enchants those who commit it and sometimes even its victims and those who observe it—perhaps those who study it as well.

This book shows that both parties to the Middle Eastern conflict—the Palestinian organizations of suicide terrorism, on one hand, and ZAKA volunteers, on the other—are captivated by the horror wrought by the Intifada. What about me, the one who closely observed the arena and compulsively wrote about it? My colleagues have commented to me about the pathological—or immoral—dimension of my breathless response to what can be defined as the heart of darkness. However, I feel that investigating the human bomb and those who deal with his body and the bodies of his victims is in fact an effort to free myself from the grip of horror. This book can be read as a disenchantment project. The ethnography of the cult of dismembered limbs implies exorcism.

Closeness to ZAKA and, through it, to the consequences of suicide terrorism, fascinated me. Repeated visits to the arena of violent death were a way to cope with the horror, perhaps an expression of primal fears or hidden desires. They apparently brought me back to traumas that lacerate my own life story. As the child of a large family that perished in the Holocaust, who lost his father at the age of two, as a combatant and officer who took part in cruel battles during three wars, my imagination explodes with a multitude of horrific sights. Moreover, I was raised in a national culture that revolves around the axis of victimhood, the inheritance of collective traumas, replete with horror. Graphic descriptions of violent death in endless series of destructions, pogroms, and genocides fill Jewish-Israeli history, mythology, and literature. The descriptions of the bodies and body parts in my book can also be read as a lament.

The terrorism of the Intifada brought the trauma of horror back to almost every home in Israel. The shock, dread, and grief in response to the suicide attacks did not spare me. The tragic death of Anna, a kind and beautiful woman, a close friend of our family's, in the explosion of number 14 bus in Jerusalem (sixteen dead, June 2003) evidently triggered my academic interest in the arena. In my effort to re-create the event in which she perished, ZAKA activists reported to me how her burned body had looked when they removed it from the scraps of the smashed bus. The connection between me and the Haredi volunteers has lasted for almost twenty years since then.

Because I lived and worked in Jerusalem during the Intifada, the presence of horror became palpable and constant for me. The terrible consequences of Palestinian terrorism touched me personally on several other heartbreaking occasions. Acquaintances, neighbors, friends, and their children were among the victims. Twenty-two people were killed in four explosions on the buses that serve my university, and an explosion took place in the campus cafeteria, where I used to eat lunch every day, killing nine colleagues and students. A former doctoral student of mine was killed in an attack in Tel-Aviv. My elderly mother, a Holocaust survivor, happened to be at the eye of the storm of an arena, where just a few inches separated her from certain death. I rushed to the site of the attack to calm her down while ZAKA volunteers were treating the bodies of the terrorist and his victims nearby.

In addition to the intellectual challenge posed by fieldwork in the arena of suicide terrorism, it was no simple matter emotionally, even viscerally—literally in the sense of the stomach's ability to digest horrifying impressions. With great caution, I have tried to spare the reader. In particular, I had to avoid the trap of the pornography of death and the vulgar treatment of pain and misery. I also had to avoid trivializing death or taking an excessively desensitized, mechanical attitude toward human tragedy. Determined clinging to professional codes was insufficient. Spiritual strength was needed. Sometimes the arena inspired ironic chuckles and a detached philosophical perspective. A bit of humor also did no harm, though this might sound incongruous in connection with sites where a cult of dismembered limbs is celebrated.

In 2005 I participated-observed a ZAKA squad tending to the body of a Jewish victim of a brutal Palestinian attack. After the security personnel left the arena, past midnight, the six of us were alone in the desert, in the dark, squatting over a disfigured body with flashlights. The Haredi volunteer who led the operation suddenly put his hand to my ear and, with a broad smile, produced a ten Shekel coin. No doubt this amateur sleight of hand was a way for him to defuse the tension we felt. It was also an exegetical statement about the status of this surreal situation. The deliberate, utter mutilation of the body left even the experienced ZAKA personnel in a state of disbelief. I could not but join the pious rabbi-cum-magician with a burst of laughter.[11]

## Postscript

Shortly after submitting the manuscript to the publisher, an official announcement was issued by the Israel government, stating that Yehuda Meshi-Zahav, the dominant figure in ZAKA, who represented it to the outside world, had been chosen to receive the prestigious Israel Prize for lifetime achievement, connected with the "holy work" of treating the victims of terrorism and other cases of unnatural death. Ten days later, the Israeli media featured convincing reports that Meshi had committed sexual crimes for many years, including rape and pedophilia.

Would it be conceivable to present this book to readers without relating to this sensational news? In order to arrive at a defensible decision, I returned to the field for several observations and interviews. I found that, aside from a few changes in personnel and minimal damage to the organization's public image, nothing had changed in the principles, sentiments, or activities of ZAKA.

I also listened to the internal discourse of central ZAKA activists immediately after the exposure of Meshi's appalling behavior. After recovering from the initial shock, they made two claims. First, Meshi was only one person, though an especially important one, and he was not indicative. Counterbalancing him were hundreds of volunteers, who were, they said, absolutely saintly, and they determined the purity of the organization. Second, even if Meshi had done terrible things, the activists believed that they couldn't obscure his marvelous deeds or diminish his achievements for the benefit of the Jewish people and the Torah. Even if he is proven to be a sinner, they argued, we may not dismiss his other side, his righteousness.

Another issue is whether the ZAKA volunteers knew about Meshi's misdeeds without doing anything about them. Most likely the majority, especially the rank and file from the periphery of the organization, heard nothing aside from vague rumors that Meshi was a "wild man," an image that he himself cultivated, which gave him a certain charm among members. A very few members of the innermost circles were partially aware of Meshi's compulsive attraction to sex, but they didn't imagine that his behavior was criminal and apparently pathological. They acknowledged that he broke boundaries and connected that trait with his ingenuity and success as a founder and head of the organization, while they were blind to indications of his tendency to break ethical boundaries as well.

When I was exposed to the allegations about Meshi, I was stunned, though I must confess that, in a troubling way, I could not dismiss them as inconceivable. While I had not had the slightest inkling of his shameful deeds, since I had gained the impression that this man stood out in his unconventionality, perhaps I ought to have considered the possibility that he was also liable to flout conventions in sexual behavior. Furthermore, throughout the book I presented ZAKA as a religious phenomenon characterized by violating taboos, particularly the taboo of direct contact with horrible death. Would it not have been plausible to expect that someone who violated taboos connected with bodies and body parts would also violate the taboos that relate to sexual misconduct?

Comments dispersed throughout the book refer to what might connect people who are pursued by demons that appear in horrific arenas of mutilated bodies with those who pursue the satisfaction of vile bodily impulses. Another insight into the morbid connection between the obsession with death and the obsession with sex is implied in the testimony of a formerly Haredi woman who accused Meshi. She claimed that when Meshi began to strip her against her will she cried and told him she was menstruating, thinking that would deter him from having his way. But he answered, "I'm used to blood."

The accusations against Meshi posed a challenge to me. Armed with hindsight, I had an opportunity to revise and resubmit the book. I reread the finished text in view of what had subsequently been made known to me about Meshi, looking for passages, lines, or expressions that contradicted what I now know. I wondered whether I would find something that would make the material that had just come to light sound improbable or impossible. I was relieved to find that the written material could explain what had not been known when I wrote it. I leave it to the reader to judge.

*

While proofreading this postscript, I received an urgent call from one of my informants. He forwarded a WhatsApp message from the ZAKA network, reporting that, just a few minutes earlier, Meshi had hanged himself.

# Acknowledgments

First, I wish to thank ZAKA ultra-Orthodox activists and those related to them. Without them, this study could not have been completed. They generously provided vital data and thoughtful insights. They hosted me among them, conversed with me at length, provided documents, and shared observations. They corroborated, corrected, or refuted information, and suggested their opinion about the conjectures I raised before them, not always agreeing with my conclusions. Many of them preferred to remain anonymous. The following is an (alphabetically ordered) list of those who let me mention their names: Adawey Shlomo, Bernstein Isaac, Brand Eliyahu, Dvir Hayim, Foxman Hayim, Gelbstein Eliezer, Meshi-Zahav Yehuda, Nebenzal Avigdor, Nissan Itay, Noygelblat Hayim, Roje Yaacob, Saviner Gedaliah, Scheinin Gedaliah, Tirenoeier Elimelech, Weingarten Hayim, Weissenstern David, Zilberschlag Ozer.

I also wish to thank many others who invested time and effort in my study. These are civil servants, public figures, journalists, and relevant professionals, like psychologists, forensic specialists, paramedics, firemen, police and army officers, ISA agents, Palestinians associated with the resistance organizations, and finally casually met Jerusalemite passersby. I decided to keep their identity undisclosed for clear reasons that involve their status and honor, and sometimes their safety.

Along the various phases of my study, I immensely benefited from the critical remarks and constructive advice of my peers and teachers in the academy: Larry Abramson, Avri Bar-Levav, Ronny Berger, Yoram Bilu, Benny Brown, Kimi Caplan, Zohar Gazit, Harvey Goldberg, Yehuda Goodman, Yuti Gurevitch, Ron Hassner, Mark Juergensmeyer, Tzipi Kahana, Adam Klin-Oron, Ziv Koren, Yehuda Liebes, Ely Lipstein, Raya Morag, Danny Schwartz, Nurit Stadler, Rina Talgam, Yitzahk Weiss, Israel Yuval, and two anonymous reviewers of the manuscript.

I would like to express my appreciation and gratitude in particular to Zali Gurevitch, a wise colleague and very dear friend, and to Bentzi Oeiring and Dano Monkatovitch, authentic subjects and reliable informers who became *de facto* research assistants without ignoring their "native" commitments.

Special credit goes to Jeff Green for translating major sections of the text with much competence, erudition, and human concern.

I am indebted also to Israel Science Foundation (ISF) for its trust and support of early stages of my fieldwork.

Finally I am thankful also to my editors Cynthia Read, Theodore Calderara, and Egle Zigaiteat Oxford University Press for their sympathetic and professional cooperation.

The book is dedicated to *N* my love.

# Glossary

**Fatah**  Founded as the Palestinian National Liberation Movement. Political party (the largest and leading faction of the Palestinian Liberation Organization, or PLO) and armed resistance movement.

**Green Line**  Internationally recognized border between Israel and its neighboring Arab countries (1948/9–1967); border between Israel and the Palestinian Authority and the territories occupied in the Six Days War.

**Halakha**  Corpus of Jewish religious laws derived from the scriptural (biblical) Torah and the oral Torah (Talmudic and later rabbinic ruling). Set of commandments (Mitzvot) binding Orthodox religious Jews. Compiles hundreds of rabbinic books concerning ritual norms and customs.

**Hamas**  Palestinian Islamist (Sunni) radical resistance organization ruling the Gaza Strip and active in the West Bank.

**Haredi (pl. Haredim)**  Ultra-Orthodox Jews. The extreme element of the Jewish religious sector centered in Israel (organically related to other Haredi communities, mainly in the United States, where they are mistakenly called Hasidic Jews). While formally citizens of Israel and practically taking part in its political and economic life, they reject Zionism in principle, oppose the secular state's values, criticize the dominant culture and the majority's norms of behavior, and avoid social contact with other Israelis. In recent years traditional Haredi solidarity with the Jewish people has developed into qualified collaboration with Israeli civil society and takes the form of chauvinistic nationalism.

**Hesed Shel Emet (HSE)**  Lit. in Hebrew, Virtue of True Benevolence, or Genuine Grace. Subtitle of ZAKA.

**Human bomb**  Interchangeable with "suicide terrorist."

**IDF (ZaHaL)**  Israeli Defense Forces; the Israeli military.

**Intifada**  Comes from the Arabic term meaning "to shake off, get rid of," referring to a Palestinian uprising against Israeli occupation. The first Intifada (1987–1993) was a popular aggressive but not predominantly lethal resistance to Israeli military rule of the Territories (West Bank and Gaza). The second (Al-Aqsa) Intifada (2000–2005) was an intensified armed resistance involving massive terrorist measures.

**ISA (ShaBaK)**  Israel's Internal Security Agency (equivalent of the American FBI).

**Jewish ultra-Orthodoxy**  Haredim. See: Orthodoxy.

**Kabbalah** Traditional Jewish mysticism. Esoteric theosophical thought and magical practice, originating in early medieval times. Rabbinic schools of interpretations of the mysterious dimension of the Torah attempting to know the secrets of Godhead and to experience unity with the Divine.

**Kippah (yarmulka)** Jewish head cap; traditional and modern religious wear.

**MaDA (acronym for Magen David Adom)** Emergency Medical Aid (the Israeli equivalent of the Red Cross).

**Orthodoxy (Jewish)** Rabbinic Judaism. A denomination in the Jewish religion that claims to be the direct and principal heir of traditional Judaism. The main defining criterion of Orthodoxy is punctilious observance of Jewish law, for example, observance of the Sabbath, *kashrut*. Divided into neo-Orthodoxy, which adapts to modernity, and ultra-Orthodoxy, which opposes modernity and is more radical in belief and practice, and more stringent in the observance of the commandments (e.g., separation of men and women). Ultra-Orthodoxy is characterized by asceticism, rejection of the secular, liberal, and materialist surroundings, and self-segregation in enclaves subject to effective social control.

**PIJ** Palestinian Islamic Jihad. The most extreme paramilitary splinter organization, based in the Gaza Strip, competing with Hamas in militant opposition to Israel. Maintains relationship with Shiite Iran.

**Rabbi** Jewish traditional religious authority. Qualified by higher studies of the Torah and ordained by rabbis of superior status, to become spiritual leader of the Jewish community, ruling halakhic decisions for his disciples regarding ritual norms, and teacher in the Yeshiva. A learned holy man, a respectable sage, expert in the sacred texts, particularly the Talmud.

**Shahid** Islamic martyr ("witness" in Arabic). Traditional term used by religious Muslims to describe those who sacrificed their life heroically and were killed by the enemies of Islam or for guarding Islamic values and promoting Islamic honor.

**Suicide terrorist** Human bomb.

**Talmud** The central text of the oral Torah, next to the Hebrew Bible (written Torah) in import for religious Jews. Primary authoritative source of Jewish law (= halakha) and Jewish theology. Contains the teachings of thousands of ancient and early medieval rabbis on a variety of topics: ethics, folklore, history, and mainly ritual binding norms.

**Torah** Broadly speaking it refers to the entire body of Jewish sacred texts, or traditional Jewish wisdom. Specifically, the Hebrew Bible, or just its first five books (the Pentateuch). The substance of the Divine revelation to the ancient Jewish people, and God's gospel for humankind. Central and most important sacred document of religious Jews. Written Torah is the twenty-four books of the Hebrew Bible, while the oral Torah is mainly the Mishna and Talmud.

**West Bank (of the Jordan River)**  The mountainous part of the historical (biblical) Land of Israel/British Mandatory Palestine. The territories bordering with Israel to the east and occupied by the IDF since 1967, populated by 2.5 million Palestinians and about 400,000 Jewish settlers. Consists of Judea and Samaria.

**Yeshiva (pl. yeshivot)**  Torah academy. Learning institution of religious studies for young Jewish men.

# 1
# Hell

## The Arena of Suicide Terrorism from a Zero Range

### A Still Small Voice

The dreadful terrorism event opens, as expected, with a ball of fire and a boom. But, contrary to expectations, the explosion is heard mainly by those distant from the site. The people who were at the scene itself usually do not hear it. To be precise, they do not remember it and do not report it, perhaps because most of them have had their eardrums torn and are deafened, at least temporarily, or because they are in trauma. According to the accounts of those close to the heart of the arena, the first, most powerful impression of the attack is silence. An eerie, petrifying silence falls on the scene of suicide terrorism. The injured, rescue workers, and bystanders confirm this impression, emphasizing and repeating it frequently.

It is difficult to estimate how long this uncanny silence lasts. It might persist only a few seconds, a minute or two, but it is experienced as prolonged. This silence is conspicuous, because it fills the gap between two huge noises—the explosion and especially the commotion that characterizes the arena after people recover from the initial shock and begin to deal with the results of the attack. The silence is broken all at once. In a moment the scene becomes one of high-volume cacophony: the wounded screaming in pain, the stunned shouting of eyewitnesses, the wailing of ambulance sirens, policemen giving orders and rescue teams passing on reports, the buzzing of two-way radios, the ringing of telephones and announcements over megaphones, shouts for revenge among the agitated crowd that quickly gathers from all over the city.

The silence after the explosion is not described as a void, the absence of noise, but as having a strong, palpable presence in itself. The silence is heard, it echoes, and it rings in the ears. Some ZAKA volunteers compare it to the still small voice (gentle whisper) in which God revealed himself to Elijah, reciting the biblical passage by heart (1 Kings 19:11–14). Thus, for true believers, the terrorism event begins in a moment of epiphany.

*The Cult of Dismembered Limbs*. Gideon Aran, Oxford University Press. © Oxford University Press 2023.
DOI: 10.1093/oso/9780197689141.003.0001

With the explosion, the world becomes voiceless, and motionless too. Everything is silent and frozen. Even the dust hangs in the air. Also, because of the first dazzling flash, one cannot see anything. The attack on all the senses paralyzes them. The next thing that is experienced, that develops and takes over the scene, is the smell. Many of those who have been there label it a stench. There is a welter of powerful odors: the smell of explosives, the smell of charred rubber and plastic, the smell of oil and burned bodily fluids, the smell of blood, and, most dominant, the smell of scorched human flesh. While the silence soon disappears, the smell remains for a long time. For the majority of the volunteers, the smell leaves a powerful impression of the attack, which does not let up even after they have left the scene.

Back home after leaving the arena ZAKA activists try hard, first, to get rid of the smell, but to no avail. They claim that the smell clings to them and penetrates beneath their skin. They throw their clothing into the garbage and shower again and again, and the smell still stays in their nostrils—the attack pursues them for many weeks. A ZAKA volunteer told me it seemed to him during the days after an attack that his children were repelled by him because of the smell. A colleague of his related that after the first attack he was involved in, he changed his clothes, but even the clean, fresh clothes he removed from the closet gave off the smells of the arena. Another volunteer testified that, when he heard the beeper summoning him to an arena, even before entering his car on the way to the distant scene of the attack, that cursed smell already filled his nostrils. Several ZAKA men claim that the horrible smell has accompanied them wherever they go, for years, since the start of the Intifada. The mass casualty event has a sharp starting point, but its end rolls on. Survivors, emergency crews, and death specialists say that it has no end at all.[1]

Several seconds pass, maybe a minute or two, before eyes open and the dust settles. Now the horrific sight is revealed. This is the stage when the rescue teams arrive at the arena of the explosion. Usually ZAKA volunteers are among the first to arrive. They listen to the emergency networks of the police and MaDA; they live, work, and study in yeshivas near downtown and close to the business centers and markets that are targeted for terrorist attacks. The motor scooters they ride on, their permission to sound the sirens on their vehicles, and their tendency to speed through the city streets in violation of traffic regulations also enable them to achieve the high level of alertness that they ordinarily maintain. Afterward they speak a lot about where they were and what they were doing when the beeper buzzed, telling them about the terrorist attack. They always seem to have been praying, at a wedding, or doing some act of charity. In some cases, they were summoned to one attack while they were still dealing with another one. Once they were summoned to an arena while they were in the midst of a banquet for the anniversary of the death of the prophet Moses, which I attended.

When the enthusiastic ZAKA activists arrive at the arena, they are disappointed if they discover that several of their colleagues got there first. Very quickly too many Haredi volunteers have gathered. They find it hard to restrain the urge to plunge into the center right away. They are all moved, eager "to merit the performance of an important commandment."

The first to enter the arena of the terrorist attack are the sappers, who make sure no explosive charges have been left behind and are liable to explode, then follow the paramedics, who try to save the lives of the wounded, firemen who locate blazes and remove debris, ISA agents and crime scene detectives who investigate details about the terrorists in an effort to apprehend their dispatchers and prevent further terrorist attacks, and masses of policemen, whose job is to help guard, evacuate, and rescue, as well as to seal off the arena, to open traffic lanes for emergency vehicles, and to keep out the crowds of curious onlookers and to prevent the lynching of passersby who might be identified as Arabs. Some Haredi volunteers violate the orders of the security forces and enter the arena, despite the danger of injury.

The ZAKA leaders beg to be allowed to bring in their men, and meanwhile they divide them into teams of three or four, under the command of experienced members. They split the site into blocs and assign tasks accordingly. The volunteers who are ready to leap into the heart of the arena fill themselves with "strength," that is, spiritual fortification by means of prayer and personal blessings and oaths, silently or in a whisper. Some of them murmur, "Blessed be the Judge of Truth."[2] Following the instructions of the rabbis, they tuck the ritual fringes (*tsitsit*), which they usually display with ostentation, into their trousers, to avoid arousing the envy of the dead in the arena, who will never be able to fulfill the commandment of wearing fringes.

A considerable number of ZAKA activists are experienced paramedics who are permitted to enter the arena and work alongside MaDA professionals. One volunteer admitted that while they were in the stage of saving lives, they were already "tempted to peek in the direction of the dead." Once they have finished dealing with the severely wounded, the Haredi volunteers can turn to the field of their original expertise and devote themselves exclusively to the task over which they have a monopoly: handling the corpses and body parts. Despite criticism from security professionals for disrupting the investigation of the event, the volunteers leap into the arena like a taut spring that is released. From ZAKA's point of view, this is when the incident begins. This moment is expressed symbolically: the volunteers turn their dayglo vests inside out. Instead of orange, with the word "Medic" on the back, they are now yellow, with the name ZAKA on it.

## Spectacle

The local journalists and photographers compete with the determination and speed of the rescue teams. They immediately transmit the sights and sounds to the entire world. Countless millions in the global village become spectators, sharing in live coverage of the traumatic events of mass terrorism attacks. The arena of the explosion becomes a full-fledged media spectacle.[3]

The image is familiar. For thirty years it has been broadcast again and again from the arenas of slaughter in Asia, Africa, Europe, and America. Particularly engraved in Israeli memory are the scenes of suicide terrorism committed by Hamas, the Jihad, and Fatah in the streets of Jerusalem. Most Israelis and a considerable number of Palestinians have viewed this image hundreds of times in variations of the same visual motives: the bleeding wounded crying for help, soot-caked survivors in ragged clothing running every which way, speeding ambulances, frantic medics and policemen, weeping passersby, their hands covering their faces. In the background: splinters of glass, twisted metal, fractured beams, peeling paint, bits of upholstery, pockmarked walls, bloodstained floors, rickety roofs, pools of oil, piles of furnishings collapsed, pulverized, and slashed, thousands of screws and nails, a shoe, leaves, and almost always a flattened school satchel, a dismembered doll, broken wristwatch that shows the time of the explosion, a lost *kippah*, or a singed bag with *tefillin* (phylacteries) inside. At the center stage, inside the sizzling bus, through the shattered display window, among the overturned market stands, are ZAKA men, deep in their work.

Several ZAKA activists, especially the most veteran and respected ones, are active in the arena wearing their ordinary Haredi black clothing. But most of the volunteers work in the arena wearing overalls, gloves, and nylon boots—all in gleaming white.[4] Their large yarmulka, their long earlocks, and their thick beards are conspicuous against this background, and the dissonance between the two components of their appearance adds to the bizarre impression. It is hard to avert one's gaze from them. They move frantically, bent over, leaning forward, or on all fours. They hold tools: trowels or spatulas, rolls of absorbent paper, and the indispensable plastic bags.

The picture of the arena of suicide terrorism is zoomed-out and blurry, often retouched or pixelized. That which is not hidden behind the images of the volunteers at the arena is hidden by other intermediaries. Only in one early case, the bombing of the number 5 bus in Tel Aviv that heralded the beginning of the first wave of suicide attacks, were close-ups of some of the twenty-two people killed made available to the public (August 1994). The photographs—filed in my private collection—are unbearable. Following the initial shock, the public reacted with revulsion and anger, accusing the media of cheap sensationalism, disrespect for the victims, and insensitivity to their loved ones. Furthermore, many protested, publicizing the images demoralized the nation as its resolve was being tested by a brutal war. Such exposure of the scene of the bombing was, said critics, tantamount to collaboration with the terrorists. Consequently, censorship was instituted—mostly self-censorship by media outlets and the photographers themselves—and such pictures were not printed or broadcast again. Since then, photographs of terrorism sites have focused on the people who tend to the victims. ZAKA thus appears as a proxy for the thing itself, as the acceptable part of it.

ZAKA's volunteers see the victims, serving as surrogates and delegates of the Israeli public. They protect the public, absorbing the trauma of watching that which is unwatchable.[5] Even in its media version portrayal it is an abhorrent, paralyzing, but also mesmerizing sight.[6] The men who handle the bodies of the attacker and his victims signal the horror, but they also conceal it.[7] The onlookers gathered in the street behind the police barriers around the site of the explosion, or the spectators at home in front of their television screens, do not see the arena from up close. Rather they see the ZAKA volunteers, who see the arena from up close.

In the vicarious gaze of the Haredi volunteers—sort of peeping toms who examine the tabooed sight on behalf of the Israeli collective—they seem to sacrifice themselves on the altar of the Jewish nation, but quite often they cannot conceal a certain pleasure that they derive from the forbidden sight, and they appropriate that pleasure entirely for themselves.[8]

The ZAKA volunteers, immersed in their work, stimulate the voyeuristic instinct that we all have, but they also thwart the possibility of satisfying it. When one observes ZAKA activists in the arena, who are occupied with what they see, they bring out but also conceal what is beneath, blacked out, and insinuated. The invisible field is the focus.[9]

*

Firsthand descriptions of the arena by ZAKA volunteers and rescue teams emphasize the massive scale and totality of devastation and carnage and, also, the chaos that reigns at the site of the explosion.[10] The volunteers illustrate the dimensions of the catastrophe by spotlighting the death of fauna and flora. They point to the bodies of cats, to the severed branches of bushes. They also describe the dimensions of the disaster by indicating the distance from the center of the explosion at which fragments of bones, scraps of flesh, and drops of blood were found. They especially like to tell, with strange gratification, about the surprising distance from the arena to which the human bomb's head was thrown.

The following illustrates the disarray that characterizes the arena of suicide terrorism, and the confusion and anomie that accompanies it. ZAKA volunteers brought the forensic medicine experts the shattered parts of a child's body, after having thrown them to the side of the arena because they were convinced they were the remains of a dog. An agonizing expression of the bedlam that prevails at the arena is not only the loss of the ability to distinguish among the victims and between them and the human bomb, but the fusing of the victims of the suicide bombing with inanimate objects and with living things that are not human. An observer of similar manifestations of horrordescribed a human body that was "so mutilated that it might be the body of a pig."[11]

One of many examples is the double bombing in Jerusalem's Mahaneh Yehuda market (July 1997). Nail-filled bombs set off in proximity within seconds of each other by two suicide terrorists killed 13 and injured 168. ZAKA found and collected body parts jumbled up with heaps of produce that cascaded from overturned stands. This early bombing incident is etched deeply in the consciousness of the organization's veterans, largely because of the memory of the way the blood of the victims mixed with the juices of smashed tomatoes and shattered watermelons, and how they found the flesh of victims interspersed with the beef and chicken meat at nearby butcher stand. Five years later, in the wake of the suicide attack of the Passover meal at the Park Hotel, the first to reach the explosion site testified, "It was impossible to distinguish between wine and blood" (March 2002).

In interviews with survivors, emergency teams, journalists, and ZAKA activists, the above themes appear regularly. In their testimony, they cling to some apparently marginal concrete detail, which attracted their attention at the time, and it has been engraved in their memory ever since. They report about the experience of dissonance in response to something that is out of place, or a combination of disparate things. Here are a number of illustrations found repeatedly in the words of the Haredi volunteers: pigeons that were struck by the shock of the explosion and fell from the sky, watches and cell phones stuck onto pieces of furniture, drops of blood on treetops, bone fragments that were thrown and went through the windows and into the apartments in nearby buildings, valuable jewelry that was thrown into a basket of potatoes, intestines soaked into Sabbath challahs scattered on the ground. At the site of the explosions, animal, vegetable, and mineral are mingled, humans and animals, males and females, adults and children, torn books of Psalms with gossip columns in women's magazines. The arena of suicide terrorism is an arena of burst boundaries. The main boundary that is broken is one's body and that between one body and another. The suicide terrorist does not only threaten the lives of Israelis, he also attacks the human body in general and removes its humanity.

## Shakshuka

The state of the bodies in the arena of terrorism is determined by the nature of the explosion. The severity of the attack and its form depend on the size of the explosive charge, its composition, the proximity of the attacker to his victims, and the angle at which he faces them, and whether the explosion happens in an enclosed and crowded place. What is termed a first-degree injury is one caused by the shock wave of the explosion. This causes death mainly by striking at the lungs and other hollow bodily organs. Injury of this kind is not always visible externally. The result is corpses that appear to be intact. This is an atypical case, which the ZAKA volunteers attracted to it regard as a miracle. Other, more common cases of death in the arena appear outwardly in their full severity, such as the severing of limbs that involve loss of a lot of blood. The main fatal wounds that are clearly visible are referred to as second-degree injuries, caused by hard and sharp objects that are driven powerfully toward the victims, especially pieces of metal, screws, nails, and ball-bearings, which the terrorists pack into the explosive charge. In addition, people are killed by fragments of glass, stones, and wooden planks that shatter and fly in every direction. Third-degree injuries are caused when the bodies are thrown against hard objects like a wall, shattering their bones and skulls. Another important cause of death whose signs are unmistakable are burns. Among the various victims of a suicide attack, the corpse of the attacker is unique in the form of his injury. Because the explosive charge is usually strapped to his chest, and according to the instructions he received, he spreads his arms to the sides (to maximize the injuries from the metal fragments in the explosive charge), his legs are cut off, his torso is crushed, his digestive system explodes, and his head is thrown far away.

The bodies of people killed by human bombs are dismembered and mashed, eviscerated and/or riddled with holes, disarrayed and scattered. Limb connects to limb in inconceivable combinations; body mixes with body in surreal juxtapositions. I have overheard conversations among ZAKA personnel in which volunteers described the state of the bodies at the site of a suicide explosion as *shakshuka*—a popular Middle Eastern dish of scrambled eggs mixed with chili peppers and cooked in tomato sauce.

A ZAKA volunteer once said to me that in the arena there is an incestuousobscenity. The impression created by a variety of testimonies is that the carnage after a suicide terrorism act consists entirely of severed limbs and mostly of genitals. The bodies of the dead are largely seen as a collection of orifices, protrusions, and disproportionate parts. In the ZAKA narrative, the pieces of the victims can only be spoken of using tropes of exaggeration, distortion, inversion, and incongruity. Internal organs—guts—are rendered visible, and body parts kept covered, such as thighs, are exposed. Left and right are reversed, front and back lose meaning, the boundary between inside and outside is crossed.[12] Body parts above the waist appear below, and lower parts appear on top. In fact, after a bombing every body part seems to be a lower one.

This is precisely the way a "grotesque body" is described.[13] In its initial moments, this awful site of death looks as if someone deliberately sought to render it ridiculous, to demean the victims and to mock those close to them. ZAKA volunteers speak in similar terms. The familiar body is distorted, which causes estrangement.[14] Indeed, once, after it was transported from the arena of the attack to the NationalInstitute of Forensic Medicine, the professionals asked, "[W]hich end of the stretcher is the head on?"[15]

## Procedures of Deathwork

In the early mass attacks, the work of the ZAKA activists was spontaneous. From event to event, the volunteers specialized in handling bodies. The heads of the organization strove for professionalization, as expressed in the development of "rules of engagement," the setting of procedures, instructional meetings, and the distribution of written directions. In parallel the equipment supplied to the volunteers has been improved, including all-terrain vehicles and powerful searchlights for effective work at night. In the latter years of the Intifada, ZAKA was already operating like a well-oiled machine in handling the victims of attacks. Upon their arrival at the arena, it was divided into sectors, which were assigned to team leaders, and different bags were distributed for various items. Each one was numbered, and notes were pasted on them indicating the contents and the place where and time when they were found. The main point was not to mix the parts of different bodies, and not to miss any body part. Despite the professionalized routine and the obligatory rules, the work in the arena still was characterized by a significant degree of independent initiative and improvisation, leading to gross violation of proper operational procedures. Damage was often caused to the bodies as a result of excessive motivation. The futility of the effort to discipline the volunteers' work is already evident as they enter the arena. They all strive to burst into the center of the arena. The order of precedence is not determined solely by seniority in the organization, but also by other criteria, mainly social and religious status (*yikhus*). Rabbis receive preference in accordance with their halakhic authority and age, increasing their chances of finding important body parts.

Immediately upon entering the arena, the skilled volunteers set to work: they survey, pick up, gather, wrap, mark, scrape, absorb, scour, remove, and transport. For long hours, they work on what they define as identification, joining together, and purification in respect for the dead. At this stage ZAKA cooperates with MaDA, with the police forensic unit, and with the ISA agents, but there is evident tension among them, and mutual recrimination, accusing one another of contaminating the arena.[16] After a while, the emergency teams leave the arena, and the ZAKA volunteers remain by themselves. From then on, they strut about "like the lords of the place" (*ba'albatim*), as they say. They and not the police determine who may enter the arena. ZAKA introduces its own religious norms in the arena. Now they impose severer rules of modesty. They make sure to cover full or partial nudity, and they replace a scarf that fell from a religious woman's head.

The volunteers close the victims' eyes so that the dead will not envy the living. The rabbis who accompany the ZAKA teams remind the volunteers also to close the mouths of the dead, to press their jaws together, and place arms that were spread against the sides of the body.

While at work, the ZAKA volunteers speak volubly. They talk on the telephone with their colleagues at headquarters and with those who are at the National Institutr of Forensic Medicine, giving them instructions. They also speak with each other—getting advice, giving instructions, sharing experiences, and encouraging one another. Some of this verbal communication is between the volunteers and their rabbis, in the arena or in the rear, asking halakhic questions. For example, Rabbi Roje was asked whether to put a certain bone fragment into a marked bag. His answer was positive, so long as it was "as big as an olive."[17] While handling the body parts, the volunteers also collect some of the objects that are scattered in the arena. The items are chosen according to their contribution to identifying the dead lying on the ground, such as documents, or according to their symbolic value. They mainly gather religious items that belonged to the dead, attributing great importance to volumes of the Talmud, prayer shawls, and skullcaps. When these are blood-soaked, they are exhibited publicly and then buried.

The precedence given by ZAKA to bodies of different kinds is determined according to two standards: the importance of findings in the arena for definitely determining the identity of the attacker and his victims, and the importance of the findings with respect to the religious tradition. According to the first standard, location and removal of jaws with teeth or hands with fingerprints takes precedence. According to the second standard, major organs such as the brain and the heart, upon which life depends, according to medical science or mystical and halakhic thought, take precedence. Apparently, the operational consideration is subordinated to the religious one, but rabbis have decreed that rapid identification and reconstitution of the body are vital for preserving the honor of the dead. Thus, the operational consideration is expressed in religious terms. On one issue the two criteria are in absolute agreement: the contribution of a finding in the arena for resolving the dilemma regarding the ethnic and religious status of the person whose organ it was, whether or not he or she was Jewish.

The first bodies to be treated are those that have been declared dead by the medical teams, though their injuries are not visible. Among the intact bodies, the most highly regarded are those identified as holy people—mostly renowned Torah scholars—and more care is taken in dealing with them. Then they pay attention to the large and undamaged body parts. At the next stage in the hierarchy of treatment are body parts that include the head as well as intact limbs. Finally, body parts are collected that are tiny or so mutilated that it is impossible to tell where they belonged on the living body. Most of ZAKA teams' time is devoted to the latter: scraps of flesh and fragments of bone. The volunteers emphasize that these are as important as an entire body. ZAKA is expert at working on a small scale. The forensic professionals of the police department say that only the penetrating gaze of a Haredi volunteer can distinguish in the blink of an eye between a grain of gravel and a human tooth. Sometimes the volunteers are seen in the arena crawling with their noses to the ground of the explosion site, holding a magnifying glass or fine paintbrush and toothpick. After stubbornly probing a crack in the ceiling or a pile of broken glass, with a cry of triumph they remove a bunch of hair or a fingernail.

## Moments of Ultra-Religiosity

A ZAKA squad commander told me that when he enters a terrorism arena he runs amok (*atraf* in colloquial Hebrew). Other volunteers claim that action in the death site makes them feel literally "high." One volunteer wondered whether this is reminiscent of the presumed "hyper" state of the Palestinian suicide terrorist when he enters the target and comes close to his soon-to-be victims.

ZAKA volunteers at the arena of the attack behave as if they are in a trance. Their mental state is evident in their behavior—they work frenetically for hours at a time. Their concentration is high, and they do their best to ignore fatigue, pain, hunger, and distractions coming from the crowd observing the horror scene. They also ignore phone calls from their worried parents and anxious wives. Frequently, a short time after leaving the arena, they find it difficult to reconstruct precise details of their work, as if they were working as marionettes and that "the hand of God operated them."

The breaching of borders in the arena is accompanied by a sense of total freedom and omnipotence. The behavior and testimony of ZAKA volunteers indicate that at the site they do not see themselves as subject to any physical or moral restrictions. They climb trees and jump over walls and other obstacles with an athleticism hardly typical of Haredim who never exercise. They shout, push, and have no compunctions about using rude language, including the use of dirty words. The volunteers are swept away in the frenzy of their work in the arena so greatly that they sometimes skip one of the three daily prayers that Orthodox Jews are required to recite. Sometimes they were aware that the time for prayer had passed (when the sun set, for example), and they received permission from their rabbis, who ruled that the commandment of honoring the dead was more important than the commandment to pray. When their conscience plagued them, they would take advantage of a short break in their work to recite a makeup prayer in place of one that was missed. Some of them, in their daily routine, might occasionally skip a prayer, but particularly in response to a mass attack, prayer seemed more important than ever to them. Some of them asserted that prayers were recited with special devotion nearby the arena, and there was no doubt that they were received by the Creator. They point out that because these prayers reach higher in heaven than usual, even secular Jews in the rescue teams join them or at least stand close to the Haredi worshipers. The ZAKA volunteers also exploit pauses to smoke a cigarette, and mainly to trade off with other teams, who are waiting for a chance to perform the commandment of handling the dead. Sometimes groups of three or four new volunteers were given a turn in order to train them, and rumor has it that once they allowed men into the arena who were not regular members of the organization—various well-connected people, or friends, as well as representatives of the Haredim who crowd the fences of the explosion site—to let as many men as possible, for a moment, enjoy the exalted religious experience.

The volunteers in the arena experience religious enthusiasm. They speak of catharsis. They speak especially of a specific "moment" in the work, into which holiness pours, a moment when they feel the presence of God physically, and He expresses satisfaction with the honor they give to the dead—a moment of enlightenment. For example, they speak of a moment of mystical essence when they gather up the limbs of a small Jewish child and place the scraps in a body bag. I heard a description of this moment in terms of several analogies. Among them: "like the moment when Rabbi Oirbach [the greatest halakhic authority in the Haredi world] comes to the climax of his ethical [*musar*] sermon in a yeshiva and burst into tears"; or "like the moment on Yom Kippur when the shofar is sounded with purity that breaks through to higher realms"; or "like the moment of the wedding night of a bride and groom, as they become one flash for the first time."

## The Inner Sanctum

In ZAKA's work at the site of the explosion there appears to be an oxymoron: exposure to the torn flesh and the blood flowing from it is a spiritual experience. The history of world religions offers us analogies for this finding. It is similar to the exaltation of worshipers who sacrificed freshly killed animals and sprinkled the blood on the altar in the ancient Israelite temple. Indeed, in the arena of terrorism, strewn with slaughter and destruction, there is the logic of a Temple. Behind the absolute chaos hides a deep structure with its own religious, ritual laws, which are bound up with the tragic irony implicit in the correlation between the horror of death and sanctity. Observations and testimony show that the greater the horror is in a certain place, the greater is the holiness there. Both the heart of the horror and the height of sanctity are at the epicenter of the explosion.

The arena of suicide terrorism, a ferocious heartbreaking mass of panic, hatred, and pain, is governed by the regularity and evident configuration of a religious cult. The arena is a central ritual stage, laden with basic symbols of the Jewish Israeli collective. It offers the national religious community an opportunity to concentrate on itself, to examine itself, and to reveal essential things to itself about itself and about its relations with its neighbors. At the center of this cult, practiced immediately after the explosion, is the horror of death, in which the Haredi volunteers find special sanctity.

In Israeli political culture—in newspaper headlines, in parliamentary rhetoric, and in civics education textbooks—suicide terrorism acts are labeled *tofet* attacks. The word "tophet" occurs in the Bible and refers to the altar where human sacrifices were apparently offered in ancient Near Eastern religions (Jeremiah 7:31). It is the site of a religious ritual, described in the sacred texts of world religions, folklore, literature, and art, as an arena packed with pieces of human flesh, bleeding and burned (as in Dante's *Inferno*). The ZAKA activists have adopted the definition of the site of the explosion as Tophet.

The police barriers that isolate the arena of suicide terror separate the holy from the profane. When the volunteers go through the bright plastic strips that prohibit unauthorized entry, they urge each other on by shouting, "Forward, to holiness!" They claim that when they enter the exploded bus, restaurant, or vegetable market, they clearly experience sanctity, like those who entered the gates of the Temple on the Passover holiday more than two thousand years ago. One veteran volunteer told me that he feels physically that God hovers low over the bodies of the dead and closely supervises the way the victims are treated.

Every temple contains areas more and less sacred. Usually, the deeper one goes, the greater is the sanctity. The right of entry to the various areas of sanctity is determined by a person's rank in the religious hierarchy. Ordinary worshipers gather in the outer quarters; from a certain point on only priests are permitted to enter, and, of course, there is a hierarchy of priests, and according to it, exclusive access to every section of the temple is defined. The priest's place in the temple marks his place in the status pyramid. This is exactly how things were in the temple of Palestinian terrorism in Israel during the Intifada. There, too, are concentric circles of sanctity, increasing in intensity from the margins to the center. The shock waves of the explosion and with them the murderous fragments of metal also spread in concentric circles from the place where the human bomb stood outward toward the margins, as did the effect of the explosion. The geometry of sanctity overlaps with the geometry of slaughter.

As with the Haredi volunteers, with the human bomb as well, along with the operational consideration, a symbolic consideration guides his behavior in the arena. Both parties relate to the implicit but compelling structure of the arena. This structure takes on a ceremonial and mystical dimension. Therefore, they strive to reach the place where the living meet the dead, the place where boundaries are transgressed.[18] To a degree the human bomb shares with ZAKA a similar and complementary conception of the holiness of the arena. Both sides wish to enter as deeply as possible, to touch the most sensitive place with respect to the effect of suicide terrorism, and thus to carry out their sacred mission in full. ZAKA and the human bomb together are priests in the temple-arena of suicide terrorism.

The closed, innermost chamber of the temple, the focus of mystery and the essence of holiness, the dwelling of the god, the inner sanctum, is called the Holy of Holies in Jewish sources. Only the High Priest is permitted to enter it, and he may do so only under very restrictive conditions.[19] Despite special precautionary measures, such as extraordinary purification rituals, entry into the sanctuary of the ancient Israelite temple was perilous and frightening, so much so that they used to attach chains to the High Priest's feet before he entered, lest he die because of the holy awe, and they might have to drag his body out. His emergence, still alive, was regarded as a miracle. The arena of suicide terrorism also has a heart of sanctity, and of danger to life, and it, too, is thought of as a holy of holies. This is the specific point where the explosion took place. The human bomb set off the explosive charge there, and most of the victims are concentrated there. In this most sacred circle you will always find the most senior ZAKA activists: Bentzi, Meshi, Roje, and a few other select individuals.[20] Being at zero range from the mutilated bodies, just like being in the presence of God, is an ardent desire and a difficult test, demanding rare religious abilities.

The ZAKA volunteers, who strive to penetrate deeply into the arena, shove each other and compete with each other, like priests who serve in a temple, who wish to rise in the hierarchy of sanctity. They hold a trowel, rolls of absorbent paper, and plastic bags, what they call "holy vessels" (*tashmishei kedusha*). Entry into the heart of the arena is the privilege of the veteran and most devoted activists of the organization, and the rabbis who accompany them. They know the holy work, with all its details, very well. Paradoxically, the ZAKA volunteers are priests in the holy arena of death, although, according to the Torah, men of priestly lineage are forbidden to approach corpses, to avoid ritual impurity. During the early attacks of the Intifada, the Haredi volunteers used to immerse themselves in a ritual bath after leaving the arena, lest they be contaminated with ritual impurity. The ZAKA volunteers say that the order should actually be reversed: they should immerse and purify themselves *before* entering the arena, like the High Priest, for they are about to be present among the corpses in the holy of holies.

## Blood on Their Hands

The attention that the Haredi ZAKA volunteers pay to every drop of blood at the site has been described by paramedics and forensic investigators who cooperate with them in dealing with the results of the explosion as "unreasonable" and "obsessive." The effort that ZAKA devotes to locating and collecting the blood of the victims is unprecedented. Before the waves of suicide terrorism, the blood of victims in mass casualty events was quickly hosed away, without a trace. Since the Intifada, the Sisyphean work of gathering blood has continued for long hours after the large body parts have been removed. It includes sponging up all the blood that has been shed and the scraping up of congealed blood, even tiny spots. The blood is intended for burial, as is the paper in which it is absorbed from the ground, and the knife with which it was scraped from walls, along with pieces of furniture and other objects stained with blood.[21] The stubborn insistence of the volunteers upon completing the blood work at the site is tested when the authorities responsible for the site of the attack in the early stages after the explosion apply heavy pressure to expedite clearing of the site as soon as possible. They urge ZAKA to finish the job so they can send in bulldozers and fire hoses to erase the signs of death and destruction. With their bodies, the volunteers resist the aggressive efforts of firemen, policemen, engineers, and local politicians to restore the routine order of the public space.

The blood work demands a lot of time and energy, especially because it entails complex distinctions. ZAKA insists, first, on the difficult distinction between the blood of the terrorist and that of his victims, between the blood of gentiles and that of Jews. Regarding the blood of the victims, ZAKA must make another subtle and critical distinction: between "blood of the soul" and other blood. The first category of blood was lost by the victims while they were still alive, and the loss of blood led to their death, whereas the other category of blood seeps out after the victim is dead. According to Orthodox Judaism, only the first category of blood must be buried with religious rites, because, according to the Torah, blood is a person's soul.[22] However, the second category of blood can be hosed away. The volunteers at the arena are assisted by rabbis to decide between the categories of blood, which are often gathered in a single pool.

The effort to return from a painful, frightening event, that shatters the social order, to the daily routine is the way of the world. For its part, ZAKA, with its actions at the scene of the attack, contributes to repressing the trauma and restoring the social order. However, at the same time, with a sort of uncontrollable instinct, only partially conscious, it also opposes denial of the horrible consequences of terrorism and the suppression of trauma. In its way, ZAKA simultaneously cooperates with the forces leading to the normalization of life in Israel after a massive explosion as well as with the forces that delay normalization by exacerbating the trauma. These two opposite tendencies are embodied in the way the Haredi volunteers treat blood. Collecting and burying the blood promotes the healing of a community in crisis. However, the volunteers find it difficult to return to ordinary life. Almost unawares they strive against making the blood disappear.

Since antiquity, the Jewish tradition has cried out in protest against the restoration of order following cruel and unjustified killing. Alongside the hegemonic tradition of healthful recovery from personal and collective grief, an alternative, counter-tradition emerges, motivated by a deep urge to preserve the memory of injustice and calamity, and to emphasize the dreadful death.

Job, the legendary biblical figure, the absolutely righteous man, begs, "Earth, do not cover my blood" (16:18). In his suffering, he cries out not to bury the blood that has been shed, but to leave it exposed. This is the cry of those who demand justice in the name of innocent people who have been killed. The verse from Job is inscribed on many of the monuments in memory of those who perished in the Holocaust in Eastern Europe. It might also imply a call for revenge. God tells Cain, who murdered his brother Abel, "The blood of your brother shouts from the earth" (Genesis 4:10). The blood exposed on the earth provokes, as it were, the eyes riveted to it. It becomes a metaphor, decisive testimony to death with which one cannot be reconciled. The natural tendency to cover the blood with earth, to make the horror disappear, is denied, and in its place comes the moral imperative to contemplate the spilled blood, to make it ferment, to retain it as a perpetual reproach. This also applies to the ZAKA activists at the site of a suicide terrorism attack. Despite the venerable tradition, and despite the constraints of modern urban life, which require the covering of the blood, from the interstices in the apparently civil behavior of the Haredi volunteers a certain urge emerges, to display the spilled blood. They collect and bury the blood, but before that they cannot restrain themselves from exhibiting it.

Observation of the ZAKA volunteers, laboring to clean up the blood at the site, easily focuses on their hands—in gloves or bare—stained with the blood of the victims. Frequently their overalls are also bloodstained. In their eagerness, they are not careful to keep them white. Sometimes one suspects that they purposely smear themselves with blood, even if they won't admit it, and even if they seek to give the impression that it is an unavoidable consequence of death work. Again and again, as though by chance, they exhibit the blood that clings to them. One volunteer admitted to me that this was the case, and from his words I understood that it was done with some degree of self-awareness.

Like the Aghori, the Hindu priests of death on the banks of the Ganges, who smear their bodies and faces with the ashes of the cremated dead, these Jewish priests of the dead in the arena of terrorism in Jerusalem smear themselves with the blood of the victims and stain their garments with it. One may propose several strata of meaning to the exhibition of bloodstains by the ZAKA volunteers. First, in this way they express the horror of the killing, which may not be ignored or forgiven. It is an index of the injustice and infamy. Against this background the call also goes forth for a violent act of vengeance. Second, in this way they show how far their devotion goes, how deeply they are immersed in their mission, and how daring and far-reaching they are in their holy work. Moreover, in this way they convince themselves and others that they are immune to death and can overcome the most dreadful challenge of all. Third, in this way they show their entire identification with the victims, even hinting that they themselves are victims. Finally, in this way the volunteers become sanctified, like the biblical priests.

Display of the victims' blood arouses an association—and perhaps it also constitutes a response—to the prominence of blood on the Palestinian side of the regional conflict: the blood of *shahids* is photo-shopped onto the testaments that the suicide terrorists film before setting out on their last journey, and the blood of *shahids,* whose bodies are laid on stretchers, is used by the masses who accompany their funerals to smear on their own living bodies. During the Intifada young men in the West Bank used to paint their hands in red and stamp the form of their hands on the white walls of the towns and villages as an expression of identification with the armed struggle and willingness to give their lives for their faith and nation.

Among the Palestinian Muslims, it is customary to dip one's hands in the blood of the sheep that is slaughtered for the dinner of *id el-adha* (the Feast of Sacrifice). Among the Jews as well the display of blood-soaked hands is a cultic act. As the ZAKA volunteers know so well, this is what the priests did in the Temple in antiquity before the eyes of the assembled people. After slaughtering the animal offered as a sacrifice and butchering its body, the priests dipped their fingers in its blood and sprayed it on the altar. This is the most important stage in the sacrificial service, providing atonement. To the complex of significance of this act, with its religious and historical depth, a new complex of meaning has been added, also rich and multi-vocal. It appears in the context of Palestinian terrorism in Israel and arouses powerful emotions among the rival protagonists in the Middle Eastern drama.

Lady Macbeth washes her hands obsessively to rid herself of the blood that stains them in her mad imagination, a reminder of her murderousness, but in vain, for there is no pardoning the spilled blood. We may assume that the words of Isaiah reverberated in Shakespeare's ears, as the prophet reproved his people for their immorality, saying that no prayer or repentance can erase their sin, which is expressed in the powerful image: "Your hands are filled with blood" (1:15). Today, "blood on his hands" has become a common term in the political language of both sides of the conflict. It expresses responsibility for murder. This is how the Israelis describe Palestinians who were actively involved in murderous terrorist attacks. In the terminology of the

Security Service, this epithet is frequently used to distinguish between two types of terrorists, according to the severity of their acts. Those with blood on their hands, for example, the dispatchers of human bombs, head the list of wanted men, and, if they are caught, they receive the maximum sentence. In prisoner-exchange agreements between Israel and Hamas, there is an Israeli taboo against freeing them under any conditions. The concept of having blood on their hands received a mocking, wicked Palestinian response after the lynching of two Israelis who accidentally ended up in Ramallah on the West Bank at the beginning of the Intifada. After they were slaughtered and their bodies were desecrated, one of the perpetrators of the horrible deed went out onto a balcony and waved his bloodied hands before Western television cameras, and the local crowd cheered with enthusiasm in the central square of the city (October 2000).

On the cover of a special edition of the ZAKA bulletin, which was published following a terrorist attack on a Jerusalem yeshiva (March 2008), a close-up of the bloodstained hand of a ZAKA volunteer appears, holding the skullcap, soaked in the blood of one of the victims. Inside the newspaper, which once again recalls the plea from Job not to cover the blood, appear more and more photographs of sacred objects soaked in blood: prayer shawls, *tefillin*, volumes of Talmud, and skullcaps, whose sanctity is multiplied because they are stained in red. In other arenas of terrorism, the Haredi volunteers also made sure to display bloodied ritual objects. Usually this is accompanied by rhetoric replete with "sanctification of the name" and mention of all the pogroms against the Jews throughout history, from the Roman conquest through the Crusades (1096), Khmelnytsky (1648), and on up to the Nazis. The Intifada is connected to the notorious bloody chain. At the arena the ZAKA activists display a book of Psalms with torn, seared, and bloodied pages, as though to say that the victims of the terrorism died because they were Jewish, and thus they are martyrs. The heads of the organization proclaim that death by terrorism serves a divine purpose. They add that if the world and the nation did not see the blood, it would be as if the victims died in vain.

The ZAKA volunteers who handle the bodies of the victims of terrorist attacks act as if sometimes they are backstage and sometimes they are on the stage, moving between the spontaneity that is possible behind the scenes and awareness that they are actors performing before an audience, and sometimes they mingle the two situations and confuse them. Not only do the volunteers conceal the horror by quickly clearing away the bodies and cleaning the area of body 'parts, but they also exhibit the horror and thus intensify collective trauma in Israel. They demonstrate the consequences of terrorism by means of startling gestures, such as grasping some large and easily identifiable body part, mainly a severed arm or leg, lifting it from the ground, and waving it at the cameras and the crowd massed behind the police barriers. Usually this is done rapidly and nonchalantly, but sometimes they display the limb without shame, even with a hint of pride, a half-smile of victory. These are episodes of macabre exhibitionism, religious extravagance, moments of fame for the ZAKA activists. Volunteers who are aware of this phenomenon and critical of it say of their colleagues that they're "posing." Maybe this is the Jewish response to the poses assumed by the terrorists in front of the cameras on the eve of their mission. Both sides understand that invisible terror doesn't exist. The visibility of terrorism is focused on bodies and severed limbs.

## The End and the Beginning

In its fundraising campaign ZAKA described its activists as the first to appear at the scene of a terrorist attack and the last to leave. For long hours after the explosion, and much after the other rescue forces have finished their job, the Haredi volunteers are still at work in the arena. They are pressured to finish collecting the remains and to clear the area to make it possible to restore the routine of city life, but they are obstinate. The tow truck approaches to pick up the smashed body of the bus and transport it to a junkyard, the bulldozer drivers wait impatiently to raze a structure that has collapsed, but the volunteers resist stubbornly, continuing to crawl on the ground or to climb walls in the effort to find yet another piece of bone or drop of blood, a tiny scrap of the victims' flesh, lest it was overlooked, even though dozens of searches had already been conducted over the hours. It is as if they refuse to part from the site of horror, to cease the death-management, to be weaned from the glory, to return from the holy to the profane.

The volunteers persist in their work even if there is only a slim chance of finding another scrap, even if their families are waiting breathlessly for their return home, and even if the heads of the organization declared an end to the event. A ZAKA volunteer compared the tarrying of his colleagues in the arena to the behavior of certain very pious Orthodox Jews who delay the Havdala ceremony marking the end of the Sabbath and the start of the work week by an hour or two, trying to extend the sphere of holiness as much as possible.

The veteran ZAKA volunteers agree that sealing the last body bag with a fastener and sending it to the National Institute of Forensic Medicine does not put an end to the event. Not even the departure of ZAKA from the arena concludes the event from the viewpoint of the volunteers. Among other things, they are responsible for the burial of the victims' blood and body parts. Some say that departure from the arena of death takes place only with entry into the depth of the following arena of death. In any case, while entry into the arena is sudden and sharp, departure is prolonged, gradual, and many-staged. Like the beginning, the conclusion also has a ritual aspect.

Many volunteers do not return home directly from the arena, even though they left suddenly, were absent for longer than expected, and are tired and dirty. Some of them delay the transition back to routine life by a series of behavior patterns characterized by abandon and wildness, a release from the high religious and operational tension that built up in the arena. They exploit the opportunity to break with order before once again conforming to the order that prevails in daily life in their community and family. One decided expression of this is their typical tendency to go out on reckless drives after leaving the arena, speeding, violating traffic laws, and ignoring caution. They leave the car windows open and overcome the roar of the wind with extremely loud music, usually Hasidic songs.[23] In the early stages after the event, many of them prefer to stay together, so as not to part from the *communitas* forged in the arena, as though they are afraid to process the experiences of the past hours by themselves. On their way to their families, they stop at a restaurant or in a friend's house, to share impressions loudly and enthusiastically. One hears quite a few bursts of rather neurotic laughter.

The sense of confidence, excitement, and impulsiveness characteristic of the orgiastic event rises and spills out of the site of the attack. Some further contradictory patterns of behavior characterize departure from the arena, perhaps another post-traumatic symptom. For instance, whereas most of the volunteers remark that, following the handling of corpses, their appetite is decreased for some time, immediately after leaving the site of horror, they are seized by a craving for food and grab whatever is available. A great deal has been written about the connection between death and eating.[24] This is a kind of recovery meal known from the tradition. A volunteer told me, "Proximity to death gives us desire to take big bites out of life." At this stage, other signs of increased vitality are also evident.[25]

In the final analysis, every Haredi volunteer must cope with the horror by himself. Many veteran ZAKA members report about private ceremonies that they adopted over the years to facilitate the transition back to normal life. Two of these ceremonies, which many of them report, are rushing to their children's beds to touch them in their sleep, and scrubbing themselves in especially long showers to remove the smell—real or imaginary—that continues to cling to them. There are also strange and idiosyncratic ceremonies: a leader of the organization told me that when he returns from the arena of terrorism, even before he showers and changes clothes, he lies on the sofa and, very slowly, eats Milki, a popular dairy pudding, enjoying every lick.

The return from the adrenaline-filled arena poses some practical challenges: how to get rid of the clothes they worked in—by burning them, by throwing them in the garbage, by burying them? How can they describe what they have undergone to their wives and children? Their sleep will certainly be disturbed. Some of the Hasidic and Mizrahi volunteers report that on the nights after a terrorist attack, they speak to God for a long time.

## The Following Night and the Day After

The vast majority of terrorist attacks took place during daytime.[26] The rescue teams and, following them, the ZAKA volunteers tried to finish most of their work before nightfall, but they often had to work under searchlights, until the official announcement of the end of the event. Even then, although the arena was already cleared, some volunteers could be seen at the site of the explosion, continuing their inspection. Sometimes Haredim who are not members of the organization join them spontaneously. They labor all night long, wearing headlamps, holding plastic bags, and even after dawn, indifferent to their surroundings, which have returned to the daily routine, they do not stop.

ZAKA made most of the terrorist attacks into religious events that extended over more than twenty-four hours. A mysterious force, which they cannot resist, draws the volunteers back to the arena on the day following the explosion. Then they climb electric poles and onto the roofs of houses over a wide perimeter to find yet another shred of a victim. After city employees clear away the wreckage and the piles of debris, the volunteers go there as well and continue their searches. Under the blazing sun, without journalistic coverage or a crowd of onlookers, they do not rest until they know that not even "the end of a Jewish fingernail" has not been properly buried. In the jargon of the organization, these volunteers are called *olnikim*, from the Hebrew word for yoke, *ol*, meaning that they bear the yoke, not for the sake of fame but for the sake of heaven. In ZAKA there are commonly volunteers who attend the arena of the explosion, and volunteers for the following night and morning. You will find the latter even after a day or two, alone, concentrated on a meticulous inspection of the creases in the burned-out bus deep in a garage outside the city.

In a survey that the organization conducted among its volunteers, they were asked to define ZAKA. One of the veterans answered, "ZAKA is the pursuit of yet another drop of blood, far from the arena, even more than a day after the attack."

## Ordinary Unnatural Death

Yom Kippur is known to be the holiest day in the Jewish calendar. Orthodox Jews spend almost the whole day (and evening before) in the synagogue, in deep and emotional prayer, confessing sins and begging for forgiveness. The holy day ends with a blast of the shofar to open the gates of heaven for atonement and repentance. Yom Kippur day is marked by a special spiritual atmosphere, and there is religious tension in the air. During the Al-Aqsa Intifada, the heads of ZAKA described every one of the 150 suicide terrorist attacks that took place at that time as if they were Yom Kippur—so greatly did they experience the religious significance of the event, its sanctity and gravity.

During the decade after the Intifada, the number of Palestinian terrorist attacks claiming many victims decreased radically, and the bulk of ZAKA's activities were devoted to many fewer charismatic cases of massive death. Concomitantly, their religious force has decreased. They compare the handling of death not connected to terrorism to that of routine observance of commandments, which, with all its importance, is regular and repetitive—several times a month, and even several times a day—like putting on *tefillin*. No Orthodox authority would underestimate the importance of this commandment, but rabbis are aware of the possibility that its normalization might make its observance automatic and decrease its religious intensity. True intention might not underlie it. In this spirit, the ZAKA rabbis express apprehension lest the routine handling of death in arenas that are regarded as normal in late modern circumstances of life might make it hard for the organization to sustain the high religious enthusiasm of its activists.

Some of the more radical Haredi volunteers have raised the opposite claim: in handling cases of unnatural death without glory, the fulfillment of the commandment partakes of pure and exalted faith. Action in an arena, which does not offer secondary reward such as fame and satisfaction of the desire for adventure, ensures pure religious motivation. The less attractive the handling of death may be, the greater is its sanctity and the higher are the Jewish qualities required of the volunteers in coping with the challenge that it poses.

The most common cases of death for which ZAKA is summoned these days fall into three categories. First are accidents, mainly road accidents, as well as work accidents, and a few other instances where there is no drama and news coverage. Suicides are a second category. ZAKA distinguishes between taking one's life by shooting or leaping from a height, which leaves torn and scattered tissue and a lot of blood, and clean suicide by hanging or poisoning. The third category is death under criminal circumstances, that is, murders, most of which are transferred to the National Institute of Forensic Medicine. There are also a few other types of death that ZAKA handles.[27]

The range of the ZAKA volunteers' feelings while handling these types of death includes mercy, guilt, helplessness, and sometimes criticism and annoyance, as well as the thought of how stupid and pointless the death was. Compared to the experience in the arena of terrorism, in other cases of unnatural death the volunteers speak of frustration because they have no one to be angry at, to blame, to regard as an abomination, and to put at a distance. They have no one to arouse hatred and the desire for revenge. Nor can the volunteers identify with the victims and see themselves as victims. In contrast, here they must make a greater effort to overcome the natural tendency, constantly increasing, to treat the bodies with contempt or indifference. They admit that, given the accretion of more and more prosaic cases of death like these, in remote arenas, with no one observing, it's hard to resist the temptation to ignore a faded drop of blood, or to drag a heavy body along the floor rather than carry it. As one volunteer put it, "These are situations where suspicion arises that if the dead person were to open his eyes, he would be insulted!"

The volunteers are frustrated by the difficulty in connecting the victims' death with their Jewishness and to find any kernel of Judaism here at all. It takes an effort to attribute sanctity to the cases of death under discussion here, to find religious meaning in them. With sophisticated reasoning, which is patently a bit forced, they manage to transfer some of the rules of conduct that apply in the arena of terrorism to arenas of death unconnected with terrorism.

In the case of an accident on the road to a vacation in the southern resort city of Eilat, the ZAKA volunteer discovered that the victims were Lubavitch Hasidim and they might have intended to make a stop on the way to light Hanukkah candles at an army base. Hence, they were immediately declared to be martyrs who died to sanctify the name of God and thus were worthy of treatment as if they were saints (*tsadikim*). Quite a few components of the practices used in handling death from a Palestinian terrorist attack were carried over to the treatment of the death of Israeli Jews caused by Israeli Jews. Typically, the religious energies born in the context of terrorism develop inertia and take over death that is not connected with terrorism. Since the possibility of according mystical meaning to standard unnatural death is limited, greater emphasis is placed on halakhic norms in handling the deaths of accident victims. Even ZAKA's treatment of suicides and murder victims is subject to an almost infinite tangle of rabbinical rulings.

When they have finished handling conventional cases of unnatural death, the chief ZAKA activist in Jerusalem pats the shoulders of his fellow volunteers and shouts out, "Holy work!" Then he repeats, "Holy work, holy work!" One sharp-witted member of his team explained that this was an expression of his fear, lest in the routine work at the uninspiring arena of death, late at night, after removing yet another body of a motorcyclist who skidded in a sharp turn on an isolated road, the exhausted volunteers might forget that they are devoted to an exalted religious mission. When they are handling death from a Palestinian attack against Israelis, there's no need for such a reminder. ZAKA lives in the tension of the inevitable comparison between the arena of death in terrorism and the arena of run-of-the-mill death.

Shortly after the waves of terror of the Intifada died down, I was invited by the head of a ZAKA team to observe the treatment of the death of a married couple, victims of murder and suicide committed with a pistol.[28] While he was removing his blood-stained overall, a veteran Haredi volunteer explained his theory, according to which the Jewish victims of Palestinian terrorism are saintly, and the ZAKA volunteers are self-effacing toward them, intending only to serve them, whereas in ordinary cases of unnatural death, "We volunteers are the saints [*tsadikim*]," who perform a mission of true compassion. Later in his monologue, he said, "If it depended on me, I'd like to die in an Intifada attack, because then death isn't so terrible. Unlike the victims of an accident, people don't pity the victims of terrorism. They even envy them a little."

## Decomposition

The term *tsadikut* (righteousness, saintliness) is common in the volunteers' rhetoric, and the topic of *tsadikut* occupies an important place in the organization's sub-culture. As is common among many ultra-Orthodox Jews, especially from the Hasidic wing, the ideal of *tsadikut* guides the ZAKA volunteers, and, perhaps more than others, they are obsessed with the aspiration to be thought of as *tsadikim*. Managing death in the aftermath of Palestinian terrorist attacks is the basis of their claim to be regarded as *tsadikim*. It has been argued that in ultra-religious groups competition develops between groups of believers and among the believers themselves within each group: "Who is the most religious?"[29] Such a dynamic also characterizes ZAKA. Even among *tsadikim* there are levels, and a *tsadik* is supposed to aspire to upgrade his *tsadikut*. It would appear that in their work in the arena of suicide terrorism, the volunteers have attained the utmost righteousness. But they want to break another record. They are trying to cope with the challenge of another arena: at a different site, they will confront a death rivaling the horror caused by the human bomb.

The competing arena awaits the volunteers in an entirely unexpected place, one that is not widely known, another site of death where the ideal of true compassion is realized. It is found in tiny apartments in poor neighborhoods, where lonely old people live, people with no ties of family, friendship, or neighborliness, and when they die, no one knows. Their bodies lie for hours or whole days, until the stench is noticed by the tenants of nearby dwellings, who call up the rescue services. However, neither the policemen nor the paramedics can stand the smell or the sight revealed to them once the fire department has broken down the door. Only ZAKA volunteers cope with this dreadful form of death. The phenomenon has an official name—the "lonesome" (*galmudim*). In ZAKA parlance, which eschews all euphemisms, the phenomenon is called simply "decomposition" (*rikvonot*).

There are *tsadikim* and *tsadikim nistarim* (the hidden righteous), who are regarded in the Jewish tradition as possessing a higher spiritual level than mere *tsadikim*. It is said that the world stands upon the hidden *tsadikim*, who also perform miracles. A *tsadik nistar* is someone whose righteousness is not publicly known or visible, that is, someone whose identity is ordinary and does not testify to his inner being, which has special religious capacities. According to Hasidic lore, throughout history there has been an unbroken chain of hidden *tsadikim* who appear in many incarnations. In every generation there are thirty-six hidden *tsadikim* (known as *lamed-vavnikim*). People have always wondered who they are and strive to locate them behind the innocent and modest impression they make. Sometimes they wear rags, make strange gestures like madmen, or earn a living by simple trades, such as cobblers. It is noted that they are not necessarily Torah scholars for whom study is their way of life. Nevertheless, their prayers and actions are particularly desirable to God.

Both in the religious and secular communities, many people pin the label of *tsadikim* on the ZAKA activists, because of their handling of death in the arena of terrorism. With some lack of modesty, the volunteers accept the title of *tsadikim* willingly, especially because it makes it easier for them to cope with the criticism of their opponents in the Haredi community for not devoting themselves to the study of Talmud in a yeshiva. According to the conventional criteria of their community, they appear to be of inferior religiosity, but in the hour of need, they prove to be superior. In ZAKA's internal discourse, the title of hidden *tsadik* is reserved for the volunteers who handle the decomposed bodies of the isolated people, for no one denies that their actions are marvelous, but they certainly do not appear to belong to the classical religious repertoire of righteous deeds. They handle this most difficult type of death on their own, far from the public eye, but, according to their feeling, they are especially close to God.

The sight of the arena of the death of a "lonely" person is absolutely horrible. The decomposed body is swollen and often it has burst, and flesh and juices are scattered all over. The acids that ooze out of it eat into the floor and leave the form of the body on it. Green flies buzz in the air, and maggots wiggle and peek out of the broken flesh. The stench is just as hard to bear. The volunteers wear masks, smear their nostrils with sharp-smelling salve, but it is no use. After a halakhic discussion based on interpretations of Maimonides, the chief rabbi of ZAKA ruled that it was permissible to spray perfume on the disfigured body. In a bizarre, almost hysterical manner, they do not refrain from joking. A ZAKA volunteer suggested that in this situation, they truly enter the depths of the world of the dead and receive a partial answer to the morbid mystery that passes through many people's minds: How does a body look in the grave?

Though the subject of handling the bodies of lonesome people has been familiar to the Haredi volunteers since the establishment of ZAKA and even before that, they did not present it as an additional area of the organization's specialization or ask for public acknowledgment for it until recently.[30] ZAKA claims to handle about five such instances of death every week. In these cases, the volunteers undergo a unique religious experience, what they describe as a kind of revelation. Having no audience, they feel that only God is with them. With great assurance they testify that they see Him while He looks upon them with satisfaction. Almost identical statements are made in internal discussion comparing the arena of terror to that of lonely persons' deaths. Their experiences in the two arenas are both similar and different. These are two extreme cases of the horror of death and of spiritual exaltation, two opposite poles that are also close to each other. Among ZAKA activists and within each one of them, they cannot decide which of the two arenas is more horrific, and of course which poses the ultimate religious test. There is a kind of tacit competition between the two arenas, noticeable only to those who are well-versed in ZAKA's inner life.

Treatment of the mutilated bodies of the victims of terrorism and dealing with the decomposed bodies of people who died alone represent two hierarchies of prestige within the organization. They are conditioned on one another: they say that someone who is capable of withstanding the challenges of one arena can also withstand those of the other. In both cases they use the same language to describe the experience in the arena, for example, "A burst of adrenaline comes from just knowing that we are doing something that no one else is capable of doing."

A central ZAKA activist testifies, "Shortly after midnight, I received a report on my beeper about the body of a solitary old man, who was found in his house two weeks since he had last been seen. The policemen who broke into the apartment retreated immediately because of the horrible stench. I was called to the arena by volunteers who complained that even they were incapable of dealing with the horror. A physician filled in the death certificate without looking at the corpse, because he, too, was unable to approach it. The body had decomposed, swollen up, and exploded. Its acidity had eaten into the floor. Maggots were swarming on it. I pressured one of the volunteers, who had vomited on the stairs, and forced him to dance and sing the verse,

'Fortunate are you, Israel, before whom you are purified and who purifies you.'[31] Thus, at the entrance to the apartment, the two of us went into a trance, and in our frenzy we entered the place, and for hours prepared the body for burial. In the morning I went home, threw my clothing in the trash, and sat in the bathtub for a long time, but the smell didn't leave me for many days."

# PART I
# INTRODUCING ZAKA
*Roots, Context, Composition, Dynamics*

Part I offers a first time comprehensive and methodical portrayal of ZAKA based on extensive field research. This part is mainly ethnographic. It provides basic information about ZAKA: the background of the organization's emergance, the circumstances of its development, its religious and political environment, its goals and worldview, its subculture, and the profile of its members.

# 2

# Fascination with Unnatural Death

## Past and Present

### When It All Began

Bus 405 travels daily on Israel's Route 1 between Tel Aviv and Jerusalem. On 6 July 1989, shortly after noon, as the packed coach ascended the hills on the way to the capital, a passenger suddenly rose, moved to the front of the bus, shouted "Allahu Akbar," grabbed the steering wheel, and swung it sharply to the right. The heavy vehicle plunged over a cliff, crashed, and went up in flames. Dozens of dead and wounded were extricated from the wreck, including the Palestinian assailant.[1] The traumatic attack brought about an escalation in the Israeli-Palestinian conflict and heralded the beginning of the first of two major waves of suicide terrorism that plagued the region for the next quarter-century.

This seminal terrorist mass murder took place just across the highway from the Haredi town of Kiryat Ye'arim. Students at the nearby yeshivas were the first to reach the shattered and burning bus, and when emergency forces arrived, the young Torah scholars helped them conduct the rescue operation. While busily struggling on the rugged terrain, the enthusiastic Haredim called friends in Jerusalem, and they, too, arrived in large numbers. Thus, most of the civilians who assisted the rescue crews were ultra-Orthodox that labored assiduously among the victims.

The horrific scene of the 405 bus received extensive coverage in the media. Sights never seen before on the country's television screens were broadcast. Besides the grisly spectacle of the violent act's aftermath, the sight of the dozens of young Haredim caring for the wounded and recovering the bodies of the dead made a huge impression. For the Israeli viewers, the juxtaposition of terrorism and Jewish ultra-Orthodoxy was startling and mesmerizing. Radical Jewish religiosity had until then been linked in public opinion to detachment, passivity, and physical flabbiness. Most Israelis thought the Haredim were indifferent to the world outside their communities, hardly

*The Cult of Dismembered Limbs.* Gideon Aran, Oxford University Press. © Oxford University Press 2023.
DOI: 10.1093/oso/9780197689141.003.0002

likely to drop their books and dash bravely into a conflict zone marked by violence. The stereotypical Haredi man represented the antithesis of up-to-date, manly, patriotic values. Indeed, the Haredi community in large measure rejected the culture of the Israeli majority, condemned cooperation with the country's political institutions, avoided displaying solidarity with Zionists committed to the Land and State of Israel, and avoided direct involvement in the armed confrontation with the Arabs. Until then, only Israel's engaged loyalists, who subscribed to a militaristic ethos and valued active citizenry and social decency, had addressed terrorism, and these Israelis viewed Haredi sectorial factionalism with suspicion and contempt.

The 405 bus attack aroused riveting dissonance in the public mind: bearded Haredim in traditional black and white garb panting, sweating, covered with mud and blood, running up and down the hillside, rappelling, and carrying stretchers to helicopters. They seemed to have emerged from the eighteenth-century ghetto to star in the kind of epic previously associated with atheist flag-wavers in army uniforms. For the first time, Israel's Haredi population had joined the Sabra fraternity of Blood, Sweat and Tears which they had avoided in the past, and which they had never been invited to join.

Just as mainstream Israel's image of the Haredim changed, so did the Haredim's view of themselves. Suddenly young ultra-Orthodox men discovered new exhilarating and addictive sensations: action, risk-taking, commitment to the country and dedication to its defense, solidarity and collaboration with secular fellow-citizens, social entrepreneurship, and pride in pioneering. They had seen themselves as pure and aloof; now they had touched bodies and encountered death—and earned praise. Indeed, chauvinism, physicality, and fame are not the least of their new intoxicating feelings. These new Haredi men could no longer be accused of being alienated or parasitical. For many Haredim, then, their response to the 405 bus attack was a total and sweeping experience, a moment of self-discovery, a revelation stimulating awakening.[2] Since the 405 bus attack, Haredim have been obsessed by horrific death, and a peculiar type of terrorism-related initiative became an integral element of their identity.

The volunteers who participated in that formative event later testified that they had initially assumed they were caring for the victims of an accident. It took time for them to realize it was a terrorist attack. At that point, they reported, their outlook underwent a radical change. In an instant, the mountainside became a holy site and their labor a sacred task. They emphasized that, even when they had thought it was an accident, they had treated the dead with all the respect that Jewish religious law requires. But when it turned out that the dead were the victims of terrorism, they became martyrs in the eyes of the Haredim, and recovering the victims' bodies became a divine calling.

An older rabbi who was among the Haredim summoned to the scene of the disaster told me that after some time, while he was taking care of the bodies of the bus passengers, he overheard someone on a walkie-talkie saying that the severely wounded Palestinian terrorist had been located and arrested. Only then did he understand that the deadly event had been caused intentionally, to murder Jewish citizens. He described that moment as a true "illumination," going on to describe it in terms of wonder, turmoil, and profound transformation. Then he went on to say, "It was as if we had gotten a huge injection of adrenaline, and we devoted more energy to the work than before. In a trance lasting hours and hours in the harsh sun, without rest, without eating and drinking, we understood we were taking part in the sanctification of the name of God." In consultation with other religious authorities, they reached the conclusion that different religious laws applied to this event, unlike those that had previously guided them. For soil soaked with the blood of an ordinary casualty is not the same as soil soaked with the blood of a martyr. For that reason, contrary to ordinary practice, they decided to bury the victims in their blood-soaked clothing, so as "to increase the dread of divine judgment."[3]

Six years later, inspired by this experience, and in the wake of a series of further terrorist attacks, a group of Haredim established ZAKA. Many of the Haredi volunteers at the site of the 405 bus attack became leaders and central players in the organization, and the attack was, for them, its founding moment. Now, some three decades after that event, these activists continue to tell and retell the story of that day, and the events have taken on mythical dimensions. In harking back to the 405 bus attack as the explanation for the birth of ZAKA, they claim that the location of the suicide attack near a Haredi community and the fact that Haredim became prominent actors in the battle against terrorism are incontrovertible proof that Providence was at work.

Within ZAKA several narratives compete regarding the origin of the organization. Other events are recorded in the collective memory of the Haredi volunteers as the moments of the emergence of this essentially revolutionary phenomenon, events that offer an alternative foundation myth for ZAKA. Some maintain that the cornerstone was not laid at the event of bus 405 but on the following days, when Haredi yeshiva students from all over the area insisted on continuing to comb the steep slope where the bus had crashed, still thrilled and diligently searching for overlooked tiny body parts and remaining blood stains for burial.

Others place the birth of ZAKA more than a decade earlier, before the appearance of suicide terror on the horizon of the Middle East, when the phenomenon of the human bomb had not yet been envisioned even as a hypothetical possibility. This was the attack on the 12 bus in the Bayit Vegan neighborhood of Jerusalem, which left six people dead (June 1978). In the collective memory of the veteran volunteers of the organization, there is confusion between that terrorist attack and the one that took place nearby on the 18 bus, with the same number of victims (1983). Identical elements stand out in descriptions of the two attacks: the amateurish incompetence of the volunteers and their enthusiasm and improvisation. They add that in a miraculous way, out of the blue, rapidly, hordes of Haredim appeared at the site of the attack. Then, for long hours, they devoted themselves to recovering the mutilated bodies and gathering their burned parts. The volunteers emphasized their attraction to the arena and the deep urge that lay in the background of their spontaneous treatment of the dead. According to eyewitness testimony, the Haredim crawled on their knees, soaking up blood from the sidewalk and scraping burned scraps of flesh and bone from the cracks between the stones of the nearby wall with matches they took from their pockets.

In contrast, others place the foundational moments later, pointing to the attacks that took place at the heights of the two waves of suicide terrorism of the Intifada. One of these attacks took place on the number 5 bus in Tel Aviv (October 1994, Dizengof Street, twenty-two victims). It made an especially strong impression, either because it took place at the symbol of the good life in the secular city, the soft home front of Israel, or because this was the first and last time that uncensored television pictures presented detailed close-ups of shattered and burned bodies, which was regarded as a kind of pornography and an insult to the honor of the dead, leaving a harsh and demoralizing effect on the entire public. According to yet another version, the double attack in the Maḥaneh Yehuda Market (July 1997, sixteen victims), was the foundational event, since its particular circumstances brought out the religious character of the treatment of the victims of terrorism. The attack took place on Friday afternoon, and because of the power of the explosion, the process of identifying and removing the bodies was not completed before the entry of the Sabbath. The question arose: Was it permissible to violate the sanctity of the Sabbath for the sake of respect for the dead, or should the bodies be left where they were until the departure of the Sabbath the following evening? They consulted with rabbis on the matter, and, at the scene of the attack, a complex halakhic discussion took place, which can be seen as the foundation of ZAKA's developing creed.

Those who propose competing versions all agree among themselves about one, primeval beginning, sanctified and binding: all the volunteers state that the act that commences the tradition of ZAKA is mentioned in their ancient, most sacred text. There one finds canonical reference to the unusual treatment of sanctified corpses. The Torah relates that the first prophet, Moses, gathers Joseph's bones and brings them to Canaan for burial (Exodus 34). As they proclaim at every opportunity, the biblical Moses was therefore the "first ZAKA volunteer."[4]

## Proto-ZAKA

With the intensification of Palestinian terrorism, and especially with the entry of suicide terrorism on the scene of the regional conflict, various embryonic procedures developed for the religious treatment of the victims of terror. The most important of these was the spontaneous initiative of a group of Jerusalem Haredim, who were summoned to the scene of terrorism as volunteers. This early organization was conservative in nature, a limited extension and adaptation of the traditional burial society (*ḥevra qadisha*) to make it suit death-management under the special conditions of a terrorist attack. From 1989 to 1995 the organization referred to itself as "Ḥesed shel emet" (HSE), meaning "true compassion."

The founder of HSE was Rabbi Eliezer Gelbstein, a graduate of prestigious Torah academies, a Lubavitcher Hasid and nearly sixty years old, with more than a dozen grandchildren. His mother and grandmother volunteered to purify women's bodies in preparation for burial, and he volunteered to take care of the victims of terrorism from the time of the attack by Fatah in Jerusalem in 1975, claiming fifteen dead. That attack, surprising in its time, proved to be a harbinger of horrors to come. Following the attack on bus 405, he gathered about a hundred volunteers; many of them worked in the burial society that he managed.[5]

Gradually the group developed primary procedures and gathered a store of equipment, though it was limited and primitive. For example, with an exiguous budget, they purchased a supply of cotton swabs from a neighborhood pharmacy to soak up blood. At the same time, they took care to provide basic halakhic backing for the volunteers, by means of occasional lectures by rabbis who happened to be available. The peak of their professional training was a brief course in the forensic department of the police force. From attack to attack, by trial and error, they put together practical know-how for dealing with the victims of terrorism.

HSE gained the approval of several Haredi rabbis and functionaries, in cooperation with mayors and government ministers. It was backed by the police and received attention in the media. The organization received prizes and honors, and in a letter of commendation the prime minister defined the volunteers as "saints with trowels" (used to remove pieces of bodies that clung to walls).

HSE was characterized by a cautious orientation toward change. It avoided full institutionalization, rejected gestures that would identity it with agencies of the state, and nurtured close connections with the institutions of the Haredi community. HSE discouraged those who advocated organizational independence and operational creativity, and it restrained the throbbing religious imagination that demanded halakhic innovation and tended toward mystical practices.

In the aftermath of the 405 bus attack, criticism of the manner of Haredi death-management on the scene was voiced, calling for increased discipline and efficiency in anticipation of future terrorist attacks. A few years later the functional disorder of HSE became more evident, and, against this background, ferment increased. A critical event was the attack on the 26 bus (August 1995). The dedication of the volunteers and their feverish activity could not conceal operational failures and inner tensions, which sometimes led to catastrophe. First, confusion arose in counting the severed limbs, leading to an error in determining the number of victims. Second, an erroneous report was made of the gender of the terrorist, who was originally identified as a woman. The following incidents were even more distressing: the arm (some say another limb) of one of the victims disappeared, and it was only found in the evening, among the affairs of one of the volunteers. The following testimony sounds even more fantastic. Though no conclusive proof has been adduced of its veracity, I heard it, with only slight variations, from numerous sources, who swore that the facts were true. The morning following the attack a Haredi volunteer showed up with a shopping bag containing a severed foot.

The excessive motivation of the Haredim who live near the sites of the explosions, who, without training or gear, and also without authorization or coordination, dealt with bodies and their parts with enthusiasm that came close to wildness, ultimately caused the desecration of the dead. This is the background of the criticism that began to be heard both from the forces of law and order and within the Haredi community. The situation became graver because two factions among the Haredim who were devoted to dealing with the victims of terrorism could not cooperate, and the old dispute between them grew sharper.

The main division was between the conservative leadership of HSE and young volunteers who had recently joined the organization. The latter disliked the association with the traditional burial society, which suffered from low public esteem, and they promoted organizational autonomy and professional expertise. The veterans defined the internal opposition as "impertinent, vociferous, and publicity-seeking." The confrontation between the two factions rapidly spread to struggles for personal prestige between the old-timer Rabbi Gelbstein and Yehuda Meshi-Zahav, who rapidly stood out as an alternative leader, endowed with charisma and organizational skills. Among the revolutionaries two apparently contradictory trends emerged: formal institutionalization along with daring and energetic religious revivalism.

During several waves of Palestinian terrorism attacks in Israel the two camps worked in parallel, with visible rivalry. At the end of 1995 a decision was made among the opposition to establish a separate organization, and in response Gelbstein and several of his followers resigned. A younger, dynamic, and ambitious group usurped the place of the veterans. The new organization received the approbation of the Rabbinical Council of the Eda Haredit, and it started to structure itself systematically, while expanding and professionalizing. It soon gained recognition from the police and other security and rescue services and found itself at the center of the life of the Haredi community and of Israeli attention. In these circumstances the name of the organization was determined: ZAKA. Within a short time, horizons opened for it which would have been difficult to envisage at the start. In parallel with the rise of a second wave of Palestinian suicide terrorism, what can be called the ZAKA decade emerged in Israel (1995–2005). This was ZAKA's golden age, during which it became distinctive, upgraded, and flourishing. Along with the human bombs, the Haredi volunteers took center stage in the

Middle Eastern public. That was when ZAKA took on the decided character central to the present book.

## Harbingers of ZAKA

Violent attacks against Israeli citizens by Palestinian organizations preceded suicide terrorism. From the time that Israel conquered the West Bank and the Gaza Strip in 1967 until the two Intifadas, 1987–1993 and 2000–2005, regional terrorism became more murderous and spectacular. In the Israeli collective memory of that period, certain violent episodes stand out, such as the grenade attack at the vegetable market in Jerusalem (leaving twelve dead, November 1969) and the bomb placed in a refrigerator in Zion Square in Jerusalem (fifteen dead, July 1975). In these terrorism attacks, Haredi volunteers led in dealing with the victims. They can be seen as the forerunners of ZAKA. Some of them remained active in ZAKA over the years, despite their advanced age. The eldest among them was Rabbi Eisenbach, who, at the age of seventy, had "preceded ZAKA by a whole generation," and in time was given the title of honorary president of ZAKA. Eisenbach gained a reputation for expertise and resilience, enabling him to deal with difficult cases of death. In these actions Eisenbach, the Haredi, also showed that he possessed national sentiments. Thus, he found himself drawn to the margins of the battlefields where the State of Israel fought from 1967 on. There, on his own, he dealt with IDF casualties whose bodies had been mutilated and remained in the field. His resume is resplendent with fantastic stories about how he scraped the tissue from inside tanks that had been blown up in the Yom Kippur (1973) and Lebanese (1982) wars. Even in old age he was one of the first to report to the sites of attacks, and, though he was not a member of the rabbinical board of ZAKA, halakhic decisions that he issued while working on the spot were accepted as binding by the organization. For nearly fifty years he evacuated corpses and specialized in the Jewish law applying to the evacuation of corpses.

Other individuals acted similarly outside of any existing institutional framework, and they were later regarded as foreshadowing ZAKA. One of these was Rabbi Eichler, an elderly Belz Hasid, who, during the battle to conquer the Old City of Jerusalem (1967), slipped into the ranks of the soldiers and helped them evacuate the bodies of their fallen comrades. Years before that, along with Eisenbach, Eichler had established a rickety body, with no members other than themselves, a burial society called "Kevod hamet" (Respect for the Dead), whose main purpose was to take care of the corpses of people who had died alone at home. Initially the two rabbis were regarded as lunatics. In time they came to be seen as saints.

Along with such private death-management initiatives of Haredim, there emerged a few institutions that are milestones on the path to the establishment of ZAKA. An early example of the tendency of Haredim to step out of their traditional seclusion and join in the care for Jewish victims of unnatural death can be found in their volunteering for para-military action in IDF burial units (YKP). At first the latter were manned exclusively by religious Zionists, but ultra-Orthodox volunteers gradually joined in and imposed a Haredi ethos.

The connections between YKP and ZAKA have several aspects. First, veterans of the former found their way to the senior ranks of the latter, including Rabbi Roje, the head of the ZAKA rabbinical council. Second, some of the practices adopted by ZAKA for dealing with shattered corpses were first developed in the military burial units, which had garnered rich experience in situations similar in some respects to the aftermath of a terrorist attack. Third, the military burial units provided ZAKA with elements of rabbinical, halakhic backing for the treatment of the dead. During the 2000s the situation was reversed: ZAKA, which had meanwhile become a major factor in Israel and among the Haredim, began to influence the military burial units. Among other things, this is evident in the insistence of the IDF upon collecting tiny pieces of bodies, even with high risk to those dealing with the dead.[6]

## Early Haredi Fixation

As a Jerusalemite police officer told me, every terrorist attack becomes a "Haredi happening." However, the connection between the Haredim and death in general existed before their fascinated attraction to the arena of terrorism. First, unlike late modern, Western urban people, who distance themselves from death by medicalizing and bureaucratizing it, the life routines of the traditional religious people who live in the Haredi ghettoes of Jerusalem are bound up with constant and palpable contact with death. Among the Haredim there is little of the professional intervention and institutional separation that makes contact with death abstract in a certain sense. Death is present in the Haredi home and neighborhood, and Haredim are exposed to it at an early age. The dead were laid on the floor of the family home and then transferred to the street. After purification, the bodies were laid on stretchers, without coffins, covered with a soft shroud that shows the outlines of the body, and accompanied to the grave. Family members and people from the neighborhood, from children to the aged, were summoned to honor the dead, including passersby, crowding close to the corpse in dense intimacy, vying for the honor of bearing the stretcher and advancing on foot, sometimes a long and tiring way, to the cemetery, where the long burial ceremony takes place. In Jerusalem, even late at night, earsplitting loudspeakers mounted on cars wend their way slowly through the Haredi neighborhoods, summoning the community to observe the commandment of attending the funerals of prominent people or people with no family. At the funeral of Rabbi Shakh, as a result of the ecstatic crowding of the masses who sought to touch or bear the stretcher, the body fell to the ground (2001). At the funeral of Rabbi Ovadia Yosef, several Hasidim sneaked through and lay in the pit that had been dug for his body, to be close to him and to identify with him (2013).[7]

Such scenes are not atypical in the Haredi world, where familiarity with death has developed organically. An almost obsessive interest focused on unnatural death is prevalent there, enveloped in the ideology of "respect for the dead," especially for the Jewish dead, and the duty to fulfill the commandment of burial according to Jewish law. The Haredi concern with death has a clear political aspect. During the seven decades of the Jewish State, the Haredi-death complex has assumed a prominent place in the public agenda.

In the early years following the establishment of the State of Israel the zealous fringes of the Haredi community took part in violent riots against the government of Israel and its agents. However, except for isolated incidents, such eruptions beyond the confines of the ghetto focused on controversial issues unconnected with the dead.[8] Mainly in the mid-1970s a series of confrontations regarding the treatment of the dead began between Haredim and the Israeli establishment. The Haredi protests were expressed in parliamentary lobbying, mass rallies, and agitated demonstrations. The cause of Haredi activism was generally the way the authorities dealt with human bones discovered in archaeological excavations, the paving of roads, or the construction of public buildings. A Haredi spokesman addressed the secular majority in Israel through the press, claiming, "For you, they are just corpses, a bag of bones. For us, their whole future lies before them."[9]

The confrontations between the Haredim and the state related to the bones of the ancient dead developed into a fierce ideological and political dispute. Behind the ultra-Orthodox fixation on respect for the sacred dead lay a broad critique of Zionism, which, at that time, saw archaeology as a central component of the civic religion, a basis for the claim of ownership of the country.[10] A series of incidents that figured prominently in the mass communication headlines in 1981–1984 related to the excavation of the City of David in Jerusalem, dating from about 1,000 BCE, where ancient human bones were discovered. Although the archaeologists determined with certainty that the dead were not Israelite, the Haredim insisted that the area was a desecrated Jewish cemetery. The Haredi demand for the immediate cessation of the excavations was accompanied by blocking major roads, throwing stones at moving automobiles, vandalism to public and private property, and even launching Molotov cocktails. They also threatened the life of the head of the excavation, a distinguished professor, excommunicating him, casting various spells against him, and performing magical ceremonies in hopes of hastening his death.[11] When he died of cancer before his time, they did not conceal their joy and declared that it was a punishment from On High. Before his death they prayed for his bones to rot, so that he would not rise from the dead when the messiah came.[12] One of the chief violent opponents of the archaeologists was Meshi-Zahav, who became the head of ZAKA several years later. In his journal he defined the struggle against the excavations as a war.[13]

In the following years there were further manifestations of Haredi violence connected with the treatment of ancient skeletons. Among others, in 1985 Haredim sabotaged the building of a hotel in Tiberias, and in 1995 they blocked heavy bulldozers with their bodies to prevent construction of the first toll road in Israel. These confrontations ended after dozens of policemen stormed an extremist Haredi yeshiva in Jerusalem, with severe beatings and arrests. Further Haredi protest broke out in 2010 after ancient bones were moved during the expansion of a hospital in Ashkelon. Although experts examined them and determined that the bones were "pagan," the Haredim ruled that it was a desecration of sanctified Jewish graves. Aggression directed against secular Jews and police agents, on grounds of respect for the dead have proven again and again to be an effective means of enlistment and agitation that enhances the status of the activists and unifies the Haredi community.

Until the 2000s Haredim accused the Zionist establishment of *hitutei shekhvi*, an Aramaic expression meaning "poking around in graves," and it refers to the prohibition against disturbing the repose of the dead. They believe that this causes suffering to the soul of the dead, which might bring misfortune on the entire community.[14] Ironically, only a few years later, Haredi circles accused ZAKA of just this transgression.

Tiny Haredi organizations, mainly Atra Kadisha, stand behind many of these mass awakenings. Their activists belong to the most radical branch of the Haredim, who also have close ties with ZAKA personnel. The most prominent figure among them is Rabbi David Shmidel, a man of about eighty, who received the blessing of the Satmer Rebbe and the Brisker Rebbe decades earlier, two of the most extreme ultra-Orthodox leaders, and who later worked in coordination with Rabbi Weiss of the Eda Haredit umbrella organization, which leads the religious opposition to the State of Israel. In some instances, Shmidel even stood in rigid opposition to the leaders of the Haredi community, who, he claimed, were compromising with the Israeli establishment. His peak achievement was a so-called victory over secular Israel, when, after bitter struggles, he took responsibility for bones from the Mishnaic period (first to sixth centuries CE), which were excavated in the northern settlement of Sepphoris, and had them reinterred according to halakha in Jerusalem.[15]

The Haredim are especially sensitive about postmortem operations. Their opposition to this practice also stirs up the Haredi community and frequently degenerates into violent responses. Occasionally they have removed bodies and organs from hospital morgues, by ruse or by force, to be buried before they are "desecrated." Some organizations and individuals have specialized in this matter, such as the Committee for the Protection of the Sanctity of the Jews of the Eda Haredit. Among ZAKA activists one finds a prominent representation of veteran militants against autopsies. ZAKA volunteers relate that in their youth they were educated to admire the rescue of Jewish corpses from autopsy, and they adulated those who seized the bodies. In ZAKA, many stories are told about fabled missions of "sanctifying the Name of God," in the form of seizing a body from the operating table at the very last moment or sneaking a body out of a police station through a narrow window after a daring climb, by means of a clever subterfuge. Another story concerns the stealing of body parts in laboratory jars from a research institute, placing them on a stretcher, and racing wildly through the streets of Jerusalem to the cemetery. According to rumors current in the Haredi community, Rabbi

Weiss issued a halakhic ruling in this instance, stating that a cement block must be placed between the limbs and the inner organs, since it was uncertain whether they belonged to the same dead person.

There is yet another legend of exemplary dedication among the Haredim, which was an inspiration for ZAKA, some of whose elements I was able to verify. At some time in the 1960s, near midnight, at the elite Hebron Yeshiva, a group of Torah scholars was concentrating on the Talmud, when suddenly a telephone call interrupted them: a Haredi man had died under unclear circumstances, and it was feared that the body would be autopsied by court order. Everyone present put aside the holy books and rushed to the operating room, from which they seized the body, despite the protests of doctors and nurses. With the body still warm, they burst into the street and hailed a taxi. The corpse was laid in the car, with its feet near the driver and the face was covered with a black fedora. Avoiding police roadblocks, they reached the yeshiva dining hall, where they kept the body for some time until it was buried, without official authorization. There were similar instances. In 1980 a group of Haredim learned that autopsies were being performed for teaching purposes in the university hospital in Jerusalem. They forced their way into a protected area, rioted there, and sprayed large graffiti on the walls: "Nazis!" In February 2006 the body of an old woman was sent for autopsy at the National Institute of Forensic Medicine. Masses of Haredim rioted in the streets of Jerusalem and some traveled to Tel Aviv and broke through the gate of the Institute in a fervor of vandalism, causing great damage.

The celebrated stories that inundate the pre-history of ZAKA contain motifs which, years later, formed the mature culture of ZAKA. One of the most important of these cherished elements is the obsessive concern with the special treatment of the Jewish dead, and the strictly observed distinction between the bodies or skeletons of Jews and those of non-Jews, again and again, even when in disagreement with the diagnosis of academic or police experts. Here is another example: Haredim from the Atra Kadisha organization besieged the home of the mayor of Acre, because two-thousand-year-old bones were discovered in the city. For years the Haredi activists delayed a large building project there, as they did not accept the professional opinion that stated with certainty that the bones were those of Roman legionnaires (2007).

After ZAKA was institutionalized, the aggressive spirit of the Haredim regarding the Jewish dead took on new hues. A conspicuous example of this is the war that ZAKA declared against an organization called Menuḥa

Nekhona (Correct Rest), which introduced the ideology and technology of cremation in Israel. ZAKA activists used detective techniques to discover the crematorium and sabotage it, and they responded violently against those involved in this practice, which is foreign to the Jewish tradition. When someone managed to burn down the crematorium, they didn't even try to conceal their joy.[16]

The veteran warriors from the proto-ZAKA era, some of whom were still active during the time of terrorism, are models for ZAKA. For their part, the central figures in ZAKA are pleased to share the stories of their lives, emphasizing the inherent connection between Haredim and death, and in many instances they hint that their fascination with death was born of a miraculous event, behind which lay a divine intention and a prophecy for the future. For example, one ZAKA activist remembers that in his early childhood he was exposed to the smell of a decomposing corpse that came from the neighboring apartment, and since then he has been obsessed with that particular smell, which still leads him from one arena of death to another. Another instance is the story of Rabbi Gelbstein, who, as a young yeshiva student, went out on a missionary journey to the north of the country, and, "miraculously," he arrived at the shore of the Sea of Galilee during a Syrian artillery barrage, which killed a resident of Tiberias at the entrance to his home. That evening, after the body was removed, and firemen were hosing down the site, he noticed a cat sniffing and sneaking into a yard just a few meters away. When he followed it, he discovered scraps of a human brain and a puddle of blood that remained on the ground. He spent long hours purifying the place, and in the morning he brought the body parts in for burial. He defined the event as "one of those holy moments in which ZAKA was conceived."

It is difficult to determine whether the unusual frequency of foundational events in the early lives of the Haredi volunteers, which are meant to explain their fascination with death-management in ZAKA as if it were fated from Above, is a credible historical fact or an apocryphal invention. Take, for example, the following testimony of veteran ZAKA activists: "My father worked for the burial society. He used to bring me into the room for purifying the dead. Once he made me drink some of the water used to wash corpses. That was like a ceremony to immunize me against the fear of death."[17]

The natural attraction to things connected with death often caused these Haredim to depart from their traditional ways and break out of the walls of the ghetto. Matters of death were among the main factors that impelled them to direct activism and violent opposition to their surroundings. They harnessed the impulse that drew them to deal with death to strengthen their anti-Israeli protests; conversely, their antagonism to Zionism and the state made use of the treatment of the dead to consolidate the community and advance its interests. Until the 1960s and 1970s, the handling of death was a factor that widened the rift between the Haredim and the State of Israel. Since then, and especially since the emergence of Palestinian terrorism, the treatment of death has strengthened the connection of Haredim to the State of Israel. At first, the hostility of the Haredim toward secular Jews and their institutions was channeled toward matters of death. Later, the effect of the Haredi fixation on death was reversed, and the sentiment became patriotic and led to cooperation between the Haredim and their secular brethren. Under certain circumstances, respect for the dead was the root of opposition to the state, and in other circumstances, it became the root of identification with the state. Rabbi Shmidel, who epitomized the Haredi obsession with corpses and skeletons, was once arrested at an illegal demonstration against the desecration of Jewish graves. Shortly afterward the police freed him so he could deal with victims of Palestinian terrorism.

## Classical Age and Recent Trends: Charisma and Its Routinization

The histories of ZAKA and that of terrorism in the Middle East are intertwined. It is especially difficult to separate the organizational career of ZAKA from that of the Palestinian armed organizations which dispatched human bombs. ZAKA appeared in its mature form with the first appearance of suicide terrorism in Israel, and it reached its zenith at the peak of that terrorism. With the decline in suicide terrorism, ZAKA lost its impetus, fame, and charisma. Diverse periods are generally discerned in the history of terrorism on the Palestinian-Israeli front, and they are parallel to phases in the life of ZAKA. The history of Palestinian terrorism is generally distinguished by the frequency and murderousness of attacks and according to their spectacularism. Hence, we have the following divisions: 1968–1980, 1980–1993, 1993–2000, 2000–2004, 2004–2007.[18] Each of these periods is reflected in the changing characteristics of ZAKA. The violent opposition of the Palestinian organizations peaked in two waves of suicide terrorism: 1993–1997 and 2000–2007. These spans of years, from the aftermath of the Oslo

Accords until the second Intifada died down, were the classic age of suicide terrorism, and, intrinsically connected with it, they were also ZAKA's golden age. The observations presented in this book focus on that period as well.

Although ZAKA has roots in the past, in the strict sense of the label and the familiar version of the organization, ZAKA is only one generation old, but it is already an integral part of Israeli life, and it is impossible to imagine the Middle Eastern conflict without it. Most likely, as long as Palestinian terrorism persists, ZAKA will continue to occupy an important place on the regional scene. Terrorism is ZAKA's raison d'être and the source of its vitality.

As this book nears completion, acts of terrorism in Israel have decreased, and we see no sign at all of suicide terrorism.[19] However, the Palestinian resistance organizations, especially the Islamic ones, promise to continue armed resistance against Israel until the last Jewish settlement is removed from the occupied territories, and perhaps until the Zionist state disappears completely from the map of the Middle East. While optimistic Israelis point to the drastic decline in the number of victims of terror in Israel,[20] pessimists call attention to the number of intelligence warnings against terrorist attacks (nearly five hundred per year). The ISA does not attribute this decline to lack of motivation on the part of the Palestinians or to a strategic decision on their part, but rather to the ability of Israeli intelligence and the army to deter and prevent terrorism.[21] In ZAKA they cite the annual reports of the ISA and point to the scores of "potential Palestinian terrorists" who are arrested to support the claim that no end to terrorism is in sight, and in any event the dismantling of ZAKA is inconceivable.[22] On the basis of this forecast, preparations are made for the day when "the holy work of the organization will be more necessary than ever." The activists and leaders of the organization are among the determinists who cannot conceive of an end to the Israeli-Palestinian conflict. Their bleak outlook on the future of the Middle East is consistent with their leaning toward the right-wing, hawkish pole of the political spectrum. Their critics argue that behind their tendency to belittle the winds of reconciliation that occasionally blow in the skies of the region a degree of wishful thinking is visible. Meanwhile, with the slight decline in terrorism, the volunteers find it hard to deny that they miss its charms. Recently alternative areas of activity have been proposed to ZAKA, but the volunteers admit in secret that dealing with them is less rewarding.

At present ZAKA is undergoing something of a crisis. However, as it has shown from the beginning, the organization continues to adapt to changing circumstances, and it insists on the continued vital need for its mission.

From the time of its establishment to this day, ZAKA has developed consistently, showing impressive resourcefulness. The number of volunteers has increased, and the organization has improved, as has its level of professionalism. They have taken on a broader variety of operational goals, fostered social solidarity, developed a typical culture, and cultivated public relations. ZAKA changed itself from spontaneous, sporadic arousal to becoming a permanent and stable phenomenon, an entity between a formal organization and a civil movement, as well as a revivalist religious cult. A peripheral impulse and sectorial interest became a central national factor; an obscure and provocative manifestation became something self-evident, legitimate, and respected.

In recent years the Haredi community has become accustomed to the presence of ZAKA, but it has not softened its critique of the organization. In the ultra-Orthodox neighborhoods people repeatedly attribute to ZAKA the "sin" of seeking publicity, bordering on hubris. Indeed, the Haredi volunteers are attracted by the spotlights of television. ZAKA employs a spokesman, and in addition it regards all its activists as effective public relations agents. Even at the arena of attacks, while carrying out the calling of "true compassion" for the dead, the volunteers respond to the requests of the media, expose themselves to cameras while they are bent over bodies, and they are not reluctant to speak to any microphone thrust in their face. The volunteers' skill in mobilizing public opinion complements the familiarity they display in relating to presidents and prime ministers, senior politicians, generals, and other celebrities. The volunteers proudly recall that in 2001 ZAKA was named the UN's volunteer organization of the year. Two years later, in the midst of the Intifada, a rumor circulated that ZAKA was among the candidates for a Nobel Peace Prize.[23]

Because it is identified with terrorism, ZAKA is a focus of attention in Israel. The organization's office houses an archive of hundreds of newspaper clippings about ZAKA, a rich collection of promotional films, television reports from all over the world, as well as self-produced still pictures and videos on events in which they starred, mainly from the arena of terrorism.[24] The heads of the organization argue apologetically that the publicity is vital for soliciting contributions. The government subsidies ZAKA receives are insufficient to cover their increasing needs. Hence, they have developed a well-oiled fundraising mechanism, which resorts to every possible mode of appeal, including emotional blackmail by intoning the melodies of existential fear and Jewish solidarity.[25] Close-ups of shattered bodies were regarded as a legitimate means of fundraising in branches of supporters that were established in Orthodox communities throughout the world, from Miami to London and Paris. A special emissary was sent from time to time to Haredi concentrations in Brooklyn, where he horrified the audiences with stories of his experiences at the arena of terrorism during the Intifada. Important visitors from abroad are invited to visit the offices of the organization in Jerusalem, where gigantic enlargements of photographs are on display, immortalizing the volunteers at the scenes of large terrorism attacks. The opposite wall is decorated with trophies, prizes, and medals. Thirst for support, connections, recognition, and further praise is evident.

With great frequency, well-produced color brochures in English and Yiddish are circulated. They contain quotations and translations of odes in praise of ZAKA along with more and more accounts of horror from the arena. The same glorifying headlines appear repeatedly: "For us, death is part of life"; "There's no knowing when the next disaster will happen, but you can be sure the ZAKA volunteers will be there"; "Facing a Gruesome Task"; "Always There When Tragedy Strikes"; "Enduring Horror." At the end of every year a chart is released summing up the numbers of "deeds of true compassion" (the treatment of unnatural deaths from disasters and terrorist attacks, accidents, and suicides). In 1999 there were 191; in 2001 there were 589; in 2003 there were 1,532; and in 2005 there were 2,065.

## Varieties of Death in the Shadow of Terrorist Attacks

An important Haredi rabbi is said to have said that God only brought terrorism down upon Israel so that ZAKA would be founded, and thus the commandment of treating the dead in the spirit of the Torah would also be observed in events less dramatic than terrorism, which probably would not have been treated properly, were it not that ZAKA existed. Indeed, ZAKA developed momentum and needs of its own, and they led the organization to continue to act, even though its original mission remains only partially current.

The decline in the intensity and prominence of Palestinian terrorism in Israel led to a degree of demoralization among ZAKA volunteers, and this is also notable in the relaxation of the religious passion that accompanies their activism. However, the heads of the organization and its activists demonstrated vitality and responded to this decline creatively. Even during the time of terrorism ZAKA expanded its activities to deal with the victims of disasters unconnected with terrorism, and, in the post-terrorism era, they continue to deal with a variety of types of death as well as with incidents not directly connected to death.

In internal discussions the ZAKA activists repeatedly refer, in somewhat jocular tones, to an imaginary future in which there will be no terrorism. They are quite ambivalent about this fantasy. For if this ideal vision were to be fulfilled, doubt would arise as to justifying the continued existence of ZAKA. The believers wonder: "And what if the messiah comes?" A Haredi volunteer responds to this possibility with humor colored by deep conviction: "The messiah will certainly come. But when he comes, he won't be riding on a white donkey, but on a motorcycle with a siren, marked with the symbol of ZAKA."

Until the advent of the messiah, ZAKA volunteers wax nostalgic over the glory days of the organization, when it was associated with the response to terrorism, and in parallel they pounce upon every new event that can be connected with terrorism, as if to show they will always be relevant and to confirm their indispensability. During the decade following the Intifada, quite a few terrorist attacks were committed by running people over, stabbing them with knives, kidnaping, and shooting from ambush or a moving car on the roads of the West Bank. Although they were not as murderous as acts of suicide terrorism, they revived ZAKA. This applies especially to the more severe attacks, which had strong reverberations, such as the murder of students while they were studying in the library of an important yeshiva in Jerusalem (March 2008, eight dead), the stabbing to death of a couple and their three children while they were asleep in their home in a settlement (March 2011, Itamar), the murder of three young yeshiva students who were kidnaped while waiting for a lift (June 2014, Gush Etzion). On the cover of ZAKA's internal newsletter a headline trumpeted in huge letters, "Terrorism is with us again!" With these sensational attacks, the organization went back to "the good old times," to use the words of various proud and newly invigorated volunteers.[26]

The decline in the intensity of Palestinian terrorism in Israel was compensated, as it were, by the spread of Islamic terrorism against Jewish targets all over the world. ZAKA received an opportunity to demonstrate commitment to preserve the honor of Jewish martyrs, wherever they were, and to flaunt its long-distance operational abilities. The Jewish Connection was the rationale for sending trained teams, with special equipment, in several incidents of international terrorism committed by Al-Qaeda, including the attack on the synagogue in Istanbul, where several members of the Turkish Jewish community were killed (November 2003), and the attack on the hotel in Taba and in resorts along the Red Sea in Sinai, where about twenty Israeli vacationers were killed (October 2004). ZAKA established branches throughout the world based on orthodox Jewish communities in various countries, such as Mexico. The organization boasted 140 volunteers abroad.

By virtue of its specialization in the victims of terrorism attacks, ZAKA regarded itself as the natural candidate for dealing with all kinds of multi-casualty events, including natural disasters and large-scale accidents. Just two prominent examples of this are ZAKA's handling of the crash of a bus full of tourists near Eilat (December 2008, twenty-four dead) and at the scene of the two train crashes (Revadim, June 2005; Beit Yehoshua, June 2006). ZAKA also received publicity and praise for its actions in the forest fire on Mount Carmel, when, bravely, they removed bodies from the flames (December 2010, forty-four dead).

The confrontation with Hizballah, which degenerated into the second Lebanese war (July 2006), seemed to revive ZAKA. The war overflowed to the home front, where ZAKA was left to deal with civilian deaths. On a smaller scale, this story was repeated during the IDF operations in the Gaza Strip.[27]

In the 2010s, from time to time, the organization's leadership presents various scenarios of mass disaster that would require emergency call-up of ZAKA: barrages of missiles, earthquakes, technological crises on the scale of natural disasters, a mega-terrorism attack with strategic consequences. Forecasts of thousands of casualties give the heads of the organization the feeling of fateful importance and participation in events of biblical proportions. Meanwhile, catastrophes of this kind take place far from Israel. The huge number of victims attracts ZAKA volunteers to there as though by a magic wand. ZAKA's participation in the response of local governments at the arenas of mass disasters in Asia and America enables them to bring "the message of holiness to the world." When the dimensions of the tsunami in Thailand were known, a delegation of Haredi volunteers set out (December 2004). The working assumption that motivated ZAKA was the high likelihood that among the victims of the tidal wave that struck the shore, there would be Israeli backpackers and vacationers. In the end, ZAKA took care of the bodies of eight Jews. Before the delegation left, they had expanded its mandate to extending professional assistance to local authorities in identifying the dead. From that point on, ZAKA regarded itself as a world expert in dealing with the victims of catastrophe. Later, at the disaster of Hurricane Katrina in New Orleans, four representatives of ZAKA were sent to help identify the corpses of Jews (August 2005). While doing so they also saved Torah scrolls that were damaged in the floods and buried them according to halakha.

The most common instances of unnatural death with which ZAKA deals are caused by road accidents. ZAKA brings the experience acquired during the decade of terrorism to this area. Every two weeks the ZAKA publication presents graphic descriptions accompanied by close-ups of the removal of bodies from smashed automobiles. Imperceptibly, ZAKA began to describe road accidents as another type of terrorism. Inferring a connection between death in road accidents and death in terrorism removes the former from banality and elevates it to the importance reserved for the latter. Thus, the bodies of the victims of road accidents receive "special Jewish treatment," and the volunteers who deal with them are imbued with sacred awe, despite the tedious procedures that threaten to erode the enthusiasm in their work.

While dealing with accident victims has taken over ZAKA's daily routine, in the minds of the volunteers, in their organizational culture, and in their public image, treatment of the victims of terrorism still holds first place. They foster the exaltation of dealing with terrorism both as a living memory of the past and as a real eventuality for the future. In this situation, many of the practices that were developed during the Intifada years and employed in dealing with terrorism flow into everyday life and are applied to the treatment of victims of accidents. Transposition of the ZAKA practices developed during the Intifada in the arena of terrorism is accompanied by the application of their religious-ritual logic to the treatment of victims of accidents. ZAKA's difficulty in parting with the complex of managing the death of the victims of terrorism is expressed in the insistence of the volunteers on the sanctity of the work of gathering small scraps of flesh, soaking up drops of blood, and having them buried according to the commandments of the Torah, in cases of accidents as well. The following episode demonstrates this. Several years ago, a man was run over and killed by a train. A ZAKA team rushed to the scene of the accident and set to work. Shortly after the accident, the train continued on its route to avoid upsetting the plans of thousands of passengers. However, the volunteers felt that they had not managed to treat several drops of blood that clung to the fender of the locomotive. For many hours they raced after the locomotive in their cars, rushing southward and northward until they caught up with it and completed their sacred task, described as sanctification of the name of God. Veteran employees of the railroad told me that no religious organization had ever intervened in such cases. According to the procedures in force until then, they used to call the fire department to hose off the remaining blood, leaving the dust, the sun, and the rain to complete the job.[28]

During the Intifada and the following decade, ZAKA volunteers coped with criminal homicides as well. Many of these were committed in circumstances not sufficiently clear. In these doubtful cases, they tended to explain the evidence at the scene as pointing clearly to terrorism, while ignoring ambiguous or even contradictory evidence. In instances of violent death in which the victim was Jewish and the perpetrator was an Arab, even though the death appeared to be accidental, or the motive for the killing was vague, they declared that it was a nationalistically or religiously motivated killing, and the bodies should be treated like victims of terrorism.[29]

Here is another example: toward the end of the Intifada, I was summoned by one of my informers to join his ZAKA emergency team in a Palestinian neighborhood. Upon our arrival at the killing field, we saw the body of a young woman whose face had been smashed and her body butchered with a knife. The crew members immediately bent over the body and began to take care of it. Our horror and grief were tinged with mystery. The police investigators discovered the identity of the attacker (Palestinian) and the victim (Jewish) and determined that the motive for the murder was romantic. This conclusion was accepted by the present Haredi volunteers. However, an alternative interpretation gradually took hold of them. When we removed the body and left the scene, it was declared that the murder was an act of terrorism, pure and simple, and that God would avenge the blood of the saintly woman who had been murdered because she was Jewish.

## Ordinary Week

The waves of terrorism in the early 2000s brought praise to ZAKA, along with abundance. The extensive public recognition that ZAKA earned was translated into a flow of contributions from wealthy individuals and masses of ordinary people in Israel and abroad. In 2003, during the second Intifada, ZAKA received contributions amounting to 3.5 million dollars. Having increasing means at their disposal, along with growing self-confidence due to their success, could not but bring a certain degree of decadence. The annual budget tripled, spacious offices were rented in the center of town, money was allocated to public relations, large vehicles and expensive equipment for communications and emergency medical treatment were purchased, and more salaried positions were created.[30] As could be expected, criticism was voiced from within and from the outside. Accusations were leveled regarding unnecessary acquisitions and superfluous officeholders, and suspicions were voiced regarding waste, nepotism, and corruption.[31]

In 2005, along with demoralization and internal disputes, ZAKA came close to bankruptcy.[32] Most ZAKA volunteers are scarcely influenced by these trends. The rank and file who are active in the arenas of death strive to maintain the consistent routine of concern for the honor of the dead, demonstratively ignoring the institutionalization and scandals.

In the absence of terrorism, the ZAKA leadership offers the activists a new definition of their task: "To sanctify the Name in public even in times when there are no headlines red with blood." The daily round of ZAKA consists of an infinite accretion of small human dramas, little tragedies, cruel fragments of life. I followed a ZAKA volunteer over a few days, mainly nights, of his routine: bending over the corpse of a lonely old man, which had rotted in his dark and moldy apartment; treating the body of a girl who was killed by a rocket fired from Palestinian Gaza; taking care of the body of a man who was killed in a drunken brawl in a public park; picking up the pieces of a woman who committed suicide by jumping out of high window; removing the body of a foreign worker that was tangled in the blades of an industrial mixer; and recovering the bodies of a couple and their children who were burned in a car that crashed on the side of a road.[33] On the beeper of that ZAKA volunteer from Jerusalem I found one or two calls to action of this kind every day.

In 2009 ZAKA responded to 2,237 cases of unnatural death: 517 suicides, 496 deaths in road accidents, 162 murders, 15 strikes by rockets fired from Gaza by Hamas, and others.[34] To demonstrate the routine of the Haredi volunteers in treating unnatural deaths, here is a selection from the weekly operations log from the main ZAKA office:

- A young woman murdered for violating family honor.
- An infant's crib death.
- A human skeleton found buried in the sand in the south of the country.
- A worker who fell from scaffolding and died.
- A demobilized soldier who committed suicide by setting off a grenade.

- A double murder in an inter-clan war in a village in the Galilee.
- The bones of Syrian soldiers, killed in the Yom Kippur War of 1973, found on the Golan Heights.
- A child who fell from a kayak and drowned in a lake.
- A young woman and man who died in their home from an overdose of drugs.
- A homeless man who froze to death.
- And, of course, quite a few pedestrians, motorcycle riders, drivers, and passengers killed in road accidents.

## Organization

ZAKA, especially the Jerusalem branch, is a homogeneous and tight-knit group, a lively community. It is a primary group whose members share many traits, know each other well, and maintain close informal contacts. Some people define ZAKA as a sect, as it is a small, exclusive, relatively uniform group with clear boundaries, whose members are totally devoted and maintain both religious tension and a high degree of commitment to the group, its members, and its values.

The varied activities of ZAKA are directed by a small body of chiefs, and in their Jerusalem offices there are fewer than ten full-time employees. Backed by a committee of rabbis and a board of trustees, they manage the volunteers who function in varying degrees of professionalism and commitment. The organization boasts about three thousand volunteers,[35] but in fact one may speak of only a few hundred ZAKA activists in the full sense of the term as discussed in this book, men who devote a considerable amount of their time and energy to ZAKA, who are prepared to go into action at any hour of the day, even on the Sabbath and holidays, and who are regularly on duty and take part in training courses and administrative work. In the Jerusalem branch, the largest and busiest one, there is a hard core of thirty to forty volunteers, who responded time after time to all the large terrorist attacks in and around the city, and they also share the burden of dealing with the other daily instances of unnatural death. The Jerusalem branch naturally received senior status because the city is a holy city and the capital of the state, the largest city in Israel, where most of the serious terrorist attacks took place, and the biggest Haredi community is also concentrated there. ZAKA was born in Jerusalem, and from there all the branches of the organization, dispersed all over the country, are managed: in other major cities, where branches were established during the local terrorist attacks based on the existing Haredi communities,[36] in regions exposed to the danger of terrorism,[37] and also in remote towns, with only a single volunteer, or at most two or three. Small branches constantly arise on an ad hoc basis in response to a certain event. Over a long period of time, they may be dormant, suddenly to be aroused to frenetic action in response to a local disaster, or the religious awakening of a local man (e.g., someone who dreamed that a holy rabbi appeared and assigned the mission to him).[38] The map of Israel circulated by ZAKA shows forty branches. The central branches tend to dispatch representatives to distant sites where disasters took place. Only the Tel Aviv branch rejected the primacy of Jerusalem and developed independently, creating tension between the branches in which personal rivalries as well as differences in style of action and public relations played a part. In general, the Tel Aviv activists were less zealous than the Jerusalemites. In time the branches of ZAKA in the two largest cities came to compete for money and prestige, and they were in conflict regarding the boundaries of their respective turfs. On occasion, volunteers from the two branches met at the arenas of disaster and quarreled over the right to deal with the bodies.

The flagship of the upgrading of ZAKA's services is the motorcycle unit. Its establishment was celebrated with pomp and circumstance, and the newspaper headline read, "Speeding to Hell." With donated money, well-equipped, fast motorcycles were purchased, and about fifty volunteers were trained to ride them. The motorcycles made it possible to reach the arena of disasters by going around traffic jams, and in more than one instance they proved to be critical in the treatment of the wounded and dead. In recent years the unprecedented sight of a Haredi Jew, dressed in black, with sidelocks and a beard, riding on a motorcycle, has already become routine in the streets of Jerusalem.

## Unique Species

There are a variety of death professionals.[39] On the one hand, there are the social functionaries: paramedics and doctors (mainly pathologists), police officers and jurists (mainly forensic), psychologists, social workers, and even the carvers of gravestones. On the other hand, there are the clergy and functionaries of the religious establishment to give last rites, purify bodies, bury them, officiate at funerals, and console the bereaved. ZAKA embodies a certain dimension of all the above. The Haredi volunteers are part of a religious system that deals with death, and at the same time they are part of a technological and bureaucratic system. In addition, they play a vital role in the national and patriotic system of the treatment of death.

Each of the stages and types of death requires particular treatment. ZAKA is unique, first, in that its treatment focuses on a well-defined stage of death, which, in normal conditions, does not attract a lot of attention, though it is fateful and problematic. This is the intermediary stage between physical and social death. This stage begins immediately after a person's last breath, and it ends with burial according to the tradition. Thus, ZAKA is responsible for a short phase which, because of its liminal nature, is potent but sensitive and dangerous. Second, ZAKA is unique in that its treatment focuses on unnatural and uncommon death, which is difficult to rationalize and to be reconciled with. This is the death connected with disasters, sometimes mass catastrophes, and mainly terrorism and suicide terrorism. In contrast to normal death, this is arbitrary, sudden, and public death, and it is seen as particularly cruel and horrifying. The death that ZAKA specializes in is also different from other types of death in the state of the bodies. They are usually cut apart, mutilated, and burned, with limbs scattered and disfigured. The death that ZAKA specializes in requires special treatment because its significance goes beyond the private and familial. Although the victims of terrorism are mostly anonymous, their death has public meaning. ZAKA deals with death that is essentially political, and, because of that, the religion also takes a special interest in it.

Every death has destructive consequences for the living environment. Therefore, all the death professionals are expected to resolve the crisis to the collective and to individuals, and to restore the situation to normal. The death that ZAKA deals with, especially death by terrorism, contains a unique chaotic and anomic potential that severely threatens the foundations of the society and its continued effective functioning. Terrorism adds to the types of death familiar from the past, a distinct kind of death that shatters the cultural paradigms that govern the idea of demise and deviates from the customary script of loss of life and the way it is handled. ZAKA, as an emissary of the injured community, is called upon to diminish the influence of this particularly bad kind of death, and to that end it developed innovative structures and original strategies for managing death. ZAKA's virtuosity is shown especially when it is handling the dead from terrorism. Then the three interconnected dimensions of the organization are expressed, and thereby the tragic event is given an interpretation that restores to those who remain alive control over the contingencies of death: ZAKA specialized in the biotechnical side of death management, along with the patriotic and defense aspect, and the priestly and cultic dimension. The management of death at the arena of terrorism is a new area of specialization, which ZAKA invented ex nihilo, gaining a monopoly over it.

While terrorism has become a global phenomenon, ZAKA, with its specialty of caring for the bodies of the dead killed in terrorist attacks, is sui generis. As such, ZAKA, like intelligence and strategic professionals and police bomb squad units, is also a terrorism expert. Among the main modes of dealing with terrorism are deterrence, counter-attack, and thwarting terrorist attacks. All of these are pre- and counter-terrorism measures. There are also post-terrorism measures that are taken immediately after the attack and intended to deal with its results, to minimize the damage, and to restore the functioning of the injured collective. ZAKA is part of the comprehensive and varied order of the organizations and disciplines of the latter kind in responding to terrorism.[40] Its work may fall under the rubric of emergency services such as first aid and firefighting, along perhaps with relief agents who move into the explosion site immediately following the attack. ZAKA can also be likened to institutions and individuals who deal with the less immediate effects of terrorism attacks, like social workers and municipal officials. Such interventionist elements constitute an inseparable part of the scene of terrorism and have a significant influence on its effects.

ZAKA cooperates with parallel organizations, sometimes submitting to their authority and according them much respect, and sometimes in friction with them, rebelling and competing with them. Such are its relations with MaDA, the IDF home front command, and the police (especially the Civil Guard and the forensic unit). For their part, these organizations express admiration for ZAKA, but they also complain that it does not consider their needs and that it works on its own, with excessive enthusiasm, which sometimes is deleterious to the general effort. Over the years judicial and administrative measures have been taken to regularize the official status of ZAKA and to define its authority according to law. Meanwhile, ZAKA's subordination to the police provides a legal umbrella for the organization's privileged status.

The surge of terrorism in our age has led to the emergence of new terrorism-related specializations, such as terrorism medicine,[41] and new terrorism-related organizations emerge like special psychological clinics that specialize in Post Traumatic Syndrome and care for terrorism victims.[42] ZAKA also represent a new model of expertise professionally attuned to the radically changing conditions that terrorism has created. ZAKA's project was fundamentally religious, but it was yoked to the needs of national defense, and thereby it adopted norms of behavior derived from advanced sciences such as genetics.

## Macabre

According to the Jewish religious tradition, Moses, the first and most important of the prophets, the giver of the Torah, was born thirty-three hundred years ago on the seventh of Adar,[43] and he died at the age of 120, exactly on the same date. The Bible does not describe his death, and mainly, the place of his grave and the identity of his undertaker are unknown.[44] Perhaps because of this very mystery in antiquity the Jews already made his death a symbol of their conception of death in general. Specifically, they adopted the seventh of Adar, the supposed day of Moses' death, as a day when death is celebrated, and the beliefs and customs connected to death are concentrated on it. Since Talmudic days, believers fast on that day, and in fear of judgment, they beg for pardon and forgiveness, reciting special prayers, and making a penetrating spiritual accounting. They perform special rituals in hope for atonement and redemption for everyone. The experts in Jewish law and mysticism believe that on the seventh of Adar the transmigration of souls takes place,[45] and one who observes the commandments connected with this day preserves the members of his community from "strange deaths." The ceremonies of the seventh of Adar were apparently influenced by various fraternities and guilds in the Christian surroundings of the Jewish communities of Europe. Thus, a ceremonial banquet was added to the fast day. It took on a sanctified character that included teachings about the Torah, moral sermons, religious hymns, and it became a *se'udat mitsva*, a meal celebrating the keeping of a commandment, like Sabbath meal. With the development of burial societies in medieval Jewish communities, they naturally adopted Moses as the patron saint, as it were, for handling the dead, and they made the seventh of Adar their holiday.[46]

The ceremonies for the seventh of Adar began with a fast which began after afternoon prayers on the preceding day. At morning prayers on the seventh of Adar, the members gathered in their synagogue, where they held a special service and recited penitential prayers. Then they went to the local cemetery and asked forgiveness from the dead, for fear some flaw, even the slightest, had occurred in treating them. After reciting psalms, they devoted themselves to the administration and logistics of managing death, such as repairing the cemetery fence. In the afternoon they returned to the synagogue for another special service and a series of sermons on death and acts of charity, given by rabbis. When the stars came out, after evening prayers, the fast was over. Then they attended a banquet accompanied by further sermons, songs, and dances, and sometimes drinking to inebriation.

Today burial societies are less inclined to emphasize the seventh of Adar. In contrast, ZAKA took over this Jewish day of the dead and made it into the holiday of their volunteer organization. ZAKA activists are almost the only ones in Haredi society who fast on the seventh of Adar, and some of them take a vow of silence for the day. The end of the fast is marked by a feast, like the ones held by religious groups on the anniversary of the death of their patron. The saint's followers believe that on this day his power expands, and his influence on the world increases. The word for the feast, *hilula*, became a synonym for unbounded festivity, including sensuality and the release of instinct. Under the influence of Hasidim, on the one hand, and Oriental Jews, on the other, these feasts, unconstrained and ostentatious, became popular and widely celebrated in Israel.[47] As in the past, today they celebrate the unity of the community. A veteran ZAKA activist reminds his colleagues that in the Hasidic tradition, the anniversary of someone's death (especially if he was a *tsadik*) is a happier occasion than the anniversary of his birth. This is because, when a person dies, he draws closer to the Garden of Eden and distances himself from the hard struggle with the evil impulse.[48]

ZAKA breathed new life into the ceremonies for the seventh of Adar, both the morbid and the festive aspects. The volunteers observe the fast day, the penitential prayers, and in the evening, they mass together from all over the country for a festive banquet, which, under the influence of Hasidism, they call a *tish*.[49] Hundreds of Haredim take part in ZAKA's annual celebrations, and the guests are mainly rabbis, police officers, politicians, and senior officials. In 2009, the twentieth anniversary of the attack on bus 405, more than a thousand men celebrated, all of them personally acquainted with one another. The guests at the *se'udat mitsva*, only men, came in their holiday clothes. Most of them wear traditional Hasidic garb: *shtraiml* (a heavy fur hat), *kapota* (a long black silk coat), or a striped Jerusalem kaftan, with a *gartl* (a broad cloth belt). Their excited meetings are full of boisterous laughter, pats on the shoulder, and reminiscences. After prayers, the event begins with blessings and, following them, reprimands: sermons from the rabbis about ethics and Jewish law. They take the opportunity to tell the volunteers about new rabbinical decisions regarding care for the dead.[50] They then head for the tables, which are laden with heavy food, and they drink copious amounts of affordable vodka and liquor, which frees their tongue and leads to somewhat rowdy behavior. Toward the end, the volunteers burst into loud song and then begin enthusiastic line and circle dancing, "in thanks to God for the honor He gave them to be partners with Moses, our master, in keeping the commandment of true compassion." Throughout the evening, videos about the activities of the organization are projected on the wall, including a mishmash of self-aggrandizing phrases, along with horrible images from the arenas of catastrophe.

In their sermons on the seventh of Adar, the ZAKA rabbis advance two other themes. The first relates to one of the goals of the annual ceremony, *dvequt ḥaverim* (cohesion of the members), as is written on the invitation.[51] The words imply allegiance, love, and solidarity, strong bonding among friends. However, *dvequt* also relates to deep devotion. This traditional mystical conception guides the ZAKA volunteers, who laugh together and hug each other until late at night. At dawn, they immerse themselves in a cold ritual bath and stand close to one another for morning prayers. This holy comradeship is often interrupted by announcements of unnatural deaths on their beepers. During one of these festivities, in which I took part, ZAKA teams rushed out twice for emergencies.

The second theme is the juxtaposition of death, sorrow, and mourning with joy and love of life.[52] This idea is familiar in a variety of cultures, which make it easier to accept the end of life by linking it with the growth of new life.[53] In traditional Judaism the relations between death and regeneration are transferred from the area of nature, genetics, and agriculture to the religious-national area where God, the believing Jew, and the Jewish people play a central role. Since the seventeenth and eighteenth centuries burial societies in Europe used to seek relief after dealing with the dead by feasting and drinking.[54] Judaism joins joy to death and death to joy. For example, at weddings, which symbolize fertility, the groom breaks a glass in memory of the destruction of the Temple, and he wears a *kitl*, a white garment reminiscent of a shroud, to be reminded that he will die in the end. On the other hand, the national-religious day of mourning for the destruction of the

Temple, the loss of the Land of Israel and of sovereignty, the ninth of Av, is also the day when the messiah will appear. These opposites alternate with one another.[55] The day of death is also a joyful day, because the deceased are liberated from the tribulations of life and from their sins.

## The Virtue of True Benevolence

ZAKA sees itself as a philanthropic initiative. As such, it is maintaining a Jewish tradition that began in the Diaspora during the Middle Ages, and which flourishes to this day in Haredi communities in Israel and abroad. In Hebrew, "philanthropy" is called *tsedaqa* (justice, righteousness) or *hesed* (grace, benevolence, compassion). The voluntary offer of material assistance and psychological, moral support is an important commandment of the Torah, which the rabbinate fostered over the generations. The Mishnah states, "The world stands upon three things: on the Torah, on work, and on acts of compassion,"[56] and it is also said in the Talmud that "charity saves from death."[57] In the second to fourth centuries CE it was already customary to solicit contributions by circulating a box in the street in which people placed food for the hungry. In the fifteenth century, volunteer confederations were established for various kinds of philanthropy such as visiting the sick and ransoming captives. In contemporary Israel, as in the rest of the modern Western world, a considerable part of these functions has been taken over by the state welfare authorities. However, in ultra-Orthodox communities, a closed network of voluntary support institutions exists, based on the historical Jewish model, which emphasized generosity and mutual support. In Haredi society, these institutions are called *gemah* (a Hebrew acronym for *gemilut hasadim*), which are based on monetary contributions and volunteer labor. Among the activities of these organizations in Haredi society are free loans to the poor, subsidized food supplies for families with many children, stalls for collecting used clothing, assistance to orphans and widows, assisting men without families to marry, help to young women to find husbands, and visiting the mourning. Prominent among the organizations are those that deal with medical assistance. Most of them serve solely the Haredi community; however, in recent years, some have emerged that aid the Israeli community at large, and they have gained the recognition of government agencies. One such is Yad Sara, which lends out medical equipment. ZAKA is also a mutation of this kind of institution. The organization is based on an infrastructure of Haredi *gemaḥ*, and many ZAKA volunteers are active in other such organizations, like ʿEzer Miʾtsiyon, which provides assistance to cancer patients and the handicapped. The original name of ZAKA was Ḥesed shel Emet, meaning "true or ultimate compassion or benevolence."[58] This is a name that burial societies in the Diaspora took from the late Middle Ages on, and to this day they act for local Jewish communities in handling the burial of the dead according to Jewish law. *Ḥesed shel Emet* is the Jewish traditional idiom for depicting care for the dead, who can never repay the kindness accorded to them. Therefore, from the point of view of the giver, this voluntary, disinterested, and unconditional gesture is pure.

True compassion is an important religious commandment. In the canonical texts of Judaism, it is presented as the ultimate commandment, whose power is greater than that of other commandments, because the beneficiary cannot recompence. Today ZAKA adds yet another reason for seeing it as an extraordinary and sublime commandment, which trumps the others: it is a commandment that is difficult to observe, or, as Rabbi Roje, ZAKA's halakhic authority, says, handling of the victims of terrorism and other catastrophes does not provide a reward in concrete form, and it is not easy to do, unlike keeping the Sabbath. He quotes from the Midrash on the Torah,[59] recounting that at the time of the Exodus from Egypt, when all the Israelites were involved in deceiving the Egyptians and plundering their gold and silver, as God had commanded them,[60] Moses raised himself above them by taking charge of Joseph's bones.[61] In a Torah lesson for ZAKA activists it was claimed, based on the ancient Jewish Sages, that *tsedaqa* (charity) is important, but more important is *ḥesed* (grace, or loving kindness), and that among the Hasidim there are various degrees of *ḥesed*, the highest of which is when the recipient does not know the identity of the donor, and the donor does not know that of the recipient. This is the case when a ZAKA volunteer takes care of a mutilated body.

While the Bible is the source of many commandments relevant to the life of the individual and the society—what may be eaten, for example, and how to deal with an adulteress, and when to go to war—the absence of an explicit commandment about how to bury the dead is conspicuous.[62] Nevertheless, ZAKA believes that it draws upon a rich and ancient Jewish heritage regarding death, and it refers to religious texts to authorize its treatment, especially in matters of unusual death. ZAKA finds the beginning of this genealogical chain in the Pentateuch. When asked about the source and interpretation of the expression *Ḥesed shel emet*, ZAKA volunteers refer to

Genesis 47:29: "When the time drew near that Israel [Jacob] must die, he called his son Joseph and said to him, now if I have found favor in your sight, please . . . deal *kindly* [*hesed*] and *truly* [*emet*] with me. Please do not bury me in Egypt. But I will be with my fathers [in Hebron]." The precedent for ZAKA's actions at the arena of terrorism is the mythic act of gathering the bones of the Patriarch of Judaism and bringing them to the promised land for burial.

Quotations from these and other sources, which lend authority to the idea of true compassion, appear in ZAKA's publications and mainly in the pamphlets for internal circulation. Every member from the ranks of ZAKA can cite the words of important rabbis, such as Rashi (from the eleventh century) verbatim, explaining and praising this commandment.

A magical effect is attributed to the act of *Hesed shel emet*. In sermons given in Haredi forums, many stories are told about the miracles and wonders that happened for those who kept the commandment of *Hesed shel emet*.

It is argued that taking care of a body is not done for any reward in this world; it is an act of generosity.[63] Death, as it were, seals the mutual connection among the members of the community: one cannot expect direct gratitude or any obligation from the dead. Thus, the Maussian gift circle is meant to be broken,[64] and absolute altruism to be attained. The conception of *Hesed shel emet* implies a determined endeavor to reject the logic of mutual gifts, to escape the deterministic chain of obligation and reward, which assumes that the deceased is still enmeshed in a series of social relationships, by means of which group solidarity is maintained.[65]

To this day, the motto *Hesed shel emet* appears beneath the emblem of ZAKA, but the organization is known publicly simply as ZAKA. Since it was first used, in 1995, the acronym ZAKA took, because it is short, fresh, vigorous, almost military, and somehow fashionable. *Hesed shel emet* was downplayed outwardly, because it is involved in a dispute regarding the organization's copyright, as it were, and because it connotes traditional Jewish burial societies.

# 3

# Culture and Personality of the Specialists in Horrific Death

## Necrophilia?

Upon the initiative of a ZAKA activist an internet forum was opened (and soon closed), with access limited by a password to trustworthy insiders. On it the Haredi volunteers shared experiences from scenes of death, without censorship. Descriptions of scraping human intestines from the pavement, which would shock and repel most people, were eagerly watched there. The internal discourse of ZAKA, orally, in writing, and in visual media, is replete with matters of unnatural death. Horrific scenes are particularly popular in the communications among the volunteers.

The volunteers seize every opportunity to present a complete picture of the site of the explosion. Their reports stand out for their attention to detail and for their concreteness. ZAKA volunteers display eagerness to rehash and recycle everything they have seen in the arena. Fervently, and with a sense that providing an exhaustive description is part of their mission, they repeat the same formulas and linger over the same specifics, generally those that are especially difficult to hear. They seem to be trying their best to shock their listeners. Their depictions display a sort of swagger. Some people who have heard them claim that the volunteers are oblivious to the horrors they have become accustomed to work with; others view the tendency to describe terror sites at length as a symptom of post-traumatic syndrome, or a therapeutic act of getting their experience off their chest.

The dominant presence of death in ZAKA's sub-culture is expressed first in the graphic medium. The volunteers take many cell phone pictures of the arenas of death and of themselves and their colleagues on the scene. They keep an abundance of photographs in their private possession, including close-ups of bodies and body parts. They also share the photographs with their colleagues. Their WhatsApp groups are crammed with such pictures. Second, death is present in ZAKA's publications, some of which are available

*The Cult of Dismembered Limbs.* Gideon Aran, Oxford University Press. © Oxford University Press 2023.
DOI: 10.1093/oso/9780197689141.003.0003

to the public, mainly the official ZAKA magazine, *NewZAKA*. Every two weeks detailed descriptions of unnatural death are published in print or digitally. In the average edition, full details of about ten incidents of death are discussed from several angles: technical, halakhic, and experiential. Third, death is also present in conversations among the volunteers on personal and social occasions outside the organization's working hours. In these exchanges, they speak a great deal about various instances of death, with vivid and long-winded descriptions of the condition of the corpses and their parts. Such conversations often reveal not only a professional interest but also a degree of emotional engagement and even excitement.

A striking example of the dominance of particularly horrible death in the internal discourse of ZAKA can be found in the volunteers' attitude toward the tsunami in Thailand (2004), as expressed in personal photographs, and the frequent, intense chats among the members. At a social event, while eating and drinking with gusto, members screened enlarged pictures of drowned corpses, swollen beyond recognition as human beings. From the loud comments that accompanied the presentation one could sense that reticence had been released. The geographical and cultural distance probably contributed to the removal of inhibitions in the attitude toward these instances of death. In contrast, conversation about the death of Jews is relatively self-aware and more restrained. Still, the volunteers converse in a whisper about the sights at the local arena, and they keep a sort of half-secret home photographic archive in their possession. These inhibitions concerning Jews who were killed are conspicuous in comparison to the entirely unrestrained talk about the corpses of gentiles, especially Palestinian Muslims. The volunteers present pictures of the bodies of the suicide terrorists with lack of discretion, even provocatively.

Over time a kind of competition developed among the volunteers: Who took part in the most incidents involving death? Where was the death the most awful? When were they closest to the heart of the horror? The volunteers flaunt their intimacy with death, and the more terrible it is, the more they boast. Within the organization there is usually consensus as to the place of each volunteer in the macabre hierarchy of prestige determined by the number and intensity of the horrible deaths to which he was exposed.

Although the ZAKA volunteers complain that they cannot free themselves of the horror of death, which oppresses them ("For many weeks after the attack, meat meals disgust me"), they are also uncontrollably attracted to it. The volunteers are eager to view the corpses up close, to touch them, if possible, even beyond the arena of the attack. As if treating the victims of terrorism immediately after the explosion was not enough for them, during the calm between Palestinian attacks, they sought permission to enter the inner chambers of the National Institute of Forensic Medicine for extra closeness to death. They were fascinated by the slides that accompanied a lecture about autopsies, and they were disappointed when they were forbidden to observe the autopsies themselves. Similarly, even when they are not on duty, beyond the many hours they invest in the activities of ZAKA, the volunteers often visit cemeteries. In ZAKA's fortnightly publication it was reported that one of the members, a teacher in a Haredi school, frequently spoke with his pupils about the deaths he had encountered at the arena, and in the aftermath of a severe terrorist attack, "he took the children for a walk in a cemetery." A veteran Jerusalem volunteer told me that he found himself dragging his small children to the local graveyard.

The activists complain that the dominance of death in their conduct and consciousness creates a barrier between them and their wives and children. The wife of a ZAKA volunteer told me that for several weeks after every attack, "I have no partner in the house." Death fills their entire being, so that they lose sensitivity to their close surroundings. Just as the effect of proximity to horrible death takes over the life routine of the ZAKA volunteers, it also swallows up and subordinates their family and friendship circles. The volunteers complain that the awful death they bear with them seems to cling to their surroundings and casts a dark shadow over them, influencing the morale of their families, whose functioning is impaired.

The wives of ZAKA activists present themselves as "stationed at the front" of the project of managing the arena of death. They complain about their distress, because ZAKA devours all their husbands' time and attention ("My husband is married to the beeper," or "There's never a holiday, Sabbath, or wedding, when, in the middle of the festivities, the telephone doesn't ring, and he leaves me and the children and rushes to a horrible incident"), and because death enters the home ("When he comes home, we have to block our ears and shut our eyes to keep living a sane family life"). But they are proud of their contribution ("Without us ZAKA would collapse"), and they see themselves as full partners in fulfilling the commandment of true compassion.

The wife of another ZAKA activist told me that when the volunteers' children play, the dead appear very frequently, and at the time of the attacks, her seven-year-old daughter was filled with pride. A ZAKA volunteer from a southern town wrote to his colleagues that he had taken his son with him to the room for the purification of the dead at the edge of the cemetery, creating "a basis for understanding and identification" between father and son. Dreadful death even takes over the volunteers' most private and protected area: their sleep. Many of them report that a lot of death appears in their dreams, and it is usually horrifying.

A central ZAKA activist confessed to me, "Sometimes, when I am in a Jerusalem cemetery, a demon wakes up inside me, telling me to dig under the gravestones. Yes, to *probe* the graves. That's my hidden weakness."

Alongside public approval in Israel for ZAKA, even admiration, there is also criticism of ZAKA and various degrees of reservation about it. Some of the opponents regard the volunteers with derision and dismissal, and some are repulsed and disgusted by them. They describe the volunteers' entry in the arena of terrorism as deviant, and they occasionally refer to the organization's members as perverts or necrophiliacs.[1] In the present book I will not discuss the mental aspects of the ZAKA phenomenon, which can, perhaps, be explained, or explained away, with concepts from the field of psychopathology.[2]

## PTSD and Gallows Humor

The ZAKA volunteers are aware of the controversial aspects of their public status, including the common claim about their ostensibly disturbed personalities. While they sustain a respectable reputation and credibility, they also concede that they are subject to some of the mental problems attributed to them. Mainly they accept the claim that they deviate from the ordinary, normal psychological profile, sometimes with reservations and in internal conversations or with their relatives, and sometimes openly in a tone of pride. They admit that they are a little insane, sometimes using slang like "We're screwed up." They are particularly fond of presenting themselves as *meshuggeneh*, the Yiddish word for "crazy."

By accepting the epithet *meshuggeneh*, they betray a somewhat apologetic attitude, overcome their embarrassment, and give themselves partial exemption from responsibility to act in a thoughtful, solid fashion. They grant themselves permission to indulge in wild behavior and transgress boundaries, without threatening the Haredi norms they are violating.

At one of the Seventh of Adar banquets, when they were in their cups, the ZAKA volunteers told about a custom of the Jewish community of Budapest in the early nineteenth century. At the burial society's festive banquets, the officiant used to place portions of meat on the guests' plates with a comb of the kind used in the purification of corpses.[3]

In response to the tendency of many Israelis to regard the ZAKA activists as sick or deviant, who should receive psychiatric treatment or moral condemnation, the volunteers pose a rhetorical question: "If it weren't for us, who would do this vital job?" To this they add a description of the high price they and their families pay for managing the death of the victims of terrorism and other kinds of unnatural death. During the Intifada, when the volunteers went from one scene of an explosion to another, they wanted to add themselves to the list of victims of the human bomb. Later they sought to define their wives and children as victims who were forced indirectly to suffer from Palestinian terrorism. ZAKA volunteers, who were exposed to the horror of the arena of terrorism, viewed themselves as survivors. As they saw it, they had survived the murderous attack just as those passengers who were in the bus when it exploded and survived, most of them wounded.

In the early time of the organization, the volunteers denied that proximity to death harmed them mentally. Gradually they admitted to post-traumatic symptoms and even accepted proposals—the initiatives of other volunteer organizations—to receive psychological treatment, although in the Haredi world there is suspicion and even hostility toward professional psychotherapy.[4] Despite the opposition of many volunteers, the leadership of the organization made participation in the support groups obligatory. During the last years of the Intifada, ZAKA became aware that even volunteers who appeared to function well over time might be "damaged." They started a workshop "for developing psychological resilience." In such forums they were given tools for coping with the trauma of handling the horrible death, and at the same time the volunteers were promised that if their faith was strengthened, the Talmudic maxim would be fulfilled: "those sent to perform a commandment come to no harm."[5]

During the Intifada, with the attrition of some volunteers, proposals were made to limit exposure to horrible death to just a short time, or to a specific number of events. But central activists blocked these initiatives, as they were not willing to give up their privilege of being the first to enter the arena and the last to leave it, again and again. They said, "The only way they'll take us out is in a body bag." There were very few cases that seemed like nervous breakdowns as a result of the trauma of dealing with the aftermath of terrorism. In many more cases, there were less serious symptoms of psychological injury. For example, the volunteers showed indifference to the normative expectations and emotions of the people around them, or they were hyper-active, arrogant, and aggressive, at the arena and beyond it. Not surprisingly, ZAKA activists were plagued by various forms of anxiety. Some of them told me that during the time of the attacks, they would wake up at night and feel their way to their children's rooms and touch them, to make sure they were breathing. An expert psychologist, who treated volunteers as individuals and in groups, reported to me that the most common post-traumatic symptoms among them are sleep disturbances[6] and states of abnormally high wakefulness. In rarer cases there were difficulties in breathing eating disorders, prolonged silences, and seclusion at home following treatment of the victims of terrorism.[7]

To cope with the tension that was liable to interfere with the functioning of the volunteers, the organization invited them to group therapy sessions. For example, three days after treating the victims of a murderous terrorist attack on a yeshiva in Jerusalem (March 2008), dozens of ZAKA volunteers met for an evening of speaking out to alleviate their distress. For long hours the volunteers spoke from the heart about the harsh experiences they had undergone. One motive that appeared repeatedly in the volunteers' words was that images from past terrorist attacks returned to them. On another occasion, at a therapeutic workshop the volunteers were asked to close their eyes, to let free associations guide them, and then to make a drawing of what they visualized. One prominent Jerusalem activist drew golden ears of grain becoming red and finally the blackest of black.[8]

In the early 2000s "ventilation meetings" were organized, providing moral support offered by experienced psychologists and spiritual support offered by rabbis, along with rest, eating, entertainment, and social solidarity. At later stages the activists were taken on short vacations for "religious reinforcement," improvement of morale, and the encouragement of team spirit. The wives and children were invited to some of these gatherings, to compensate them for the frequent absence of the husbands and fathers, and for the psychological pressure to which the men are subject and which they project onto their families. An effort to create a formal framework for the volunteers' wives encountered opposition from rabbis. Even a course in first aid for women raised a storm in the Haredi community, and to calm things down ZAKA had to promise that the wives' use of paramedical training would be limited to the home. One function of the wives about which there is general agreement is "to preserve their husbands' sanity." At the same time, psychologists who are familiar with the doings in ZAKA believe there is a certain probability that these women will be subject to secondary post-traumatic stress (and that the children will develop the second-generation syndrome, like the children of Holocaust survivors).

Racing from one arena to the next and being confronted with mutilated bodies for months and years could not but affect the volunteers. Some of them could not stand the pressure and withdrew from activity in the organization. Others reacted in the apparently opposite way: quite a few volunteers coped with the horror by banalizing it. They treated the corpses nonchalantly; they manifested indifference and role distance typical of experienced professionals. Sometimes they smoked and gossiped next to the corpses, and while handling death they smiled, even posing for the camera. This was only done behind the scene, and never in terrorist incidents.

Following the 9/11 attack in New York City, there was growing awareness of the effect of horror on the rescue teams, and also on the mental health of those who were not present at the arena.[9] Research done at the height of the Intifada in Israel found that about half a million citizens of the country suffered from PTSD, expressed in impaired functioning.[10] Surprising was the low proportion of psychological damage among ZAKA volunteers, a dramatic finding: only 2.1 percent[11] This stands out especially in comparison to the damage to other professionals who are in direct contact with the horror, such as the staff of the police forensic laboratory. During the Intifada there was a wave of departures from its ranks due to "nervous breakdown from the horrible sights" at the arena of terrorism.[12] Sappers called to the arena (and even newspaper photographers) who were exposed to "the accumulation of sights of the horror of bodies in a terrible state" were recognized by the Labor Court in Jerusalem as shell-shocked and eligible for compensation.[13]

The efforts to explain the resilience of the ZAKA volunteers in the face of horror repeat the same reliable recipe for psychological strength. First, they mention the self- and organizational selection of those who enlist to work at the arena of death. The volunteers have a high level of resistance from the start, and the weaker ones naturally drop out. Second, great weight is attributed to the social climate in which the Haredi volunteers live: they are connected with their families, involved in various jobs, and accepted in their community. They also mention their commitment to the cohesive and supportive group of activists, with its ethos of mission. Of course, religious faith plays a considerable part. The volunteers state that the Torah gives them strength to resist. They claim that coping with the horror is a test of the strength of their devotion to God. Hence, they are drawn to the horror and approach it with peculiar joy. Researchers propose an additional explanation of ZAKA's resilience: characterizing the volunteers as "sensation-seekers": people with a tendency to seek action, who enjoy coping with emergencies, who seek to break boundaries, to test themselves in extreme situations, and to shatter frameworks.[14]

These factors of psychological resilience enabled the ZAKA volunteers to function optimally even at times of intense terrorist attacks.[15] They apparently developed effective defense mechanisms such as clowning and joking. Psychologists have confirmed that in the case of ZAKA volunteers as well, this is a proven strategy for coping with post-traumatic stress.[16] It appears that the death professionals, even when they are religiously radical have a sense of humor.[17] The Haredi volunteers often release tension with black humor.

The organization's old hands amused themselves with witticisms and wordplay about the severed body parts they dealt with in the arena of terrorism. In their internal newsletter they published all sorts of "sentences you wouldn't want to hear from ZAKA volunteers." For example, "Friend, you're a bit scattered"; "He picked up his feet and ran"; "I'll pick you up tomorrow morning"; "Give him a finger, and he takes the whole hand"; "I need help—give me a hand"; "The situation is tense, don't lose your head." They gave a nickname to forms of unnatural death: *riki* is used for a moldering body (*rikavon* means "rot" in Hebrew); *tali* is used for a person who hanged himself (*talui* means "hanged" in Hebrew). They also tell jokes at their own expense: each volunteer imagines his own death in an explosion and chooses among his colleagues who will have the honor of scraping his body parts off the pavement. And there are also jokes at the expense of the enemy: a hungry Palestinian human bomb goes into a restaurant and he tells the waiters that they'd better bring him what he ordered quickly, or he'll blow himself up. For the organization's annual banquet, they had a T-shirt printed with the slogan "ZAKA—Collecting People."[18]

## Fun, Miracles, Sex, and Scandals

At the family celebrations of ZAKA activists—weddings, circumcisions, and bar mitzvahs—tables are set apart for the host's fellow volunteers. The groups that gather around these tables stand out especially in their sweaty closeness, their vociferous merriment, and in the quantities of cheap alcohol that they down.[19] Although ZAKA volunteers are obsessed with horrific death, they know how to free themselves from the tyranny of chronic melancholy. Over long periods of time, in the offices of the organization and the homes of the activists, there is no sign of gloom and doom, or of fatigue. On various occasions, the outside observer is surprised by the death-managers' spirit of happiness, perhaps even euphoria. In some instances, ZAKA volunteers have been caught by their Haredi opponents joshing with each other in the very arena of death. ZAKA culture abounds with episodes of laughter, singing, dancing, and feasting, characteristic of Hasidic culture.

Another typically Hasidic custom prevalent within ZAKA is the recounting of stories of miracles and wonders. These are mainly connected with terrorist attacks and were spread especially during the Intifada. The random nature of terrorism is regarded as a decree of divine providence.[20] I heard innumerable legends in ZAKA of the following sort: a man missed a bus that blew up because he had been detained to join in prayers, and someone else was saved from death because he moved a few meters away from the center of the explosion to give alms to a beggar. Many fantastic stories hint at a mysterious connection between the dead person and those who handle his corpse. It is told that a week after a terrorist attack in a Haredi neighborhood, a volunteer returned home, and on the balcony that looks out at the site of the explosion, he found "holy remains" of one of the victims.

In chats about death among ZAKA volunteers many supernatural motives appear, including stories about ghosts and demons. In the internal ZAKA bulletin there was a report about a team of volunteers who remained on the scene to handle the body of a man whose death had been confirmed by a doctor, and a death certificate had already been issued. While putting the corpse in a body bag, they suddenly heard a soft groan, and the dead man moved his hand. "He's alive!" they shouted and fled in a panic. In interviews with volunteers about their experiences at the arena of suicide terrorism, I heard things like "When I was putting a woman's body in a bag, she grabbed me, as if refusing to depart" and "I leaned over a mutilated body, and I felt as if the victim's soul was looking at me from above. For three days it didn't let me go and kept looking at me from heaven." Following terrorist attacks the volunteers feel pursued, especially by fears of guilt and remorse. For example, "In my sleep, the dead man shook me by the shoulder and bit my finger. I realized that I hadn't respected him enough, and maybe I sinned by arrogance toward him." Several volunteers told me that at the time of the Intifada, they were afraid that "bodies would rise up against them." In those nights, they would see "white figures," living-dead, possibly Hamas terrorists, possibly Israeli victims (both of these are represented in the Middle Eastern repertoire of images enveloped in shrouds). In similar spirit, before entering the arena of terrorism, the volunteers employed various protective measures based on ancient magical practices and beliefs deriving from Jewish mysticism. Some volunteers, when they were called upon to deal with the victims of an attack, repeated the name "Amtelai Bat Karnevo" seventeen times while grasping the doorpost of their home. As very few outsiders know, according to the Talmud this is the name of the mother of Abraham, the patriarch of the Hebrew nation.[21] In the Haredi world, they pronounce this esoteric name as a charm against the evil eye. Experts in Kabbalah state that by doing so one is guaranteed success in fateful encounters and challenging events, such as coping with the dead in a violent event.[22] After finishing their work in the arena, the volunteers recite the blessing for having escaped from the danger of death.[23]

In the early days of ZAKA, the Haredi volunteers worked in the arena of death without gloves. Later, when they were required to use gloves while touching bodies and body parts, some of them protested and wanted to touch the flesh without any separation. One may say that they are carnal. In the language of Orthodox Jews, the ZAKA volunteers are *ba'alei guf*, "bodily" men, physical. This epithet implies more than a hint of condemnation. This corporeal nature of ZAKA, which relates to the numerical and cultural dominance of Hasidism in the organization, is expressed in two tendencies regarded as gross and deviant, arousing criticism within the community from which the volunteers are recruited. First, they are rather openly preoccupied with matters of a sexual nature, which are taboo in ultra-Orthodox Jewish society. Second, their mischievous behavior sometimes overflows into unruliness that has, on occasion, involved ZAKA in public scandals.

Haredi society is known for the puritan standards it imposes on its members, including extreme ascetic practices. For example, married couples sleep in separate beds, set apart from each other, and marital relations are permitted only once or twice a month, in the dark, partially clothed. Even exposure of a married woman's hair or listening to a woman singing are proscribed. Many of the ZAKA volunteers adopt moralistic norms like these, which associate them with the most radical Haredim. Even from early childhood, boys and girls are sent to separate educational frameworks, and in the public transportation that serves the Haredim, and on the sidewalks of

Haredi neighborhoods, separate areas are allotted to the two genders. Some of the ZAKA volunteers go further and even advocate postmortem prudishness, which has surfaced in several Israeli towns: insistence on separate areas for the burial of women and men, lest, beneath the earth, the naked skeletons might be revealed to each other. In the purification of bodies before burial, they make certain that male bodies are washed only by men, and female bodies, only by women. In the Haredi neighborhoods of Jerusalem people tell about a rare incident, when no woman was available to wash a woman's body, so an old man was called upon to perform the task, with his eyes blindfolded. All the ZAKA volunteers, including the most pious, are men, and they are often exposed to nakedness, including women's nakedness. This gives rise to acute tension.

As a result of the explosion, the seams of the victims' clothing burst, and they are scattered, and as a result of the heat of the explosion, they are burned. Consequently the arena of terrorism inevitably occasions the sight of and often physical contact with women's intimate parts. This is one of the reasons why mature, married men are preferred when enlisting new volunteers. But an educational effort is still needed, the investment of psychological energy, as well as religious virtuosity, to cope with this sexual challenge. Quite a few sermons by rabbis have been devoted to this topic. In instructional talks the obligation to adopt a "professional gaze" is emphasized, and not to distinguish between the corpse of a man and that of a woman. They suggest aspiring to an ideal situation in which the volunteer, like a gynecologist, cannot remember the color of the panties worn by a woman whose body he handled. In ZAKA I heard a sermon about "the ability not to look at a dead woman's vagina." A central volunteer confessed to me about how hard it was to abide by that obligation, and that success in meeting this high standard was the source of a feeling of elevation. In internal conversations within ZAKA the sexual organs of women victims are spoken of as a temptation, an act of Satan, placed in the path of the holy men at the arena. Overcoming this temptation is a supreme test for the volunteers. Several volunteers spoke about the difficulty in coping with the sight of "pieces." They are fully aware of the double meaning of this word: it refers both to severed (body) parts, as well as to attractive young women ("chicks" in Hebrew slang).

Along with Haredi puritanism, there is also prurient interest among ZAKA volunteers in the nudity so noticeably present in the arena. The motive of sex is evident in ZAKA in the obsessive moralism of the rabbis and activists of the organization, and in other sublimated ways. In a coarse manner, it appears in dirty jokes. Most of the locker-room talk is at the expense of the Palestinian terrorist's penis. Here is a typical one: in heaven, after an explosion, a suicide bomber runs quickly past the spirits of his victims, who call out to him, "Don't rush to the seventy-two virgins—ZAKA has your organ." Such gags are generally derisive and malevolent, testifying to a degree of anxiety. The volunteers are preoccupied with their adversaries' potency, and specifically with the virility of the bomber who lies before them. They report, for example, with a mixture of scorn and embarrassment, details about the size and shape of the attacker's penis. ZAKA volunteers believe that suicide bombers also think about their sexual organ and what it will look like following the explosion. They claim that some bombers wrapped their organ with thick layers of toilet tissue.[24]

Haredi volunteers relate more hesitantly to the sexual aspects of the victims' bodies. For example, they joke about an erect male member that ejaculated semen as a result of the explosion, and they point out a body whose scrotum swelled up during the terrorist attack as an index of the victim's sexual appetite.

The sexual associations that arise among the ZAKA volunteers in connection with the bodies of Israelis are hinted at and delicate. Jewish sexuality in the arena is largely denied and transferred to the non-Jewish dead. The sexuality that is negated from the Jewish body is mainly invested in the body of the Palestinian suicide terrorist. The dead terrorist is entirely sexualized.

The more foreign the victim of terrorism is, and therefore the less the volunteers feel solidarity with him, the more the sexuality aroused by the sight of his body comes out. When ZAKA volunteers were dealing with the body of a woman, whom they identified as "Christian," adding, "apparently a whore," they exempted themselves from the obligation to regard her as holy, and they loosened all restraint.[25] Seeing her half-naked body, they spoke about her with coarseness that expressed their ambivalent attitude toward sexuality: disgust along with arousal that they could not disguise.[26]

## Pious Masculinity

Quite a few cracks are visible in ZAKA's wall of morbid seriousness, and vitality bursts through them, expressed in energetic activism, as well as mischief. Even at the arena of death, while they are doing what they define as holy work, among the volunteers there are signs of mischief that sometimes are so unruly that they go beyond good taste and tact and threaten the decent image of the organization. Usually the disreputable gestures are made far from the public eye, but on several occasions thoughtless acts that shame the ZAKA volunteers have come to public knowledge, giving rise to a scandal. More than once a photograph of Haredim in white overalls, posing for the camera with broad smiles on their faces while putting a mutilated body into a bag, has slipped beyond the inner circle. In one case, a local paper published a picture of senior ZAKA activists, including an elderly rabbi who was known for his halakhic rulings about respect for the dead, making vulgar gestures at the body of a Palestinian whose head and limbs had been blown off in a work-related accident while he was making an explosive charge for use in a terrorist attack.[27]

These signs of coarseness and bullying on the part of ZAKA volunteers re-inforce their problematic status among their Haredi brethren, who see them as an organic part of a notorious phenomenon, young men whom they call *shababnikim*. The term is a compound of an Arabic noun (*shabab*, youth), and it refers to young males with the potential for deviance and rebellion. The Haredim apply this pejorative epithet to youngsters who have dropped out of Torah studies in the yeshiva but remain part of the ultra-Orthodox community. The *shababnikim* congregate in bands on street corners in Haredi neighborhoods and are identified by their idleness, overflowing hormones, and destructive delinquency. Some hardcore Haredim see ZAKA as a *shababnik* phenomenon.

Surplus youthful energy bursting into the quest for action and violence is a familiar social problem. The Haredi community found ways to incorpo-rate it partially, and to channel it for a religious project. Some of the young *shababnikim* became Modesty Guards, a kind of moralist vigilante squad, situated on the fragile boundary between hooliganism and puritanism. The guards are a spontaneous initiative that could have become subversive or criminal. When the rabbis realized they could not eradicate the squad, they co-opted it and gave it a certain direction and a wink of encouragement. These young men wander about the Haredi neighborhoods by day and night, seeking deviants from the puritan codes of the radical wing of the com-munity, to set them straight by deterrence, warning, and punishment. The guards aren't loath to administer brutal beatings to girls who walk about with short sleeves, to unmarried couples, or to yeshiva students who spend too much time loitering in front of falafel stands. These gangs spread fear in their surroundings and are reminiscent of the cliques that were active in the streets of Teheran after the Shiite revolution in the 1980s. They are also somewhat similar to other instances of semi-patronized internal terrorist groups in tyrannical theocracies such as sixteenth-century Calvinist Geneva. These are all ultra-activist improvisations acting in the name of radical religion, which usually regards them with ambivalence. ZAKA is a partial example of this kind of holy delinquency.

The Haredi *shabab* phenomenon is identified with the inability to release the frustrations of developing masculinity. The heart of Haredi society, the yeshiva, is an exclusively male brotherhood, but it does not offer models of physical, assertive, or adventurous masculinity, and it does not offer legitimate paths for forming and expressing masculinity as is customary in the West. Young men in the Haredi community are subject to a regime that denies impulses and forbids sexual release, restricts athletic activity, and condemns physical aggression. The ideal of the Torah scholar is the opposite of the macho style available to secular Israelis, who glorify health, entrepreneurship, practicality, courage, and other qualities that are cultivated in military service. Against this background, ZAKA represents a revolutionary ideal: Haredi macho.[28]

The Haredim who, in their youth, found no answer for their desperate search for ways to develop and experience their masculinity carry their frustrations into their thirties and forties, and then, as ZAKA volunteers, they find a solution: in the arenas of death they are given an opportunity to realize that forbidden and enchanting masculinity. Late, but with enthusiasm, they adopt the traits of the new Jewish man, representing patterns of behavior that Zionism initiated and monopolized. This is Sabra manliness that is stereotypically regarded as rough but charming: the masculinity of a fighter, brave, strong, handsome, determined, confident, exemplified in the IDF. Like the vast majority of the Haredim, the ZAKA volunteers avoid military service, but they have incorporated in their absolutely Haredi appearance and behavior a selection of Zionist-military embellishments and mannerisms.[29] The ZAKA admixture of styles attracts attention: a mishmash of items of clothing and apparatus of two entirely different types. The impression made by ZAKA volunteers is dissonant: the black *kippah* and ritual fringes, the beard and earlocks, interwoven with a bunch of cellular phones and walkie-talkies, rappelling carabiners, a baseball cap, hiking boots, and a pistol.

An illustrative element in this jumble of Haredi-military mannerisms is the jargon typical of ZAKA. It is a language with many strata: Yiddish/ Hebrew, religious/secular, traditional and anachronistic/current, Diasporic/

national, ritual/instrumental. The dominant dialect, its melody and words, is that of the synagogue, the yeshiva halls, the ultra-Orthodox alleys and ghettoes of northern Jerusalem. It is characterized by Ashkenazi intonation, a rising and falling drawl, that emphasizes the penultimate syllable of words (accompanied by Talmudic casuistry hand-gestures), combined with rabbinical homilies, concepts from the world of prayer, halakha, and medieval Midrash, seasoned with witty *vorts* and quotations from the weekly Torah portion. But within this there is an increased presence of up-to-date bravado in staccato, with the accent on the last syllable (as in modern Hebrew), as well as the use of vulgar terms and those taken from Zionist mythology and local politics. In addition, there is also slang influenced by Arabic, and especially expressions used by the security forces (in whose company they enjoy palling around and boasting) and combat soldiers, and even idiosyncratic acronyms taken from the operational and technocratic jargon of the IDF and ISA.[30]

The ZAKA sub-culture is characterized by a dynamic language, which develops rapidly and changes according to circumstances. The variation is mainly in the mixture of sacred and profane idioms. There is a notable difference between ZAKA's language when the organization is in the center of the public stage, at the arena of terrorism, or in contact with institutions of the State of Israel, and its language when its members are by themselves or among Haredim. The multiplicity of languages and the constant and sharp transitions among them reflect the informed sophistication of the volunteers as well as the duality and confusion in their identity. A sign of this is found in the use of two types of body language and in their combinations. On the one hand, there is the ultra-Orthodox body language, which polices and restricts the body, even denies it, and on the other hand there is the Israeli body language, which is free, relatively aggressive, and imposes itself on the space around it.[31] The bodies of the ZAKA volunteers, which shrink and expand by turns, is an index of the inner tension of their existence and of their complex relations with the two segments of the population between which the organization functions.

ZAKA sees itself as sharing the Israeli defense ethos, and like various religious (fundamentalist) groups within the three Abrahamic religions, the Haredi organization internalizes images and patterns of behavior tinged with militarism. Research on the Haredim has discussed their attraction to matters of army and warfare, and this is the context in which we must examine the quasi-military tone that characterizes ZAKA.[32] Like the self-image of Habad Hasidism, which regards itself as "the army of the Lord" and operates "mitzvah tanks" (to persuade Jewish men who happen to pass by to lay *tefillin*), and like the children in the ultra-Orthodox neighborhoods of Jerusalem who dress up as IDF pilots and paratroopers on the carnivalesque holiday of Purim, in ZAKA as well the fantasy of serving in the army surfaces from the unconscious. Several volunteers confessed to me that, despite all their reservations, they dream of being true warriors. Envy and admiration of soldiers suits the political leanings of many of the ZAKA activists, who support right-wing political parties and hawkish foreign and defense policies.

ZAKA activists address one another as members of the "holy organization," and at the same time they present themselves in the press as "an elite military unit." During a combined exercise of ZAKA volunteers and an IDF battalion, the ZAKA rabbi told the colonel commanding the soldiers, "It seems there's a point of contact between the most Haredi men and the most combat-ready soldiers." The religious experience of the ultra-Orthodox organization that deals with the dead has a decidedly martial tone. Here I will present several examples, which quite a few critics of the organization, both among the Haredim and among secular Israelis, regard as unseemly adolescent behavior. On rare occasions the volunteers were able to wear items from army field uniforms for a few hours, and they couldn't restrain their pleasure and pride. Once they were invited, upon their request, to take part in anti-terrorist training that included elementary instruction in hand-to-hand combat. More than they actually trained (as their bodies were cumbersome and heavy), they photographed themselves and immediately made the photographs public. The instructors snickered. The volunteers are proud of their knowledge of desert trails and cliff-climbing, of the police i.d. that gives them access to scenes of disaster, and of their skillful and nonchalant driving of motorcycles and four-wheel-drive vehicles. In the training of the volunteers and evaluation of their abilities, emphasis is placed on perseverance, goal-oriented action, the formation of regular practices, and command of equipment, techniques, and also of emotions in challenging situations. Like soldiers and similar specialists, they aim to develop an ethos of keeping cool in action charged with adrenaline, in the presence of danger and horror. As an index of their professionalism, they present self-control—the separation of their action from feelings and sentiments such as frustration and anger, on the one hand, and pleasure, on the other—as the alternative to paralysis or loss of control. Nevertheless, instructors have reported to me that the Haredi volunteers who train at the firing range go into a frenzy, waste amounts of ammunition far beyond the norm and the quantity allotted to them, and that it is difficult to stop them from shooting more and more in their fury. They particularly like to carry weapons, and firing captivates them. A Haredi volunteer confided to me that participation in ZAKA projects enabled him and his companions "to do at the age of thirty to forty what we didn't do when we were eighteen."

The ZAKA volunteers have an adventurous tendency that sometimes borders on negligence. For their part the ZAKA volunteers often speak about the dangers they assume. On the one hand, they exaggerate them, while, on the other hand, they dismiss them. They dramatize their exposure to delayed explosive charges that might be attached to the bodies of the terrorists, to being shot by a wounded terrorist, and to catching a fatal disease that the terrorists were infected with. They also mention the threat to their mental health because of their habitual proximity to the horrors of death. But they return to the arena time after time, demonstrating what the organization's publications define as courage. The ZAKA volunteers claim that keeping the commandments protects them from all evil. They view the degree of risk, which, the greater it is, the more enthusiastically they assume it, as an index of the strength of their religiosity. Some ZAKA activists compared themselves to the Haredi movement of Bratslav Hasidim, who have developed new ways of expressing their faith in God in the past generation. Among other things, they joyfully accept risks to their lives that border on suicide, in order to show how much they trust in divine providence, which will reward them for their religious devotion by saving them from danger, against all odds. It is known that Bratslav Hasidim have ignored military orders and rabbinical prohibitions, avoiding checkpoints and clambering over border fences, unarmed and totally visible, in order to pray at the tomb of Joseph the Righteous, which is in the outskirts of a hostile Palestinian city, whose residents often killed Israelis in the past. According to stubborn rumors, some Bratslavers sped in their cars with their eyes closed or went through busy crossroads against a red light to prove their religious trust to themselves and to others.[33] This is a particularly extreme form of asceticism, self-mortification in the literal sense, a variation on martyrdom. A Haredi admirer of ZAKA stated that entering the arena of suicide terrorist attacks was an even greater religious challenge, testimony to the volunteers' saintliness.

## Violent Group

Despite its passive and defensive image, the Haredi community has a history of militant activism. ZAKA draws upon the tradition of Haredi violence.

The Haredi tendency toward aggression does not contradict its tendency to cloak itself in victimhood. According to the Haredi ethos, those who are faithful to halakha today, as throughout all the generations, are martyrs who suffer from the oppression of their gentile neighbors and various regimes. This also applies to the secular Zionist state, where they are ostensibly subject to discrimination and persecution. Jewish religious sources contain expressions of hatred and even the commandment to act violently toward the other. However, the oral and written traditions that instill and sanction aggression were developed in circumstances entirely different from the present ones, when the Jews were a minority group in an environment dominated by foreign powers and dependent on their goodwill. The traditional community of believers could not implement, or even conceive of applying the least of such violent ideas. An Israeli observer compared the recurrent recycling of these aggressive motives in the sacred texts and customs to what a weak child, suffering from bullying, might utter only alone, at night, in whispers to his pillow.

In the protracted exilic period, which provided the roots of religious Judaism as we know it today, violence on the part of Jews was rare, and a legacy of victimhood developed. But in this same period new canons and rituals emerged, which undoubtedly had a grain of violence in them. The two most prominent examples are the Passover Haggadah, which was compiled during the Middle Ages and Purim celebrations that drew on the biblical Book of Esther. At the ceremonial Seder meal, religious Jews repeat the line "Pour out your wrath on the nations that refuse to acknowledge you—on the peoples that do not call upon your name. For they have devoured your people Israel." Participants sing hymns of victory accomplished through cruel acts of violence against Egyptians (who are often identified with contemporary villains). They also recount with triumphalism each of the ten plagues with which the Egyptians were afflicted, including the killing of their firstborn.

There is a clear gap between the halakhic, theological, and ceremonial preoccupation with violence and the ability to commit that violence. Indeed, the certainty that violence could not be exercised gave free rein to violent fantasies. One can speculate that the textual and ritual acting out of violence betrays impotence as an overcompensation for the inability to take violent action. As soon as conditions changed for the Jews, and the practical possibility of acting upon hatred arose—in the sovereign State of Israel—these texts and rituals changed their meaning. This raises questions about the relationship between symbolic and physical violence: Are they unconnected, is their connection reversed, or might they be correlated?

The seventy-plus years of the State of Israel are replete with Haredi violence against non-Jews and against the Zionists and their institutions, and also against their fellow Haredim. In many cases, this violence was approved explicitly or with a wink by the rabbis. I will now present a partial list of incidents of Haredi violence:

Attacks against Christian religious institutions and Christian clergy (such as demonstrations against construction of the Mormon university, graffiti saying "Death to Christians" on the Via Dolorosa, and an attack on an Armenian monk in the Old City).

Attacks on Jewish businesses that violate the Sabbath (such as movie theaters and cafés and burning cars that drive on the Sabbath).

Attacks on institutions that do not observe *kashrut* (such as burning down butcher shops that sell pork products).

Attacks on places that are seen as immodest (such as demonstrations against the opening of pools where men and women swim together and against the Yad Vashem museum for exhibiting photographs of naked victims of the Holocaust, and killing a participant in a Gay Pride parade).

Attacks on businesses that are liable to have a bad influence on members of the community and bring them to adopt a degraded lifestyle (such as fast-food stands).

And of course blocking central traffic arteries on the Sabbath and physical opposition to autopsies and archaeological excavations in cemeteries.[34]

There have also been severe incidents of intra-Haredi violence, such as those between splinter groups of the Toldot Aharon yeshiva and between Belz and Machnovka Hasidim. An illustration of Haredi violence against other Haredim is, of course, the modesty patrols, the gangs of bullies from the margins of the yeshiva world who circulate in Haredi streets and, possibly on their own initiative, possibly with rabbinical approval, have cursed, sent threatening letters, and even sprayed acid and broken the arms and legs of those regarded as deviating from the norms. Soon after the establishment of the state, an underground movement called Brit haqanaim (The Covenant of Zealots) operated, attacking various sites and waving the flag of a halakhic state, and fifty years later, a group called Yad Laaḥim (Hand to the Brethren) was active, employing the same aggressive methods. Many ZAKA veteran activists, headed by the organization's chairman, took a central part in a variety of the incidents mentioned above. To this day the ZAKA volunteers are proud of their connection with these manifestations of Haredi violence.

*

In many suicide attacks, the body of the terrorist is blown to smithereens. I heard several volunteers complain that in the absence of a fragment of an object that retains or recalls a (hated) human figure, against whom they can direct their rage, the fury that has built up in them finds no release, and it is hard for them to cope with their rising frustration. During a long night that we spent together in the ZAKA operations room, one of the heads of the Jerusalem branch confessed to me that on rare occasions "we were lucky, and something we could hate remained." Indeed, after a mass attack during the Intifada, in the ambulance bringing the rather intact body of a Hamas terrorist to the National Institute of Forensic Medicine, the volunteers shouted at it, cursed it, and kicked it. Most expressions of ZAKA violence are more subtle. It may be argued that the very attraction to the arena of terrorism and the meticulous handling of the bodies of the victims entails various degrees of sublimated aggression.

The volunteer organization devoted to handling the victims of violence is itself infected with some violence. Rabbis from the hardcore Haredi world are aware of this apparent paradox. Whereas in the Haredi community many kinds of violence are expressed, this community shows strong sensitivity to the violence of groups that it opposes, such as the violence accompanying the realization of the national vision in the Land of Israel. The Haredim oppose Zionism because of the violence attributed to it, and because Haredim oppose Zionism, they attribute violence to it.[35] This also applies to their attitude to ZAKA. Within the Haredi community, there are those who explain their opposition to ZAKA by identifying it with violence. At the Simḥat Torah[36] celebrations in a synagogue in a Haredi neighborhood, an elderly member of the congregation pointed at a circle of dancers and said to his neighbor, "The most enthusiastic ones, the loudest singers, the ones who sweat, stamp their feet, push, and trample on the others are men from ZAKA." During the Intifada, posters were glued to the walls in Haredi neighborhoods, saying, "ZAKA is a Violent Group," Hebrew words that begin with the same letters as ZAKA.

For a long time, emissaries of ZAKA searched for the secret location and clandestine operation of a private company that arranged secular burials and cremations. Someone did manage to burn down the company's installations (August 2007). The evidence indicated that activists of the Haredi organization had committed the arson. ZAKA's chairman avoided taking responsibility for the act, but he blessed whoever had done it and stated that no Jew could remain indifferent to this "insult to the honor of the dead." There are other clear expressions of the violent tendencies of the ZAKA volunteers in the context of dealing with the dead and in other contexts, such as in their street fights with representatives of competitive rescue organizations.

Violence has many aspects, some of which are hidden or unacknowledged.[37] Violence can also play a role in places that appear to be the objects of violence, the opposite of violence. It could be that the treatment of victims, especially dead victims, is an indirect manifestation of a violent instinct. ZAKA's violence should not be surprising, as the organization is an integral part of the scene of the most horrible terrorism. The volunteers are experts in violence, in that they are experts in terrorism and in unnatural deaths.

There are various ways of understanding the connection between ZAKA and violence. Of course, it is possible that from the start the ZAKA volunteers had a tendency toward violence. Because of it, perhaps, most of them dropped out of regular Torah studies in yeshivas and then chose the option of serving in ZAKA. Some of them were known as tough guys in the community. It is a fact that the careers of many of the volunteers are studded with active participation in violent incidents that are not connected to ZAKA, mainly aggressive protests against the State of Israel and confrontations with its agents of law and order. The head of ZAKA has a past especially rich in delinquent and brutal action against Zionist institutions. Perhaps the personalities and life histories of the volunteers contained a hidden seed of dormant violence, and an opportunity was needed, such as that provided by ZAKA, to bring it out. Some of the volunteers acknowledge the violent potential within them. On this matter, they offer with a smile a variation on a Talmudic Midrash that deals with the roots of the differing personalities of human beings and with determinism. Many of the ZAKA men, they claim, were born in the month of March (Maadim, in Hebrew, from the root for "red"), and people born in that month are destined to be spillers of blood. Though predestined, some free will is left for them. They quote the sources, saying that if they direct the inborn traits of their soul well, they will be circumcisers or surgeons. If they act in the middle way, they will be ritual slaughterers or butchers. And if the Torah does not make them gentle, they will be murderers.[38] The ZAKA volunteers argue among themselves as to where they belong on the scale.

It is no less likely that the tendency to violence develops among the volunteers during their service with ZAKA. First, at the arena they are exposed to the results of the most terrible kind of violence, at zero range, in large scale and high frequency. In time, this exposure desensitizes them to violence. Once people become used to violence, it becomes easier for them to employ it without inhibition. It is claimed, for example, that brutality among policemen and jail guards is heightened due to exposure to violence.[39] Perhaps exposure to violence influenced the volunteers the way a child of parents, one of whom acts violently against the other, adopts the model familiar to him and becomes violent himself. Even if he is the victim of his parents' violence, he might identify with his aggressors, according to the model familiar from the literature, as in the case of the prisoners in concentration camps who identify with their cruel guards.[40] In ZAKA's surroundings there are effective agents of violence, who can be imitated, whose ways of acting in the world can be adopted. Not only the men of the IDF but also the Palestinian terrorist, in especially ironic fashion, play a role in this Middle Eastern matrix of mimesis.[41]

Second, since the natural identification of the ZAKA volunteer is with the victims, he internalizes their pain, and thus frustration arises within him, anger, and the desire for revenge that can lead him to violence. As a victim or someone who feels close to victimhood, it can be expected that he will develop fantasies of (vindictive) violence and perhaps try to carry them out. The volunteers who act in a violent environment become victims themselves. They identify with the primary victims and gradually become at least secondary victims, and thus they absorb a lot of violence. The connection between receiving and applying violence has been proven. This connection is exploited, for example, in training soldiers for military units that are called upon to exert severe violence in accomplishing their missions. They are made into effective appliers of violence by having systematic violence inflicted on them, as in the training of US Navy Seals or the IDF Duvdevan unit.[42] There they learn the ability to bear pain and live with pain, to be able to inflict pain on others. Absorbing violence and inflicting it are acquired abilities.[43] Violence emerges with the possibility of bearing pain and not only with the ability to inflict pain. The ZAKA volunteers also absorb violence and learn about it. They learned how to be violent just as they learned how to be victims. In time they became not only professional handlers of the victims of violence but also professional victims of violence, and, consequently, they also become professional appliers of violence.

In scenes of violence there is a constantly repeating chain of stimulus and response. The links in the chain are made of attacker and victim, who exchange roles. One can enter this vicious cycle either as an attacker or as a victim. This is the cycle of suicide terrorism. ZAKA activists are an integral part of this cycle. The human bomb enters the cycle as an attacker and becomes a victim. The Palestinians present him first as a victim, and this explains and justifies his aggression. The Haredi volunteers initially appear as victims, and then their aggression is also revealed.

Study of the arena of suicide terrorism shows that the distance between attacker and victim can become short, and the difference between them can be blurred.[44] (In no way can this statement be understood as denying the ethical difference between attacker and victim.)[45] ZAKA operates in areas of especially intense violence, replete with points of contact with victimhood. In violence the attacker and victim meet, on either side of a thin line, and sometimes the two interchange or become one. This contact between what appear to be two opposites draws to it the Haredi volunteers in a way that recalls the attraction of terrorists to this tense coupling. Like the Palestinian human bombs, ZAKA activists find both the charm of victimhood and the charm of violence in the arena of terrorist attacks in Israel.

## Selection and Initiation

In ZAKA's formal announcements, the high standards required of the organization's members are laid out. They must stand out in knowledge of Torah, in observing all the commandments, in love of God, in integrity, and in responsibility. To reinforce the demands, they quote the bylaws of a burial society from the past in the Diaspora, where other demands are made of the members: they must observe family purity; their treatment of the dead must not be accompanied with a smile, idle conversation, or distraction, but it must be done in "awe and dread."[46] These demands were presented in ZAKA's effort to enhance the prestige of their volunteers in the eyes of other Haredim. The heads of ZAKA are sensitive to this issue, since some of the volunteers are dropouts from the yeshiva framework, tough guys, adventurers, and impulsive. ZAKA responds that even if they did not come to the organization for appropriate reasons, during their activity they internalize the ideal intention, and their membership in ZAKA is testimony to their rehabilitation. They add that not every God-fearing man is capable of dealing with the dead, but that everyone who devotes himself to dealing with the dead fears heaven. Even those who appear to be lowlifes in fact are sanctifying the name of God, select individuals who fulfill the injunction from the Mishnah: "Where there are no men, endeavor to be a man."[47]

Despite the organization's declarations regarding their orderly method for enlisting volunteers, the process of selection and acceptance is random, and it takes place via informal social networks, mainly friends bringing friends and relatives. There are no activists in the organization who did not know some of their colleagues before joining, and there are quite a few brothers, fathers and sons, and brothers-in-law. Each volunteer has his personal story about how he came to the organization. Common to most of the accounts is the mention of something miraculous that brought them to the arena, something that has stayed with them for years, since their childhood, or that they just happened to come to an arena, but they were immediately "infected," and ever since they have become addicted. Each of the volunteers connects himself with a certain arena of death as the start of his ZAKA career. In most cases it is a terrorist attack. Even after years of activity it remains engraved in his autobiography as a life-changing event.

Quite a few of the candidates drop out at the beginning of their path with ZAKA. These are the men who are unable to stand the sights and smells of the arena. Some of them fled for their lives upon their first encounter with the horrible deaths. In fact, there is a kind of entry test that can be described as an initiation rite: the novices are asked to take part in the purification of bodies at the cemetery, and to show composure. The ones who vomit or avert their gaze are eliminated. Those remaining join the experienced volunteers as apprentices, and for some time they participate in handling the dead only in a passive manner. This is an unofficial stage of training and testing that is not clearly defined in time. In a documentary film on ZAKA, one Haredi activist says, "We are an exclusive club. A sect. Not everyone is accepted. No one wants to leave it."[48]

## Collective Profile, Hasidic Hegemony

The photographs of a few dozen volunteers alternated on ZAKA's official website: all men, none beneath the age of about thirty, some fifty or sixty years old, and some even older, wearing black yarmulkas, with long beards, many with earlocks, and wearing glasses. Not a single secular person appeared there. Some secular men are allied with ZAKA, but only irregularly. None of them belongs to the inner circles of ZAKA or shares its organizational culture, and, mainly, none of them takes part in treating the corpses. The secular men serve as divers, rock climbers, and specialists in other skills connected with evacuation and rescue, and they are called up on an ad hoc basis. I heard it claimed that some secular men wanted to volunteer to be in the group summoned to the sites of violent death, but they withdrew when they came within zero range of the mutilated bodies.

The Hasidic hegemony in ZAKA is noticeable and seems natural. ZAKA volunteers come from various branches of Hasidism, mainly those relatively less structured, which do not have a regime based on ambitious Torah study or tight supervision of people's schedules and effective monitoring of behavior in public, such as Shomrei Emunim. "Lithuanians" (also *mitnagdim*, the catchall term for Haredim who are in opposition to the Hasidim) are a minority in the organization. They explain this not only as a consequence of their commitment to yeshiva life, but also of their meticulous observance of halakha, because of which they are reluctant to have contact with the dead, out of fear of ritual impurity,[49] and also as a result of their preference for a delicate bodily style, which values restrained movement and cleanliness, which are impossible in the arena of death. There are Torah scholars in ZAKA, like those associated with the large Mir Yeshiva, but there are no sworn *mitnagdim*. The differences between Hasidic and Lithuanian volunteers are evident in their styles of action. In contrast to the total devotion of the former, who roam about restlessly between incident and incident—in the headquarters, in the streets, in acts of charity, at the graves of *tsadikim*—the latter come unquestioningly to an event or to report for duty, scrupulously do what must be done, and return to their yeshiva and family.[50] The increasing closeness between these two Haredi sectors in recent years is evident in ZAKA, but a division of labor between them remains: the Lithuanians provide a halakhic umbrella and are satisfied with being simple soldiers in their work at the arena, quietly and modestly doing their religious duty. The enthusiastic, boisterous Hasidim provide the operational, spiritual, and impulsive momentum.

Among the ZAKA volunteers, the "Jerusalemites" (*chalmers* in Haredi parlance) predominate, mainly because of the roots of the senior members of the organization. People make fun of them for being idlers, unsophisticated, and short-fused. They are descendants of the Old Yishuv, whose ancestors arrived in Palestine during the Ottoman Empire rule, and who were characterized by fanatical anti-Zionism and social self-segregation even before the establishment of the state. Today they have a local ethos whose center of gravity is less in ideology than in their unique style, and in their way of praying.

A significant characteristic of many ZAKA volunteers is their difficulty in defining their specific Haredi identity, and not only because they impatiently reject all efforts to link them with one or another faction of the Haredi community. The human composition of ZAKA is a mixed multitude of individuals, each one of whom has a confused or divided identity. They tend to introduce themselves as "general Haredim." This might be an expression of their marginal or problematic personal status within the various factions, and it could also be an expression of the unconsolidated and non-consensual status of the organization within the Haredi community. It might also be an indication of a dynamic of blurring the intra-Haredi boundaries and the emergence of a supra-factional Haredi identity, in whose recent development ZAKA plays a role.

Hasidism is torn by tension between the ascetic and mystical and the worldly and bodily. Alongside the tendency to spirituality, it also gives an important place to the corporeal and the carnal. Mostly Hasidic ZAKA volunteers differ from other Haredim in that they express the earthly and sensual elements of Judaism. At the arena of terrorism, the Haredi body, usually repressed and inhibited, comes to the fore. Below I mention several manifestations of Hasidic physicality that also characterize the behavior of ZAKA volunteers outside the arena of terrorism and not in the context of death. ZAKA men are prominent among the escorts of Hasidic rabbis on their way to prayers at the Western Wall. They climb fences and surround the rabbi as he walks through the Muslim Quarter, a combination of bodyguards and fans. When the rabbi rides to meetings on community matters, ZAKA men run panting before his cars to clear the way in the streets of Jerusalem, and to honor him. They are boisterous and frenetic when they dance at the weddings of community notables, shooting their arms and legs in every direction, and at feasts they eat with their hands without self-restraint. At night they immerse themselves in freezing springs in the wilds, and from pushing and shoving to get close to the marriage canopy of a rabbi's grandson, they emerge scratched and bruised. Many ZAKA volunteers also behave like Hasidim in matters not connected to physicality. For example, they frequently visit the graves of *tsadikim* and make pilgrimages to holy sites.

A Hasidic custom that characterizes most of the ZAKA volunteers is going to extremes in observing a certain commandment, to which transcendent importance is attributed, although performing it might entail the neglect of other commandments. Orthodox Jewish men put on *tefillin* upon rising in the morning in obedience to a commandment. Some of the Hasidim in ZAKA wear *tefillin* on their forehead and arm all day long. Some Hasidim emphasize the commandment of eating in the *succah*. [51] They break their tight daily schedule and take the trouble to go to the *succah* outside their houses to eat even a crumb of food. The ZAKA volunteers claim that, similarly, they emphasize the commandment of honoring the dead. They know that when they crawl on the asphalt of a street with a magnifying glass, looking for tiny pieces of bone, they are doing more than is expected in their community: *lifnim mishurat hadin* (beyond the letter of the law).

## Individual Profiles

### Bentzi

Bentzi isn't strong, handsome, smart, or especially talented, but he's always there, in the center of the action, colorful, embodying the phenomenon with all its aspects and complexities. Not a good speaker or elegant, and not sophisticated, but a noble person, cordial and liked by everyone who knows him. He has no official function, though sometimes honored with the title "operation officer of the Jerusalem Branch". Not a born leader, but experienced in the field, someone whom everyone respects and whose authority they accept.

Since the attack on bus 405, there has been no large terrorist incident in which he did not participate, often first to enter the arena and last to leave it. He is not sophisticated, he's just a simple man, but a noble person, cordial, respected and liked by most who know him. He has no official function, not a born leader, but experienced in the field, someone whose authority others accept. He never turned his back on the less brilliant events that don't receive public attention, several hundred cases of unnatural death. Sometimes he is there by himself. For nearly thirty years he has been on call, 24/7, and solely as a volunteer.

Camera lenses are attracted to Bentzi: heavy-set, large, red-faced, with a thick beard and long earlocks, ritual fringes outside his shirt, with the cuffs of his broad trousers stuffed into his long stockings, wearing a gigantic black yarmulka on his bald head. Photographs of him are familiar, despite his anonymity, giving artificial respiration to a wounded child, scraping blood off the sidewalk. The day after a murderous attack in Jerusalem, in the Palestinian newspaper *Al Fajer*, the picture of the female suicide terrorist appeared, and, next to it, a photograph of Bentzi carrying her body in a bag.

Bentzi's terrible death memory, which he bears in his heart more than others, and to which he returns repeatedly, is the suicide terrorist attack in the Beit Yisrael neighborhood, near his house (March 2002). He heard the explosion, saw huge flames, and immediately ran to the arena. It was a Haredi incident: dozens of Haredi men treating the eleven Haredi victims. Bentzi knew many of them. He worked without gloves there, as though touching his own burned and mutilated flesh.

Bentzi Oering, fifty-five years old at the time of my fieldwork, was a mediocre student in the Lublin yeshiva in Bnei Brak, entered an arranged marriage at the age of twenty, is the father of eleven, and his health is not good. He served for a short time in the IDF as a gravedigger and *kashrut* supervisor, but he requested to be excused because he was unable to adjust to the secular atmosphere and especially suffered from witnessing what he defined as sexual wantonness. He will not let his children join the army. For ten years he taught reading, writing, and the Pentateuch (*ḥumash*) with Rashi's commentary to children aged four to six in a *ḥeder* (yeshiva for young children, the ultra-Orthodox equivalent of elementary school)). Bentzi does not study Talmud regularly, he is not an expert in halakha, and he does not pretend to spiritual depth. He frequently consults his rabbi and receives his guidance and rulings in personal and public matters. He also gives his rabbi notes with questions from other Hasidim (*kvitlakh*), and he passes on the answers: what to name a new baby girl, whether to have an operation in the hospital, what percentage of the family income must be given to charity. Regarding the halakha concerning the treatment of the dead Bentzi goes to a different rabbi, who specializes in that area, although he belongs to the Satmer Hasidim, with whose extreme anti-Zionism Bentzi disagrees. On the Sabbath and holidays Bentzi wears a splendid *shtraiml*, a black silk *kapota*, and three-quarter-length trousers that show his snow-white, high stockings. Beneath his broad sash, which serves as a separation,[52] he places his three telephones and his walkie-talkie. In the pocket of his holiday coat there is always a pair of rubber gloves, ready for use.

Bentzi belongs to a group called Shomrei Emunim (Keepers of the Faith), a Hasidic faction rather depleted in size, self-assurance, and influence, the remains of a group after three generations of disputes among the leaders' heirs, leading to split after split. The eldest and most prestigious branch is Toldot Aharon, known for its zealotry. Bentzi's branch, in contrast, moderated its positions regarding the State of Israel in the past generation. These Hasidim maintain three principles: "worship in weariness," a prolonged style of prayer at high volume, accompanied by vigorous bodily movements; "the devotion of friends," emphasis of close relations of love and mutual responsibility among the Hasidim in the community; and "sanctity of eyes," insistence on puritan modesty, including the prohibition against looking at women.

Bentzi and his large family live in a meager, crowded sixty-square-meter apartment, with almost no furniture or equipment. Clothing hangs on door handles. Since there are no desks, the children do their homework kneeling on the floor. At night mattresses are spread on the floor and in the corridor. The apartment is on a high floor in a tenement belonging to Shomrei Emunim. A narrow, dark, and dirty staircase leads to it. There is no television in the apartment, though there is a computer—for the purposes of ZAKA, mainly used in correspondence with courts regarding postmortem examinations—but it is hidden from the neighbors' eyes.

Bentzi's family is below the poverty line. He has no steady work, and he is sometimes unemployed for a long time. During my research he worked as a supervisor in a chicken slaughterhouse and as a *kashrut* inspector in a catering service, and he is also deep in debt. Bentzi's wife is a cashier in a store, his brother is a slaughterer, and only one of his three adult sons is steadily employed as a kitchen assistant in a yeshiva. A second son studies Torah in the daytime and washes dishes at night. From time to time Bentzi goes to Brooklyn to raise money, for charity and also for himself (though he doesn't speak any English). Many of the people around Bentzi wonder how he gets along. His constant answer does not solve the mystery: "The Holy One takes care of me."

Bentzi's busy day begins with *tefilat vatiqin,* a special service for those who are particularly meticulous concerning certain customs, beginning before dawn and ending at sunrise. From the synagogue he rushes to immerse himself in the ritual bath every morning. At one time he used to immerse himself several times a day to cleanse himself from the impurity of the dead. Then he begins a hurried round of errands he has taken upon himself: to draw blood from a lonely old woman and deliver it to a laboratory, to give an injection to a bedridden man in his home, to give a massage to a sick-child, to collect money for the wedding of a widow's daughter, and the like. The errands are interrupted again and again by emergency calls from ZAKA headquarters, and he rushes in an ambulance that is at his disposal from one arena of death to another: the crib death of an infant, a road accident, a suicide. While driving from one incident to the next, Bentzi negotiates with the police by telephone to get permission for a Haredi demonstration, and he intercedes with the burial society to make them hurry to bury someone before dark. In the evening he attends the wedding of someone who was severely wounded in a terrorist attack, and Bentzi was the one who saved him. After that he might finish his fortnightly shift as a paramedic at MaDA.

The ZAKA routine that fills Bentzi's days is broken by particularly dramatic events. One such case is that of a young Haredi man, apparently mentally unstable, who abused his infant physically and caused its death, and the police wanted to have an autopsy performed (2006). In response, hundreds of Haredim gathered and demanded the father's release and the immediate burial of the infant, without forensic intervention. The situation got out of control, until Bentzi picked up the infant and brought it to the father's cell. The father recited the kaddish, and calm was restored. In another incident, he was suspected of cooperating with the police, and when he was surrounded by masses of Haredim, they vented their fury on him, though he was on duty. They dragged him out of the ambulance he was driving, beat him, and nearly lynched him. In ZAKA, by contrast, no one is better liked. His children's weddings are holidays for all the volunteers. Within a few hours all the activists of the organization contribute money for the celebration. He hides in a corner, but they drag him into the circle and dance around him. At other people's weddings they seat him at the head of the table, despite his efforts to slip away.

In ZAKA Bentzi is described as a one-man charity industry. In addition to his involvement in various charitable associations, such as raising money for dowries and providing clothes to the needy, he also established his own charitable organization to return lost children to their parents. The high point of Bentzi's charitable missions is his open Sabbath meals. It is known in his community that at Bentzi's house one can always get a free meal with *kiddush* (sanctification of the Sabbath with blessings) over wine and Sabbath hymns. Whoever comes is welcome. He hosts about forty guests in his tiny apartment. Most of them are Torah students far from their families. On Thursdays he and his wife ask for donations of chickens and other foodstuffs from the neighborhood stores, and all the night before the parents and children cook. They also bake sixty *challot*. As the Sabbath approaches, they bring folding tables and benches from neighboring apartments. The crowding is intense, and the singing is contagious. Bentzi and his children serve the food, and he pours wine that he made himself in the corridor to his apartment. He has done this every week for thirty-two years.

The connection between Bentzi's volunteering and acts of charity and his immediate contact with the dead has made him into a *ba'al nes*, a miracle worker. In the Haredi neighborhoods and beyond them people regard him as a miraculous healer and one who fulfills wishes. People stop him in the street and ask him to bless them. Once I saw Palestinian workers address him in hopes that his powers would benefit them. He placed his enormous hands on their heads and murmured something.

## Meshi

Yehuda Meshi-Zahav, a sixty-year-old Jerusalem Haredi, known among both the pious and the secular by his nickname, "Meshi," was, until the shocking scandal that brought him down, an Israeli cultural hero. On several occasions he said of himself, with typical lack of modesty but to a large degree of truth, "Meshi is ZAKA, and ZAKA is Meshi." For many years he was the actual head of ZAKA, and he may be said to have established the organization. Meshi was an effective manager of ZAKA both on the operational front and on that of public relations, as well as behind the scenes. He has a vision for the organization, which guides its daily operations. He is responsible for the relations between the organization and the institutions and persons who make policy and provide financing, and he speaks for the organization, bringing it to every house in the country and in world Jewry.

Meshi's biography is marked by a dramatic turning point. At the halfway point in his years, he passed from the pole of being a zealous warrior against the state and secular society to the opposite pole of being someone who receives official recognition as a figure who symbolizes what is positive in Israel. He performed this turnabout while mounted on the back of ZAKA. From a ruffian he became a man of charity, from a curser to an extoller. In retrospect, Meshi speaks of his two incarnations, and in answer to the interviewer's question, he says that the earlier Meshi would undoubtedly demonstrate in front of the present Meshi's house, and even disconnect the electricity from his apartment. Meshi's personal transformation fits into the transformation in the character and status of the Haredim, and specifically in the image of ZAKA.

Meshi comes from the most radical Haredi aristocracy, the eleventh generation in Jerusalem. His mother's father was Rabbi Amram Blau, the leader of Neturei Karta in the first years of the state who became famous for his violent protests against the apparatus of the state. He was regarded as a martyr because he was severely beaten by the police in Jerusalem several times. He put a sign on his door saying, "Here lives a non-Zionist Jew." Meshi's paternal grandfather was Rabbi Yossele Shainberg, the secretary of the Eda Haredit, with the most extreme ideology of separation and opposition among the Haredim. Meshi recalls that in his childhood, the members of his family used to fast on Israeli Independence Day. At that time, he pictured himself as a soldier in the armies of God, confronting those who profane His name, and when he encountered a policeman, he called him "Gestapo." When he and his friends were beaten by the strong arm of the police, they believed this guaranteed them a place in the Garden of Eden, the more painful, the better.

In his youth, because of his tempestuous nature, he found it impossible to devote himself exclusively to regular studies in the yeshiva, and thus he was known as a wild kid in the alleys of Meah Shearim. As he says of himself, he was "a *shababnik* but not an *epikores* [heretic]." Along with his aggressiveness, he also stood out in creativity and leadership ability. He gradually channeled his anarchistic, not to say delinquent energies into semi-legitimate action. He became a *makher* (a Yiddish term meaning someone who gets things done, an activist who arranges matters outside of official procedures) in the service of the leaders of the Eda Haredit. They exploited his abilities but were forced to distance themselves from him in public. Using unconventional methods, he promoted their interests in their struggle against the government and mainly in intra-Haredi struggles. At the age of sixteen he was already the editor of a newspaper, *Ha'Eda*, and at night he went out into the street to paste up provocative wall posters and to extort contributions. At that time he learned the *shticks* (Yiddish for inelegant and half-legitimate manipulations) of behind-the-scenes politics, including the art of exploiting personal connections and inciting public opinion, and of combining clandestine and violent activity with symbolic protest acts.

When Meshi was in his twenties, the Israeli press called him the operations officer (*kamba'tz*) of the Eda Haredit. His charisma attracted dozens (he claims hundreds) of ultra-Orthodox young men, including yeshiva students, who took part in urban guerrilla action aimed at Zionist targets, or those that were defined as immoral or non-Jewish. They set fire to a sex shop, broke the windows of a bus that bore an advertisement with the picture of a woman, vandalized buildings of Christian missions and churches, and harassed and threatened archaeologists who were excavating in areas presumed to be ancient Jewish cemeteries. They covered the walls of buildings in Jerusalem with black graffiti, signed them *Keshet* (bow). According to one source, this is an acronym for the Hebrew words meaning "Torah Guardians Group," while others claim that it stands for "Group that won't be reconciled."

The Haredim called that thuggish cell the "Meshi Commandos," and twenty years later they applied that epithet to ZAKA. Meanwhile Meshi aroused and enlisted masses of Haredim to go out into the street and demonstrate against autopsies and violations of the Sabbath. Major roads were blocked, and cars traveling near Haredi neighborhoods in Jerusalem on the Sabbath were stoned. Some people were wounded, and there was one death. In the "Sabbath Wars" Meshi caused escalation in the physical confrontation with police armed with clubs and mounted on horseback. The arsenal of the Haredi activists contained a weapon that proved to be particularly effective: dirty diapers that were thrown and smeared on the police. In the folklore of the community this invention is also credited to Meshi.

Meshi was arrested thirty-six times for his actions against the agents of law and order.[53] He frequently mentions this as a certificate of honor (every time he was arrested, he repeated the phrase, "How fortunate to be arrested for keeping the Torah"), and he used it as an alibi against those who accused him of being a *moiser* (Yiddish for an informer, a halakhic concept referring to Jews in the Diaspora who informed on other members of the community to the gentile authorities; this is considered a contemptible crime, with a heavy penalty, including excommunication). The accusation of collaboration with the "Zionist police" arises against the background of his developing relations with its heads. Alongside direct confrontations, fruitful dialogue also developed between them. Personal relations progressed into professional relations. Senior officials in the state administration, the municipality, and the security forces approached Meshi and used his leadership to advance agreements and truces with the Haredim. In so doing they also raised his standing in the community. The covenant between Meshi and the police was one of the foundations of ZAKA's success. As the head of ZAKA, Meshi held a police identity card, but this did not prevent him from launching religious wars that sometimes led to head-on collisions between the Haredim and the authorities.

In 1989 Meshi took part in handling the victims of bus 405. This was a formative experience for him, too. From 1995 until his death Meshi was the head of ZAKA, though his official title changed during that period. In the past twenty-five years he has been ZAKA's initiator and planner, carrying out plans and acting as spokesman. When circumstances changed, he adapted and reinvented ZAKA anew. ZAKA reached its peak during the Intifada. Meshi managed to garner most of the credit for that. After September 11, at the height of Palestinian suicide terrorism, Rudolph Giuliani, then mayor of New York City, visited Jerusalem as a gesture of solidarity between two cities beset by terrorism. The Israeli mayor said to his guest, "You in America have everything you need to cope with the challenge of future terrorism, except for one thing, that only we have: Meshi."[54]

On Israel's fifty-fifth Independence Day, in the most difficult period of the Intifada, because ZAKA was identified with Meshi, the government invited him to be one of the twelve people to light torches at the central ceremony of the holiday, the ultimate symbolic expression of loyalty and contribution to the state. The invitation posed the dilemma of his life to Meshi. On the one hand, not only was it an enormous personal honor, but it also implied recognition of ZAKA's national and human mission and its success in penetrating the heart of the Israeli consensus. On the other hand, it was impossible not to see the occasion as granting legitimacy to the secular state and glorifying it, which implied betrayal of Meshi's religious principles and his loyalty to the Haredi community, turning his back on the tradition upon which he was raised, and in whose name he had done battle. On every Independence Day, his family had worn sackcloth as a sign of mourning. The ceremony is held every year on Mount Herzl, named after the founder of Zionism, one of the fathers of the nation, and exactly on that spot, not many years previously, Meshi had desecrated Herzl's grave in a coarse act of vandalism. His relatives, his Haredi friends, and respected rabbis put heavy pressure on him to reject the invitation. Some ZAKA volunteers called upon him to withdraw until the last moment.

Only Rabbi Nebenzahl, the rabbi of the Old City of Jerusalem, a well-known radical, particularly stringent in keeping the Torah commandments, the one who rigorously supervised the ZAKA volunteers to make sure they observed all the strictures of the halakha at the arena of death, said, "Go and sanctify the Name of Heaven." Meshi lit the torch. As part of the ceremony, which was broadcast live to millions of viewers in Israel, he was required to recite a text that was written, like all the other personages who lit torches. He found it particularly hard to swallow the last sentence, and he considered avoiding it, against the rules of the ceremony, and without warning. In the end he decided to go all the way. In the name of ZAKA he read the final chord of his declaration loudly and clearly: "for the glory of the State of Israel."

That night the walls of Meah Shearim were covered with libelous posters against Meshi and ZAKA. They said, "For the glory of the State of Israel and the shame of religious Judaism." In Haredi neighborhoods the tires of ZAKA's motorcycles were slashed. The reactions in his family were particularly harsh. He was boycotted, and they asked him to change his name so as not to shame them. His parents, his siblings, his sons-in-law, and his brothers-in-law refused to visit his home or to be seen with him for more than four years. His grandfather cursed him, insulted him, and drove him away, screaming that he had destroyed everything the Haredim had built in several generations. Rumor has it that his children were afraid to be seen next to him in the street. The little ones were separated from their grandparents and uncles, and the older ones were threatened with expulsion from school. His friends shunned him and complained that after fighting against the heretics together, he had joined with them. Meshi received summonses from the rabbinical court of the Eda Haredit and was warned that he would have no part in the world to come. Even Haredi members of the Knesset, who themselves maintain close connections with the secular political establishment, disavowed the far-reaching step he had made.

Meshi justified his decision by claiming that he only did what he did in honor of all the volunteers, who worked for long hours handling decaying bodies, whose sight and stench are repulsive, that he had not gone for himself but in the name of his comrades in the organization, who know neither day nor night. At the ceremony he announced that he was representing 195 victims of terrorism, who have no one to speak for them.[55] Meshi added, somewhat apologetically, that he had not become a Zionist, but he had come to the conclusion that Israel had to be recognized, that secular Jews must be respected, and that it was better to work alongside the establishment for the sake of Jewish security and out of concern for the interests of the Haredim.

The response of the Israeli public was prompt. Meshi became a sought-after celebrity. He was recognized in the street and honors were showered upon him. He became a popular lecturer and interviewee, who responded to growing curiosity about the Haredim. He wanted to be seen as a symbol of rapprochement between secular and Haredi Jews, claiming that he was responding to a need felt on both sides. In addressing Israeli public opinion, he presented the lighting of the torch as an effort to atone for everything he had committed against the secular state over the years. Meanwhile, the reaction in the Haredi community gradually became milder. For many Haredim, especially young men, he redeemed their injured pride, and they saw him as a model to be imitated. Older and more official Haredi spokesmen, along with condemnation, found it hard to conceal admiration and gratitude, in that, by his means, they had finally achieved legitimacy. The ambivalence of their attitude toward Meshi and ZAKA became sharper. To illustrate, Meshi himself said that once Rabbi Katzenelbogen, one of the heads of Neturei Karta, called upon ZAKA volunteers to handle the death of the head of his family. While he was sitting in the ambulance with the volunteers, as it took away the body, he burst out in a torrent of insults against the organization, whose sin was greater than that of the Zionists.

Meshi was born in Meah Shearim, one of thirteen brothers and sisters. He was married to a younger girl at the age of eighteen in an arranged marriage (he claimed that he saw her for the first time just a few minutes before the ceremony). At nineteen he was already a father and ultimately had seven children. From the age of two he was sent to a *ḥeder* and then to a yeshiva *ktana* (for boys under bar-mitzvah age) and then to a yeshiva *gedola*, after which he spent three years in a *kolel* (a yeshiva for married men). He did not persist in his studies. His admirers in ZAKA said that if he had devoted himself to the Torah, he would have become the head of a major yeshiva. He slipped into other activities, which clashed with yeshiva life. In addition to public activism and work to support himself (from 1983 to 1989 he worked in marketing, specializing in introducing products in the Haredi sector), and he was tempted by actions forbidden in Haredi society: from an early age he secretly read secular literature, mainly stories of heroism in the wars of Israel. When he grew older, he read adventure stories with a macho element, which were the sole province of secular Zionists, such as books about challenging trips in the desert. Later on he took training courses in paramilitary skills such as parachuting, diving, and karate.

Meshi was smart, cunning, quick thinking, and fast moving, a methodical thinker, eloquent, and endowed with social skills. He was an enterprising man, original, energetic, and daring. Meshi is also affable, and a magician in public relations. He has abundant self-confidence. Meshi is short, with red hair and beard, and he emphasizes his individuality and visibility. He is never in a fedora hat and always in a gleaming white shirt. He does not hide his long earlocks behind his ears. Meshi is also emotional. He puts his whole self in songs and dances. Every Friday evening, before the Sabbath, he goes up to a spot overlooking the Temple Mount, where he stands alone, swept away until sundown while listening, with earbuds, to his personal but famous playlist of Hasidic music. Meshi is an action-seeker, excited by physical, organizational, and religious extremes. From his childhood he retains a provocative element, seeking challenges. Under the aegis of rabbinical permission, given with a wink, because of his insistence on respect for the dead, he allowed himself to cross red lines for Haredim. For example, he could not restrain himself and for a few hours he put on an IDF uniform, an infraction as grave as eating pork. He also developed relations of mutual trust with Professor Hiss, a pathologist and head of the National Institute of Forensic Medicine at the time, which was like waving a red flag in front of a raging bull. Meshi told me that the flip from anti-Zionist militancy to ZAKA was actually not so great, since at both the opposite poles there is a flirting with crossing boundaries, and action remains action. Many of the qualities that made him so admired—his appetite for risk, penchant for extreme behavior, and willingness to cross red lines—likely also played a part in his crimes and ultimate downfall.

In the Haredi community Meshi has opponents no less ardent and vociferous than his supporters. He is criticized for his vulgarity, his hunger for publicity, his foppishness, his bullying manners, and other traits, that are symbolized in his black Jeep with its special gadgets and antennas, which arouses the envy of his sworn enemies and doesn't sit well even in the eyes of his sympathizers. Everybody knows that Meshi isn't without his faults, and his public image vacillates between the most righteous of his generation and a lawless and dangerous man, or a buffoon. Not surprisingly, even before the abuse that would lead to his undoing, Meshi's career in ZAKA was full of scandals. He was accused of running ZAKA negligently and improvidently, with nepotism and even actual corruption—apparently with some merit to the charges.

In a sincere conversation with Meshi, his secret dream arose, of being an IDF general. He is sure that, had he not been born Haredi, he would have had a successful career in the army. He immediately shifts away from that fantasy and returns to the experience of ZAKA. He points at the wall before him in his office at the organization's headquarters. There, between maps, charts, and graphs, hang two large pictures. He says that his faith lies in the combination of the two. In interviews, he quotes a verse used in Jewish funerals: "Look upon three things and you shall not enter into sin: Whence have you come? Where are you destined to go? And before whom you must stand in final judgement."[56] In answer to the first question, he points at the photograph of the Rabbi of Satmar, the leader of the most extreme Haredi sect. In answer to the second question, he points at an enlarged newspaper photograph of the day after a terrorist attack that claimed many victims, showing a long row of bodies wrapped in bags with the ZAKA symbol. In answer to the third question, he points upward.

One of Meshi's sons is tending to pass over into the secular world, and, with his encouragement, three of them enlisted in the army. His critics see this as proof that their claim was correct: the path that led to lighting the torch ended in heresy. Rumors about poor management that led to a financial crisis in ZAKA, and persistent criticism for constantly ignoring the rulings of rabbis during the work of the ZAKA volunteers, have contributed to the turmoil that arose in the community following the "sin" of participating in the Independence Day ceremony. Haredim in the organization and outside it demanded Meshi's removal from the leadership. A newspaper headline proclaimed, "Meshi lit a torch, and he was burned." In 2006 Meshi was deposed, and his in-law was appointed as his successor. Shortly afterward, he was restored to running the organization.

## Rabbi Roje

Rabbi Yakov Roje is the rabbi of the dead no less than the rabbi of the living. He is the highest authority in Israel regarding the death of Jews, and especially an expert and the final decisor on the treatment of violent and unnatural death according to the Torah. I saw hundreds of books on halakha in his office, as well as sixty thick binders crammed with halakhic disputes on the field of his specialization, which he calls "What is between the closing of eyes and their covering with earth."

Roje is the rabbi of a dull and middle-size city in the center of the country. In addition, he bears four titles, all of which refer to death. He is the rabbi of the burial society of Tel Aviv. He is a veteran in the military burial unit, and in his many years of reserve duty he has reached a high military rank and serves as an advisor to the chief rabbi of the IDF in handling casualties of war. He is also the rabbi of the National Institute of Forensic Medicine, and he is the intermediary between the Institute, the burial society, and ZAKA. Finally, Roje is the head of the ZAKA rabbinical council, the chief halakhic advisor of the volunteers, and the ruling authority on halakhic issues that arise during the treatment of bodies at the various arenas of death.

Roje is seventy-five years old, learned in Torah, meticulous in keeping the commandments, and the graduate of the best Lithuanian yeshivas. For many years he was a teacher and school principal, and he was also the head of a religious Zionist yeshiva. He gradually went from modern Orthodoxy to ultra-Orthodoxy. He told me that he doesn't go to funerals, because he can't stand seeing people cry.

While working with the burial society, he made several innovative halakhic rulings regarding the interface between death, technology, and architecture. Among other things, he approved of a system of burial which has become common: burying family members in a single grave, one above the other. In his work at the Institute, he encountered difficulties because the medical employees there perceived him as intervening unprofessionally and restricting their action, whereas his Haredi friends regarded him as a traitor who assisted the desecration of the dead. Ultimately the former understood that his presence quieted the belligerent religious opposition, and the latter realized that he diminished the chance that the Institute would violate the laws of the Torah.

Until he was thirty, there was no connection between his religiosity and dealing with the dead. It happened suddenly and powerfully. A few days after he enlisted in the army rabbinate, the Yom Kippur War of 1973 broke out. The next day he was sent urgently to the IDF logistical center at the southern front. Immediately after his arrival he found himself in a tent with a dozen bodies of soldiers. With no preparation or training, he was forced to take them by the legs and place them on a table for identification. He was then sent to a helicopter landing pad to help unload the wounded and the dead, to clarify and separate them, and to handle the latter. In the following two weeks, he dealt with a few hundred dead soldiers When he removed the blanket from one of the bodies, he discovered that the victim was his cousin. He left the war in shock. In time he became experienced and professional at identifying the dead.[57]

After the war, for more than thirty years, he was frequently called up to help handle IDF casualties. Our last meeting took place a few days after he oversaw a complex religious, military, and political operation: the removal of a cemetery in Gush Katif, which the Jewish settlers had to abandon when the government decided to withdraw from the Gaza Strip (2006). The bodies were removed from their graves and reinterred in several sites in Israel. During his service in the army reserves, he was also responsible for developing a military-Torah doctrine for handling the bodies and body parts of casualties. He summed this up in a book entitled *Kevod hamet* (Respect for the Dead) in Hebrew and *Yeqara deshekhavei* in Aramaic, but the IDF prevented its circulation. Later he published a digest of his rulings in a pamphlet distributed to the members of ZAKA.

Roje's connection with ZAKA was formed before the organization's official establishment, in the suicide terrorist attack on bus 5 in Tel Aviv (October 1994). He was one of the first to be called to the arena and, along with other Haredim, he handled the bodies of the twenty-two victims for long hours. When that task was finished, he rushed to the National Institute of Forensic Medicine to continue treatment of the dead there. Since then he has taught halakha to the Haredi volunteers, admonishing them to treat the bodies of Jews with sanctified awe, as if they were touching a Torah scroll that had been burned, and as if they were offering a sacrifice in the Temple.

During the long time I spent in Roje's company, his two telephones and two walkie-talkies never ceased ringing. Our conversation was often interrupted by rabbinical questions addressed to him by ZAKA activists, who encounter problems requiring an immediate halakhic solution at various arenas of unnatural death. I followed in real time one such question and answer. A Jerusalem volunteer asked what to do with a pool of blood around the toilet after a woman had miscarried a dead fetus. Unhesitatingly and authoritatively, the rabbi answered: there is no need to collect the blood and have it buried, since it was the blood of a living person. In contrast, they must look carefully for remnants of the fetus, which must be buried according to the law of the Torah. The conversation took only two minutes.

## Rabbi Avigdor Nebenzahl

I never saw Rabbi Avigdor Nebenzahl at the arena of an incident. Because of his advanced age, his fragile health, and mainly because of his exalted status, he is not summoned to routine events, but he summoned himself several times when he heard on the radio news about a terrorist attack with many victims. Among those I interviewed for this research, he was one of the hardest to reach. He lives an ascetic life and spends his time only on the study and teaching of Torah. It is said that once he was riding in a car that was involved in an accident. When the rescue forces came to evacuate him, they found him sitting in the totaled car, studying a volume of Talmud.

At the time of the Intifada, he was already in his eighties. He was born to a well-known religious Zionist family. His father was the first state comptroller, his sister was a senior official in the Ministry of Justice, and his wife came from a prominent Lithuanian rabbinical family. When his wife died, he married again at the age of eighty-three. He was a learned scholar, a halakhic authority, and an admired and influential head of a yeshiva. He was the rabbi of the Old City of Jerusalem, and when he retired his son succeeded him. In the Yom Kippur War he was called up to serve in the IDF burial unit. His homilies on the biblical portion of the week were popular. His political positions were right-wing and hawkish. He ruled that anyone who gave up any part of the sacred, whole Land of Israel (anyone who called for withdrawal from the West Bank, which was occupied in 1967) was subject to *din rodef* (literally, "the law of a pursuer"), meaning that it was permissible to kill him.[58] Among his well-known rulings were a prohibition against holding Christian ceremonies, such as Christmas parties, in Jerusalem hotels and public facilities, and a prohibition against Jews visiting churches, even for sightseeing. He also forbade women from studying Jewish religious books and teaching the Bible based on the scholarship of secular Jews.

Nebenzahl is famous for being extremely rigorous in observing halakha, even according to radical Haredi standards. He does not enter cemeteries, for fear of impurity. He does not even visit his father's grave. Nevertheless, he insisted on taking part in the handling of the victims of terrorism, and he had no inhibitions about touching their limbs and blood. He states that proximity to the dead pollutes, whereas proximity to the victims of terrorist attacks sanctifies. The matter of respect for the dead is particularly important to him, and he defined the ZAKA activists who climb electric poles to scrape off tiny pieces of flesh and bring them to burial as devoting their souls to sanctify the name of God. Because of his fragility, his proud bearing, and his elegant appearance, he stood out as unusual at the arena of terrorism. He behaved modestly and wanted people to relate to him as a simple low-ranking soldier. However, he received special treatment there. Despite the limitations of his age and his partial professional experience, the volunteers cleared the way for him and accorded him the honor reserved only for the senior members of ZAKA, to perform the supreme commandment and enter the inner circle, closest to the point of the explosion.

The ZAKA volunteers describe his conduct at the arena as that of a *mashgiaḥ*, the religious and moral supervisor of the yeshiva students for whom he is responsible. No less than he bends over to locate the body parts of the Jewish victims; he observes his fellow volunteers, lest some detail in their behavior might violate a halakhic rule or dishonor the dead. He goes from one volunteer to the other to examine them closely as to whether they took the trouble to conceal their ritual fringes inside their trousers, so they won't be visible to the dead. Nebenzahl described himself to me as walking about in the arena and truly "experiencing miracles"—the acts of ZAKA on the site appear supernatural to him. Nebenzahl is proud because once he "merited" the fulfillment of a great commandment: he found the leg of a Jewish victim in the arena of a terrorist attack.

## An Assemblage of Randomly Sampled Characters

*Rabbi Elimelech* is known for not being at all afraid of the dead. Hence, when it is necessary to watch over bodies at night—the sensitive and dangerous time when, it is believed, evil spirits are liable to enter the body, which is empty of the soul, for it has already risen to heaven—he volunteers to do it. While he was a yeshiva student, he gained experience in violent action against autopsies, including snatching bodies from operating rooms ("I held organs in my hands that had just been removed from a body, and they were still warm"). From that he naturally found his way to ZAKA. He is proud that he has never missed an attack with many casualties. He is nostalgic for the days before the institutionalization of the organization, when it was possible to burst into the arena without permission from the police, and when it was permitted to touch the bodies without gloves. The more the work involves wallowing in blood, the more satisfying it is in the end. Shortly before our last meeting he had worked all night, scraping thousands of scraps of flesh from the walls of a room where a young man shot himself in the head with an M16 assault rifle. He attended the best Lithuanian yeshivas but became a Gur Hasid. He consults a rabbi on nearly every matter, large or small. He is unusual in his community, as shown, among other things, by his custom of bathing in the sea at beaches with mixed men and women, and by his refusal to tuck his trousers into his stockings like the other Hasidim. He volunteers in an organization that provides day camps for children with cancer. He was one of the organizers of demonstrations by Haredim against the Israeli Supreme

Court. He is the educational supervisor of an institution for Torah studies in poverty-stricken areas. At the age of fifty-four, he is athletic and good-humored. He is the permanent emcee at ceremonies for ZAKA volunteers.

*Rabbi Gedalia* introduces himself as a member of the ZAKA family "who is enlivened by terrorist attacks." Rumors about the attack on bus 405 reached him in his neighborhood. Since the road was blocked, he arrived there by foot, a distance of several kilometers. Since then he has been a ZAKA volunteer. Once he withdrew to the edge of the arena in the midst of the handling of bodies—at the terrorist attack against the Sbarro pizzeria—because he no longer had the emotional strength. He volunteers for duty with ZAKA on holidays so as not to miss Torah studies. He is fifty years old, father of ten children, one of the heads of the Yad Laahim organization where he acts, often clandestinely and violently, against Christian missionaries in Israel, and pressures Jewish women married to Arabs to return to their families, and even kidnaps them. He was an outstanding student in the prestigious Hebron Yeshiva for fourteen years, and he spent another seven years in the Mir Yeshiva, the pinnacle of the Lithuanian world. He established a yeshiva for boys with learning disabilities and teaches lessons in ethics there—"spiritual reinforcement," as he calls it. He claims to sleep only three hours a day and finds time for acts of charity such as intervening in conflicts between parents and children, spending time with isolated old men, and collecting contributions for the needy. His brother and grandfather work in the burial society, and his wife teaches computers. At home they insist on speaking only Yiddish.

The terrorist attack in Beit Yisrael caught *Rabbi Eliahu* at prayer in a nearby synagogue. From that evening on, for two weeks, he dealt with the consequences of the explosion full time. He took part in the incident of the 405 bus, and, following it, he was one of the rebels against the old leadership of ZAKA, claiming that it wasn't sufficiently innovative and enthusiastic. He also rebelled as a volunteer for MaDA by instituting a paramedic training course for men alone (so that Haredim could take part). He is a Karlin Hasid and lives in poverty. His wife doesn't work, and ten people live in his apartment, with its two minuscule rooms. He studies Torah eight to ten hours a day, and he is responsible for the Torah studies of ZAKA volunteers throughout the country. He is active in charity and specializes in obtaining medical assistance and subsidizing flights abroad for surgery. During the Intifada he dealt with many victims of attacks and would wake up in a panic several times a night to make sure his children were safe and sound. He has been a devoted activist in ZAKA for twenty-five years, ever since, in his youth, he was confronted with the death of a small child who fell from a high balcony. He does not want his sons to be ZAKA volunteers but rather great Torah scholars.

*Kobi* is a ritual slaughterer and the logistics manager of an abattoir under the supervision of the extremely severe Haredi rabbinical court of Jerusalem. He tells me that when he first began to work as a slaughterer, he had flashbacks that brought him back to the first time he entered the thick of the arena of a terrorist attack that claimed many victims. The explosion took place in the Maḥane Yehuda outdoor produce market in Jerusalem, near the butchers' stalls. When he was already an experienced ZAKA volunteer, he was the first one to arrive at the scene of an attack and handled the body of a Jew who had been murdered by a Palestinian worker in his workshop, which was close to the slaughterhouse outside the city. Kobi stayed close to the body throughout: as it was transported to Jerusalem and examined in the hospital, during the legal battle to prevent an autopsy, and, finally, at its burial. After the Sabbath he went to the widow's home to take the victim's blood-soaked garments for burial.

*Shlomo* was once a petty criminal. At the age of thirty, after hearing a lecture from a charismatic Haredi preacher, he went home and threw the television set out the window. Thus began his "return" to religion, along with his family. Over the years he became increasingly extreme in his Haredi religiosity. He became an absolute follower of Rabbi Ovadia Yosef and an ardent supporter of SHAS, the Sephardi Torah Guardians party. While beginning to dress like a Haredi, he also became the head of a ZAKA team in Ofakim, a development town in the south, most of whose residents are deprived. In his community he became known as a holy man whose blessings worked miracles. He does not see Judaism as based on study of Gemara but rather on prayer and acts of charity. He is a great believer in the healing power of the pure prayer of holy small children in Talmud Torah (a Haredi elementary school). His activity in ZAKA is his way of repairing the world. In the arena of death he is not meticulous in observing the halakhic rules, but rather on deep intention accompanied by magical, mystical gestures. He arrives on his motorcycle at every case of unnatural, violent death in the large peripheral area of the southern part of the country. Often, on his way to deal with the dead, he weeps.

*Israel* works as the assistant to a local rabbi in a medium-size city in the north of the country, and he is the head of the ZAKA team in the region. He has been a volunteer since the age of twenty-seven. He joined the organization after encountering a terrorist incident in Jerusalem by chance and spontaneously helping the Haredim who were working at the arena. Since then he has taken part in dealing with every terrorist attack in the northern region. Most of his activity is less dramatic. For example, recently a man died in his city right before the entry of the Sabbath, and the burial society refused to bury him, because they were in a hurry to greet the holy day, when work is forbidden. The volunteer took the body down in the elevator, transported it to the cemetery in his private car, purified the body there, and finally buried it with the help of the rabbi.

*Gedalia S.* was born into a family of Gur Hasidism. He rises every morning at four for prayer at the Western Wall. He is an extreme hawk. He is ordained as a rabbi and trained as a religious judge, but he works as the administrator of a yeshiva. His father was an IDF gravedigger who was wounded by a mine when he volunteered to remove the body of a pilot after the 1967 war. Gedalia lives in a desirable neighborhood, most of whose residents are neo-Haredim, in a roomy and attractive apartment. His wife is American, and they have four children. He volunteered for ZAKA under pressure from fellow Gur Hasidim, and he is connected to the organization mainly through his close connection with Bentzi. He is different from most of the volunteers in his bourgeois and modern background, but mainly in his attitude toward handling bodies. He does everything required of him with great devotion but without mystification, excessive excitement, or exaltation. He says that ZAKA did not change his personality or religiosity. He does not involve his family in experiences connected with death. When he returns from the arena, he takes a shower and goes to sleep. In many other respects he exemplifies the opposite of the norms of behavior in ZAKA. He raises the possibility that his exceptionality might derive from the fact that he never had occasion to deal with a multi-casualty terrorist attack, and he contents himself with minor cases of death such as suicides and accidents. Once, he told me, after treating with great meticulousness the body of a Haredi child who was run over by a school bus, he went by himself to the parking lot of the bus company, and there he crawled under the vehicle for a whole day, scraping off traces of flesh and blood. He is convinced that he fulfilled a great commandment, but he kept it in secret, and he did not "experience a religious orgasm."

# 4

# Torah Study vs. Deathwork

## Motorcycles

Secular Israelis regard ZAKA as representing Haredi society, but that is not how the Haredim see it. Quite a few Haredim, including influential figures such as the heads of leading Lithuanian yeshivas, take a dim view of ZAKA and repudiate its identification with Haredi ideals. During the Intifada, when ZAKA's fame was at its height, posters were glued to the walls of buildings in the Haredi neighborhoods of Jerusalem, claiming the organization was sinful and heretical. Making a pun on ZAKA's name, they wrote, "This is a Disaster with Victims," words beginning with the same letters as ZAKA. However, along with the condemnation and resentment of ZAKA, one also finds manifestations of Haredi support and admiration, as displayed in the costumes the children wear on the traditional carnivalesque Purim holiday. On that day, once a year, the pious allow themselves to throw off the yoke and express themselves spontaneously, and they are even encouraged to act impulsively in ways that are forbidden during the rest of the year. For example, they are supposed to get drunk. Naturally the costumes embody Haredi fantasies. Along with legitimate ideals such as the vestments of the High Priest, they portray the objects of forbidden desires, which are usually censored, such as a police uniform. One popular costume for children in the streets of Meah Shearim during the time of the Intifada was that of a ZAKA volunteer: a yarmulka, a beard and sidelocks, with a white cloak, a yellow vest, and rubber gloves. The moment signs appeared that the ZAKA volunteers had become Haredi cultural heroes, the reaction came: wall posters condemned the disguise as glorifying "the abominable organization called ZAKA, which corrupts our young men and sends them to hell."

ZAKA occupies a central place in the internal discourse of the Haredi community, and it is a bone of contention in the ultra-Orthodox world. Children are perceptive guides to lead a researcher to important crossroads in their parents' culture, to call attention to sensitive points charged with contradictions, and to locate potential fault lines. The sub-culture of Haredi

*The Cult of Dismembered Limbs*. Gideon Aran, Oxford University Press. © Oxford University Press 2023.
DOI: 10.1093/oso/9780197689141.003.0004

children is drawn to foci of simultaneous attraction and repulsion. Boys gather around the motorcycles of the ZAKA volunteers parked in the streets of their neighborhood. An important rabbi defined this gleaming provocation as "an idol in the sanctuary." But with their sharp senses, the children feel the magic appeal of the motorcycle—its masculinity, action, extravagance, extremes, arrogance—and they are riveted to this alien and seductive object. Only the scolding of parents and neighbors shames them and forces them to move on. As for the adults, whenever the motorcycle drives through the neighborhood, roaring and speedy, they're fixated on the sight, but they immediately recover their wits and pretend to ignore this mobile sign of vanity. The children, by contrast, find it hard to repress their desire, and they ask the volunteer motorcyclists for a short ride: the height of forbidden pleasure.

The children of ZAKA motorcyclists proudly stand at the top of the prestige ladder in their kindergartens. Other children envy them. But when they grow up, their fate is liable to be reversed. Their resume will probably by flawed, and their status will be low. In interviews, the volunteers of the ZAKA motorcycle unit express satisfaction and pride in their activity at the arena of death. However, at a certain point their self-congratulatory rhetoric changes and becomes skeptical and mournful. With variations, they conclude with the same wistful confession: "But, after all, it will probably be hard for us to find good husbands for our daughters."

ZAKA motorcyclists evidently know the Haredi marriage market, a sensitive and cruel barometer of the differences in status of various categories in ultra-Orthodox society. It is absolutely forbidden to marry certain people (*psulei ḥitun*) because, according to halakhic definitions and old traditions, there is doubt as to the purity of their ethno-religious origins. Others, although they are within the bounds of the collective according to the formal and declared standards, and are "permitted," still have some flaw in their religiosity, and thus their chances of finding a worthy Haredi match are slim. This is evident in the fate of the newly religious (born-again Jews, *hozrim beteshuva*) in this exchange marketplace. Even when there are no reservations with respect to their faith and their virtues, and no one doubts their perseverance and achievements in Torah study—notwithstanding the lip-service paid to their great piety[1]— Haredim are reluctant to intermarry with them, so they are forced to wed among themselves, even to the second and third generation. The situation of ZAKA activists is rather similar. Despite efforts to plaster over this fact, quite a few Haredim regard them as a kind of low caste, whose members are not worthy of marriage, and restrictions are placed on social ties with them in general.

There is a feeling of dissonance in ZAKA: on the one hand, the snobbery of an elite group, the elect, and, on the other hand, insult, contempt, and partial ostracism. This duality has various characteristics as they both carry out a noble mission and are outcasts and pariahs. Similarly, some of the chosen have characteristics that are faulty according to various Haredi standards. They may be divorced men who have remarried, Jews of Oriental descent (Mizraḥim), or yeshiva dropouts, whose volunteering for ZAKA is apparently consistent with their somewhat defective status. Some of them regard themselves as taking additional risks by joining ZAKA, further damaging their flawed image, or, seen from another angle, their affiliation with ZAKA might be regarded as an opportunity to upgrade their image in the Haredi community.

The head of ZAKA's rabbinical council reminded the Haredi community that the holy sources rule that manual laborers are not required to stop work in honor of a Torah scholar, but they must rise in honor of someone who takes care of the dead.[2] Over the years, the Haredi community has increasingly recognized the exalted Jewish values that ZAKA embodies and become aware of the dividend that the organization brings to the ultra-Orthodox community in general. The opposition of the rabbis of the community, including the heads of yeshivas and their militant students, is becoming more moderate. From a priori rejection and condemnation they have moved to a more nuanced relation, which has a degree of reconciliation, though understated. The Haredi leaders realize that there are no clear signs that the volunteers have crossed lines and left the community, having thrown off its norms, and they also acknowledge the organization's contribution toward the creation of a more tolerant and sympathetic public attitude toward the Haredim in Israel, which enables them to live their lives and promote their interests without encountering contempt and hatred. The volunteers are condemned and admired at the same time.

The first of the open accusations against ZAKA made by the Haredi rabbis and their followers is *bitul torah* (idleness from Torah), meaning that the volunteers are busy with all sorts of matters, which, while they may be important, are infinitely less important than the study of Torah, day and night, with devotion, in a yeshiva. The ZAKA volunteers concede that they sin by not obeying the commandment of studying Torah, but they argue that they do so in order to fulfill other important commandments, primarily the commandment of respecting the dead. The response is "Study of Torah is equivalent to them all," meaning that it is more important than all the other commandments, including performing acts of charity, honoring parents, and reconciling people with one another.[3] Most of the Haredim who work instead of studying in a yeshiva also have to apologize for not persisting in Torah study. Although, as they are not idle from Torah study for the purpose of fulfilling another commandment but to make a living, they are not subject to such blunt attacks as those leveled at ZAKA. For the Haredi establishment, to subvert the hierarchy of the commandments' importance is a more severe challenge than neglecting the commandments. That is to say, to prefer making a living to devotion to the service of God is a considerable threat. However, to serve God in an alternative manner, not in the established way, is a far greater threat. The first instance is one of mitigated religiosity. The second instance contains a seed of heresy.

The members of ZAKA find it easier to cope with the second reproach leveled against them: that they "cut corners," that is, that they are lenient with themselves in observing halakhic norms. In this matter, they do not apologize. Rather they emphasize their clean consciences. Among the Haredim there are evident efforts to catch the volunteers neglecting a commandment in flagrante. However, these efforts to discredit them have ended in failure. The ZAKA people are aware of this sensitive point. Therefore, they make certain to demonstrate that they obey both minor and major commandments. They are proud of emphasizing their observance not only of the commandment to act with charity toward the dead and the living but also in a variety of other areas, including some ritual matters of secondary importance. The extra effort made by the members of ZAKA to impress the community with their observance of the commandments sometimes arouses ridicule. For example, they often prolong prayers indefinitely with vigorous physical gestures, in a manner that causes the people around them to question their sincerity.

The third Haredi argument against ZAKA concerns the cooperation of the organization with the institutions of the state, and the close connections of the volunteers with secular Jews. Not only are the rabbis loath to grant tacit legitimacy to Zionism, but they also fear exposure to foreign influences and the infiltration of undesirable norms into their community. Ironically, ZAKA's most effective response, that, thanks to their contribution to the Israeli public in various arenas of death, the attitude toward the Haredi community has changed and it receives respect and admiration, is precisely what worries the extremists in the Haredi community. The editor of a newspaper and a Haredi political activist said with sarcastic wit, "The day when the secular media begins to praise the ZAKA project without reservations, then we'll know that the process of the community's assimilation has reached a particularly perilous stage."[4]

## Explorations in Religious Zeal

ZAKA challenges the established text-based yeshiva model of ideal Haredi religiosity by offering an alternative way of divine worship. The death specialist volunteers have created a brand-new this-worldly ascetic piety.[5] They did this with a conscious effort to avoid a head-on confrontation with the rabbinical leadership of the Haredi community. With their acute senses, the leaders and activists of ZAKA honored the option of full-time Gemara study, proclaimed the superiority of yeshiva students, and at every opportunity they conceded the inferiority of their volunteers in relation to them. To minimize the feeling of threat that they posed to the world of Torah, they tried to convince Haredi public opinion that the course chosen by ZAKA was only good for a few isolated, marginal individuals that have no alternative. On the declarative level, they were cautious to avoid being thought of us competitors of Torah scholars and their rabbis, and, with a healthy instinct, they blunted the edge of the opposition between the two paths of religious excellence, directing attention to their ability to coexist and complement one another. With somewhat affected modesty they neutralize the criticism against them by admitting that they simply are not good enough at it to devote their lives to Talmudic casuistry.

It is difficult to determine how sincere the ZAKA men are, when they exploit various opportunities to confess that they hope their sons will not be members of ZAKA who rush to scenes of death, but rather Torah scholars, who, despite the temptation, remain glued to the sacred texts. In ZAKA they know that the dream of many a boy in *heder* is to have a ZAKA beeper when he grows up, and they add that the father of every boy in *heder* dreams that his son will be a precocious genius in Talmud. However, at the same time, I heard ZAKA activists criticize the yeshivas for lacking any system of supervision or an orderly regimen of examinations, leading to a decline in intensity. In secret, activists in the organization point out flaws and demoralization in the world of Torah, along with the small number of gifted and serious students, and they concede that the majority exploit the system to cover their parasitical idleness. To support their claims, they quote the Talmud, saying that every day the Holy One weeps for those who do not study Torah, although they can, and for those who do study Torah, although they cannot.[6]

It would be relatively easier for the Haredi community to be reconciled with the existence of ZAKA volunteers who were incapable of studying Gemara and were not expert in it. In contrast, they are frustrated by the challenge posed by ZAKA volunteers who are devoted to fulfilling the commandment of honoring the dead, after "filling their bellies with *Shas u'foskim* (the entire Talmud and halakhic rulings)." One of them reviewed a Talmudic text with me, which is relevant to the issue of the relations between ZAKA and the Haredi establishment. An important rabbi sent his son to study Torah in another city. After a while the father sent agents to spy on his son, and they found that instead of studying Torah, he was performing acts of charity, meaning that he was burying the dead. The father reprimanded his son, saying, "Study (of the Talmud) takes precedence over action." Other rabbis disagreed and ruled that if there were already people who were occupied with honoring the dead in any event, then those capable of it should turn to study of Torah, but if there was no one who took it upon himself to do acts of kindness by burial, then even those capable of study should give preference to action over study.[7]

Many people in the Haredi community are in doubt as to whether the ZAKA men are loyal to the community and the tradition, or whether they should be seen as defectors. This is typical of the perplexing question that always arises regarding anyone who is deviant in appearance or behavior: Is he still one of us? People look for external signs that will testify to the inner essence: Does he let his earlocks grow? Does he display or hide them? The pious ZAKA activists are proud of their long earlocks, while their critics call them "heretics with earlocks."

The insecurity that arises among the Haredim regarding the blurred status, full of contradictions, of the ZAKA volunteers recalls their difficulty in coming to a clear position regarding the conscription of their young men in the IDF. The Haredi soldiers leave the community's zone of control, they are absent from Torah studies, they are exposed to temptations such as the availability of non-kosher food and the presence of unmarried women, and of course they are surrounded by secular Jews and subject to the authority of the Zionist establishment. Although many of the Haredi conscripts were originally lackadaisical yeshiva students, and even *shababnikim*, the rabbis regard enlistment as apostasy, and some of the conscripts' families mourn for them as if they were dead. But during their military service, quite a few of those who were already on the verge of crossing the border into the secular world become increasingly insistent on keeping the commandments. In parallel fashion, prominent among ZAKA volunteers are those whose service in the arena of death was accompanied by strengthening of religious observance, and they adopt increasingly extreme Haredi manners.

Haredi opposition to ZAKA focuses less on the violation of the halakha than on deviance from the traditional patterns of behavior and the accepted customs. It mainly targets abuse of puritan Haredi values. Exposure to women's bodies and handling them is thought of as especially scandalous. However, this provocative behavior is performed with the permission of rabbis whose authority is too high to be denied. This situation of breaking a taboo with a strong religious alibi completely perplexes the Haredi extremists.

Avigdor Nebenzahl is one of the highly respected rabbis of ZAKA. He is venerated in the Haredi community because of his erudition, his abilities as a halakhic decisor, his integrity, and the intensity of his piety. Nebenzahl is so meticulous in observing the laws of modesty and purity that, when he is teaching Torah to a class of girls, he gazes only at the floor or covers his eyes with his hand, lest he sin by seeing a female silhouette. Yet he ruled that the Haredi volunteers were permitted to handle the bodies and body parts of women, even when their intimate parts are visible. A rabbi who is an opponent of ZAKA confessed to me that he wished Nebenzahl had ruled differently, or, alternatively, that a rabbi of lower prestige had issued that decision. My interlocutor also agreed with me that he would be more comfortable if the ZAKA activists cut off their earlocks, and he admitted that it was easier to deal with Jews who converted to Christianity and assimilated among the gentiles than with Zionists who had abandoned the religion but not Judaism. On the contrary, the insistence of heretical and sinful Israelis on their Jewish identity, the pride they take in their Judaism, and the use they made of Jewish symbols for their nationalism were what made life difficult for religious extremists. Some people in the Haredi neighborhoods pray that the ZAKA volunteers will abandon their Haredi identity and proclaim that they are departing from the community.

## Radical Religion and Psychopathology

The Haredi suspicion of ZAKA bears an echo of orthodox folklore surrounding the possible gap between outward appearance and inner essence. Every Orthodox Jewish community has some members of whom it is rumored that "they shave under their beards," upending the reassuring assumption that the piety of every believer is public knowledge. That Haredi attitude toward ZAKA is laden with two-layered doubt: first, the volunteers socialize with secular Jews, are exposed to women's bodies, and break other Haredi taboos—will they continue to keep the commandments? Second, the Haredi volunteers observe the commandments meticulously, though their customs are innovative and strange—do they have faith in their hearts? Haredi culture is a public and overtly expressive religious culture. Their religiosity is extroverted, monitored, and supervised. It is common knowledge that Judaism (like Islam) is a normative, ritual religion, unlike a religion based on faith or dogma (like Christianity). In the authoritarian Haredi society, there is only partial awareness of the possibility of inconsistency between one's state of mind and one's behavior, and, furthermore, there is a certain ability to accept a situation in which a person might be wild and irreligious within, so long as he conforms to the visible rules of the game. For a person to be recognized as deviant, it is not enough to guess what is concealed in his mental structure, but he must demonstrate it by his actions. True, it is commonly assumed that the inner level determines outward appearance and behavior, and that the latter reflects the former. However, the emotional and intellectual factors are not determining. While there is a rhetoric of the importance of faith and inner intention, a person's religiosity is measured by what is visible. Whether a man is Haredi is determined by where he lives, his occupation, the way he spends his spare time, the number of his children, and of course his severity in observing visible commandments such as praying in a prayer quorum or not sleeping under a roof during the Sukkot (Tabernacle) holiday.

The presence of ZAKA in the heart of the Haredi community does not merely undermine the convention that identifies ritualistic piety with authentic piety. ZAKA is also subversive by its very recognition of the existence of an inner space, which Haredi society tended to suppress and deny, or at least to see as a congruent expression of the normative code. In itself, a separate and autonomous internal space is alarming, especially if there is a difference between it and the external space. As noted earlier in the book, in the discourse of the Haredim who volunteered to deal with the victims of terrorism, the expressive and emotional elements surrounding the axis of trauma stand out. This may be defined as proto-psychotherapy. In the ZAKA milieu and in interviews with activists in the organization, expressions like "anxiety," "ventilation," and "self-awareness," taken from clinical jargon, are thrown out into the air. In particular, by means of the therapy workshops for ZAKA, which are intended to deal with post-traumatic stress, ideas and practices from psychotherapy have penetrated Haredi discourse. The introduction of modern Western methods of treatment arouses opposition in the Haredi community, among other things because it implies recognition of the function of the inner space in the life of the pious, who are used to largely "behavioristic" religiosity.[8]

The traditional Jewish way to cope with trauma, and especially with death, always sought consolation and strength through the classic combination of prayer and the study of sacred texts. The option proposed since the Intifada of treating fragile situations by free expression and the regulation of emotions, as in the ZAKA workshops, is revolutionary. The presence of terrorism—a new experience—brings a new authority with it to the Haredi world: science and popular psychology, which were anathema until the arenas of horrifying death became part of the lives of the pious. ZAKA became an agent in the adoption of systematic knowledge of emotion management, and this aroused apprehension among the Haredim, lest phenomena like admitting frustrations and failures or the expression of criticism of authority might go beyond the focus of terrorism-related trauma and crop up in other focuses of great tension in Haredi society, especially sensitive institutions like authoritarian yeshivas and perhaps in the patriarchal family, too. This is another example of the challenge to the Haredi ethos posed by ZAKA from an unexpected direction.

The rabbinical opposition to the introduction of innovations such as these in the Haredi world is an automatic reaction, but with the passage of time, since the innovation has acquired a place in broad circles of Haredim, and especially if it turns out that the leadership can exploit the innovation, and that it is likely to bring a dividend to the community, the opposition becomes more moderate and can even be replaced by encouragement, although partial and tacit. This was the case with ZAKA in relation to some of its innovations. The invalidation was more bitter and the adaptation more difficult since the innovation appeared in the name of religion. Regardless of the motivation for the proposed change, when it is formulated in religious terms and bears religious aspiration, it is harder to swallow. In such cases, the feeling of threat is especially acute, but it is impossible to declare all-out war against the innovation, and inner contradictions and ambivalences develop, which necessitate restrictions on a priori rejection. A Haredi authority explained to me that when confronted with two bad alternatives, it is preferable to be swept out of the community than to blow it up from within. My interlocutors in ZAKA interpret his words with an analogy: the initiatives of Haredi women who wish to open the gates to academic studies encountered only minor difficulties compared to those that arose in response to Haredi women's initiatives to study Talmud.

The rabbis were less troubled by delinquent girls than by girls who wanted "to live in sanctity." Changes bound up with the penetration of concepts from the secular world are less compromising for the Haredim than changes that seek authorization through resort to alternative canonical components of the rabbinical tradition. Accordingly, dealing with dead bodies as a legitimate and exalted option for worshiping God is intolerable for the heads of the yeshiva world. Regarding the volunteers' treatment of the victims of terrorism as "holy work" is what makes ZAKA problematic for the Haredim.

## Betwixt and Between

ZAKA is an agent of modernization that introduces values from the fields of technology, psychology, and the politics of civil society into the Haredi community. ZAKA is also an agent of Zionization, introducing values of national solidarity and patriotism into the Haredi community. But primarily ZAKA is the potential seed of religious revival—a reform, or even a revolution—which subverts existing religious values without abandoning the community.

It has been commonly assumed that the line separating Haredi society from modern surroundings—both secular and religious—is clear and rigid. In recent years this view has changed in light of research that revealed phenomena showing that the boundaries of Haredi society are blurred, shifting, and penetrable.[9] Lately a new path has been opened, the possibility of living on both sides of the boundary simultaneously, or to pass from one side to the other and back, again and again. There emerges a hybrid creature, drawn to the open life of the majority in Israel but unwilling to deny its Haredi identity.

One could view ZAKA's death-related practices as indicating a path of departure from the Haredi community. But departure is not necessarily absolute or final. Transition to the secular world can be partial and tentative, or reversed. This is an open-ended or dialectic dynamic. Certain prominent rabbis claimed that ZAKA will end up out of the community. None of the volunteers agrees with this prognosis. ZAKA might also lead to a process in the opposite direction, to the heart of the Haredi community, and breathe new life into it by introducing variety and perhaps radicalization.

Among those who prophesy that ZAKA will split from the community, or that individual members will abandon ultra-Orthodoxy altogether, some of the best-informed say that the process is possible not only because the volunteers have adopted Zionist ideals and a modern spirit, but because in their activity in the various death arenas they have acquired proficiencies that enable them to function in the capitalist, cosmopolitan, digital Israeli environment. They admit that the path of yeshiva students who might wish to abandon a life of Torah is blocked, because they lack skills that would enable them to survive in a modern urban setting, from the use of automatic banking facilities to the ability to read English or find a partner of the opposite sex. Most of the veteran ZAKA volunteers possess, in addition to the above, the ability to improvise and experience contact with outsiders and negotiations with government officials. They also know their way around the country and how to operate gadgets. Nevertheless, not a single instance of leaving the community is known. Moreover, among the volunteers, only a very few possess any of the characteristics that might make them suspect as potential deserters. They do not confess to harboring heretical thoughts, nor are they known as skeptics, dreamers, seekers, of unstable character, alienated from their environment, and so on.

Nevertheless, in some senses ZAKA is in limbo between their Haredi society and their Israeli surroundings. They are liminal.[10] Anthropology identifies the liminal stage in the life of a collective with separation from the existing social order and with the adoption, at least temporarily, of its opposite, with dense symbolism, mystery, autonomy, anarchy, experimentation, criticism, and protest. In the liminal stage, members of the group are enthusiastic and drunk with power, but also sensitive and vulnerable, and from the viewpoint of the establishment this is an explosive situation that requires vigilance and supervision. This is an empowering and invigorating episode, which offers an opportunity for searching and new experiences, and it has creative potential. Liminality is crisis-laden and dangerous, but it can lead to renewed and strengthened integration into the mother group. Ultra-Orthodox society, despite its fears and rigidity, might display tolerance and liberality and give ZAKA a free space for acceptable deviance for a certain time, until the liminal process plays itself out. In conversation with me about the place of ZAKA in the range between the heart of the Haredi community and what lies beyond it, a central activist told me, "Just like in the desert [a decidedly liminal space between enslavement in Egypt and settlement in the Promised Land] you feel close to God,[11] from the moment we enter the arena of death, inside the café, the dance club, or the shopping mall, far from the Haredi neighborhood, totally disconnected from the yeshiva and the family, we feel our religiosity more strongly." I cannot say whether the following quotation describes a real situation, or whether it is fabricated, but in any event, it certainly is telling: "Some argue that our devotion to the treatment of the victims of terrorism might come from our religious weakness. But years of activity in ZAKA have strengthened our religiosity. Some volunteers were strengthened so much that they threw away their beepers and returned to the Gemara."

## Haredi Heart Surgeons

ZAKA activists frequently use expressions that convey awareness of their inferiority and subservience to yeshiva students. This is often accompanied by the promise or expression of the desire to return to full-time Torah studies, as if the activity in ZAKA were merely an episode, required by an emergency that was expected to come to an end. According to a less common argument that contains a particularly sophisticated rationalization, abandoning yeshiva life for the sake of "providing true compassion" is the volunteers' greatest sacrifice. ZAKA counters the presumed heroics of the world of Torah with that of giving up the world of Torah. In this casuistic manner the ZAKA volunteers can offer the rabbis the honor they deserve and, at the same time, escape their grip. In public the volunteers accept official Haredi rhetoric, but privately they do not let their honor be impugned.

The attitude of the Haredi community to ZAKA is laden with tension. In the streets of Meah Shearim I spoke to ordinary Haredim who described the ZAKA activists as doing jobs whose value cannot be ignored, but they are constrained to admit that there's something problematic about ZAKA. My informants compared the ZAKA volunteers to heart surgeons, whose life work is of exalted significance from both the human and Jewish point of view, but, after showering praise on them, they add openly that, nevertheless, they would prefer for "others" (i.e., non-Haredim) to perform this important mission. This reflects a familiar ultra-Orthodox outlook: the division of labor between the believers and their Israeli surroundings. Secular Jews see this as self-indulgent hypocrisy, while the Haredi explain it in terms of historical purpose and the messianic mission of different types of people. Jews, they believe, have a separate and more exalted mission than gentiles, and, among the Jews, the Haredim bear responsibility, imposed by heaven, for preserving the fate of the Jews and the entire world by means of Torah study. They are aware of the possible contradiction between the sanctity of Torah study and the constraints of life, and, in a routine manner that does not betray deep conviction, they declare that study of Torah will bring redemption, and then there will no longer be any need for heart surgeons.

In internal Haredi discourse, it is accepted that if a young man from the community insists upon fulfilling his ambition to become a heart surgeon, they will not stop him, but they wouldn't recommend it, and they wouldn't encourage him. This also applies to those who volunteer to serve at ZAKA's arena of death. A Jerusalem rabbi put it this way: "The organization's volunteers fulfill an important commandment. I don't dismiss the possibility that on the day of judgment, the heavenly court will acknowledge that they are holier than their brothers, who spent their time in yeshiva. Nevertheless, if my son were to come and express the desire to volunteer to serve in ZAKA, even if he isn't among the most gifted scholars, I wouldn't give him my blessing."

The apologetic and conflicted attitude of the Haredim toward ZAKA is translated into an educational dilemma. It is tacitly assumed that even though ZAKA may be absolutely kosher and even fulfill a holy mission, it still must not be presented as a model for the boys of the community. It is one thing to admire ZAKA, but it is an entirely different matter to allow the system of social control to permit enlistment in the organization, and, worse still, to establish a system of socialization that would support enlistment and prefer it to the accepted options.

They resolve the dissonance between praise for ZAKA and negating the option it offers as an educational goal by means of the conceptual distinction between *lekhathila* and *bedi'avad*, terms that are similar but not identical to "a priori" and "retroactive," between something that has not yet been done and something that has already been done. These concepts are taken from the realm of halakha and refer to the status of a commandment that has been fulfilled, and only retroactively does it come to light that it was not done properly according to the defined criteria. For example, according to halakha, one is supposed to wash one's hands before eating bread, and this must be done by pouring water from a vessel whose lips are intact. The rabbis ruled that the vessel must be intact, *lekhathila*, but if, after one has washed one's hands, one discovers that the vessel was damaged, the act of washing and the blessing recited over the act are still valid, *bedi'avad*. In the present time, this halakhic principle is transferred from ritual matters affecting the individual to public and political issues. The distinction has become popular among traditionalists who live in a changing world. Orthodox and ultra-Orthodox Jews use the distinction to cope with phenomena which are regarded as undesirable, but which, by force of circumstance, have become a part of life. Because continued opposition is liable to be more damaging than useful, especially as the innovation might also have positive consequences, the rabbis who initially condemned it tend to approve it retroactively. With respect to ZAKA, which initially aroused criticism but meanwhile became a fait accompli and part of the Haredi world, it is thus logical to approve of it. The question remains: How far should one go on granting legitimacy to ZAKA? The organization's leaders respond: our test is to move from the status of approved and praised retroactively to approved and praised initially.

The Haredi arsenal contains further techniques for coping with phenomena that are difficult to digest but impossible to disgorge. One option is to define a religious phenomenon as exclusive and appropriate for select individuals with distinct religiosity, and thus to exalt it while at the same time negating it as a widespread and dominant possibility. This is not absolute and final negation, but merely putting it off. Such is the case with ZAKA. Defining it as the province of select, exalted individuals forestalls the possibility of its spreading, but it reinforces its explosive potential by inadvertently making it an elite company of God-fearing men.

ZAKA cannot be condemned, but encouraging it is dangerous. Suspicion arises regarding the anarchical potential of sanctifying the name of God by violent deathwork, making it an institutionalized and legitimate pattern. The heads of the Haredi community understand that making membership in ZAKA an established religious track would threaten the primacy of the study of Torah. Several Haredi informants expressed themselves like a rabbi whom I interviewed: "Driving one's wife, who is in labor, to the hospital on the Sabbath is *kosher*, but the professionalization of keeping drivers on duty to drive women to the hospital to give birth on the Sabbath is *treife* ['forbidden food' in Yiddish]." The rabbi presented the analogy as though it was self-evident: "It's one thing to respond ad hoc to an emergency and to come to the arena of death to show compassion for the dead by bringing their severed limbs to a religious burial, and it's something else to make the collecting of body parts into your calling."

## State Religion Priesthood

Most often ZAKA appears in public discourse in conjunction with the idiom "holy work," referring to the death management in the arena of terrorism. In the Jewish tradition, the phrase "holy work" refers to the service of the priests in the ancient biblical Temple, the pinnacle of the worship of God. The first to apply this phrase to ZAKA were not members of the organization or necessarily religious. It first appeared in newspaper reporting; it was immediately adopted by politicians, and quite soon the combination of the three words—ZAKA, terrorism, holy work—became common in Israel. Identification of the deathwork in the arena with the priestly service in the Temple connotes admiration, but it also implies distancing, relegation to a separate realm that does not directly touch upon life in contemporary Israel. One gets the impression that the Israeli public are comfortable with having radical religious men deal with the victims of terrorism. A central figure in the organization told me, bitterly yet proudly, "Secular Jews want the handling of severed limbs in the wake of mass disasters to be our problem, not theirs. Apparently, Israelis prefer this awful job to be accomplished by 'aliens.'"

In descriptions of terrorist attacks during the Intifada, on television and in the press, the expression "holy work" is repeated, attached to pictures of the Haredi volunteers bent over the bodies in the arena. Mayors and ministers also rattle off this expression ad nauseam, while expressing their appreciation of ZAKA. I photocopied a letter to the chairman of ZAKA containing words of gratitude, praise, and self-effacement in response to the "holy work." The document is signed by the prime minister of Israel (March 1996). Shortly afterward ZAKA received a medal of honor from the president of Israel, and on it are engraved the words "holy work."

Secular Jews who speak of ZAKA's "holy work" do not refer to the full complex of religious meaning of the term, and perhaps they are not even aware of it. However, after what had become a cliché was used in reference to the volunteers, they adopted it enthusiastically, and henceforth it appeared as a core concept in ZAKA's rhetoric. Although the volunteers' experience of sanctity was acute from the beginning, until they made the term their own, the idiom and the idea behind it were not fully integrated into their religious system. Once they appropriated it, however, not only did the term "holy work" figure prominently in the discourse of ZAKA activists, orally and in writing, but it also gave depth and complexity to their authentic feeling of sanctity. The Haredi volunteers' religious instincts received recognition and validation from outside, and in the self-awareness of the organization, "holy work" receives its original profundity and vigor.[12] Once the volunteers became attached to the idea of holy work, they didn't let it go, and they find more and more dimensions in it that are appropriate to their basic feeling. In the history of ZAKA one takes note of the development of the volunteers' self-understanding of their sense of mission: at first the work in the arena of death was humanitarian and patriotic. Later it became sanctification of the name of God, devotion to the Torah, and demonstration of Jewish values at their best. Finally, it was interpreted as a ritual act, worship.

During the Intifada, as the intensity of terrorist attacks increased, the reports in the media ceased to be framed in political terms and began to speak in terms of fate, and ultimately they came to use traditional religious terms.[13] The expression "holy work" and the sanctification of ZAKA's project is no less indicative of the organization and its volunteers than of Israeli society and the place it gives to religion and the organization's deathwork in the local civic culture. ZAKA plays a role in the re-Judaizing of the Zionist state. An expression of this can be seen in the posthumous subjection of the victims of terrorism to halakhic norms even if they did not observe the halakha in their lifetime.

ZAKA's activity in the arena of horrific death brings together the two Israeli religions: the traditionalist Orthodoxy and the new civil. There is a close connection between the two religions and a significant degree of overlap.[14] The Western Wall, for example, is central for both religions: the faithful pray for atonement and redemption, and IDF soldiers are sworn in there. ZAKA is a religious phenomenon which is conscripted by the civil establishment for national use. Conversely, it is a national phenomenon that reinforces itself by means of the traditional religion, from which it draws values, symbols, and energy. In the division of labor between secular and religious Jews in Israel, ZAKA supplies a sacred canopy for the national project of coping with Palestinian terrorism. ZAKA was a vital factor in the development of the collective security creed that characterized Israel during the Intifada.[15]

The Haredi volunteers regard themselves as priests serving in the religious temple at the heart of the Jewish tradition, spoken of by the Bible, the Talmud, and halakha. In secular Israel, the volunteers are also seen as volunteers serving in the temple of Zionism. In Israeli nationalism, and not only in the Jewish religion, offering sacrifices plays a key role. The secular state largely assigns the role of the priests, who handle the torn flesh and spilled blood of the victims, to religious believers, who, in turn, accept the sacred task with devotion.

## Alliance

Terrorism links the Haredi community to Israeli society, and ZAKA is the intermediary between the two sides. The combination of secular Jews–terrorism-Haredim responds to needs and desires of both parties. Let's begin with the interest of the state and the general public in bonding with Haredi ZAKA. First, the Haredi project presents effective tools for dealing with distress in the presence of horrific death: it offers comforting meaning. ZAKA exempts others from the demanding task, takes the responsibility upon itself, and even dyed-in-the-wool secular people take solace in these miserable and chaotic moments from the confidence that it imbues and the time-honored consoling script that it offers to those who are perplexed and stunned by the Intifada's gruesome lethality. Moreover, ZAKA, unlike other religious initiatives in Israel, is not seen as threatening secular Jews with religious coercion or as exploiting its status for efforts at proselytizing. The Haredim of ZAKA do not demand entry into areas of central interest in Israel such as foreign affairs, the economy, or public education. Rather, it is content with its monopoly of the area of unnatural death.

Regarding the Haredi community, we have already noted that there are widening fissures in its opposition to Zionism and modern secular life. Isolation and absolute rejection are replaced by conditional legitimation and expressions of solidarity and sympathy, which the believers no longer seek to conceal. Efforts are being made to establish contact and cooperation between the sides. ZAKA embodies a Haredi effort of this kind. The volunteers yearn for fraternity, which would respond to their desperate need for recognition. They seek to absolve themselves of blame for enjoying privileges without contributing anything to their surroundings. The ZAKA activists point out their self-sacrifice for the dead and the living, and they repeatedly ask their partners in the arenas of death and those who observe them from the side, "Are we shirkers?" One veteran volunteer places a sarcastic heading over his weekly schedule, crammed with events of deathwork and acts of charity: "The journal of a Haredi draft-dodger."

It has been argued that a principal motive behind the effort of another radical religious group to intervene in Israeli public life—the Jewish settlement movement in the occupied territories on the West Bank—is the hidden yearning to escape from marginal and despised status and link up with the Israelis who had ignored and mocked them up till then. Underlying the dream of taking over the whole Land of Israel is an older dream of getting close to the secular Zionists and sharing the experience of Israeli life with them.[16] In this sense there is some similarity between the Gush Emunim movement and ZAKA. Beyond these two God-fearing incursions into public life in Israel lies a feeling of rejection and deprivation. From the Haredi point of view, ZAKA's activity brings a dividend in the form of upgrading the status of ultra-Orthodoxy in Israeli society. It also has intrinsic value, since it is bound up with rewarding ties with government institutions and secular individuals. In the arena of death there exists an island of harmonious coexistence between the Haredi volunteers and policemen, sappers, ISA agents, medics, politicians, municipal officials, and journalists—most of whom are secular. The veteran activists in the organization do not deny the pleasure they experience at that moment of grace, in the intimate companionship that characterizes the aftermath of a murderous explosion.

Central activists in the organization regard themselves as standard-bearers of coexistence with secular Jews. They emphasize that they are not by any means calling for assimilation, but for establishing an alliance. In his campaign of lectures about ZAKA throughout the country, the head of the organization calls this bond "All Israel are Fellows." Some volunteers have found hidden meaning in the name ZAKA, making it an acronym for words meaning "bringing brothers together." Gradually one more aspect of the charm of terrorism comes to light: redemption of the Haredim from their feeling of solitude and inferiority. A Jerusalem police officer described his relations with the ZAKA volunteers as a "covenant of blood." A photograph hangs in the ZAKA headquarters showing a Haredi man with a secular man next to him, with the caption "Terrorism = Shared Fate = Mutual Responsibility."

A large portion of Israelis harbor the sense of brotherhood between the two segments of Israeli society, which ZAKA takes pride in exemplifying. The dissenting minority belongs to the atheist leftist-liberal branch, who spice their criticism with disdainful mockery. They regard ZAKA as fetishists and pagans who make a farce of Judaism. Ironically, this secular critique is incredibly similar to that of the extreme Haredi rabbis, mainly Lithuanians, who also regard the actions of ZAKA in the arenas of death as "non-Jewish." They focus on the ruling of ZAKA rabbis that permits the removal of the bodies of the victims of terrorism on the Sabbath, which is to say, violation of the sanctity of the day, for the reason that leaving the bodies on the site would expose them to public view and thus strike a blow to national morale and shame the state before the nations of the world. The Haredi critique goes on to say that the ZAKA rabbis are not from the first rank of halakhic authorities, and there is no consensus regarding their rulings, and that respect for the dead and the integrity of the body belong to a bizarre, marginal, and negligible area of halakha.

Haredi criticism aims its arrows at ZAKA's initiatives, which fit into the national project and advance the interests of the state, such as the efforts of the leadership of the organization to send the burned-out body of a Jerusalem bus, which had been blown up in a Palestinian terrorist attack, to the International Court in the Hague, in coordination with the Information Department of the Israeli Foreign Office (January 2004). For their part, the heads of ZAKA are sensitive to Haredi criticism and aware of the bear hug of Zionism, which is pleasing but liable to deprive the organization of its rabbinical legitimacy. On the one hand, they flaunt the flattery lavished upon them by the Zionists, while on the other hand they conceal it from Haredi eyes.[17] The dilemma is reflected in the stormy discussion among the volunteers as to whether to wear police uniforms while active in the arena of terrorism. They can hardly resist the temptation to appear in uniform. Having opposed enlistment, they are well aware of the symbolic meaning of the uniform. The decision between fulfilling a dream that partakes of patriotism and militarism and subverting the authenticity of their Haredi identity has not been resolved. In a course on evacuation given to them by the home-front command of the army they did wear uniforms for a few hours, and they couldn't conceal their pleasure. To deal with corpses, they continue to appear in their traditional Haredi garb.

## Violent Death in Israel

Death plays a significant role both in traditionalist Jewish religion, the varieties of orthodoxy, and in the national civil religion, the religion of the state. In the pre-state Zionist past and the first two decades of the state, these two Israeli religions were separate and parallel, and there was some tension between them. Since 1967, and even more so since 1973 and 1977,[18] elements of the traditional religion were absorbed into the civil religion, and vice versa. Two new religious variations have emerged: Orthodoxy penetrated by Zionist national values, and nationalism tinted with elements of the Orthodox religion. Naturally, these two religions tend to approach one another and mingle. One result of this mix is emphasis on the centrality of death in Israel, especially death connected with building nationalism and preserving the security of the state, fundamentally violent death. Death in wars and disasters figures on center stage in many societies, especially for the purpose of augmenting a collective identity and encouraging political engagement,[19] but in Israel this culture of death is particularly prominent, to the extent that some scholars speak of the cult of violent death as typifying public life in Israel.[20] The two most important days in the Israeli (as opposed to the Jewish) calendar are the Memorial Day for the six million victims of the Holocaust and the memorial day for fallen soldiers, providing a dramatic illustration of this.

The Israeli death discussed here relates to the notions of trauma and martyrology that are prominent in Israeli political culture. Victimhood is also an important resource, a political asset in both the internal and international fronts. A related corpse-and-bone cult has developed in Israel.[21] The scene described below could have taken place only in Israel of the 1980s. Many years after they were discovered in an archaeological excavation in an inaccessible cave in a far desert canyon, bones—regarding which it was conjectured, though never proven, that they were the remains of Jewish rebels against the Romans in the second century CE—were buried in the presence of the prime minister, rabbis, and generals, who were brought to the site in air force helicopters, in a full military funeral, which was broadcast live to every household in Israel.[22]

In the past generation, the cult of death in Israel was nourished by the trauma of Palestinian terrorist attacks. These reached their peak during the violence of the Intifada, which gave rise to ZAKA. Riding on the waves of terrorism, ZAKA conquered an important place for itself on the Israeli stage, and with it swept the Haredi community from outsider to insider status, and thus intensified the cult of violent death in Israel and gave it a Jewish tone. ZAKA continued an existing national and religious heritage, but it also gave it renewed vitality and changed its face in unpredictable ways.

No less than ZAKA claimed a monopoly over this specific deathwork for itself; the Israeli establishment withdrew from fulfilling this duty, distanced itself from the arena, and abandoned it to the Haredim, who exploited the opportunity and saw it as claiming a right. ZAKA's entry into the arena of handling the victims of terrorism encountered no opposition, and their taking over of that arena was almost called for. In ordinary death, the relatives of the deceased are asked about their preference with respect to the treatment the body receives and the type of burial. Not everyone chooses the Orthodox version of a funeral.[23] In the case of death in a disaster, especially terrorism, treatment and burial of the bodies is automatically placed in the hands of the Haredi volunteers.

The natural way that the Haredim slipped into terrorism-related deathwork and their smooth takeover of the area are also expressed in the details of this deathwork behind which lies concern with the integrity of the body. A body without flaw is a Jewish obsession as well as a Zionist obsession. ZAKA inherited both these traditions and combined them. It developed an element that was already present in the storehouse of Jewish and Israeli culture, retrieved it selectively from the depths of the reservoir of the values of the past, and brought it up to the surface, to center stage, and fostered it.

## Prayer for the Safety of the Nation-State

Like the ISA, ZAKA is identified with the struggle against terrorism, and terrorism has been an integral part of Israeli life in the past forty years. Notwithstanding its Haredi essence, ZAKA is no less an Israeli institution than the ISA.[24] ZAKA is viewed favorably by most of the Israeli public, and its recognition by the governmental authorities has given it legal status and budgetary subsidies. ZAKA frequently participates in official ceremonies, where it is honored, and the activists of the organization have adopted Israeli patterns of behavior. The volunteers also display social solidarity and civic accountability. ZAKA fits into the national culture and the civil society that is arising in Israel. On Israel's fifty-fifth Independence Day, at the height of Palestinian terrorism, between one attack and another, a Haredi representative of ZAKA was invited to light a torch at the central official ceremony to express the appreciation of the establishment for the organization and the volunteers, who proved their devotion to the state. This event is commonly seen as the ultimate manifestation of ZAKA's Israelification. There is another symbolic act that demonstrates an extreme step toward identification with Israel. At the organization's headquarters in Jerusalem high-ranking visitors and generous donors are given a silver plaque with the Prayer for the Welfare of the State engraved on it. This revolutionary national prayer explicitly states that Israel is "the beginning of the emergence of our redemption." Haredi zealots can agree to cooperation with secular citizens and to implied recognition of the state, but in the sanctification of the sinful and heretical political entity, by understanding it as the realization, even if only partial, of their messianic vision, the Haredim of ZAKA have gone far.

## Second-Class Corpses

Like the New York City firefighters of 9/11, the Jewish death priests who handle the corpses in Jerusalem are honored as heroes—coping with evil while taking risks, endeavoring to heal, console, and restore order. In that way, the repulsive Haredi, at best a gravedigger, gains a moment of fame. Soon he will try to collect a dividend in terms of improvement of his image as a "weakling and parasite."

However, after the enthusiasm that comes with terrorism-related deathwork dies down, it becomes clear that the arena has another side, and the connection with this horrific fatality is of a dual nature. Along with grief, a feeling of humiliation creeps in. The trauma in the presence of the shattered and burned bodies arouses solidarity but also bespeaks failure. ZAKA has realized that its association with terrorism is a blessing mingled with a curse. Death in terrorism is not particularly honorable; at best there is bad luck in it, at worst it smacks of humiliation, a reminder of weakness. The region knows another kind of death, the death of fighters, the active death of people who consciously run risks for that which is believed to be a good cause. The latter death is regarded as honorable and one that complements those who deal with it. The Zionists keep this death for themselves, and they do not make room for the Haredim, who wish to share in the handling of that death, which is magnificent and bestows splendor. The Haredim are left with treatment of an inferior sort of death. Israel sends citizens without prestige to deal with death devoid of glory. This death perpetuates the marginal status of those who handle it, and, because they handle it, it becomes even more marginal. Second-rate death is related to second-rate citizens. Those who die by terrorism do not enter the national pantheon, and their memorialization takes second place in public attention and official investment. The monument and memorial ceremony industry, which flourishes in Israel, provides testimony to this. Monuments to the victims of terrorism are modest (usually a small marble plaque bearing the names of those who perished), local (under the responsibility of municipalities, dispersed in the urban space, at street corners, on the walls of houses, in the bus stop where the attack took place), and private (usually erected upon the initiative of the families of the victims). In a few years, many of them become dirty and broken. The memorial ceremonies for the victims of terrorism are not highly organized, there are few participants (only relatives and friends), and in time they cease to be held. This is in polar contrast to the monuments and memorial ceremonies for soldiers who died in combat. They are central and official, subsidized and imposing. The relatives of the victims of terrorism have been trying for years to upgrade the status of their dear ones, to make them equal to military casualties, but in vain. Their initiatives to raise the victims of terrorism from their inferior status were strongly opposed by the government, the press, and mainly the parents of the military dead.[25]

ZAKA plays an active role in the negotiations with the authorities and with public opinion on the status of the victims of terrorism in the hierarchy of patriotic death, for it has consequences for the status of ZAKA and of the Haredim. The organization has tried time and again to penetrate this respected and exclusive tragic circle, to enjoy the highest degree of honor. But it is repeatedly rejected, both because it is involved with terrorism and not with war, and because it is Haredi.

Like other nation-states, Israel needs heroes, dead heroes included. However, those who die in terrorism are not the heroes that Israel is looking for. Some people try to force them on the country, but it resists. Israel is enamored with its dead soldiers and minimizes the value of citizens who died in terrorist attacks. In the Israeli past, soldiers were sent to the front to sacrifice themselves in battle, in order to defend the lives of the citizens at home with their bodies; civilian lives were thus more precious than those of the soldiers. With the increase in Palestinian terrorism during the Intifada, it has turned out that the lives of soldiers were more valuable than the lives of civilians.[26] The hierarchy of Israeli grief was overturned. Furthermore, most of the citizens who died in Palestinian terrorism in Israel belonged to the weaker strata of society: old and poor people, foreign workers, and new immigrants, since they are the ones who use public transportation and shop in the markets and in the streets in the center of town during the day.

Frequently these victims have no affluent, well-connected relatives with skills that can help them become effective agents of memory and improve the status of their dead kin.

A ZAKA volunteer told me that, since the Haredim are a sort of outcast, they are forced to squeeze into all the niches that the state has abandoned and left to be handled by anyone who is willing to, for example, care for poor, sick, or isolated old people, and for the less prestigious dead. However, ZAKA reinvented the handling of shameful death and enlarged it to become a matter of religious and national importance. Thus, it once again gained an honorable place for itself in Israeli life.

# 5

# New Torah

## Terrorism-Centered Sacred Norms

### What Is to Be Done with a Plastic Bag after Severed Human Organs Have Been Emptied Out of It?

Answer: Since it is likely that bloodstains and tiny body tissues cling to it, the bag must be buried, but in a grave separate from the body, because it might prevent the earth from touching the body (*ḥatzitza*).

In their deathwork at the arena of terrorism, ZAKA volunteers occasionally encounter situations they don't know how to cope with. They ask the Torah scholars among the colleagues at their side in the field how to proceed. Those they ask are older, more experienced, known for their piety, and graduates of many years of study in elite yeshivas. The volunteers mainly seek instruction from the well-known rabbis in the organization or from other rabbis whom they respect, including Haredi figures with great prestige as learned scholars of Torah, with whom they communicate by cell phone. I have documented cases in which questions were asked of rabbis while a volunteer was bent over a body or while he was driving, even late at night. Following is a typical selection of questions that the volunteers asked of halakhic authorities in real time and some of the answers, according to which the volunteers conducted themselves in the arena.

Question: What is to be done with hair pulled out of the heads of corpses because of the explosion? Answer: It must be gathered and buried along with the other body parts. Among the rabbis of the Mishnah, the Talmud, and the Middle Ages, there is a difference of opinion on a similar matter. Some say that it should not be buried, and that it is even possible to make use of the hair of a dead woman (as opposed to the hair of a dead animal), while others argue that one may only make posthumous use of a person's hair if it is a wig. Recent rabbinical authorities have concluded the dispute by ruling that what is connected permanently to a body must be gathered and buried, but that which can be separated from the body is exempt from that obligation.

*The Cult of Dismembered Limbs*. Gideon Aran, Oxford University Press. © Oxford University Press 2023.
DOI: 10.1093/oso/9780197689141.003.0005

Therefore, they directed ZAKA volunteers to deal with a dental crown like a body part, unlike jewelry, watches, and spectacles. There is no dispute regarding finger and toenails: they must be buried.

In answer to a question addressed to the rabbi of the Southern District of ZAKA following a terrorist attack in Beersheba, it was ruled that handling death in the arena does not exempt one from prayer. However, in this and similar matters, there were different and even contradictory rulings. Once a volunteer was called to deal with one incident and immediately afterward to deal with another one, so that he missed the time for afternoon prayer. The question was raised: Should he recite the evening prayers twice to compensate (*tashlumin*)? The answer: if the volunteer is observing the commandment of dealing with the dead from the beginning of the time for prayer until the end, he is exempt from the obligation to pray. If he is called to another incident after the time for prayer has already come, he must recite the following prayer twice.

The volunteers in the arena also ask: Is it permitted to bury severed limbs separately from the bodies and to gather the body parts that were collected in the arena and bury them in a single grave? The answer: a supreme effort must be made to place the parts with the bodies they belonged to, and if this is impossible, then it is permissible to bury the body in one grave and the limbs in a separate but nearby grave. The question: If one of the wounded from the explosion dies while ZAKA volunteers are close to him, are they required to tear their garments as a sign of mourning (because someone who dies in a terrorist attack is regarded as a *met mitsva*, an unidentified corpse, which one is required to bury, and anyone who happens to encounter the body is tantamount to a relative). The answer: they are exempt from the obligation to tear their garment according to the laws of mourning, for were they to rend their garments for every dead body they encountered, their clothing would be in tatters. What is the law regarding a tiny piece of flesh or bone found in the area of the explosion? If it is larger than an olive, it must be buried according to halakha. Upon this followed a discussion of exactly what that dimension was, and recently it was determined to be twenty-seven grams.

Some of the rabbinical rulings connected with deathwork are not answers to practical questions posed by the volunteers in the field. Rather they are theoretical and relate to hypothetical situations. The responses are circulated among the volunteers to guide them in future work. Here is an example of a situation that the rabbinical imagination forestalls: the scenario of a nuclear attack. The danger of radioactive contamination necessitates burial in sealed concrete coffins, but this prevents contact of the body with the earth, which is required by halakha. According to the ruling, in such a situation the coffins must first be buried, and afterward the corpses are to be placed in them.

Other rulings by the ZAKA rabbis explicitly dictate practices well known to the volunteers from previous experience, ritual procedures that have become routine for their deathwork. The familiar directives are sharpened, and explanations are appended to them. A prominent example relates to the *tallit katan (tsitsit)*, a four-cornered fringed garment worn by religious Jews. While the fringes are generally kept visible, ZAKA rabbis call for them to be tucked in while in the presence of the dead. The explanation for this is to avoid the possibility of *la'ag larash* (mocking the poor): not to provoke the dead by arousing their envy when they see living people racing among them and observing the commandment of wearing a fringed garment, whereas the dead are unable to observe this important commandment. The ZAKA rabbis add further restrictions. Thus, one must also observe this prohibition next to the body of an infant (who is not required to wear ritual fringes), because the soul of a great person might dwell in it. In contrast, some authorities maintain that there is no need to conceal one's ritual fringes from the body of a woman, since, were she alive, she would be exempt from this commandment. On other occasions ZAKA rabbis add that, for the same reason of avoiding frustration of the dead, one may not pray or even study Torah near their bodies. Rabbi Elyashiv adds that the commandment to avoid mocking the poor applies only to a whole body or one who is mostly intact, including the head, as opposed to a truncated limb. Another ruling by the ZAKA rabbis, which in fact merely corroborates traditional practice, is, for example, the obligation incumbent on all the volunteers to close the corpse's mouth, so that air or a demon cannot penetrate it. Another matter touches upon the state of the victim's hands. In the distant past it was customary to lay them upon the victim's heart, as was done for Moses, according to an ancient myth. Later this custom was altered because laying the hands of the deceased over his heart became a Christian custom, symbolizing the cross. Therefore, in ZAKA they decreed that, following the opinion of rabbis in recent centuries, the arms of the dead should be placed against their sides.

Sometimes the volunteers' questions do not receive an unequivocal answer, or they receive different answers, which might not be consistent. For example, what should be done with a fine and expensive carpet that was stained by a few drops of the dead person's blood? Those who ask are aware of the conflict between two relevant commandments. On the one hand, it is customary to bury every drop of blood, but, on the other hand, to bury the carpet would violate an explicit prohibition of the Torah, not to destroy.[1] Sometimes the rabbis' instructions do not satisfy the volunteers who ask, or they find it difficult to obey them. In such instances, a certain crisis of trust can emerge between the questioner and the respondent. An example of the tension between the sides regards treatment of the Palestinian terrorist's body, while it is lying in the arena of the explosion. Although the veteran volunteers are aware of the unpleasant duty incumbent upon them, before they perform it, with reluctance, they occasionally ask again how to treat it. The answer of the head of the ZAKA rabbinical council is unshakable: the body, with all its parts, is to be removed with great care. The volunteers are offered a few explanations, which persuade them only partially, and then they do the job reluctantly, despite strong internal resistance. They are told, first, that removing the body will prevent danger to the ritual purity of men of priestly descent who might approach the site, since the bodies of Jews are liable to contaminate them, and, even more so, the body of a non-Jew. Second, they are offered the explanation based on the principle of "the ways of peace." That is to say, the need to treat one's enemies in a worthy manner so as not to arouse anger and criticism, lest the nations of the world might respond aggressively. Without conviction, they mention a third reason: after all, even the Palestinian terrorist was created in the image of God.

Respect for the dead is derived from respect for the living, who were made for the glory of Creation. This traditional value also derives from the conception of the body as the sanctuary (*nartik*, literally "sheath") of the soul. The body is comparable to a holy book, a Torah scroll, and to a sacred vessel in general. Hence, the law applying to a Torah scroll, which must be buried if it is irreparably damaged or defiled, even applies to scraps of bone or scorched flesh.[2] Moreover, respect for the dead is intended to console the bereaved family and to ensure "correct repose" to the soul of the deceased (in the world to come) and to increase the chances of its resurrection.

ZAKA also translates respect for the dead as preserving the modesty of the corpse.[3] The ZAKA rabbis ruled that if a person's body is exposed, it is as if he were murdered twice. In a sermon given by a ZAKA rabbi on the day of the organization's holiday, he quoted the Book of Proverbs (25:2): "It is the glory of God to conceal a thing." In similar spirit Rabbi Roje published a ruling stating that volunteers who see corpses "in various strange states" are forbidden to tell others about what they saw, because of respect for the dead.

For that reason, it is forbidden to photograph corpses except for the purpose of identifying them.

Another characteristic issue relates to the blood of people who die a violent death. They recite the halakha about this matter in countless forums: if the "blood of the soul," that is, blood that a person shed between being wounded and his death, which is caused by loss of blood, is soaked into his clothing, it is not removed, his body is not ritually washed, and he is buried in his blood-soaked clothing and shoes. ZAKA also applies the laws of burial to objects soaked with the victim's blood. If blood has flowed onto the earth next to the victim, they dig it up and bury it with him. If the victim has already been buried, it is forbidden to open his grave to bury the blood, but they dig into the earth above the body and place the blood-soaked items there, so long as it is at least ten inches deep. There is no disagreement as to whether the victims' blood, like their severed limbs, must be buried, but a minority of rabbis permit the burial of the blood in any grave, not necessarily along with the victim's body.

If the victim was severely wounded and died several days after his clothing was removed, his body may be washed, and he may be dressed in a shroud. Only if he was wounded by non-Jews and died, and his body was then washed, the blood-soaked clothes he was wearing must be buried. If the victim's "blood of the soul" stains a living person's garments, specifically those of a ZAKA volunteer working in the arena of death, the garment must be soaked in water, and the water must be poured onto the victim's grave, and if that is not feasible, into a pit as close as possible to the grave. A considerable number of volunteers were even stricter in observing this halakha and buried their blood-stained garments. Several veterans proudly state they have buried more than one pair of trousers. In cases of doubt regarding the identity of the body that shed the blood or when the blood of several Jewish victims has mingled, they bury the blood in a separate grave. As for the limit for collecting the blood, it was determined that it was obligatory to gather and bury all the blood of the victims in the arena, until the final drop, even if this requires a supreme effort. However, when this is impossible because of time pressure and the scattering of the blood over a wide and inaccessible area, the minimum amount is known as a *revi'it*, a quarter of the biblical measure of a *log*, about a cup of the blood from the arena. If drops of blood remain in the arena which cannot be soaked up to purify it, the area must not be hosed with water, but it must be covered with earth. Once a veteran ZAKA activist told me, "A volunteer who puts the body of a small child in a bag but leaves a drop of blood on the ground has failed the test. Leaving one percent of the blood in the arena is not fulfilling ninety-nine percent of the commandment, but zero!"

ZAKA defines the victims of terrorism as *metei mitsvah* (literally, "commandment dead"), a halakhic category defining corpses found without relatives or friends who would see to their burial, in which case members of the community must make sure they are buried with respect. This is a sacred obligation which must be fulfilled at any cost, even the suspension of another important commandment. It even applies to *kohanim* (men of priestly lineage), who, under ordinary circumstances, avoid contact with the dead to avoid ritual pollution. Fulfillment of the commandment of honoring the dead grants immunity from contamination to *kohanim*, while to others it confers the status of *tsadikim* (righteous). The expression *met mitsva* ordinarily refers to a situation that seldom arises, a marginal and idiosyncratic religious subject that is not widely discussed, whereas ZAKA has made it a central and practical matter.

## Tractate Terrorism in the Making

One of the venerated judges in Jewish mytho-history is Jephthah, a general who rescued the Israelites in a time of trouble. On the eve of a crucial battle against the archenemy, the Ammonites, he made an oath to God that, if he triumphed, he would sacrifice the first living creature who came to greet him when he returned home. Great was his religiosity, and great was his victory too. Crowned with glory, full of gratitude and a sense of obligation, determined to keep his oath, he headed toward his home. The first one to greet him, with drums and dances, was his only daughter. Although she was more precious to him than anything, and despite his compassion, he fulfilled his vow and sacrificed her. After leading the nation for another six years, he died and was buried in "the cities of Gilad" (Judges 11–12). Why is the plural used in the expression "cities" rather than the singular?[4] The traditional commentators could not ignore this dramatic episode, which develops like a Greek tragedy, combining an exalted manifestation of faith with unparalleled cruel rigidity. They conclude that Jephthah was buried in several different cities because he did not go to the high priest to annul his oath, and, as punishment, his limbs fell from him one by one while he was alive. Wherever he went, a limb fell off, and it was buried where it fell.[5] This is the point of departure for a rather morbid discussion among generations of rabbinical authorities from Maimonides in the twelfth century to Rabbi Feinstein in the twentieth. ZAKA volunteers asked their halakhic authorities how to deal with the limb of a living person, and they were referred to this biblical precedent.

While there is no dissent from the obligation to bury a limb torn from a corpse, the rabbis disagree about limbs severed from a living body. The culmination of a complex discussion is that there is no commandment to bury them, but, at the same time, their burial is recommended to avoid contempt for the person who has lost the limb and to avert the possibility that a man of priestly lineage might encounter the limb and be contaminated. The head of ZAKA's rabbinical council adds that the severed limb would be liable to contaminate only if it contained a bone, but if it has no bone, it does not have to be buried.

The rabbis' deliberations in response to problems posed to them and the explanation of their decisions are one of the principal ways in which halakha has developed since the time of the Mishnah. The questions and answers have been accumulated, edited, printed, and circulated among faithful Jews for generations. This is the classical dynamic that produces the traditional Jewish literature known by the Hebrew initials *shot* (questions and answers) or "responsa." This is a central component of rabbinical creativity (in addition to biblical exegesis and commentary on the Talmud), and it is the basis for a considerable amount of halakhic literature. The questions of the Haredi volunteers and the responses of their rabbis provide the foundation for the body of halakha that guides ZAKA's activity. Thus, in the past thirty years, a full code of laws has been compiled concerning the treatment of unnatural death in general and especially of the victims of terrorism. It is composed of layer upon layer of precedents, additions, corrections, reservations, specifying, explanations, and counter-explanations. The result is a body of dynamic interpretations and rulings that makes possible the elaboration and application of sacred principles under changing conditions.

Once the parents of a young woman who fell victim to violent death wanted to cut off a lock of her hair to remember her by. The head of the ZAKA rabbinical council was in severe doubt as to whether to agree to their request (and he shared his considerations with me). Finally he refused permission, only because of the commandment to bury the entire body, though he admitted that his decision seems harsh and might be unpopular. Later the rabbi's assistant published the decision, and it was included in a collection of decisions on similar matters. As he said, one halakha and then another steadily become a consistent doctrine. Before our eyes, religious literature regarding the handling of death in the arena of terrorism and other disasters—mainly the treatment of corpses and body parts—is gradually amassed. Caring for victims of violent death is an original area of rabbinical expertise, though several of its components are based on generations of prior rulings, sometimes hundreds of years old. A new tractate of the Oral Law emerges.

The rulings of the ZAKA rabbis are often quite daring. Their focus on horrific death entails a change. Until recently, there were relatively few laws relating to the areas of death in which ZAKA specializes, and the old rulings had to be adapted to new geo-political and cultural circumstances, and to advanced technology. For this purpose, customs are examined and translated into written halakha, and contradictions between written halakhot are resolved. In so doing, earlier marginal, sketchy, even obscure rulings are made into a wide-ranging, relevant, trendy, vibrant matter. The terrorism-related halakha, invented by ZAKA, has become a monopoly of the Haredi organization. The growth of ZAKA's halakha has aroused criticism on the part of both extreme and liberal Haredi circles. These two parties admit that the sections of halakha that deal with death are short and under-studied.[6] They argue that it would be proper to leave the halakhot of death hazy, numerically small, and little-known. To support this claim, the critics refer to a traditional wisdom, according to which Torah study regarding death leads to calamity for those who engage in it. They tell about a rabbi who devoted an entire year to study of the laws of mourning, and, at the end of that year, his wife died.[7] The ZAKA rabbis understand that they must contend with the primal fears that their specialty arouses.[8] They cite a twelfth-century book that advocates the loving treatment of those areas of halakha which most people shun or depreciate.[9] Those who advocate systematic Torah study of death claim that it is a particularly great source of merit to study commandments that few people deal with. This is stated in the foreword to Jewish books about death from the seventeenth and eighteenth centuries, as well as in ZAKA's manuals.[10]

The consolidation of ZAKA halakha does not lack difficulties and disputes. The organization's halakhic decisors cannot ignore the predicaments of life in a modern city. Therefore, they must acknowledge the legitimacy of burial arrangements that seem to violate the dictates of the Torah. For example, they rehearsed time and again that the victims of terrorism ought to be buried where they were killed, which they, as it were, purchased with their spilled blood (*met mitsva kone' mekomo*). Nevertheless, the bodies are removed from the arena. Those who permit this refer to a different ruling, according to which the victims should not be buried "in a grave that is harmful to the public."[11]

ZAKA's halakhic creativity is far from finished. I came into possession of a first draft that was lying on the desk of the head of the ZAKA rabbinical council. Under the heading "Laws of a Killed Person" were written quotations and interpretations pertaining to the question of whether the body of the victim of terrorism should be wrapped in a shroud over his blood-soaked garments. After a detailed discussion of the pros and cons, based on precedents from the sixteenth and eighteenth centuries, extending over four pages, the bottom line appeared in the form of a clear and short halakha. In my archive I have a tentative version of "Laws and Customs Applying to Respect for the Dead," published by the ZAKA rabbis. This is a thick book in which, among the densely printed lines, there are handwritten corrections, deletions, and additions. The book underwent several readings and has not yet received approval for circulation among the volunteers. Here is one example among many for an optional addition suggesting an exception to the prohibition of delaying burial: it is possible to delay the burial of a married woman to enable her newly widowed husband, who wants to marry her sister in her place, to arrange the engagement before the burial, and thus to comfort the deceased woman, who would most likely be happy to know that her sister is replacing her.[12]

Meanwhile other pamphlets have been published, detailing the ZAKA halakha. Some of them are in pocket-size format, meant to be brought to the arena, such as the booklet entitled *The End of Days*. This is a practical summary of the halakhot regarding treatment of unnatural death. Appended at the end are the operative and administrative procedures regarding conduct in the arena of terrorism. For example, it defines three levels of certainty in identifying a corpse: according to fingerprint—absolute identification; according to tattoos and scars—intermediate; according to height and hair color—weak. It adds that according to the halakha, two intermediate-level identifying signs are equivalent to one absolute sign. Another pamphlet is entitled *Identification of Corpses According to Halakha*. It refers to visible signs such as lumps on the nose. The pamphlet sums up a training course held for the volunteers following their failure to identify the victims of the attack on bus 26 in Jerusalem (August 1995). A third pamphlet presents instructions regarding order of preference for removing corpses from the arena. It states that one must relate to the following variables in descending order of importance: the influence of the corpse's presence in the area on the security and functioning of the teams devoted to the saving of life, danger of deterioration in the condition of the corpse that might lead to its humiliation, fear of the loss or blurring of identifying signs on the corpse, and finally preference is to be given on the basis of religion (priests, rabbis, and Torah scholars take precedence). Another pamphlet, which was distributed to the volunteers for the seventh of Adar, contains a collection of petitions and penitential prayers to be recited on the Haredi organization's holiday as well as emphatic reminders of the customs and laws that must be learned by heart for the needs of deathwork in the arena.

The compilations of ZAKA halakhot may be viewed as a variation on the traditional Jewish literature of death written by rabbis in the Middle Ages and especially in the Early Modern Period. A ZAKA rabbi defined their compilations as an extension and specification of the widely circulated and authoritative book *Gesher haḥayim* (The Bridge of Life), the ABC of the burial societies.[13] To complement this project of the ZAKA rabbis, the volunteers are required to attend lessons in halakha. At a certain stage in ZAKA's history, its heads decided that volunteers who did not regularly attend lessons would be expelled from the organization. A donation was also used to finance the establishment of a yeshiva for married men in the ZAKA office. A stipend was offered to men who spent several hours every day studying halakhot related to death. I discovered that this initiative petered out within a short time, though this was denied by the organization's officials. The establishment of the ZAKA rabbinical council was a more successful initiative. This body is composed of about ten members, headed by Rabbi Roje, who is a kind of guru who derives his authority from his vast knowledge of halakha, from his many years of experience, and from his close association with Rabbi Auerbach, the leading halakhic authority in the Haredi world. The council is responsible for the Torah education of the volunteers and for maintaining the halakhic rules in the arena, and it gives traditional legitimacy to ZAKA, a moral and halakhic umbrella that protects the organization from the criticism of the Haredi community. The members of the council are highly respected in the organization and referred to with the honorific title of *geonim* (geniuses). Various camps in ultra-Orthodoxy are represented in the council. Most of them are Lithuanian, to counterbalance the Hasidic tendency among the ZAKA volunteers.

## The Invention of the Tradition of Violent
## Death Management

I stood by the cradle at the birth of ZAKA's doctrine of corpses and body parts and followed its growth. Under radically changing circumstances in the world and the region, wide-ranging innovations have been introduced in halakha regarding other areas as well, including medicine and biotechnology, use of the internet, participation in democratic elections, and the army and warfare.[14] The recent decades have seen a dramatic rise in concern within the world of Torah, in all its varieties, in halakhic issues deriving from the conflict in the Middle East. These include questions connected with terrorism and counter-terrorism. For example, in the early 2000s rabbis were asked: Is it permissible for a social worker to travel on the Sabbath to administer urgent psychological treatment to the residents of an isolated Jewish settlement who were suffering from post-traumatic stress after a Palestinian terrorist attack that slaughtered an entire family of their neighbors?[15] A considerable number of those who pose and answer questions regarding halakhot connected with terrorism are religious Zionists, mainly settlers in the West Bank, who tend to hold rightist political views and a messianic religious outlook. Like the ZAKA rabbinical council, a council of rabbis of Judea and Samaria was established to issue halakhic rulings regarding defense and offense in response to increasing Palestinian militancy. One of the fruits of this rabbinical effort is a book of responsa entitled *Hilkhot intifada* (halakha rules for the Intifada time).[16] While a body of Jewish law related to terrorism developed in parallel within the two organizations on the front in facing the Intifada, the settlers and ZAKA, a similar development took place on the Palestinian Muslim side of the confrontation. Sharia authorities in the Arab world issue fatwas concerning the battle against the Israeli occupation.[17]

*

Whereas in the past, the entire Jewish universe subjected itself to the regulations of halakha, currently only a minority of the Jews do so. However, in other important respects, contrary to expectations, with modernization the rule of halakha has become stronger. The influence of halakha on the lives of the sub-group that has remained faithful to it has become deeper and more comprehensive. I refer to the Orthodox and especially ultra-Orthodox communities. First, this religious sector imposes halakha on more areas of its life. It creates new halakhot, which can be applied in the changing world with its unprecedented phenomena such as organ transplants, supersonic air travel, as well as the smashing of bodies in terrorist explosions. Second, the directives by which halakha regulates the public and private lives of this sector have become more specific and rigid. While most Jews have thrown off the yoke of halakha, about a tenth of them adhere more strongly to a more severe and demanding version of halakha. This paradox can be explained by the weakening of the communal framework, which formerly supplied examples of correct Jewish behavior. Since it was no longer possible to imitate other people's customs, to examine and study the customs prevalent in one's immediate surroundings, Orthodox Jews could only turn for instruction to rabbis who issued halakhic rulings or to books of halakha. Thus, the written halakha and its interpreters received a status they had never had. This phenomenon is notable in the flourishing of the responsa literature, including innovative manuals that teach how to deal with violent death. To sum up: the increased recent halakhization of Orthodox Judaism has two dimensions: expansion of the application of halakha, and the tightening of its grasp. These are clearly expressed in ZAKA. In the past the dead were mainly handled according to custom. Now they are handled according to halakha. Subjection of the activities of ZAKA in the arena of death to the severe regime of halakha imbues the volunteers with confidence and makes it easier for them to cope with the paralyzing horror and with criticism on the part of more conservative Haredim.

*

Most ZAKA volunteers are not exemplary Torah scholars. Their halakhic expertise is limited, including their knowledge of halakhot pertaining to the dead. Their attraction to the arena of death, especially violent death, and their enthusiastic activity there do not derive from the discipline of extreme obedience to the halakha, but rather from an authentic impulse, which seeks religious channels of expression, out of a spontaneous need to cling to permanent and significant patterns of behavior that make it easier for them to cope with the new situation in a time of crisis. Nevertheless they, who do not belong to the scholarly elite, were the primary factor in religious creativity, which ultimately found expression in innovative halakha. The source of ZAKA's doctrine is the ritual predisposition of the ultra-Orthodox, who found themselves in the heart of suicide terrorism during the Intifada, and since then they have not relaxed their grip on it.

At first the Haredi volunteers shaped their intervention in the arena according to patterns of behavior familiar to them, which were acceptable and respected in their community. These were prevalent customs which seemed appropriate to them for application to circumstances they had never encountered. After they had already begun to play a significant role in managing death, they addressed rabbis, out of their desire to anchor their intuitive procedures in the tradition and to give meaning and approval to their largely instinctive response. On some occasions the questions addressed to the rabbis came from the field in real time, when they were called upon to respond to the murderous results in an emergency.

The response of the ultra-Orthodox rabbis was mixed. Many of them remained indifferent or dismissed the importance of the phenomenon as an episode that would pass quickly, a quirky and superfluous wrinkle in the Haredi way of life. In those early days, in the Haredi neighborhoods of Jerusalem, one could hear mocking responses to the volunteers. A minority of rabbis, usually not influential ones in the Haredi community, responded positively to the challenge posed by the volunteers and were excited by the opportunity that had come to them. They promptly embraced the volunteers and gave them what they needed: making the procedures that the volunteers had employed in the arena of death, procedures that became increasingly and almost imperceptibly fixed from event to event, into precise and legitimate rituals deriving their force from their connection with the tradition. Within a short time, these rabbis issued halakhic rulings that were compiled as the ZAKA doctrine. The backing given by these rabbis to the ingenuous and relatively ignorant volunteers developed into a polished method, dependent on authoritative sources, and integrated into a well-ordered and prestigious system. These halakhic decisors are rabbinical entrepreneurs. They are innovative, though at first they responded to requests from below, to needs from the grassroots. The most active among them later became members of the ZAKA rabbinical council.

The dynamic of halakhic backing and patterns of action that are created while adapting to a changing environment is known in the history of the Jewish religion. An illustrative paradigmatic analogy to the case of ZAKA is provided by the development of the halakhic concept of the "Sabbath goy," rabbinical permission to employ a non-Jewish neighbor to perform necessary work on the Sabbath. In principle, if a Jew is not permitted to perform an action on the Sabbath, he is also not permitted to ask a gentile to do it. However, employment of Sabbath goys became routine at the beginning of the Early Modern Period, imperceptibly, with the approval of genuinely observant Jews who were not recognized as experts in Torah and who were not authorized to issue halakhic rulings.[18] These dilettantes, who played a key role in the development of the halakha, did not act in a vacuum, according to their own whims. Rather, they were guided by a ritual instinct, which many believers, loyal to the Torah, developed over the years. When ordained rabbis were called upon to make rulings on this matter, they tended to approve of the custom, so long as it did not openly violate the spirit of the Torah and its explicit words, especially since this pattern of behavior had already become widespread. The circumstances of time and place impelled the decisors to make an intellectual effort and effect a compromise between what had already become customary and the expected permission.

The bonding of the organization's volunteers to the rabbinical decisors and the application of halakha to the scene of terrorism mainly fulfilled three vital functions. First, in this manner the challenge of the horrific murder in the arena of Palestinian terrorist attacks during the Intifada was transformed into a phenomenon that could be subsumed in the religion. The rabbinization of the spontaneous response to death in terrorism led to its annexation by the religion—more specifically, to its becoming a monopoly of the Haredi sector. A second function of the rabbinical umbrella provided for ZAKA is legitimacy, which provides it with the ability to withstand the attacks of important parts of the Haredi establishment, which viewed the organization as a threat to the traditional way of life of the community, especially as a threat to the supremacy of Torah study in yeshivas.

A third function of the halakhic ritualization of ZAKA's actions in the arena was less expected but no less important. The rabbinical responsiveness to the appeals of the volunteers made it possible for the first time to control and restrain them. The rabbinical rulings gave a traditional aspect to the work with violent death and thus made this seminal enterprise easier for the volunteers. At the same time, however, it restricted them. The area of death is sensitive and explosive and thus needs to be tamed.[19] Moreover, the incursion of the organization in the arena is a charismatic, even wild act, which leaders responsible for maintaining the religious tradition felt obligated to subdue. Ardent creativity coming from below has anarchic potential that must be suppressed, at least partially, with the help of the bear hug of halakha.

Negotiations develop between the Haredi rabbinate, the core of the religious establishment, and enthusiastic upstarts from the sidelines of the community. Will the latter gain recognition by the former? Will the latter accept the command of the former? Both sides made a visible effort to translate the innovative and subversive discourse into one that is acceptable and admissible into the canon. The establishment responds cautiously. It knows that if it co-opts the threat and enlists it in its ranks, it will avoid competition, pre-empt revolt from the outside, and thus can also exploit this primal vigor to strengthen itself. The establishment needs the energy of the new margins, but it also fears it and requires ingenuity that will enable it to absorb the potential danger and thus moderate and regulate it. The institutionalizing of charisma is incomplete. Tension remains between the center and the periphery. The challenging factor is left with a relatively autonomous living space, free from neutralizing supervision, while the ecclesiastical establishment changes without realizing it, becoming an agent of radical transformation under the aegis of its conservatism.[20]

A group of Torah scholars, hardly an integral part of the rabbinical upper stratum, chose, unlike the Haredi establishment, not to ignore the representatives of ZAKA who were emerging on the horizon of the community. Instead they sought to co-opt the new phenomenon, which seems promising to them, and to embrace it before it slipped out of their grasp and took an independent route. The halakhic ritualization of the handling of death was yet another illustration of the new professionalization of the rabbinate, making possible the manipulation of the religious community. As with matters of women's menstruation, so, too, with the handling of corpses, in this way the dependence of the faithful on their rabbis increases.

As soon as they received halakhic backing, the pioneering volunteers, who had been seen as threatening the old Haredi hierarchy of values, were given approval to continue their groundbreaking initiative. Paradoxically, this enabled some of the volunteers to enjoy the luxury of not studying the halakhot relevant to their work. They handled death from the routine of customs that were embedded in their DNA, and in cases of doubt, they asked their rabbis to decide. Once I tested the knowledge of a senior ZAKA volunteer in halakhot related to his daily work for years. I discovered that his command of the matter was vague, and, mainly, he had not taken the trouble to learn the rationale foundation of the commandments that he obeyed.

It quickly became clear to the volunteers that the rabbinical backing they had received also had another aspect: a rigid system of laws that restricted their freedom to act in the various arenas of death. Along with the confidence that the halakhot of death gave them, the volunteers also were frustrated. In some instances, especially when they went into a trance during their work with the dead, several ZAKA activists expressed bitterness because of the efforts at imposing discipline and the restrictions that the rabbis levied on them, and they seemed to be ignoring their instructions. The zealots in the group were the ones who expressed impatience with the strictures of halakha. At one time a sentiment bordering upon a call for rebellion against rabbinical rule was expressed, as if it were blocking the momentum of collecting severed limbs and blood spots.

The religious dynamic of ZAKA is characterized by tacit tension between the rabbinical council, which is controlled by Lithuanians, and the volunteers on the operational level, most of whom are Hasidim. The former seek to impose a culture of books on the organization, whereas the latter cling to the remnants of a living culture.[21] In the arenas of death of the end of the Intifada, ZAKA was vacillating dialectically between custom and halakha, preserving a division of labor and delicate equilibrium between legalistic, scholarly religiosity and popular religiosity.

*

The halakhization of ZAKA activism is a kind of invention of tradition.[22] The invention of a tradition of death in Judaism has a precedent.[23] The sixteenth and seventeenth centuries were a period of flourishing religious creativity in the Jewish communities of Palestine and Europe. Among other things, customs still practiced today, such as *tiqun ḥatsot* (midnight prayers of mourning for the destruction of the Temple) and *kabalat shabbat* (hymns and psalms recited in the prayer of the Sabbath eve), were crystalized, as well as ceremonies of death and burial. Regarding death, as with marriage and birth, books of customs were more influential than rigidly binding books of halakha. Rather than initiating customs, the rabbis mainly embraced existing customs, contributed to unifying variants of them, connected them to canonical literature (mainly Kabbalah), explained them by means of earlier sources, and circulated them in print. This new genre was simply a response to the demand of individuals such as members of burial societies, who did not belong to the scholarly elite. The rabbinate tried to supply the need of the faithful for rituals that helped them overcome crises. The religious literature such as the books of the dead, which were written at the start of the Early Modern Period, bear some resemblance to the halakhic writing of the ZAKA rabbinical council. The bi-weekly column of halakhic innovations published by Rabbi Roje on the internet during the Intifada specified matters treated in the classic work *Ma'avar Yaboq* (Crossing of the Jabbok) by Rabbi

Modena in 1626.[24] In both of these analogous cases, we find religious creativity in the new area of handling the dead by developing religious practices rather than by theological speculation and spirituality.[25] Against the background of the changes in the Jewish community and its surroundings, the need arose to give shape to death and to give it a set of ritual patterns. More than three hundred years ago, for the first time a coherent model of proper death was presented, which does not relate only to the stage of mourning, as had been the case in the past, since the Bible and the Talmud. Rather it relates to the very moment of dying and to the first minutes afterward, until burial.[26] ZAKA presents a new model of proper dying, adapted to the circumstances of the 2000s. Below I present outstanding examples of religious innovation by means of the ritualization of Jewish violent death.

## Two Chapters in the New Halakha: Purity and Goyim

The connection between death and ritual impurity is familiar to scholars of religion. In the ancient sources of Judaism ritual impurity, particularly the impurity of death, is discussed at length. Several passages in the Bible treat matters of purity and impurity,[27] and the Mishnah devotes an entire order, *Taharot* (Purities), to the subject, the largest of the six. The Jewish religion distinguishes among several degrees of impurity, the most serious of which—"the father of the fathers of impurity"—is the impurity of death, which is conveyed by a human corpse or the body of a dead animal, and it is transmitted not only by contact with the body but by contact with even a tiny part of the body, and also, indirectly, even by the shadow of the tent in which the body was laid.[28] Against this background it is surprising to find that in ZAKA interest in the issue of impurity is largely secondary. Obsessive concern with purity and impurity, which would be expected in an organization entirely occupied with death, is conspicuously absent. Occasionally one sees signs indicating a blasé attitude toward these questions.

ZAKA activists who go to the ritual bath upon returning from the arena of terrorist attacks take care to explain that they do not immerse themselves for the sake of ritual purity but to detach their souls from the horrific experience. As they say, purifying the body is merely optional, but it is impossible to go on without purifying the soul.[29] Sometimes the volunteers do not even wash their hands after a death incident (whereas they make certain to wash their hands after a funeral, in which they didn't touch the body).[30] ZAKA volunteers relate with a hint of mockery to the Lithuanians (even those who are not of priestly lineage) who are strict with themselves and refrain from entering cemeteries to visit the graves of their relatives. Very few people attended a lecture on ritual purity organized by the ZAKA rabbis, mainly out of a sense of obligation and courtesy. In an only partially apologetic tone, they maintain that, while one should not ignore the commandments relating to the impurity of the dead, the commandment to honor the dead is so much more important that it overrides the former.

The trivialization of the impurity of the dead in ZAKA discourse and practice can be explained in the context of developments within rabbinical Judaism that partake of Orthodox and ultra-Orthodox characteristics in recent generations. The turning point apparently occurred between the sixth and eighth centuries, and it is evident in the Babylonian Talmud, which was written after the completion of the Mishnah, and today it is the central text in the Haredi world of Torah. The Talmud's treatment of the laws of ritual purity and impurity, aside from the question of menstruation, is quite minor. These laws were of pivotal importance while the Temple stood and the priestly service took place. After the destruction of the Temple and the exile, animal sacrifice was replaced by other forms of worship, and gradually, over more than a thousand years, the question of impurity and purity lost its urgency and was relegated to the margins of the believers' consciousness.[31] It is still a current issue of relevance only with regard to sexual relations and the status of women, and, to a lesser degree, regarding the prohibition, which applies only to men of priestly descent, against approaching the dead. Sensitivity to the issue of ritual impurity today is also reduced by the fact that, according to the traditional view, in any event all Jews are ritually impure, since it is inconceivable that they never encountered dead people, even if they never entered a cemetery, for example, without being aware of it, when they entered a hospital. According to the halakha, immersion in a ritual bath is insufficient for purification, which can only be accomplished by the ritual of the Red Heifer: sprinkling of water mixed with the ashes of a cow without even a single hair that wasn't red. In other words, only a genetic miracle or complete redemption can make it possible to overcome the impurity of the dead.[32] At the conclusion of a stormy disagreement, it was ruled in halakha that even retaining the impurity of the dead was not prohibited. On the contrary, it was a great honor to carry the bier during a funeral, and, in general, to handle a corpse for the sake of respecting it. The ZAKA volunteers, who observe halakha, are free of inhibitions regarding physical contact with bodies.

*

In the ordinary cases of death with which they deal, the ZAKA volunteers act according to the dictates of traditional death books such as *Gesher heḥayim* (Bridge of Life) . They obey the precepts, according to which, for example, even a tiny bit of dead flesh, "which is squashed and has turned to phlegm," conveys impurity, whereas the fingernail, hair, or tooth of a dead person does not convey impurity. In contrast, in the arena of terrorism, the ZAKA rabbis and volunteers apply different rules of impurity. Because "in their death, *tsadikim* are called living,"[33] the Jewish victims of attacks by gentiles are not infected with impurity. Therefore, those who handle their bodies do not have to purify themselves at all. Sanctity spreads and is transmitted like impurity, and the blood can serve as a medium to spread sanctity. In some cases, blood has the potential to sanctify and purify possible impurity. Just as the blood of the sacrificial animal on the altar in the temple sanctified the priest, so, too, the blood of the sacrificial victim in the arena of the explosion in the bus or café sanctifies the Haredi volunteers.

ZAKA's perspective on the issue of purity and impurity at the arena reaches a peak, which is the absolute opposite of the ordinary order of things. According to several volunteers, not only must one not purify oneself after contact with the victims of terrorism, but one must purify oneself *before* contact with these bodies. A veteran activist in the organization explained, "Just as before the funeral of great rabbis, a car passes through the Haredi neighborhoods of Jerusalem and announces over a loudspeaker that someone who hasn't immersed himself must not approach the bier, I fantasize that five minutes before every terrorist attack, the heavens open and a voice will announce what is about to happen, and this will enable us to purify ourselves hastily, lest we contaminate the bodies of the holy people scattered at the site of the explosion."

*

In ZAKA's religious culture, the impurity of gentiles that necessitates keeping a distance and separating from them plays a larger role than the impurity of the dead that relates primarily to priests and their descendants.

ZAKA's conception of non-Jews is influenced by Jewish mysticism. A statement in the Mishnah expresses God's unconditional love for all human beings: "Beloved is man, for he was created in God's image" (Avot 3:17). But this was interpreted by several leading rabbis as referring to Jews only. In the sixteenth century, Rabbi Judah Loew of Prague argued, "Though it says

'Beloved is man' this does not include all of mankind, because the sages said 'You are called man and gentiles are not called man.'" ZAKA activists paraphrase such quotations in modern Hebrew slang. Some Haredi volunteers are inspired by the neo-kabbalistic ideas of Rabbi Yitzchak Ginsburgh. Advocating a religious doctrine linked to an extreme radical right-wing geopolitical agenda, he encourages Jewish settlement in the West Bank even if it severely infringes on the basic rights of local Arabs. Furthermore, he promotes a campaign of vengeance against the Palestinians. The charismatic, American-born Ginsburgh, who became religious in his youth and later turned into a follower of Lubavitch Hasidism, upholds the distinction "between blood and blood" (i.e., between Arab and Jewish blood). In his view, Jews differ from Arabs not only spiritually but biologically as well. Many ZAKA volunteers adhere to this quasi-genetic racist mystical theology. Such teachings partly explain the alarm evinced by ZAKA volunteers when they see Jewish and gentile blood mixing at a bombing site.

ZAKA's halakha maintains the Jewish traditional attitude toward gentiles—"non-Jews," "strangers," "nations of the world" in the terminology of the Haredi volunteers—applied to the unique historical circumstances of the present-day Middle East conflict. The point of departure is typically Haredi: between Jews and gentiles there is an abyss and a hierarchical relationship. Jews are chosen, superior, and holy. Contact with others is subject to severe taboo restrictions. The separation from gentiles, which must be maintained in life, must also be maintained in death. Just as a gentile is impure while alive, a fortiori he is impure while dead. However, gentiles do not convey the impurity of death. Among the rabbis a dispute has developed. Some argue that the impurity of a dead gentile is less than that of a dead Jew, who, while alive, was far more holy. Therefore, they ruled that contact with the corpse of a gentile conveys impurity but being in a room with it does not. There are other halakhic disputes, such as whether it is permissible to "benefit" from a gentile corpse (by using its hair, for example), unlike the corpse of a Jew. In general, the ZAKA rabbis ruled that it is worthy to honor the gentile dead, both because they, too, were created in the image of God, and because of "the ways of peace." This reason expresses reluctance to arouse the antagonism of the world against the Jews, reluctance that developed over hundreds of years of exile as a minority that suffered from dependence, discrimination, and persecution, and apprehension lest Israel might be accused of racism. In the public announcements of the heads of ZAKA, they emphasize that the body of a gentile, including that of the suicide terrorist, deserves respectful treatment as much as that of a Jew. In fact, observations show that the relation to the corpses is differential, as reflected in specific halakhic rulings. The ZAKA rabbis have collected old precedents and repeat them emphatically. Several examples follow.

If a Jew dies, and he has lost no blood—for example, if he froze to death, drowned, or choked to death—his body is purified, and he is buried in a shroud, as if his death was natural. But if he was drowned or strangled by a gentile, he is buried in his clothing (as if his blood had been shed). ZAKA relates to the gentile as other, even if he is neither the aggressor nor the victim. A man who is uncircumcised is forbidden to touch the bier of a dead Jew, lest the divine presence depart from the body. They quote medieval religious works from Central Europe and from a book of the dead from the sixteenth century, stating that it is forbidden to allow a gentile even to look at the body of a Jew laid in his grave, so that he won't contaminate it with his impurity, just as it is forbidden to allow a gentile to look at a Torah scroll standing in a Holy Ark, so as not to impair its sanctity.[34] The ZAKA rabbis add, bringing the ruling up to date, that one must be careful not to let a gentile handle a Jewish body. Thus, the driver of the vehicle that transports the body must observe the Torah commandments, and if this is impossible, then a religious Jew must at least sit in the vehicle.

Once a hypothetical question arose in a ZAKA deliberation: How were they to act at a terrorist incident that began on Shabbat, and it is known that all the victims are non-Jews? Whereas on the weekdays there is no obstacle to removing them, this is not self-evident on the Sabbath. The question is moot, since in Israel, it is most likely that non-Jews would be a minority of the victims. This was indeed the case in more than one incident when tourists or foreign workers (who are often in places liable to be attacked by terrorism, such as markets and public transportation) were struck. As mentioned earlier, in the course of their work with the dead, the volunteers are concerned with the religious and national identity of the casualty.[35]

A halakhic ruling was needed regarding use of the services of non-Jews as Sabbath goys for removing bodies from the arena on the holy day, when Jews are commanded to refrain from all work. While the rabbis granted permission to the faithful for the purposes of saving a life (e.g., boiling water on the Sabbath for a person who is mortally ill), they always feared that it might be used for purposes that are not vital, thus marring the sanctity of the Sabbath. There were many doubtful cases, such as whether it was permissible to make a business transaction on the Sabbath, if it was vital for the livelihood of the community. The halakhic decisors tried not to expand the loopholes in the law, but on various occasions lenient interpretations were given. The ZAKA rabbis also struggled with this dilemma. They did not disagree as to whether it was permitted to employ a gentile to save lives, but what about doing so for the sake of respect for the dead?

In the following instance, no opposition, not even any apologetic contortions were expressed regarding the employment of a Sabbath goy by ZAKA. On the day of rest, it was discovered that a popular baby formula was poisonous.[36] An emergency announcement about the danger of poisoning was transmitted to the Israeli public on all the radio and television networks. However, the Haredim are not exposed to the media on the Sabbath. ZAKA took it upon itself to drive back and forth in the streets of ultra-Orthodox neighborhoods and warn mothers with an announcement over loudspeakers. The ZAKA ambulance drivers who were employed for this emergency initiative were local Arabs.

The ZAKA rabbis ruled that it is permitted to ask a gentile to move a corpse on the Sabbath, if this is necessary for preserving respect for the dead.[37] For such purposes ZAKA maintains a reserve of non-Jews who are instructed and prepared to be employed on Sabbaths and holidays. In addition, ZAKA considered the idea of enlisting Bedouin Muslims from the south and Druze from the north as permanent volunteers to handle the bodies of their coreligionists according to their customs. They added that, in cases of need, they could also handle Jewish bodies, so long as they observed the directives of halakhic authorities.[38] Once I heard an important Haredi rabbi state that not only was it permitted for ZAKA to go to the arena of a terrorist attack on the Sabbath, but it was in fact a religious duty (saving lives and respecting the dead). Hence, given the choice between using the services of a Jew or a non-Jew for this purpose, preference should be given to a Jew, so that he can gain the merit of performing this important commandment.

## Sabbath Challah Bread

The Maḥane Yehuda produce market in Jerusalem was attacked by Palestinian terrorism several times, including what is known as "the double attack," one of the earliest and most murderous incidents dealt with by the Haredi volunteers (July 1997).[39] However, in ZAKA's collective memory another attack that took place there stands out, though it was nearly swallowed up in the series of Intifada attacks. This was the attack at a bus stop opposite the door of a bakery, which took place on Friday afternoon, soon before the entry of the Sabbath (April 2002).[40] This event made a unique impression because not only did it pose an operational and mental challenge to ZAKA, but for the first time it also raised fundamental religious questions, requiring serious discussion and a difficult decision regarding ethical and halakhic issues.

The rescue teams and police squads, along with ZAKA volunteers, had to act in the confusion of collapsed buildings, overturned stalls, piles of smashed fruits and vegetables, torn shopping bags, and, in the midst of all this, corpses and body parts. Minutes passed, the medical assistance to the wounded and their evacuation to hospitals took a long time, and the secular week was over. When the holy Sabbath entered, the handling of the bodies had just begun. The volunteers were stuck in a situation they had often imagined but never experienced: the need to finish the holy work of gathering the bodies, identifying them, and removing them during the holy day, when labor is forbidden by the Torah. The ZAKA men were permitted to violate the Sabbath to save lives, but how could they honor both the sanctity of the Sabbath and the dead, who lay in the arena? The volunteers were confronted by a contradiction between two central values in their religion. The rabbis accompanying them in the arena provided partial solutions on the spot. It was permissible to use ambulances to transport the bodies to the pathological institute, if they made certain the drivers weren't Jewish. But the burning question remained unanswered: How were they to move the bodies and their parts from the ruined and blocked-off site of the explosion to the parked ambulances? Upon consultation with the rabbis a solution was found that applied traditional rulings to the given situation.

Almost no discussion of this subject fails to begin with reference to an ancient precedent taken from a rabbinical interpretation of the Bible. According to legend, King David died on the Sabbath. His body was exposed in the city square, and the sages of the Talmud debated whether it would have been permitted to move it to protect it from public humiliation, because of decomposition in the sun, and from dogs that approached it and threatened to lick it.[41] They ruled that the body must not be moved until the departure of the Sabbath. One Mishnaic Sage said of this, "For [the sake of] a living one-day-old infant, one violates the Sabbath; for [the sake of] David, the King of Israel, [after his death] one does not violate the Sabbath."[42] It is generally accepted in Jewish law that a corpse has the status of *muqtse*, an object one is not permitted to handle on the Sabbath (*tiltul*), in that it cannot be used on the Sabbath, like money, key, or stone. This is a severe prohibition, derived from the Torah, but the rabbis modified it and ruled that if one places something that may be handled on the Sabbath, such as a loaf of bread, or an infant(!), next to the dead person, it is permissible to move the body on the Sabbath. The rabbis added that placing a bag of candies or a pair of clean gloves on bodies is accepted too. Moreover, it is permissible to place objects on a base such as a tray or a plate, which one may or may not be permitted to move, depending on the object placed on it. A stretcher is such a base and can be moved if what is on it is not *muqtse*. The blown-up bakery in the Maḥane Yehuda market provided a ready supply of such permitted items, particularly scattered loaves of challah, the special bread of the Sabbath. The ZAKA rabbis consulted halakhic precedents and issued an ad hoc ruling: the challot were to be placed on the stretchers, which served as a base, preferably before the entry of the Sabbath. Then, even when the Sabbath was already in, they pushed bodies and body parts onto the stretchers, and it was permitted to pick them up.

Following this event ZAKA's Council of Rabbis was established. This is one reason why many members of the organization view this bombing as a milestone in ZAKA history. Work at this site on the Sabbath, under rabbinic sanction, was a particularly potent experience. What felt like a crossing of sacred boundaries was an unsettling experience and yet—as the volunteers could hardly deny—also an exhilarating one. Other attacks that occurred on the Sabbath are recorded in the organization's sacred history.[43] I documented the treatment of a body that had been burned on the Sabbath (December 2008). The head of the ZAKA team in Jerusalem brought his son with him and summoned his neighbors, and together, still wearing their Sabbath clothing, they went through the streets of Jerusalem on foot, from the center of the city to the funeral center, which is on its outskirts, bearing the stretcher with the body and a loaf of bread on it.

*

From the story of Creation to the explicit directives in the Ten Commandments, the Bible reiterates the idea of the sanctity of the Sabbath and its observance, and it is emphasized again in the Prophets, the Talmud, and halakha. According to the Torah, a person who violates the Sabbath is to be stoned. The ZAKA rabbis, like the rest of the ultra-Orthodox community, are zealous about the Sabbath. The ultimate importance of keeping the Sabbath is tested when it conflicts with another important Jewish value. The highest of the values that compete with observing the Sabbath is that of preserving the life of a person who is in danger (*piquaḥ nefesh*). In the Jewish legacy, since ancient times, no one has challenged the ruling that preserving a person's life overrides observing the Sabbath.

When a person's life is in danger, not only is he permitted, along with those who are helping him, to violate the laws of refraining from work on the Sabbath, but they are even required to do so (Leviticus 19:16). The commandment to save lives is so strong that even a doubtful case of danger to life requires violating the Sabbath. Not only that, on the Sabbath one is required to answer a summons to save a life without waiting for authoritative rabbinical sanction. On the contrary, "he who asks [i.e., consults a rabbi] is a spiller of blood."

The era of terrorism in the present-day State of Israel gives the laws of saving life greater urgency. The organization's rabbis demand of the volunteers that they must be expert in the halakhot of saving lives, and they constantly repeat certain passages to the activists such as the order of priorities in saving lives (e.g., men take precedence over women because they are holier, in that they are obligated by all of the commandments). They are in full agreement that they must save every Jew, even if he is a heretic and a sinner, but they disagree as to how far the obligation to save a gentile goes if it entails violating the Sabbath.

ZAKA heads explain that the saving of people injured by terrorism during the Sabbath is not its violation. Rather, it sanctifies the Sabbath. They add that suspending the Sabbath to save lives is not a liberal halakhic ruling that makes allowances, but rather it is a permission that is a commandment whose gravity must not be underestimated. The ZAKA men declare, "We are not lenient in observing the halakhot of the Sabbath; we are strict in observing the halakhot of saving lives."

Halakhic rulings giving preference to the saving of life over observing the Sabbath were routine among the Orthodox and ultra-Orthodox, but their practical consequences were generally limited to several common test cases, such as the permission to drive a woman in labor to the hospital on the Sabbath. In the present generation, the variety of cases in which this halakha is applied has grown. This is conspicuous with respect to rabbinical rulings regarding military operations that are defined as defending the lives of Israelis. Religious Zionists lead in the increasing tendency to cite the principle that saving lives takes precedence over the Sabbath, and this is mainly in relation to public security. Only in recent years has the rabbinical principle that saving lives overrides the Sabbath appeared in the Haredi world to its full extent. ZAKA, mounted on the waves of terrorism, is the central agent for introducing this explosive halakha in the Haredi world.

The collision of the ideal of the Sabbath and the ideal of respect for the dead is less familiar, clear, and agreed upon. This is the halakhic dilemma with which ZAKA especially wrestles. Here the hierarchy of values is equivocal and requires fundamental clarification, which ZAKA advances.

ZAKA activists, accompanied by rabbis, have been summoned to a mass terrorism attack on a Sabbath. First, they devote themselves to giving medical aid to the wounded and evacuating them quickly to hospitals. It can happen that, while the Haredi volunteers are in place at the arena and serving as paramedics, one of the wounded passes away. They immediately cease treating him, just as they ignore handling the death of the other victims, whose bodies lie around them. They are even forbidden to close his eyes.

ZAKA circulates a leaflet among the activists entitled "Treatment of the Dead on the Sabbath—Forbidden, Permitted, and Obligatory." The first ruling states that in principle handling of the dead does not override the Sabbath. It points out that "to respect the dead is not to desecrate the Sabbath," meaning that violating the Sabbath to handle the dead in fact is contemptuous of them. They go on to quote "the greatest halakhic authority of the generation," Rabbi Elyashiv, who ruled that the Sabbath is so holy that during it one may not even employ a gentile to handle the dead. The introduction to this compilation of rulings acknowledges the natural inclination that impels people to act for the sake of respect for the dead, especially at the time of great excitement following a terrorist attack. Therefore, they saw fit to caution the volunteers once again regarding possible desecration of the Sabbath.

The ZAKA rabbis review the Halakhot regarding the handling of death at the site of an explosion that took place on the Sabbath. Unlike cases of saving lives, for the honor of the dead it is forbidden to use walkie-talkies and cell phones. If there is a possibility of saving lives, it is permitted to leave the walkie-talkies and phones on, so they can receive messages, but it is forbidden to answer calls, and one must not hold the devices in one's hand. It is permitted to ride to the arena, where the victims lie, only if the driver is a gentile, and only within the "Sabbath area."[44] It is permitted to go there on foot or to ride on a bicycle, so long as no use is made of the headlight or the bell.[45] It is permitted to bring plastic bags to the arena, to collect the bodies, and gloves, but it is forbidden to bring a trowel there, a vital tool for ZAKA's work. They can close body bags with string, on condition that it was cut on a weekday and a slipknot was prepared. In identifying the bodies, it is forbidden to write anything down. At the request of the police, it is permitted to collect valuables if an authorized rabbi determines that they are vital for identification, but they can only be picked up by pushing them from the side. Scattered body parts must not be carried, only covered. But if exposing them is liable to make the dead person's relatives faint, it is permitted to place them in a bag. Bodies may only be moved by rolling them, pushing them with the back of the hand.

A ZAKA activist is permitted to ride to the site of the attack on the Sabbath if he is an authorized medic and it may be assumed that some of the victims will be alive, for then it is a case of saving lives. Once he is at the site, he can turn to handling of the dead. It is permitted to move a body only if there is fear of its desecration. It is only permitted to move a body under special circumstances that might cause harm to it, such as a fire that threatens to burn it. While there is disagreement regarding the treatment of the Jewish victims of terrorism on the Sabbath, everyone agrees about treatment of the body of the suicide terrorist: if the ISA must identify it in order to prevent further attacks, the body must be removed immediately, also on the Sabbath. Still, volunteers ask: Do the instructions applying to corpses also apply to body parts?

Halakhot pertaining to terrorism became a trademark of ZAKA and guided the organization's actions in the arenas of death, while they continued to develop. The rabbis consider further issues, and the volunteers pose further questions. Here is the ruling of the head of the ZAKA rabbinical council in response to a question raised by a volunteer from Beersheba, who returned home close to the entry of the Sabbath after treating a body that had already decomposed, and whose smell clung to the volunteer's body. It is permissible in such a case to take a shower on the Sabbath either in cold water or in water that had been heated before the entry of the Sabbath. He could wash his hair and hairy parts of his body, preferably with liquid soap, but it was forbidden to wring out the wet hair.

In certain situations, the question of respect for the dead touches upon the saving of lives. This is the case regarding the permission to remove corpses on the Sabbath because their presence might demoralize Jewish soldiers if they were exposed to the sight of the victims, which would achieve the enemy's purpose in employing terrorism.[46] The rabbis who oppose this view maintain that halakhic leniencies of this kind are precisely the true aim of the Palestinian adversary, who understands, in his cunning, that the Jews are only assured victory if they observe the Torah.

Underlying ZAKA's halakhic discussions is the assumption that current terrorism is like war. The ancient laws of warfare are applied to this situation, including rulings related to doing battle on the Sabbath. For example, according to the Talmud, one may only lay siege to a gentile city three days before the Sabbath, and if a battle has already begun, one does not stop fighting when the Sabbath enters. This was done when Joshua conquered Jericho. Therefore, it might also be permissible to deal with the victims of terrorism on the Sabbath if it was begun beforehand. Pronouncements of this kind by rabbis do not get by without doubts and criticism. The main apprehension is that defining the situation as a state of war might create an atmosphere of holy emergency, and that in the excitement of performing important commandments, the framework of halakha might break down.[47]

The ZAKA rabbis are very apprehensive about authorizing sweeping halakhic permission in the Haredi response to terrorist attacks, especially on the Sabbath. As a countermeasure they implore the ZAKA activists to make certain to employ a religious mechanism known as *shinui* (change). This is a kind of halakhic niche used in response to urgent needs requiring actions forbidden on the Sabbath. A *shinui* is the performance of a routine action, which is normally forbidden on the Sabbath, in a clearly unusual way. For example, if a right-handed person may use his left hand, despite the awkwardness, to heat water to heal a deathly sick person. A familiar *shinui* is touching an object with the back of one's hand rather than the palm. The halakha permits certain actions, if they are vital for existence, in an unusual manner, for the purpose of bringing out the difference between weekday routine and the uniqueness of the Sabbath. *Shinui* is meant to be a reminder and to emphasize the Sabbath, making sure that the believer is aware of the halakhic prohibition and avoiding the danger that, by inertia, he might be drawn into violating the Sabbath. Like the Sabbath goy, *shinui* is a mechanism which, although recognized as valid, has an odor of Sabbath subterfuges.[48] Nevertheless, this mechanism, precisely because of its manifest arbitrariness, is a manifestation of Orthodox piety. ZAKA's versions of *shinui* are less a liberal interpretation of religious law than a sign of the seriousness with which religious law is taken and an effort to test its limits. In the arena of terrorism, on the Sabbath, ZAKA volunteers move things with their teeth and press light switches with their elbows.[49]

## The Lord is Too Great

I tried to compare ZAKA to other religious phenomena in Israel, some larger, more prominent, and more influential by far, especially Gush Emunim (the faithful bloc, the hard core of the settlers' movement in the West Bank, followers of Rabbi Kook),[50] and also to Habad (Hasidic movement faithful to the Lubavitcher Rebbe).[51] Despite their differences from each other —the one being ultra-nationalist and the other being Haredi—they have a common denominator: messianic doctrine and missionary drive. Both are crusades that promote the gospel of imminent redemption and attempt to proselytize fellow Jews. In contrary fashion, not at all self-evident, ZAKA is neither actively messianic nor missionary (beyond the standard rhetorical norms and mannerisms, sterile by nature, that characterize Orthodox Judaism in general). Furthermore, both Gush Emunim and Habad have a radical political interest, which is expressed in their efforts to impose their religious values and conservative way of life on their surroundings by means of exhortation, political and social manipulation, and, if necessary, violent coercion. By contrast, ZAKA seldom seeks to intervene in the agenda of the State of Israel, and it refrains from efforts to exert influence in the controversial area of the relations of religion and the state. ZAKA does not exploit the credit it has accrued in the arena of terrorism to advance the interests of religion or of the religious.

In contrast to ZAKA, the other two religious movements have a solid religious doctrine. Not without connection to the lack of messianic and missionary elements, ZAKA has almost no theology, and no dogma. The lack of a comprehensive, systematic, and explicit theology is surprising, considering the organization's focus on death, which usually arouses questions about the nature of God and the relations of man and God. ZAKA continues in the Jewish tradition, which, unlike other ancient traditional cultures such as Pharaonic Egypt, attributes only secondary cosmological significance to the world of the dead, and to a large degree separates it from the world of the living.[52] Theology is notable in its absence, especially since terrorist attacks cause an especially bad death, of a kind that would naturally be expected to encourage elaborate rationalization or theodicy. Only closer examination reveals that ZAKA indeed has a stratum of religious thought, which is invisible, largely because it is a way of thinking that long ago became part and parcel of normative Jewish religious life, an organic component of Orthodoxy of all shades. Perhaps a theological or mythological system will yet emerge in ZAKA, revolving around death. Meanwhile, the activists are only partially aware of the relative lack of discussion of the question of the connection between divine providence and violent death of traumatic effect. Somewhat apologetically, the Haredi volunteers explain, "We're simple Jews. God is too big for us."

This sort of statement is quite characteristic of the Haredi world. In ultra-Orthodox Judaism, of which ZAKA is an organic part, the theological and mythological dimension exists only in latent, fragmentary, and indirect fashion, and it is often denied. In ZAKA one can identify traces of a theology that once existed and have long ago faded away as well as components of a potential theology. ZAKA's religious space, devoid of theology, is filled by what the Haredim called "innocent faith." This is largely an unarticulated theology. A colleague who is an expert on contemporary Jewish thought defined it as "somewhat childish."[53]

The innovations of the organization's rabbis and volunteers are often inhibited by lack of confidence and fear of criticism. An initiative to compose a special prayer for the safety and success of ZAKA volunteers, to be recited when they enter the arenas of death, encountered resistance, and was nipped in the bud.[54] The conservatism of the Haredim, including that of ZAKA, is not expressed solely in rules of behavior (the halakhot, which are constantly issued and pile up, are not regarded as innovative, but as implementation of the ancient normative system), but also and mainly in belief. At the focus of this religious conservatism stands innocent faith, which in recent years has become not only the standard but also an ideal. It is emotional, instinctive, and anti-intellectual. It is simple, if not to say simplistic faith, free of all reflective thought and without metaphysical arguments. In ZAKA and among other Haredim, there is no inquisitive examination that seeks to understand and find a basis for the principles of faith, nor is there a methodical and consolidated formulation of the belief. Religious creativity specializes in expanding the halakha, commentary on the Torah, and ethics.

Simple faith opposes itself to informed faith, which was once important for apologetics in response to the external challenges to Judaism, while today it is seen as superfluous and even dangerous, since it is liable to lead to thoughts with a kernel of heresy. In medieval times, an impressive effort was made to place faith on the foundations of Jewish philosophy, but since the end of the Middle Ages faith found a broader basis in the competitor of philosophy, Jewish mysticism (Kabballah), whose influence on Jewish life is seen in prayer and in customs, including the customs of burial and mourning. With the modernization of Judaism, the status of Kabballah, which had been a kind of substitute for theology, declined, and its place was taken by innocent faith, which asks no questions, and which does not strive to understand what is beyond it. Rather, it is based on a priori acceptance of the laws of the Torah as interpreted by the rabbis. Cleaving to halakha requires neither logic nor explanation, and it is connected to loyalty to a closed group and to subservience to the law and to charismatic authorities. The Torah is embodied in the rabbinate and the community, and this is their faith in a nutshell. The Torah, not God, is central to the religion of the Haredi volunteers,[55] and in place of heaven there is obedience to halakha and insistence of customs, what they call *yiddishkait*.

The simple believers eschew philosophizing, and they are rather impatient with deep and nuanced religious rationalizations. ZAKA volunteers usually are satisfied with the bottom line, with a practical directive—what should be done, precisely and in brief. The volunteers are obsessively preoccupied with the concrete, applied aspect of the commandments, while the rabbis try to nourish them with some of the reasons for these commandments (*ta'amei hamitsvot*). For this purpose, they are constrained to touch upon esoteric literature to some extent, as well as legendary, mytho-historical literature. Kabballah and Aggada (rabbinical tales), at whose heart is myth, gives vitality to the dry halakha, and they offer justifications for customs that sometimes seem arbitrary and odd. The more learned of the ZAKA activists admit that "Kabballah is in the air" of the organization.[56]

From here and there ZAKA people pick up some Kabballah and Aggada to convince themselves of the logic of the customs and halakha. Here is one example: corpses must be removed with their legs facing forward, and if they are placed in a room, they should face the entrance, and if there is no opening to the outside, they should face Jerusalem. All of this is done so that they will be ready for the resurrection of the dead, to rise and be redeemed in Zion. Here is a second example: the volunteers are ordered to open the hands of the corpses lying in the arena awaiting removal. The reason for this custom is given in a Midrash: "When a person comes into the world, his fists are clenched, as though to say, 'the whole world is mine. I inherit it.' And when he leaves this world, his hands are open, as though to say, 'I did not inherit anything from this world.'"[57] The rabbis quote an ancient ruling, which permitted the opening of a sealed grave to open the hands of the dead person, which had remained closed because of negligence.

The ZAKA activists manage to maneuver and function effectively with an abundance of halakha and a paucity of theology. The volunteers can permit themselves to avoid going deeply into the ideas behind the commandments, because they are always accompanied by rabbis and learned scholars, even in the arena. However, on several occasions I had the feeling that they presented themselves as knowing less about the foundations of the halakhot and customs than they actually did. Once I found they were trying to conceal ostensibly sensitive quasi-theological information from me, and another time they confessed to me that they didn't want to share esoteric material with me. The Haredi volunteers are more ritualistic than propagandistic.[58] Unlike other priests of death, such as the Hindu Aghori, they do not accompany their conduct in the arena with explanations of their peculiar acts concerning life and death. Except for a few erudite scholars, the ZAKA activists are quite ignorant. In any event, they are not eager to offer explanations of the rituals that seem irrational, and when they are asked directly to provide an explanation for the precise and fastidious rituals, they answer laconically, "That's the custom" or "That's what's written." Sometimes they admit that they can't offer an answer and in fact do not tend to raise questions, without embarrassment.

Underlying ZAKA's substitute for theology are two elements: one is relatively elitist, Kabbalistic mysticism and casuistic Midrashim; the other is popular folktales. The elements with theological potential, which touch on Kabballah, as superficial and random as they may be, put off the heads of ZAKA, because they arouse the explosive theological potential concealed behind the mysteries of the divinity, and similarly it is feared that outsiders might see the organization as misguided by superstition. At an early stage of the organization's development, some volunteers lit candles next to the bodies while they were removed from the arena. The heads of ZAKA intervened and forbade the practice, when they realized it was decidedly inspired by a kabbalistic tradition.[59] Suppression of the instinct of curiosity and the desire for religious understanding is supported by invoking fear of the evil eye. Volunteers have addressed a question of the head of the rabbinical council: Is it wrong to study the laws that deal with violent death? The answer is self-contradictory, reassuring, and also anxiety-provoking.[60] While it states that one is obligated to be expert in the halakhot and customs that guide behavior in the arena of death, it also presents an anecdote about an admired rabbi who was asked to answer questions about death, which were sent by his son-in-law. When he saw the letter, he took it as a bad omen. Sure enough, immediately afterward he was told that his mother had died.[61]

## Ghosts

According to anthropological intuition, the abundance of directives and regulations in any area betrays social tension. However, such a normative and juridical concentration is hardly self-sustaining. It requires support from another cultural system to supply relief from the burden of laws and demands and provide meaning to them. Given the profusion of rabbinical rulings determining the management of violent death in the arenas to which ZAKA is called, Jewish mysticism plays the requisite auxiliary role. As a necessary support for halakha, Kabballah, even a rather vulgar version of it, offers the volunteers a web of meaning that helps them cope with the horrors of death in terrorism and decomposition. The ZAKA activists who use mythical concepts taken from the Kabballah—mainly Hasidim and Mizraḥim—have no articulated mystical doctrine. Alongside the Haredi, and especially the ZAKA tendency to reject grand theological systems, they unthinkingly adopt an incoherent assortment of symbols, formulas, and stories of a mystical nature. Mystical-messianic elements have been unreflectively and gradually absorbed into prayers and ritual so that the volunteers are not necessarily conscious of their kabbalistic character and origin. ZAKA's mystical theology is not a whole corpus of Kabballah laid out in texts. Rather, it is a popularized assemblage of general, vague ideas plucked from their context and ever changing, and it is treated largely in a reflexive, nonchalant manner. Most of the volunteers draw it from secondary or tertiary sources, randomly. Very few of them have read, even at an elementary level, the Zohar (the classic mystical text, of the thirteenth century), or the writings related to Isaac Luria (the central sixteenth-century kabbalist). Nor have they studied deeply the Jewish literature of death, which was considerably influenced by Kabballah, such as *Ma'avar yaboq* (seventeenth century).[62]

Most of the mystical Jewish ideas pertaining to death are conventions within Haredi society. For example, the dead, especially the *tsadikim* among them, are seen as living: having consciousness, senses, will, and the ability to communicate.[63] Below I discuss a selection of beliefs and practices inspired by the Kabballah that are connected to unnatural death and are fostered by ZAKA. For example, the physical state of the corpse is seen as an index of the moral stature of the deceased. The teeth of time do not affect the bodies of the righteous.[64] Bacteria, worms, and rodents do not injure them (similarly, in Muslim belief, the body of a Palestinian *shahid* gives off the fragrance of roses years after its burial). According to holy sources, certain habits, such as eating persimmons during one's lifetime, assure preservation of one's corpse, but they will not work for people who were not holy in their lives or who did not sanctify themselves in death.[65] ZAKA's collective memory maintains instances of corpses that were preserved because of the sanctity of the deceased. Another example is justification of the need to reassemble the body parts of the victims of terrorism. Bringing the dead to burial in identifiable and integral form helps guarantee that, when redemption comes and along with it the promised resurrection of the dead, the souls of the dead will be able to reoccupy their former bodies.

The Jewish tradition has much to say about the relation between the human body—living or dead—and the soul.[66] ZAKA is preoccupied with the soul of the dead in the most palpable way, while the dead are lying before them. Many Haredi volunteers report a truly physical feeling of the presence of the souls of the dead, which hover near the bodies. While they lean over the body, the soul, which has just left it, touches them. Sometimes it helps them stuff a large limb into a plastic sack, and sometimes it grabs the volunteer's arm to stop him when it seems he has behaved rudely toward a piece of flesh. The victim's body, and mainly his soul, also serves as a medium, an intermediary in the dialogue between the volunteer and God. While handling death in the arena, they speak about the souls and to the souls. The ZAKA activists agree that at the moment of death, the soul leaves the body but stays near it for some time. They disagree about what the soul undergoes in the following moments: some believe that it rushes up to the higher worlds; others believe that it remains near the place of death to make sure the body is properly treated. Some ZAKA rabbis, influenced by the Kabballah, state that, with physical death, the soul does not leave the body all at once. Rather, it remains during the week of mourning, and then for the entire month of bereavement, until the end of the year of mourning. They add in a whisper that during the first year after death, the soul ascends and descends without rest, and also, during thirty days before physical death part of the soul begins to leave very slowly, and while this is happening a person utters comments that betray certain awareness of imminent death. According to a different version, in standard death the soul leaves the body gradually while in a death inflicted by terrorists the soul ascends to heaven in one fell swoop. In a branch of ZAKA in the southern periphery, the team broke up because of contradictory views of the soul's behavior.[67]

The soul of the deceased sees, feels, and scrupulously examines the volunteers' relation to its body. Sometimes it is experienced as protecting those who handle the body and sometimes they are afraid of its ability to harm them. The soul's relation to the people treating the body, from which it has flown up but not abandoned, is in response to the handlers' relation to the body. ZAKA volunteers believe that when they die, they will be received in heaven not only by the Holy One and His retinue of angels but also by the long series of dead souls that departed from the bodies they handled. If they didn't collect all the body parts, the soul will testify to that. If they respected the body, the soul will be a *melits yosher* (sponsor) for the volunteer, who stands before the heavenly tribunal. It is believed that the most effective sponsors are the victims of terrorism, who are particularly holy. The volunteers report that the thought about the role the soul will play with respect to their future passes through their minds while they are handling the body. One ZAKA veteran put it this way: "The dead we took care of in the past will take care of us in the future." Every volunteer has "his own" dead that "envelops him" in this world and in the world to come.

*

While the more rationalistic of the ZAKA volunteers speak about the soul, other volunteers speak about ghosts and demons.[68] The volunteers use many other parallel terms, such as *mezikin* (harmful), *ḥitsonim* (aliens), and other malicious spirits found in the arsenal of Jewish mythology.[69] It is commonly believed that until burial vigilance is necessary to protect the dead from such creatures. The demons in ZAKA's repertoire of associations sometimes appear in the volunteers' imagination as Palestinian suicide terrorists as well.

The world of the dead arouses ghosts and demons and brings them to the world of the living.[70] Ghosts and demons are particularly attracted to the situation represented by the arena of horrific death: liminality, an experience of being on the edge, betwixt and between. Those who deal with the bodies of the victims of terrorism, accidents, or decomposition are confronted with a particularly vulnerable and explosive situation between this world and the world to come, between the closing of the eyes and burial, between physical death and ceremonial, social death. The soul has already left the body, but it has not yet reached heaven. This is the time for the ghosts and demons to attack. The ghosts and demons are especially attracted to the orifices of the body, through which they can penetrate it. In addition to the mouth, the eyes, and the other members of the corpse that are exposed to penetration of evil powers,[71] the arena is full of mutilated bodies and severed limbs that invite penetration. Wounds that penetrate the body and especially blood, which is neither part of the body nor external to it, are especially attractive to the dangerous entities.[72] This is the reason for a ritual that ZAKA performs in the arena: the closing of orifices, the covering of wounds, reassembling limbs, gathering and rejoining body parts, collecting the blood. This is another reason for prompt burial.

According to the belief that ZAKA adopted, the corpse is a pure vessel that was emptied and thus became available for the entry of malicious spirits, who seek to appropriate the small amount of sanctity that remains in it. They compare the body lying in the arena to a honey barrel, which, even after it has been emptied, retains its sticky sweetness, and insects and vermin rush in to suck on it. There is another reason for the spirits' desire for the dead body, which motivates the forces of impurity. According to Kabballah, no bodies were created for them. Therefore, they strive "to complete their creation."

The head of the ZAKA rabbinical council explains to the volunteers that if they are not meticulous in honoring the dead, the evil spirits that manage to penetrate the body are liable to pollute the relatives of the deceased and mainly to cling to the men who handle the corpse. The ghosts and demons detach from the dead and harm the deathworkers in the arena. ZAKA volunteers complain that sometimes ghosts come and disturb their sleep at night, and the next day they feel impure and are afraid of all kinds of disasters that might happen to them. Therefore, during the deathwork in the arena, they are doubly cautious in observing the relevant halakhot. Thus, the plague was prevented in the past,[73] and thus, in the present, they managed to prevent further terrorist attacks. The righteousness of the dead, who have the power to perform miracles and wonders, also helps in the volunteers' battle against ghosts and demons. In the world of ZAKA's imagination, the *tsadikim*, like the demons, are unwavering mythological figures who set out on a journey full of tribulations. After they have overcome temptations and trials, they incapacitate the forces of evil.

The ZAKA activists' fear of the demons that appear near the dead in the arena leads them to adopt the traditional custom of guarding the dead (*shmira*).[74] The head of the team of volunteers in the port city of Ashdod, which suffered from suicide terrorist attacks and the firing of Palestinian rockets, asked the ZAKA rabbis, "Since the men handling the bodies are very busy, is it enough just to look at the assembly point for the bodies from time to time to examine the state of the bodies?" The answer was categorically negative. A halakhic ruling was issued requiring the stationing of a ZAKA man whose sole duty would be to guard the bodies, and he would do nothing else. The reason for this was fear of desecration of the dead. Another factor with malicious potential is the gaze of gentiles, who might be near the bodies. The guard must defend the dead against this threat as well.

Some ZAKA volunteers are afraid to guard and try to evade fulfilling that duty. Others, bolder, volunteer to guard, even at night, after the arena has been cleared. The laws governing the guarding of the dead are read to them repeatedly. The bodies must be guarded by day and at night, and on the Sabbath, too. The guard must refrain from smoking, eating, and drinking, as well as from talking too much ("Lest he be drawn into a quarrel or taking the name of God in vain"). The guard should ask for mercy for the dead by reciting psalms. Because of the importance of guarding, the guard is exempt from other commandments, including prayer and putting on *tefillin*. It is preferable to station two guards, one who only is on watch, while the other studies Torah (in another room, to avoid mocking the dead). Women, too, can serve as guards. One question remains open in the halakhot of guarding the dead. It is known that the spirits of pollution "have no grip in water." Does a body placed in a boat require guarding?

*

It is difficult for those who are handling a corpse to look at its face, and it is no less difficult for the deceased. Therefore, they cover the faces of the dead in the arena, as required by the responsa of the ZAKA rabbis.[75] There are several reasons for this. First, so that the dead person will not be seen by the living in his shame, and so that he won't see the living and envy them, because they can still merit observance of the Torah. Second, it is written, "He who looks at the face of a dead person forgets what he has studied."[76] According to the Talmud, looking at the face of a dead person is one of ten things that cause difficulty in studying Torah.[77] Third, according to the Kabballah, all the sins a dead person committed during his life are written on his forehead.[78] In this state, he is exposed to the evil spirits and to his accusers, and both add to his pain.[79]

## May God Avenge Their Blood

The blood-soaked bodies of the Palestinian *shahids* are borne in mass funeral processions and buried that way.[80] Similarly, the ZAKA volunteers bury the victims of violent death in their blood-soaked clothing. Usually they go to extremes in observing this halakha, beyond the letter of the law. For example, corpses that were removed from the arena of terrorism and stripped for the purpose of identification at the National Institute of Forensic Medicine are dressed again in the clothes they were wearing when they were killed in the explosion. Furthermore, in preparing the victims of terrorism for burial purification was not performed, regardless of the condition of the body. Ordinarily bodies are washed and wrapped in white shrouds, unless they died because of loss of vital blood (*dam nefesh*), in which case the blood-soaked bodies are buried as they were found (since the blood is regarded as part of the body). In the ZAKA variant, the bodies of the holy victims are not washed, even if their death did not involve loss of blood.

I documented several reasons for refraining from the purification procedure usually required by the halakha.[81] First, whereas standard purification is performed with water, it was determined that people who died from terrorism "merited" (thus in the original) purification by fire. Singeing a body is a means of purification higher than washing. The second reason is based on the traditional belief that when the messiah comes, all the dead will appear before him and look exactly as they look when they were buried. In ZAKA it is believed that, in contrast to the sight of a cleansed body in a white shroud, which would only attract ordinary attention, the sight of a body wrapped in blood-soaked clothing will impress the messiah more, causing him to give special honor to a Jew who merited such a horrific and glorious death. "The blood on the bodies of saints will be their medal of honor at the hour of redemption."[82] Put differently by a Haredi volunteer, "The blood of saints is in itself like an explosive; it raises to heaven in a storm and arrives like Elijah right up to the Throne of Honor."

A third reason for burying the holy dead in their blood-soaked clothing refers to Ezekiel's reprimand: "That it may raise up fury and take vengeance, I have set her blood on top of a rock, that it may not be covered" (24:8). According to standard Jewish Orthodox understanding of this biblical verse, the anger that the sight of blood will arouse is the anger of the community of mourners. Haredim explain that if those killed by terrorism were to be washed, those who remain alive might see the murder as something routine, whereas direct exposure of the body whose spilled blood is conspicuous as it is buried in the grave will assure that the community will not be indifferent but will arise and demand vengeance. Even central activists in the organization are completely unaware of another stratum of meaning in the idea that blood arouses fury, whereas the ZAKA rabbis are familiar with it and state that it is the most important of all: the spilled blood is meant to arouse God's fury.

According to various ancient sacred sources, when the Jewish victims of massacre reach heaven their blood spatters and stains God's robe (*porforion*). Drop is added to drop until at last the divine garment goes sour from the blood. When that moment arrives God will no longer be able to hold back, and He will take revenge on the gentiles. In a garment red with the blood of Jews, God will go out to shed the blood of the gentiles. Then His garment will be red again, but this time with the blood of non-Jews.

By being murdered by gentiles, a Jew becomes a martyr, and martyrdom will bring about vengeance against the gentiles. In the personal prayer book of a Jew who preserved the traumatic memory of the pogrom that destroyed his community, he addresses God in the following way: "Be zealous for your great name and take vengeance before our eyes for your Torah and vengeance for the blood of your servants, shed to sanctify your name."[83] Parts of this sentence appear in an important, canonical Jewish prayer recited in the synagogue every Sabbath morning after the reading of the Torah.[84] This is one of the sources for the phrase "God will avenge his blood," frequently appearing in the Hebrew acronym "HYD" (*Hashem yinqom damo*), which for nearly a thousand years has been placed on the tombstone of every Jew murdered by gentiles. Today it is attached to the names of the victims of Palestinian terrorism in Israel. It is a kind of honorific title, and behind it lies the prayer, the wish, perhaps the promise, the taking of responsibility. The acronym "HYD" is not placed on the graves of IDF soldiers who died in battle. It is reserved for citizens who had the misfortune of being killed in a terrorist attack. Curiously, those who were killed on the battlefield, in a war in which they participated actively and consciously, are not regarded as martyrs, as opposed to innocent passengers in a bus whose death was random.[85]

Beyond the magical potential of the blood of martyrs is the theurgical effect: mysteriously the blood can influence God and make Him act. This religious mechanism touches upon the secrets of the divinity and the essence of the inner connection between man and God. A blood accounting is opened in the arena of terrorism. Every drop of the blood of Jewish martyrs is collected and registered in a heavenly account book. When the total number of drops reaches fullness and becomes intolerable, God will be aroused and begin his campaign of revenge. A reservoir of blood is gradually filled and awaits its moment. When that moment comes, it will prove that the death of the victims was not in vain. It had a purpose. The blood accounting is maintained by God, and the faithful, the volunteers who gather the drops of blood, play a vital role. Without them, without their ritual actions in the arena of death, the divine campaign of revenge cannot begin.

The ultimate revenge is blood revenge. The connection between blood and vengeance, a universal idea, appears in Jewish texts from antiquity. Judaism is obsessed with blood: the blood of the covenant of circumcision, the blood of ritual slaughter, the blood of ancient sacrifices, and menstrual blood, too, as expressed in a rich halakhic corpus devoted to these subjects. However, the connection between blood and killing is relatively thin in Jewish sources, and only recently, in present-day Israel, has it grown richer.

Blood serves in atonement and redemption. The familiar connection between blood and redemption touches upon the regenerative capacity of blood, which not only kills but also makes new life flourish. There is another, less well-known connection between blood and redemption by means of the intermediary variable: revenge. In Hebrew, blood revenge and blood redemption (*ge'ulat dam*) are synonymous. Not only does revenge redeem, but redemption avenges. There is a redemption that is preceded and preconditioned by vengeance, redemption that is combined with blood vengeance, redemption that is essentially blood revenge. So that blood may have redemptive and vengeful power, it must be pure. Therefore, in the arena of suicide terrorism, the ZAKA activists try to distance and wash away the polluted blood—the blood of the Palestinian attacker—and to isolate, gather, and bury the blood of the holy victims. The Haredi volunteers are convinced that the blood of the victims of violent death goes up to heaven, where it atones, and on various levels of awareness they acknowledge that it also avenges.

Some redemption revolves around the axis of revenge upon the gentiles. An important Jewish historian, whose work inspired these passages, called it "vengeful redemption."[86] In many prominent messianic visions throughout Jewish history, the repertoire of collective hope for a more brilliant future contains not only the people's return to its land, its Torah, its Temple, and its kingdom, but also the defeat of the gentiles, killing them, and wiping them out. This is so in Aggada, in Kabballah, in the prayers, in liturgy, in apocalyptic literature, and in belief in miracles. This is a well-known dream, the mirror image of and compensation for life as a helpless minority, discriminated against, and persecuted by the gentile surroundings because of its Jewishness. In times of Jewish distress, as in the Middle Ages, and as in the period of the Intifada, the identification of redemption with revenge, an idea that always existed but was negligible, comes to conquer the religious imagination. In difficult times the messianic age is first seen as destruction of the gentiles. Revenge, the revenge of spilled blood, is a central component in the yearning to restore order and justice to the world. The ZAKA activists confess that they are pursued by desire for revenge while they are dealing with the blood of those who died in terrorist explosions.

*

The ZAKA rabbis compare people who died in terrorism to the *harugei malkhut* (literally, "those murdered by the kingdom"). These were the ten great Torah scholars of the Second Temple period who remained faithful to their Judaism despite the Romans' decrees and were executed with extreme cruelty. According to the Talmudic legend, reiterated in an elegy recited on Yom Kippur, these martyrs were executed by the enemies of the Jews in extraordinary ways whose details are similar to horrific death from terrorism, such as turning the body into a sieve after "three hundred iron lances were plunged into it." These are the first people of whom it is said in Jewish religious texts that God will avenge their blood. Another mytho-historical precedent that appears in ZAKA's world of associations is that of sanctifying the name of God in Europe during the Crusades. In particular the trauma of the violent events that took place in Germany in 1096 is recalled. Incited Christians attacked flourishing urban Jewish centers, burned down synagogues, looted property, and massacred the faithful who refused to betray their religion. In response to the threat of forced conversion, rather than be coerced into heresy, the Jews slaughtered their wives and children and then killed themselves by burning or by the sword.[87] This Jewish response aroused amazement and admiration at the time and in succeeding generations, and to this day it is held up as an example of particularly bold martyrdom and religious faith.[88] The Haredim compare the martyrdom in the arena of Palestinian terrorism in the streets of Jerusalem during the Intifada to martyrdom in the arena of the pogroms in Mainz, Worms, and Speyer during the First Crusade. In both cases, according to the believers, the spilled blood of the sanctified victims serves as atonement and revenge. We may add that in both cases the sanctification of the victims did not escape criticism from within the community itself, though it was largely silenced.[89]

According to the official version prevalent in sacred Jewish historical documents, the medieval martyrs in Europe sought their own deaths and, by means of it, redemption and revenge. This was the conscious and purposeful suicide of particularly pious believers. In contrast, the martyrs during the Intifada in Israel probably did not wish to die or take vengeance. On the face of things, the victims were killed involuntarily, passively, and randomly. They merely went out shopping in the market or dancing in a nightclub. Many of them were not at all religious. The intention of sanctifying the name of God and the desire for revenge were attributed to them posthumously by ZAKA. In fact, perhaps in the model precedent of 1096, the dead were not trying to arouse the ire of God so he would take retribution against their persecutors. We have no full, objective, and reliable information about the medieval events that were defined as sanctification of the name. We have only elegies that were included in the religious canon, especially in the prayers for the ninth of Av. The explanation of the events in terms of sanctification of the name, which certainly glorifies them, though it is somewhat apologetic, appears only after the tragic events, when it figures in a few biased Jewish chronicles and mainly in religious poems. In both the distant and the recent past, the ones who describe and explain the events are not the dead, who testify about themselves, but those who survive, their descendants, or those who deal with their bodies. In the case of the slaughter of Jews in the present, in the arena of terrorism, it is certain that the interpretation is retroactive, attributing an intention to the victims, as though they had it initially. ZAKA alone enjoyed confidence in knowing exactly the degree to which their death was voluntary and the bus passengers' intentions before they were killed while riding on the line to the university campus in the early 2000s.

*

A leading scholar of the events of 1096 pointed out that the acts of the men who killed their children and committed suicide, the legendary sanctifiers of the name of God, as interpreted in the Jewish canon, might be seen as an effort to force God to take vengeance against the gentile murderers.[90] By spilling their own blood, they might have been trying to force God's hand into making order in the world and enforcing justice according to their view. In what is regarded as this model of faith, he finds a kernel of "political pro-test" against God's management of the world. I maintain that ZAKA's project in the arena of terrorism is a clear instance of manipulative intervention in the divine order, intended to hasten redemption and revenge. One of the organization's activists admitted to me that handling the blood of the victims of terrorism was both fulfilling a commandment and, at the same time, a gesture of chutzpah toward heaven.[91]

Collecting the blood as a provocative act intended to induce God to abandon passivity, the appearance of being reconciled to the death of Jews, and embrace murderous activism, revenge against the gentile murderers, blurs the differences and changes the relations between aggressor and victim in the scene of Middle Eastern terrorism. The first stage, defining the victims of Palestinian violence as sanctifiers of the name of God—that is, people whose spilled blood will assure redemption and revenge—changes them from simple victims to victims who are also aggressive, from victims to victimizers. Responding to death by causing death, they enter the murderous vicious cycle of terrorism. In the second stage, the ZAKA activists also become participants in a cosmic dialogue of blood and vengeance. The Haredi volunteers deal with the consequences of Palestinian aggression in the arena, and afterward they take part in the heavenly counter-aggression in store for the Palestinians.

# PART II

# THEMES IN THE ANTHROPOLOGY AND SOCIOLOGY OF ZAKA

While Part I consists of a thick description of various aspects of ZAKA, Part II offers an essentially analytic point of view on the organization. This part is an exploration and appraisal of ZAKA in a few theoretical contexts, mainly those of the sociology and anthropology of religion, the human body, death, terrorism and Judaism. It tests hypotheses related to additional fields of study like Israeli society, Middle-East conflict, myth and ritual. Each of the following chapters could be read/stand by itself/alone as an independent essay with a different conceptual center of gravity.

# 6

# Strange Pairings

## Muslim Human Bombs and Ultra-Orthodox Jews

### Lethal Embrace

At the height of the Palestinian suicide terrorism in Israel, a poster was tacked to the bulletin boards of police stations around Jerusalem. Its title was "Identifying Features of the Haredi Person." Underneath was a silhouette of a man, surrounded by legends such as "Brimmed hat or black *kippah* (skullcap)," with an arrow pointing to the appropriate item in the image. Many of the contours were easily identifiable markers of Haredi dress and grooming, such as "white shirt, never colorful or T-shirt." When an expert guest speaker presented a PowerPoint briefing for patrol officers, he called the audience's attention to those items that "only one of *us* can tell; gentiles wouldn't notice." For example, "no rings on the fingers."

The lecturer in the police station zoomed in on small details that betrayed their wearer as a counterfeiting suspect, like sneakers. Of course, the real purpose of the poster was not to identify genuine Haredim but to expose Palestinian human bombs disguised as Haredim.[1] That intention was obvious from the recommendation printed at the bottom of the poster: if a policeman suspected someone who looked like a Haredi man of being a suicide terrorist in disguise, he should ask him something about Jewish tradition, like "What is the weekly Torah portion?" Having adopted a stereotypical macho aggressive stance during his many years of service as a law-and-order agent, the lecturer added, "If we spy a 'Haredi' who doesn't sway while reading a prayerbook, he should be shot on the spot."[2]

Following a series of terrorist attacks in which the perpetrator wore Haredi clothing, the security guards stationed at bus stops in Jerusalem complained that it was hard for them to distinguish between real Haredim and men in disguise. ZAKA activists offered to stand in the bus stops themselves to help out.

*The Cult of Dismembered Limbs.* Gideon Aran, Oxford University Press. © Oxford University Press 2023.
DOI: 10.1093/oso/9780197689141.003.0006

The expertise of ZAKA's Haredi volunteers in locating disguised human bombs stands on the foundation of an ancient sacred legacy of uncovering gentiles who have masqueraded and attempted to pass as Jews, pretending to be an organic part of the Jewish community.[3] The Talmud tells of a gentile who plotted to gain access to the Temple so that he could experience what it was like to offer a sacrifice. How could he be identified? The canonical solution is identical to that proposed by local specialists in our own day who seek a way to identify human bombs. In the Talmudic story, the counterfeit Jew is asked which cut of the sacrificial animal he wishes to offer to God. Innocently, he says the fat tail of the sheep, which seems to him the choicest part, most worthy of heaven. In doing so, he reveals his ignorance, for Jews know that the sheep's tail is not acceptable as a sacrifice.[4]

The ancient gentile's effort to gain access to the Temple is parallel to that of the Palestinian human bomb to penetrate the Jerusalem pedestrian mall, the heart of Israeliness. They do it in the same way: by mimicry that enables total assimilation. ZAKA volunteers cooperate with security forces in locating them just as ancient Jews identified those who sought to infiltrate into the Temple and pollute it. They quote, "God, heathen have entered your domain and defiled your holy temple" (Psalms 79:1). According to the accepted interpretation of the Book of Numbers, the ancient Israelite priests of low rank were actually policemen who guarded the area of the sanctuary to make sure no one crossed the boundary protecting its sanctity.[5] The Haredi activists are like the priests who purified Judaism.

*

Haredim and suicide terrorists: strange bedfellows. The police poster is one of many manifestations of an intriguing linkage. This peculiar blood relation is multi-dimensional, with macabre aspects. The encounter between these committed Jews and committed Muslims offers insight into the Haredi community and Israeli society as a whole, as well as its fraught relations with its neighbors. It also has much to teach us about Palestinian culture and politics. By extension, examination of this encounter can also offer new insights into suicide terrorism in the Middle East.

The seminal event that first linked Haredim and suicide terrorists took place in 1989, on Route 1, the suicide attack on the 405 bus. From that time on, thirty years later, they have not parted. Suicide terrorism twice targeted the Haredi community itself, both times in Jerusalem: the attack in the Beit Yisrael (March 2002) and the bombing of the 2 bus (August 2003). The first assault killed eleven persons, most of them children and women who had congregated at the gate of a yeshiva, waiting for the men to emerge at the end of a bar-mitzvah celebration. Twenty-three Jews were killed in the second attack, which struck a bus carrying worshipers from the Western Wall to the Haredi neighborhoods in the city's north after the end of the Sabbath. In both attacks, almost all the victims were Haredim. ZAKA volunteers found themselves tending to the bodies of relatives and acquaintances. One of the volunteers reportedly shouted in Yiddish, "*Unzera*—They're ours!" Among the members of ZAKA, the two events are called the "Haredi attacks," and they affected the volunteers profoundly, and added another fatal dimension to the connection between Haredim and suicide terrorism.

The ZAKA volunteers view themselves not only as bearing the burden of direct engagement with the consequences of terrorism, but also as victims of terrorism. The motif of martyrdom is an important trope in the Jewish tradition, beginning with Rabbi Akiva and the other Sages executed by the Romans in ancient times. It continues through the Jews of the Rhineland murdered by Crusader armies and those slaughtered in pogroms in Russia in the Early Modern Period, and culminates in the Nazi genocide. The Haredim also include their fellows, who were persecuted and beaten by the Zionist police force in Israel's early years. They draw a direct line from the past martyrs to the Haredi victims of Palestinian terrorism.

This final component in the Haredi ethos of the martyr has three strata. First, the Haredi volunteers identify strongly with the Jews killed and injured in terrorist attacks. Second, they view themselves as putting their lives on the line, because in some cases, a second bomber might blow himself up while rescue crews were tending to the victims of the initial explosion. They also risk their mental health and cause their own families to suffer. For these reasons, ZAKA volunteers regard themselves as metaphorically losing their lives in terrorism attacks. Thus ZAKA volunteers see themselves as exemplifying martyrdom, forming another link in the historical and religious chain of Jews who accepted death to glorify God.

The Haredim were chosen as victims by Hamas and—as they truly believe—by God, and, among them, it is the ZAKA volunteers who bear the brunt of victimhood. ZAKA volunteers emphasize the trauma they undergo, and they are proud of their victimhood, which provides them with a social resource in their struggle with yeshiva students for legitimacy within ultra-Orthodox society, and in their struggle for more tolerance from general Israeli society.

Third, the Haredim genuinely believe that the Palestinians have specifically targeted them as the ideal victims of suicide terrorism, chosen as targets because the Palestinians see them as the ultimate Jews. In this respect, they are projecting their conception of themselves upon the terrorists, for in their view, they are the true Jews, the only members of Israeli society who are legitimate heirs of the ancient heritage of the Sages and rabbis. For them, and presumably for the Palestinians as well, the real Jew is the one with a beard and earlocks. In other words, the Haredim conform to a stereotypical (antisemitic) image of the Jew, the same image held, ironically, by radical Muslim Palestinians. It is generally assumed that the arch-enemy of the Palestinian resistance movements is the Zionist soldier or the settler in the West Bank, but it might be the Haredi Jew, their polar opposite who personifies their true anathema.[6] An article was published in a widely circulated Haredi newspaper under the headline "The Eternal Jew" (the title of an antisemitic Nazi film made in 1940).[7] At the end of the article, a direct appeal to the Palestinians appeared (in Arabic), asking them to refrain from striking at Haredim, since "they are not Zionists at all."

The Haredim believe that suicide terrorists see them as the preferred target because of their uncompromising Jewish faith, and therefore they accept the choice of the human bomb to focus on them as reinforcement of their determined ultra-Orthodox stance. The Haredim assumed the role of victim with a degree of understanding and submission. Some of them even explained suicide terrorism in terms bordering on the acceptance of divine judgment, implying that the human bombs were sent by God to punish them for their and other Israeli Jews' sins. The suicide attack on the number 2 bus, which claimed many victims in a Haredi neighborhood, was specifically attributed by the organization's volunteers to a Gay Pride Parade that had taken place in Jerusalem exactly one year before, which had not been effectively stopped by the Haredim though it was characterized by what they regarded as sexual licentiousness.[8]

There is no precise way to count how many Haredim have been physically hurt by suicide terrorists, but it is not unreasonable to assume that the number is disproportionate to their approximate 10 to 12 percent share of the local Jewish population. In Jerusalem, the city worst hit by suicide terrorism, Haredim are more than one-third of the population. A few Haredi neighborhoods lie close to the city center, where most of the attacks have occurred. Haredim also heavily patronize the city's open-air markets and bus system, the targets of most of the bombings. Whatever the precise statistics, many Haredim are certain that their particular vulnerability is a fact, that this fact is no coincidence, and that it cannot be explained merely in sociological terms (their socio-economic and demographic profile), or by terrorism tactics. In their view, the Palestinians know very well that the Haredim are not Zionists and do not serve in the occupying army. Hence, the Palestinians' ostensible preference for Haredim as targets for slaughter must have a deeper rationale. They believe that singling them out as the victims shows that the Palestinians wish to strike at the fundamentally Jewish substance of the enemy's entity. That is why, in the Haredi view, the terrorists deliberately attack at the most Jewish of times—on holidays and, especially, the High Holy Days.[9]

The Haredim call the attack on the worshipers returning from the Western Wall a "desecration of the Holy of Holies." One important rabbi labeled the two attacks on specifically Haredi targets "quality attacks," using an Israeli military idiom that refers to an especially effective raid with strategic consequences beyond its tactical success. Palestinian resistance organizations employ the same term in reference to terrorism operations that hit religious Jews. Hamas publications emphasize that the human bomb penetrates the innermost core of Israeliness, which is what gives suicide terrorism a special quality. Thus, Hamas proudly announced that the *shahid* Saed el Jatari (November 2001) "carried out his qualitative martyrdom operation in the enemy's heart, and then ascended to heaven."[10]

## Ideal Targets, Ideal Disguise

One must, of course, distinguish between the views that Israelis project upon the Palestinians and the real motivations of the Palestinians, which are a matter of conjecture. However, we have some evidence of what supporters of Hamas and Islamic Jihad in the West Bank and Gaza view as the ideal terrorism attack.[11] A special exhibition, held at An-Najah University in Nablus, to mark the anniversary of the outbreak of the Al-Aqsa Intifada and to lionize its martyrs[12] included a huge mural depicting the suicide attack on the Sbarro pizzeria in Jerusalem (August 2001). In the picture, the human bomb's spirit, wrapped in a white shroud, hovers over pools of blood while his maimed victims burn. Most of the casualties have beards and wear skullcaps.[13] The students at this Palestinian institution of higher education constructed a realistic model of the entrance to the bombed pizzeria emblazoned with a large number of "kosher" stamps resembling the ones used by the official Israeli rabbinate to label meat slaughtered for use by observant Jews. In one of the inner rooms a crafted installation displayed a Muslim martyr bearing a Koran and AK-47 rifle, sheltered behind a rock. Loudspeakers blared a taped *hadith*: "The Day of Judgment will not happen until the trees and stones will say: O believer, there is a Jew hiding behind me, come and kill him." On the other side of the rock the students placed a mannequin made up to represent a Jew. This life-size human figure was dressed as an ultra-Orthodox Hasid.[14]

Al-Masri, the human bomb dispatched by Hamas to blow up the Sbarro pizzeria, was accompanied by a female terrorist, Ahlam Tamimi, to make sure he would reach the target and to allay the suspicions of the police. After she was apprehended, in a prison interview she reported that they had walked all the way without exchanging a word, but when they were close to the target al-Masri suddenly asked her if she were sure that religious Jews would be killed in the attack. He was pleased when she replied that in an earlier reconnaissance trip she had seen that this restaurant was patronized by men in *kippahs*.

Another connection can be found in the interrogations of suicide terrorists who were captured or who gave themselves up before carrying out their plans. It turns out that a significant number of the aborted attacks targeted Haredim; one case in point is that of a cell in Bethlehem that planned to stage an attack in Mea Shearim because "it's the only way to be sure that the victims will be Jews."[15]

Haredim are not only a preferred target; their garb is also an effective disguise. Many suicide terrorists chose to dress like typical modern Israelis of various types, sporting, for example, the colorful shirt and bleached hair of a Tel Aviv beach boy, or the khaki fatigues of a reserve soldier on his way home after duty. However, the Haredi costume of dark slacks, white shirt, black *kippah,* and black suit jacket, even on hot days, is especially effective and popular. The common wisdom in the Haredi public is that almost half of Palestinian suicide terrorists were able to pass and reach their targets because they were disguised as Haredim, hiding their explosive belts under their black jackets. While acknowledging the operative advantages of the disguise, the Haredim claim that it was employed even in the early days of the Intifada, when people who were clearly Arabs could still ride buses and walk on the street without arousing suspicion. Suicide terrorists did not need to go undercover then, the Haredim argue. Yet the human bombs chose this costume so they could blend in among the Jews and hit "where it hurts most."

The suicide terrorist preoccupies ZAKA obsessively. The human bomb is the Haredi volunteers' arch-nemesis. His cunning worth for them is expressed, among other ways, in their need to inspect his dead body close up and actually touch him, and, of course, to display him. They say, "It's good to feel him in your hands." Since the human bomb is perceived as the embodiment of evil, examination and physical contact are aids in coping with him. There is always the fear that evil is omnipotent and omnipresent, even within us, and that it is sly and elusive, and so can catch us by surprise. Only when evil takes on tangible form and concrete dimensions can one be sure that it is contained, controlled, indeed, defeated.

## Two Icons of Suicide Terrorism Meet

A man from a refugee camp near Nablus wearing an explosive belt and a man from an ultra-Orthodox Jerusalem neighborhood wearing a day-glow yellow vest have become emblems of the Israeli-Palestinian conflict, parallel and alternative symbols of the same cruel reality. The attacker, a green band wrapped around his forehead, and those who care for the victims' bodies, capped with big black *kippah*, are automatically associated with each other.

The ZAKA volunteer and the human bomb meet in the arena of terrorism. They have several characteristics in common. For example, both come from a marginal social position, and terrorism redeems them from anonymity and a sense of worthlessness. They upgrade their status in their respective societies through their encounter at the site of the attack. The suicide terrorist belonged to an oppressed people and lived in a poor neighborhood in an obscure town or village in the occupied territories. He generally had no personal achievements to his credit and had no affiliation with an influential family or prestigious community institution. The explosion turns him into a role model and saint, the pride of his relatives and community, his photographs plastered on every wall in the Palestinian areas.[16]

Likewise, the position of the ZAKA volunteer is often problematic within his reference group, Haredi society. Furthermore, that group suffers from denunciation within Israeli society at large. The volunteer's willingness to enter the bloody havoc following a suicide attack improves his self-esteem and status in Haredi society and enhances the reputation of the Haredim in the eyes of other Israelis. The terrorist act moves both the attacker and the handler of his dead body from the margin to the center. In both cases, their involvement transforms them into exemplary figures in their communities. During waves of terrorist attacks, they become objects of admiration and emulation.

The suicide terrorist sent by Hamas or PIJ and the Haredi ZAKA volunteer are generally termed "fundamentalists."[17] Both are perceived as pious and observant who view militancy as intimately related to an ascetic and literalist religiosity. Since they oppose the idea that any other faith might bear religious truth, Islamic and Jewish fundamentalists are naturally bitter enemies, and this animosity is found in its most extreme form at the site of a terrorist attack. Yet, at the same time, the site also reflects a certain vague mutual awareness and consideration, a kind of raw pan-radicalism, since both parties share a somewhat similar set of values, even though they derive from distinctly different traditions, harnessed to conflicting forces. They are unwitting partners who unintentionally collaborate to foster and renew a discourse based on concepts such as devotion, martyrdom, and sacrifice; holy body, holy suffering, and holy death; rebirth and redemption, atonement and revenge; holy land, holy war, and the war of light against darkness. The scene of a terrorist attack makes these concepts concrete and imbues them with a peculiarly charged meaning.

The opposing fundamentalists share similar views of the Middle East conflict in general, and of the terrorist death arena in particular. The market, which stands for base quotidian materialism, or the restaurant, that represents abundance and leisure, are sanctified at the moment of the explosion by both parties. The Haredi volunteers are aware of the dissonance between this sanctity and the previously profane nature of the site. Furthermore, they point out that many suicide terrorism attacks occurred in places contaminated by sin and heresy, and often places of perceived lewdness, as in the attacks on pubs and cafés, and especially at the Dolphinarium Club in Tel Aviv, where there was mixed dancing, the drinking of alcohol, and revealing dress (June 2001). The Hamas movement, which began in the Gaza Strip as prude squads of enforcers who struck at Palestinian women in immodest dress and at parties where there was loud Western music,[18] presents Israel in general as a country of vulgarity and obscenity and refers to the immorality and wantonness in the targets chosen for suicide terrorism attacks. Behind the similarity between the religious views of the Islamic and Jewish organizations are concealed parallel beliefs that the attack is punishment from heaven for abandoning traditional puritan values.

While they never meant to be allies and would never admit that their ideals are comparable, in the end the Hamas suicide terrorist and the ZAKA volunteer do pursue similar and related goals. They reinforce each other in their effort to impose a religious agenda on the world around them. They seek, by implication, to transform the Middle East conflict into a religious conflict. More specifically, they seek to make death, particularly violent death, a religious event, as it was in the past. They impose another level of meaning on an event that would otherwise be seen as primarily ethno-national. Each party contributes to translating the communal conflict between Israelis and Palestinians into a conflict between Judaism and Islam. In this, they make the conflict more profound and primal, and as such more brutal and difficult to resolve. Together they shape the head-on collision between two nations into a complex rite of worship rich in symbolic meaning.

Modernization has privatized, medicalized, and bureaucratized death. These processes shunt death, especially in the West, off into far institutional corners out of the public eye, and to a large extent desecrate or secularize it. The actions of both the human bomb and the ZAKA volunteer at the scene of the terrorism restore death to a prominent public position. This renewed visibility brings old-new symbolism with it: death is once again manifested as an important public ritual. The suicide terrorist fashions a central stage for himself, on which he plays a key role in a bloody ritual. ZAKA joins in, taking advantage of the horrific drama to sanctify the contest between them and death itself.

The Hamas human bomb and ZAKA volunteer meet at the terror site as the emissaries of two distinct cultures of death, each with its abundance of rituals. At the site, two dormant but precedent-rich martyr traditions become vibrant and aggressive. They interpret themselves to themselves and to the world in the context of this encounter, and in so doing they gain momentum and take the form of two full-fledged death cults. The struggle at the site between the different kinds of martyrs develops into a grand scene of sacrifice. The Palestinian-Muslim and Haredi-Israeli death cults clash and compete, but at the same time engage in a tacit dialogue. Their complexities and the fullness of their meanings can be appreciated only in the context of their encounter.

In some sense, the ZAKA activist and the suicide terrorist are bound up with each other. In the associative world of each side, the other plays a significant role. In the imagination of the Palestinian human bomb and of the Haredi volunteer his enemy and counterpart appears in palpable form, connected with the arena of death in which they will meet. Each one's fantasies nourish those of the other. Even in the planning stages of the attack, the terrorist and his dispatchers already imagine the way ultra-Orthodox Jews will treat the mutilated body. The filmed testaments left by Hamas human bombs make use of photomontage techniques to show them holding their own severed head, just as ZAKA volunteers will soon be holding it.

In the videotaped last will and testament of the Hamas aspiring *shahid* Mohammad al-Hindi, he addressed his parents and promised them that they would be proud and happy when they envisioned the moment of his death, "his body blown to smithereens, bits and pieces of it pulled down from trees, and scraped off the sidewalk, and collected in plastic bags by the ultra-Orthodox Jewish ZAKA."[19]

ZAKA volunteers claim that they often think (and dream) about suicide terrorists. They speak of them a lot in conversations with their colleagues. One of the motifs that appears in ZAKA discourse on the suicide terrorist is speculation about his motives. They distinguish between Palestinians who were compelled under threat to carry out a suicide mission (unmasked collaborators with Israel, for example) and those who offered themselves for the task in the absence of any pressure. Surprisingly, they express certain respect for the latter.

The Haredi volunteers also compare the suicide bomber to themselves. They develop the contrast between (the angel of) death, represented by the suicide bomber, and life, represented by ZAKA. They put the lethality and devastation that the terrorist wreaks next to the rescue, healing, and repair that they bring to the world. Another characteristic comparison, aimed to stress their advantage in the contest, is between themselves, who demonstrate "true compassion," having no anticipation of receiving any reciprocal favors from the dead person they care for, and the suicide bomber, who would not have set out on his mission had he not been promised an attractive afterlife. In this regard, they never miss an opportunity to make chortling reference to the seventy virgins who, so the suicide terrorists are allegedly promised by their dispatchers, await them in Paradise.

By juxtaposing the ZAKA volunteers with the suicide terrorists, while pointing out the similarities between them and the reciprocity, even tacit cooperation, between them, I do not wish to imply that human bombs and ZAKA volunteers are morally equivalent. Nor do I wish to in any way minimize the responsibility and the ghastly murderous brutality of the former or to disparage the compassionate work of the latter. Viewing the two as macabre twins would be wholly intolerable—and pointless—without recognizing the moral abyss that separates them. Nevertheless, suicide terrorism does bring the Palestinian terrorist and the Haredi ZAKA volunteer together in a Gordian knot.

## Martyrdom: On the Verge of Heresy

ZAKA volunteers feel profound hostility and loathing for the human bomb. They often declare this publicly. Their anger at the perpetrators of suicide terrorism is focused on the terrorist's corpse. They whisper, sometimes shout abuse at the body; when they think they are unobserved, some kick it. When they are certain that they have identified parts of the terrorist's body, they handle and pack it roughly, in stark contrast to the tenderness and care they use with the bodies of the victims. Especially apparent is the difference in their care for the bodies' modesty. Unlike the bodies of the victims, the terrorist's corpse is left bare, or sometimes deliberately stripped, as an outlet for wrath and frustration, a kind of revenge. Since the waning of the wave of suicide terrorism, ZAKA volunteers complain that "there is no one to hate and blame." One can display disrespect for the terrorist's remains by nonchalantly smoking a cigarette while collecting the pieces, and by hurling the plastic bag containing his body parts onto the floor of the ambulance. Accidents and natural disasters offer no such opportunity for catharsis.

While ZAKA volunteers don't deny their anger and resentment toward the enemy, they also boast of the evenhandedness that both Jewish and universal ethics mandate toward all human bodies, including that of the suicide terrorist. Sometimes ZAKA's treatment of the bodies of suicide terrorists evinces a trace of understanding, even appreciation. At the site, the volunteers realize that the suicide terrorist's project has certain moral aspects to it, and that the values that guide the suicide terrorist are reminiscent of Haredi values. At this point, attitudes toward the other side become more complex. At the height of the wave of suicide terrorism, an Israeli cultural critic's reference to a central ZAKA activist's "interfaith openness" was widely quoted. In a television interview a ZAKA official marveled at how the Islamic terrorist calls out *Allah hu akbar*— "God is Great"—at the moment he blows himself up alongside his victims. He added, "The Palestinian terrorist believes that he has been sent by God. I act out of similar religious motives."[20] This was another sign of the reserved empathy and limited solidarity with the attacker felt by those who care for his victims.

The human bomb is, for ZAKA activists, the absolute inversion of themselves, but at the same time he is the object of some jealousy. Regarding themselves as men of faith, the Haredi volunteers perceive the suicide terrorist's act of faith as a kind of insult, so they feel a certain need to mitigate the slur they feel that the terrorist has leveled against them. Already on the defensive from the attitude of their fellow Haredim, who devote themselves exclusively to Torah study, they cannot disregard the religious zeal displayed by the human bomb.

The fascination the human bomb arouses in them does not abate at the site, and even after leaving they remained caught up. While riding back from one of the death arenas in the ZAKA ambulance, I witnessed an animated conversation concerning what motivates the Palestinian human bombs. The Haredi volunteers ascribed the human bombs' evil and brutality to their "inferior Muslim religiosity." But then, one of the young ultra-Orthodox Jews in the vehicle hesitantly ventured a daring speculation that the terrorist who sacrificed his life for a cause he considers sacred acted out a venerable kind of religiosity, maybe even more elevated than their own. One could sense traces of reserved admiration, with a shadow of repressed envy. A tense moment of complete silence followed.[21]

ZAKA activists cannot ignore the true belief of the Hamas suicide terrorist, and, contrary to their ideology and against their will, they acknowledge his martyrdom. With instinctive defensiveness, they respond by sharpening their conception of themselves as martyrs as well. An implicit contest ensues: who sacrifices more, a competition of victimhood. The Palestinian terrorist is a victim in three ways: of the Israeli occupation, of the organization and community that sent him to his death, and, of course, of his own act, for he killed himself. In contrast, the Haredi volunteer puts forward the three levels of his own victimhood: first, he identifies completely with the dead people whose bodies he handles, as if he had died with them; second, he repeatedly emphasizes that, as someone who enters the thick of the arena of death, he is risking his body and his soul, and, indirectly, his family is injured; third, he exploits the opportunity to declare to others in the Haredi community that he pays a heavy price for honoring the dead, in that he gives up a life of Torah in a yeshiva.

Within the Middle Eastern conflict and particularly at the scene of suicide terrorism, victimhood becomes an asset, even an advantage, and each side is interested in having the other side and the world acknowledge that. The unstated regional competition is not only on strategic objectives; it concerns alleged virtue, justice, uprightness, equated with victimhood. The arena in the wake of the explosion is a microcosm of this competition. The victor, as it were, is given a pretext for claiming ethical superiority. The sides challenge each other around the issue of who is the ultimate martyr. The human bomb has a claim to be the ultimate victim and as such he bids for the moral high ground. He is regarded by his supporters as holier than his victims, and this in turn legitimizes the act that generates further victimhood. The Palestinian human bomb works to inflict maximum suffering on the Israelis and at the same time to outdo them in the suffering index. The claim to excel in suffering gives the victim the right to cause suffering to the other.

The Haredi volunteers join this implicit discourse, too, by contrasting themselves with the suicide terrorist as moral rivals. This is the background for the frequent mention of the psychological price the volunteers pay. Exposure to horror causes them to suffer from anxiety, and even nervous breakdown. Many of them testify of themselves, with a bit of boastfulness, that they have gone crazy. When Haredi rabbis rebuke ZAKA volunteers for abandoning the ideal of yeshiva study, they feel the need to apologize by paraphrasing the well-known idiom, according to which yeshiva students "die every day in the tabernacle of Torah." The volunteers say of themselves that they "die again and again in the arena of suicide terrorism." This is the ammunition of the Haredi volunteers in the dual competition in which they are engaged: on the one hand, with those who study Torah, and, on the other hand, with the Palestinian human bomb.

The martyrdom that developed on the Israeli side during the waves of suicide terrorism in the Intifada was probably influenced by the groundswell of martyrdom (*shuhada*) among the Palestinians. ZAKA especially presents the Israeli victims of suicide terrorism as martyrs—devotees whose violent death sanctifies the name of God—and this is to create a kind of balance or canceling out of the Palestinian martyr, the *shahid*. They create symmetry between the suicide terrorist and the people he killed, as if they actively and consciously had sought their own death for a goal more exalted than life.

In the internal discourse of ZAKA, suicide terrorism is described as a wrestling ring in which Islam and Allah, the god of deceit and murder—according to the volunteers—grapple with Judaism and the God of Israel. But there are moments at the site in which a hint of insecurity about which side is stronger steals into the speech of the ZAKA volunteers. Despite everything, they find themselves dumbfounded by the terrorist's willingness to sacrifice himself, and are unsettled and challenged by his act of self-immolation. They are compelled to think about the human bomb using terms such as *mesirut nefesh*, a term that in Jewish tradition means "absolute devotion" and which is often used in contexts involving Jews who give up their own lives or well-being in order to save others, or for the sake of heaven. It is a quality that ZAKA volunteers ascribe to themselves as well. Despite self-evident condemnation of human sacrifice, and precisely because they themselves take pride in their own willingness to sacrifice so much without hope of reward, the volunteers find themselves in doubt, and feeling somewhat inferior, when faced with the shredded body of a Palestinian who volunteered to die. One ZAKA activist confessed to me that, faced with the acts of suicide committed by Hamas terrorists, he found himself increasingly critical of his own Haredi society, where idealism was waning and which was unwilling to make necessary sacrifices, not even to go out to the streets to protest against the secular Zionists.

ZAKA volunteers go to great lengths to convince themselves of the moral superiority of preferring life to death. But they cannot help but be captivated and impressed by death, and their encounter with the radicalism of the human bomb makes them, as it were, irresolute. The body of the human bomb seems to taunt the volunteers with the charge that they are less religious and patriotic than he was.

In the arena of the suicide terrorism two opponents contend for championship in martyrdom and for top ranking in religious virtuosity. The attack site is a stage on which to display ardent devotion, measured by a willingness to kill and to be killed. ZAKA volunteers acknowledge, grudgingly, that the man whose mutilated body they see before them, for all his loathsomeness, beat them in the game of ultimate religiosity. One ZAKA rabbi admitted to me that a Muslim human bomb is measured not only by the extent of the destruction he wreaks and his effectiveness in forcing Israel to change its policies, but also, and principally, by his ambition to exalt the value of self-sacrifice. According to this rabbi, the act of suicide terrorism is largely a matter of religious braggadocio—it seeks not only to annihilate Jews, but also to humiliate them by setting a higher religious standard than they can meet.

# 7

# God-Fearing Acrobats

## The Most Pious Will Violate the Sabbath

Once the ZAKA volunteers were summoned to a multi-casualty incident on Sabbath morning. They cut off their prayers in the synagogue, and, without saying goodbye to their families, who were waiting to have the festive meal with them, they rode out to the distant arena in the team's emergency vehicle. As they passed through the Haredi neighborhoods in northern Jerusalem, they spontaneously began to sing with increasing enthusiasm. The passengers report that they sang with devotion (*dvequt*).[1] The song they chose is a central part of the Sabbath morning service, a Sabbath hymn. The melody is a traditional Hasidic one, and the words are "May the keepers of the Sabbath, who call it a joy, rejoice in Your kingdom, the nation that sanctifies the seventh day."

Haredim who knew about this scene responded with a mixture of wonder, embarrassment, and distaste. In contrast, the ZAKA activists exhibit more than a hint of self-congratulation when they report it. Singing in those circumstances, its content and its power, is not at all something to be expected.[2] Singing a hymn while on the way to the site of a disaster on the Sabbath contains a double dissonance. First, there is a jarring opposition between what appears to be celebration and joy in the vehicle and knowledge that in a few minutes the passengers will arrive at an arena permeated by suffering and death. Second, the contrast between the sanctity of the Sabbath and the commandment to rest and what appears to be a desecration of the Sabbath and a violation of the halakha is equally jarring.

By singing the hymn, ZAKA signaled to itself and to the other Haredim, unmistakably, that the Sabbath was intact, and its sanctity was meticulously observed. Moreover, the charged contradiction between the emphasized sacredness of the day and the wholly profane trip showed itself, surprisingly, to be uplifting. That Sabbath, in which the boundaries were shaken, is remembered by the volunteers as especially holy.

*The Cult of Dismembered Limbs*. Gideon Aran, Oxford University Press. © Oxford University Press 2023.
DOI: 10.1093/oso/9780197689141.003.0007

On the legalistic level, that ride received authoritative rabbinical approval, but on the behavioral level, there was a departure from the norm. That departure made a strong mark on the volunteers' experience. The religious song did not contribute to harmony; rather it exacerbated the dissonance and heightened the inner tension between the feeling of desecration and the feeling of greater sanctity. In this instance and others, one gets the impression that the ZAKA Haredi activists derive enjoyment and religious inspiration from moving among contradictions of this sort. Some of the volunteers used the word in Hebrew slang, *keif* ("pleasure and satisfaction" in Arabic), to describe their feeling when they are acting in a way that appears to violate the ultra-Orthodox rules of the game, while at the same time taking care to assure its legitimacy. The passengers in the vehicle commented that the powerful impression made by that experience derived from the connection between the sanctity of that day and what appeared to be a desecration. This juxtaposition, or the joining together of opposites into a single organic whole, was, from the religious point of view, both destabilizing and enthralling.[3]

Here is yet another example of the paradoxical nature of ZAKA's religious conduct in the arena, which bursts at the seams with many inner contradictions. In some cases when the volunteers were called to the site of a disaster on the Sabbath, the question arose as to who should drive the emergency vehicle. According to the rabbis' directives, it is best to employ a local Arab for this purpose, as a Sabbath goy. However, several volunteers objected to this solution, which they saw as "too easy and relatively low," from a pietistic point of view. They argued that the driver should be a Jew, for it is a great privilege to serve God by violating the Sabbath to save lives and to give honor to the dead. In the ensuing discussion, they agreed that the act of violating an important commandment for the sake of observing a more important commandment should be reserved for the most pious among them. Only he could withstand the inner tension, and he was worthy of being honored with that privilege. The man chosen could not deny the pleasure he received from the permission he had received to break through the restrictions of the Sabbath.

## Taboo-Ridden Arena

Religions present models of worthy behavior to their believers. No less than they recommend what one must do, and they proscribe what one must not do. Normative-ritualistic religions have an abundance of restrictions and prohibitions. Central to some of them—especially Judaism and Islam, like Hinduism—is a set of taboos. These are categorical directives of avoidance, which dwell at central psychological and social crossroads, and they are reinforced by severe negative sanctions. These behavioral rules mark boundaries, the crossing of which effects an undesired change in the status of the transgressor. The option of the infraction of a ritual prohibition threatens the social order and arouses dread. The taboo appears in vague situations and touches upon the extremes where holiness and pollution meet. Thus the relation to the taboo is ambivalent—violation of a taboo both repels and attracts. Examples of Jewish taboos are eating pig, marrying a gentile, and working on the Sabbath. They all bear an important symbolic burden, embodying desire and, at the same time, threatening with horror.[4]

Most religious people are conformist; they keep a distance from the boundaries of the religion and refrain from challenging taboos. In contrast, certain individuals and groups choose to deviate from religious normality by breaking through boundaries and violating taboos. Some of these people are seen by the establishment as sinners or heretics, and they are excluded from the religious collective or abandon it by themselves. Others break through boundaries and violate taboos without forfeiting their full participation in the religious group.

In certain social situations the establishment permits, even encourages, the violation of important taboos. These situations can be rituals of transgression, ceremonial situations in which the normal rules of the game are suspended, and in their place is a regulation with peculiar logic, laden with symbolism.[5] Such a situation is well defined and restricted in time and place, and, despite its wild appearance, it has a decided structure (which is by nature anti-structural). In this situation powerful human energies with creative potential are released, and an effort is made to prevent their subversive effect from overflowing into the realm of the normal society in an unsupervised manner. In the annual Jewish carnivalesque holiday of masquerades, Purim, for example, true believers can fulfill fantasies that involve what seems to violate taboos.[6] Second, certain social types receive permission, even encouragement from the establishment to cross borders and violate important taboos. These individuals belong to a chosen group of specialists who play a ceremonial role bound up with assuming demanding duties and mainly with taking risks, but they are rewarded with a privileged status. They are few, with special personalities and skills, experts to whom the society grants the prerogative of conditional exemption from the tyranny of the law. They are a type of genius who embodies supreme characteristics, such as the high priest of the ancient Jews, who alone was permitted, under certain conditions, to violate the taboo against entering the most sacred inner sanctum of the Temple, without dying.

The site of a Palestinian terrorist attack in Israel is a taboo-ridden arena. ZAKA's deathwork in the arena is a festival of Haredi boundary-breaking and the violation of Jewish taboos. Concomitantly, the ZAKA deathworkers are religious virtuosi, who are drawn to challenge the boundaries of ultra-Orthodoxy, and they specialize in violating Haredi taboos, under the supervision of Haredi rabbis.[7] They are priests who do what others in their community do not dare to do and are not permitted to do. The arena is exterritorial, and certain basic religious laws do not apply in it. It is a closed enclave with intensification and ritualization of the challenge of borders. The arena offers exposure to the heights of pollution and of sanctity, and mainly the thin border between them, bringing the Haredi volunteers to states of ecstasy. It is a Dionysian space permeated with the Eros that characterizes intimacy with taboos.

In classical anthropological terms, organized crossing of borders[8] and established violation of taboos characterize the liminal moment, that which is betwixt and between two situations of social order, a kind of rite of passage bound up with psychological and social transformation. The ZAKA deathwork has liminal elements, and the Haredi deathworkers are a type of liminoid person.[9] Liminality can have a revolutionary—even suicidal—effect on the social order, but it can also create possibilities of trial and error and promote options of reinforcement and renewal of the system.

The combination of the new fields of activism and the channels of self-fulfillment offered to the pious members of ZAKA and the security given to them by rabbinical sanction gives these men a rare opportunity for religious experimentation, which enriches their ultra-Orthodox life. Although going out on the escapade of violating taboos seems supervised and contained, and measures are taken to secure a return to the normative-ritual haven, the energetic outward leap might still veer out of control irrevocably. Despite the careful efforts at delimitation, those who break the boundaries might not return home safely. Hence there is a sense of adventure that intoxicates the action-seeking volunteers in the arena.

The paradigmatic instance of ZAKA's violation of taboos in the arena is performance of deathwork on the Sabbath. The Haredi rabbis who permit this delicate and explosive game with the laws of the Torah warn against the error of seeing their ruling as a cynical exploitation of the religious law, with the appearance of insisting on observance while acting against its spirit to sanction acts of wrongdoing (called "a villain with permission of the Torah"), or as trickery and the manipulation of normative loopholes to make religious life easier by circumventing demanding laws (called "Shabbas subterfuges").[10] On the contrary, the ZAKA rabbis' permission to violate the Sabbath is granted only for the sake of heaven, and it poses a grave challenge to the faithful. It is regarded as a heroic act of sanctifying the name of God.

The transgressor is a martyr.[11] Violation of the Sabbath is a sacrifice offered to God by the volunteers. With the Sabbath, they sacrifice themselves. Giving up observance of the sanctity of the Sabbath, like refraining from observing other commandments such as Torah study in a yeshiva, is an act of forgoing normal religiosity, and it entails risk. The ZAKA volunteers endanger both their bodies and their souls, risking damage to their status in the community, and mainly risking loss of the boundaries of their religiosity. All this is in addition to the danger of direct contact with horrific death. Their intimacy with violence and lethality testifies to their ability simultaneously to contain the observance of the Sabbath and its violation in their religious imagination, and also to heighten the tension between them, in which they find the secret of supreme devotion.

## Disrupting Habitus

While some ZAKA rabbis maintain that riding to the site of disaster on the Sabbath is not just permitted neglect of a commandment but in itself a commandment, in the ultra-Orthodox surroundings of the organization doubt and criticism are voiced, and even the most radical volunteers confess to some perplexity and discomfort. The activists are not only slightly disturbed by this but also excited and proud. The upsetting experience of performing forbidden-permitted acts on the Sabbath is both undermining the volunteers' confidence and thrilling. Participating in holy tasks, which, under other circumstances, would be regarded as transgressions, is bound up with inner drama. Riding on the Sabbath, be the reasons and justifications what they may, is not a trivial religious moment, and when it is enveloped in traditional religious sanction, the order of the universe seems to be turned upside down. The forbidden-permitted religious act might be more defiant— but electrifying—than a prohibited act.

Despite the rabbinical backing for actions ostensibly forbidden, performing them is grasped as particularly demanding and conditioned on stronger than usual piety. Accordingly, the effect of performing these actions is seen as religious improvement, as an ascent in the spiritual ladder. Activity in the arena of disaster has the taste of non-conformism, not to say deviance. However, precisely because of this, it is pleasurable and exalting. The forbidden-permitted terrorism-centered activism has a far-reaching religious impact.

What obstacles must the ZAKA volunteers who violate the Sabbath and other taboos overcome? First, they must cope with the suspicious and condemnatory responses of the community to which they belong. In the ultra-Orthodox milieu, a person is not judged by his or her intentions, as pure as they may be, and it is not enough to know that the behavior received rabbinical approval. The conformism must be visible in public. ZAKA's rabbinical authorities make certain to preserve the appearance of observing the commandments (*mar'it ayin*) and to avoid creating the impression that a volunteer has violated the halakha, although he did not do so. On this matter they cite an example from the Talmud: if someone's clothing got wet on a rainy Sabbath, he may not hang them to dry outside of his house, lest people might think he had laundered them, in violation of the prohibition against working. The logic of the importance of appearances guides a variety of Haredi behaviors that seem to run counter to common sense.[12] In this spirit, one could expect ZAKA to downplay acts of deathwork that appear to violate commandments. However, contrary to the advice of the rabbis, volunteers find it difficult to overcome the instinct that draws them to flaunt such acts.

Second, the ZAKA volunteers must cope with the inner inhibitions of the pious. These are often gut feelings and not intellectual or ethical in nature. Rabbinical permission is insufficient for approval of a certain religious act. The act must be consistent with the tradition, customs, and ways of life, which are expressed, among other ways, in routine bodily practices in which people are trained, or which they have adopted for years. After all, religion, too, is a habitus. One of the essential characteristics of ZAKA's religious experience is that underlying it is habitus-disrupting behavior. Hence, although the action is legitimate, it is difficult to perform.

A devout volunteer shared with me his experience while performing acts of rescue and removal of corpses at an incident that took place on the Sabbath.

"On the intellectual level, it was as clear as day to me that there was no dese-cration of the Sabbath in the arena. The Torah and the rabbinate backed me. Nevertheless, there was something new and surprising there. Habit has its way, and deviation from the routine of the Sabbath drove me mad. As the graduate of a yeshiva, I understand that I was maneuvering within the bounds of the Torah and faith, since observing the Sabbath and not observing it in special, permitted circumstances are equally lawful. However, as a Jew who had been pious since birth, I felt very strange."

This experience is analogous to that of one of the very few volunteers who served in the IDF with religious Zionists. Because of the necessity of defending the borders of the state, they operate radios and carry crates of ammunition on the Sabbath. These actions are defined as *piquaḥ nefesh* (the saving of lives) and are sanctioned by the rabbinate. Nevertheless, here, too, according to this informer who attended yeshivas, this is no trivial matter. The time the Sabbath was violated—with halakhic approval, of course—is remembered as a searing experience, a significant event in his religious life. He did not feel as if he was casting off or abandoning the sacred mo-ment and replacing it with a secular one. On the contrary, when its borders are pressed outward, the sanctity is enhanced. Whereas among the neo-Orthodox, suspension of the Sabbath is a familiar and widely discussed phenomenon, among the ultra-Orthodox, this religious privilege is still a matter that requires further processing. Haredim are learning only recently to derive the full religious capital from suspending the Sabbath under special circumstances. This development is an indication of the modernization and the Israelization of the Haredim, and it shows that these processes are not necessarily bound up with secularization.

The analogy of the soldiers offers more precision in diagnosing the unique feeling of those who simultaneously violate and keep the Sabbath. Religious combatants who experienced this report the erosion of order and the vio-lation of harmony as something physical. The experience of the Sabbath is sensory, and, even more so, the experience of breaking its boundaries. Both sanctity and its profanation are permeated by Eros. This is a delicate flirtation with permitted and prohibited. A pious Orthodox described the first time he rode on the Sabbath as the piercing of a membrane, despite the approval. His friend spoke about the "inebriation of space" that opened before him then. The formulations of other ZAKA activists are usually less articulate, but they point to a remarkably similar experience.

## Slippery Slope

The volunteers specialize in violating taboos and repeatedly perform actions that challenge halakha and stretch the boundaries of the religion. The organization's rabbis express fear lest the sanctioned violation of the Torah—sanctioned by themselves—might become routine. In that case, erosion of the observance of the Torah and its commandments might ensue, and who knows where that might lead. They recall the popular aphorism "The heart is drawn after deeds." Consequently, they recognize that their problem is educational rather than halakhic.

The halakhot that regulate the behavior of the volunteers in the arena also serve as an umbrella, under which the boundaries of the religion are liable to crack, and then the dam of halakha might burst. To counter this threat, the rabbis adopt a strategy of heightening awareness, increasing restrictions, and painstaking regulation. Within the organization one hears repeatedly the warning against deviating "beyond the bounds of the permissions." In an apologetic tone they point out that the volume of halakhic restrictions is far greater than that of the permissions. The ZAKA rabbis and many of the volunteers show instinctive sensitivity to what they themselves define as a slippery slope, extending from the arena in a direction that is liable to defeat the original intentions of the decisors.

ZAKA has launched a new channel of religious action, horror deathwork, the dangers of which it acknowledges. The volunteers generate energy, the rabbis join in and encourage them, and later, when it gathers impetus, they make a huge effort to rein it in. Behind this impossible effort lies understanding of the seductive power inherent in halakhic permissions that make it possible for Haredim to intervene in the arena of disaster. Both the rabbis within ZAKA and those outside of it are particularly aware that in the frenetic activity of the volunteers in the presence of the dead there are moments in which the "natural religious impulse" bursts out, and then, exactly then, one must "be in awe of the sanctity."[13]

A halakhic article written by one of the ZAKA rabbis justifying permission to save the wounded and clear away the dead on the Sabbath provoked an aggressive reaction from other ZAKA rabbis. The criticism focused on the tendency to issue "sweeping permissions" which naturally "are created from the particular atmosphere" prevailing among the ZAKA volunteers while they are dealing with the victims of disaster.[14] They explain that the Jewish tradition is aware that momentum and habituation play a decisive role in religion.[15] The ZAKA activists cannot ignore the fact that their activity, especially on Sabbaths, although it has formal approval, is still deviant with relation to

what the members of their community are conditioned to see as natural, self-evident, and proper. Jewish religiosity, they concede, depends on habits. They add that the sweeping permissions, fed by the spirit prevailing in the arena, are precisely the goal of the terrorist and his way of striking at Israel and Judaism. Meticulous observance of the halakhot of the Sabbath is a recommended response to terrorism. Indeed, they maintain, it is itself the victory over terrorism.

The rabbinical rulings that regulate ZAKA's conduct in the arena are intended, among other things, to share the infringements of halakhic norms equally among all the volunteers, so that none of them will accrue a substantial burden of transgression. This is another reason why, on the Sabbath, a division of labor by rotation is practiced among the volunteers who are occupied with forbidden-permitted labor such as moving a corpse. In this way they also want to prevent the volunteers from becoming accustomed and losing the feeling of the uniqueness of the Sabbath and its sanctity.[16] One ZAKA activist offered a different interpretation: they don't want there to be a situation where a few volunteers seemingly violate the Sabbath a lot, while others hardly do so at all, so as to expand the circle of those who are privileged to fulfill these explosive commandments.

ZAKA has developed an internal control mechanism meant to make certain that the deathwork proceeds in the spirit of the Torah and in accordance with all its details. Alongside the activists in the field, a body of voluntary *mashgiḥim* (supervisors) is active. The term *mashgiaḥ* belongs to the Haredi sub-culture, where it refers to inspectors of the *kashrut* of food and to the spiritual superintendent in yeshivas, the man responsible for the discipline and ethical behavior of the students. The supervisors are mainly members of ZAKA's council of rabbis, along with other Haredi rabbis who act on an ad hoc basis. These rabbis rule on the halakha whenever doubt arises in the arena. In cases of disasters with many victims, they take the trouble to come to the arena themselves. There they oversee the observance of the commandments, while they also help in the deathwork like the rank and file of the organization. The supervision becomes intense and is seen as particularly necessary when the volunteers go into a frenzy of activity, seized by religious enthusiasm. That is when they are liable to violate halakhic rules. Some of the volunteers testify that when they are among the dead, the rabbinical supervisors "sit on their tails" so that they won't deviate in the slightest from the dictates of halakha.

The volunteers emphasized that the rabbis' presence in the arena imbues them with the assurance that enables them to perform the deathwork while free of fear of neglecting small details. Some of them admitted that because they understand that someone will restrain them before they are swept away, here and there they allow themselves some *shpil* ("play," in Yiddish), that is, freedom to deviate a bit from the standard procedure. More than once a deathworker has been caught "cutting corners," as they say, by pouring some sand on a small spot of blood instead of scraping it up for burial. Sometimes when the volunteers feel that there are no outsiders among them, they express some resentment against the rabbis' *frumkait* (a Yiddish expression used by the Orthodox in reference to pedantic piety, insisting on dotting every "i" at the expense of true and full religiosity). It has happened that hair-splitting Haredim known to be "holier than the pope" were perceived as interfering with the sacred work. People in ZAKA are sensitive to the built-in tension that emerges in the arena between excessive adherence to halakha and religious authenticity. It is told that one of the rabbis, a veteran volunteer with enormous credit, walked close behind the deathworkers at one of the gruesome attacks and cleaned the bloodstains left by their shoes. He cleaned, and they dirtied; they dirtied, and he cleaned, repeatedly. The responses to this description were a mixture of self-effacing admiration and chuckles of ridicule.

## Tightrope Walking

Some ZAKA activists consistently refuse to abbreviate their prayers in the arena of disaster, without skipping any minutiae. In their ordinary lives, the same men seldom make no bones about missing a prayer because of quotidian concerns. While dealing with a terrorist incident, most Haredi volunteers are severe in observing the commandments. However, on these occasions they might also refrain from performing important commandments, consciously and ostentatiously, in order to dedicate themselves exclusively to the holy work. In ZAKA two standard and contradictory religious tendencies are in evidence, both of which demonstrate a super-religiosity. Although they appear to contradict each other, they appear side by side, combine with one another, and complement and compensate for each other. Both behaviors are performed with pride and enthusiasm. They can appear in the same arena, represented by different volunteers, but sometimes by the very same volunteers. Some of those who are usually the most severe in observing the halakha are the ones who go farthest in violating its laws in the arena.

Behind the radicalism and religious enthusiasm that characterizes ZAKA's deathwork lies the duality of the antinomian and hypernomian trends. The assumed sanctity of the volunteers is related to both. In the arena there is a tacit struggle for religious excellence between those who sanctify the name of God by observing every single commandment and those who, while sanctifying the name of God, and for its sake, ignore certain commandments. When the volunteers take a short refreshing break from the deathwork on the edge of the arena, some of them, before drinking, recite the benediction, moving their bodies, praying out loud, at length, while closing their eyes with intense devotion, although frequently, in daily life, they don't bother to recite the blessing at all. Others drink on the edge of the arena and completely neglect the blessing, which they view, under the circumstances, as a petty nuisance. The former enjoy a feeling of religious assurance as guardians of the borders, and the latter revel in the religious freedom of boundary-breakers. The test of the volunteers' virtuosity is not only in hypernomy or only in antinomy, but mainly in the ability to contain both of them simultaneously and to foster the tension between them.

*

ZAKA volunteers' behavior, especially in the arena of disaster, has an essential characteristic that is non-conformist, even dissenting in ultra-Orthodox terms. Their deathwork deviates from the Haredi norm. They are both within the bounds of the religion and the community and outside them. The mixture of a smidgen of sin and heresy together with true religious fulfillment confounds them. The ZAKA activists genuinely wonder whether their way is that of *mitsva habaah be'aveira*—a commandment that is conditioned by and entails a sin. While they have allowed themselves to benefit from the doubt, critics arose from the Haredi world and rebuked them explicitly by calling them "Sabbateans."

Apart from Christianity, Sabbateanism (mid-seventeenth century) is the most notorious incident of antinomianism in Jewish history. This messianic-mystical awakening movement swept through significant parts of the Jewish world, including important communities and rabbis. The leader of the movement, Sabbatai Zevi, was believed to be the messiah, directly connected to the divinity. At the axis of his exemplary religious behavior were ritual acts that appeared to be "alien deeds," or "strange acts" (*ma'asim zarim*), and so they were classified. Among these were the mixing of dairy and meat foods, shifting the Sabbath and holidays to other dates, public sexual activity, and pronouncing the name of God—acts that violated central taboos. According to the Sabbatean interpretation of the Kabballah, these acts of desecration embodied the path for seeking God, and they were intended to bring redemption. After the messiah failed to deliver the promised goods—freedom from the rule of the gentiles, abundance and security, the ingathering of the exiles in the Land of Israel, and the building of the Temple in Jerusalem—and he was also imprisoned by the Ottoman authorities and even converted to Islam, the majority of his ardent followers abandoned him and his teachings. The remnants of his devotees were persecuted and excommunicated, and all overt traces of the movement were wiped out. In retrospect Sabbatai was called a false messiah, and Sabbateanism was considered an appalling sacrilege. This religious episode has been inscribed in Jewish memory as particularly traumatic, and in the ensuing generations it has served as a warning sign against any change in doctrine or ritual that claims to embody consistent and pure Judaism. Religious phenomena of this kind, which suggested deviation from the norms of what subsequently became orthodoxy, are labeled Sabbatean to this day.[17] Ultra-Orthodox have no tolerance for those who break taboos, especially when they claim to cling to their Judaism. No wonder Haredim see the details of ZAKA's deathwork in the arena as alien and strange deeds.

The appearance of a religious option that bears Sabbatean connotations on the horizon of the Jewish world suggests not only a scenario of threat but also one of promise. Despite the efforts at denial and condemnation, it exerts strong attraction upon even the most pious, offering the powerful religious experience of shedding the yoke of Torah, liberation from the burdensome tradition, overturning the existing order—all in the name of heaven. The unspeakable negativity of Sabbateanism is not exhausted solely in transgression, but in the idea of a transgression committed for the sake of a commandment. The ZAKA volunteers are sensitive to the possibility that their conduct in the various arenas of death might be interpreted as deviance in the form of the deterrent precedent of a commandment performed through transgression. This acute awareness enabled the volunteers to maintain their equilibrium in the era of terrorism-related religious enthusiasm. The Haredi volunteers are like acrobats on a high wire between the poles of hypernomy and antinomy, while beneath them yawns the chasm of Sabbateanism, both frightening and seductive.

The first time that the ZAKA volunteers rode on the Sabbath on their way to the arena of terrorism, where they moved bodies and body parts, they looked upward, expecting the heavens to fall. They feel the same to this day, every time they touch the blood of the dead—after the catharsis that accompanies the breaking of taboos. When the heavens don't fall, they are relieved. But then they also feel some disappointment and loss of confidence.

## Deathwork on a Religious Holy Day Is Worth More

ZAKA's violation of the Sabbath is in no way the only taboo that the Haredi volunteers break. The taboos violated for the purpose of dealing with the victims of disaster and other types of unnatural death fall into three categories: those that touch upon challenging the ascetic way of life of the ultra-Orthodox community, those that touch upon challenging the puritan norms relating to body and eroticism, and those that touch upon violence and death.

The most intriguing violation of a taboo is direct contact with fatality, especially brutal fatality. Touching the mutilated bodies of the casualties of a terrorist explosion with bare hands invites a peculiarly thrilling religious experience. I received no unequivocal answer to the question of which was the most extreme abhorrent-attractive taboo of all: unmediated contact with the holy bodies of Jewish victims or with the abominable body of the Palestinian attacker. And one still wonders: the violation of which proved to be more rewarding?

*

The transgression of taboos is a source of tormenting pangs of conscience but also of pleasurable stimulation. The ZAKA volunteers are thirsty for the violation of ritual prohibitions. Sometimes it seems as if they are seeking ever more taboos to violate for the sanctification of the name of God. I observed several nearly Sabbatean incidents, when they enthusiastically embraced a commandment whose fulfillment was bound up with a transgression. For example, in parallel with the holy war for respect of the dead, some veteran ZAKA volunteers declared holy war against Christian missionaries. They vandalized churches and monasteries in Jerusalem. To do so they violated an Orthodox prohibition against entering gentile places of worship. This was an alien and strange deed. Although they presented it as a sacrifice on their part, they could not conceal the satisfaction they derived from it. Their critics maintain that they could have battled against the Christians without the action-filled adventure of crossing the border and penetrating to the depth of the adversaries' holy place. A central activist in the organization told me, "The adrenaline that flows in the veins of a yeshiva student as a result of the risk of arrest by the police is negligible compared to the adrenaline that flows in the veins of a yeshiva student who sins by standing in front of a cross."

The Haredi volunteers display publicly the severity of their observance of the commandments, and they also display proudly the violation of commandments which is permitted to them. The invisible violation of a taboo is of little value and misses the point. They mainly flaunt the ability to contain the contradiction between enhancement of a commandment and behavior that appears to be the violation of a commandment. The organization's newsletter describes the handling of the victims of a mass accident that took place at the entry of the Sabbath. The headline says in huge letters that the Haredi activists worked in the arena while wearing their festive Sabbath clothing.[18] When a ZAKA delegation was sent to Haiti to treat the victims of the earthquake, they reported to their colleagues in Israel that they "violated the Sabbath with pride."[19]

ZAKA's self-presentation contains self-congratulatory dramatization of the challenge it poses to the boundaries of the religion by violating halakha with rabbinical sanction. Many both in the organization and out of it present the same illustration, which, ironically, they call "the Sabbath beeper syndrome." ZAKA's activists appear at public prayer in the synagogue on the Sabbath and holidays with a selection of cell phones and two-way radios hanging from their garments. Some of them conceal these devices beneath their Hasidic gaberdines, while others purposely make them conspicuous. Despite the halakhic permission—and perhaps because of it—these shining devices in the festive services are seen as foppish and teasing the Haredi community. The volunteers who violate the Sabbath barely feel uncomfortable; their embarrassment is trumped by their excitement and their feeling of advantage over their fellow worshipers. For their part, the others do not ignore them. They find it hard to accept but are unable to condemn, and they conceal more than a bit of admiration and envy. Outwardly and in an apologetic tone, the volunteers express their hope that there will be no need for the electronic gadgets, that they won't be called to an arena of disaster. In the depths of their hearts they would prefer for the devices to buzz, for all the other worshipers to notice and watch them rush off to their deathwork. The Haredi critics of ZAKA joke, "On Sabbath, some people pray for their barren wife to get pregnant, others pray for their businesses to prosper, but the volunteers pray for their telephones to ring loudly, interrupt the prayers, and call them to their holy task."

The ZAKA volunteers rush to the arenas of disaster on the Sabbath even if they receive notice that there are already more than enough of them. They refuse to forgo the special kick of violating the Sabbath with permission. It is known among the activists that, religiously speaking, an incident that takes place on the Sabbath is more exciting than one that takes place on a weekday.

## The Streets of Jerusalem and the Banks of the Ganges

Many millions of Hindus adore their death priests, called Aghori.[20] They are an idiosyncratic phenomenon, and in the West some people say they are bizarre, even hideous. The Aghori are a small, radical religious sect that specializes in presiding over an ideal Hindu mortuary rite. It is centered on the cremation sites on the banks of the Ganges in the pilgrimage city of Varanasi and in a few other places where the faithful come to die or are brought soon after their death. They are a type of *sadhu,* monks who renounce the vanities and material pleasures of the world, as they demonstrate, among other things, by their custom of walking about in nudity or semi-nudity. They worship Shiva, the god of destruction and death, as well as regeneration, and they have a traceable history of over three hundred years.[21] Their worldview is harmonious and monistic. They practice peculiar yoga techniques reaching full bodily self-control, which enables them to overcome the passing of time. They enter ecstatic states that allow them to transcend the conventions of their surroundings. To emphasize their denial of common values they practice extreme rituals, most prominently ostentatious displays of defilement, notably drinking urine and eating feces. By means of rites of this kind the Aghori testify to their utmost asceticism, their disavowal of ego, and their devotion, which comes almost to self-sacrifice. Furthermore, the consumption of human excretions implies blurring the differentiation between the body's inside and outside and obliterating the boundaries of the body. The latter are the metaphoric parallel of horizontal and vertical social boundaries, for example the lines that separate Brahmins and Dalits (untouchables). Traditional Indian society strictly observes bodily boundaries, caste boundaries, as reflected in ritual purity laws. The Aghori challenge these laws.

The practices by which the Aghori seek to attain religious distinction are deviant in relation to Hindu orthodoxy. Nevertheless, these practices afford them honor and prestige. Their worship entails the violation of severe ritual prohibitions, such as sexual relations with prostitutes, in public, and around temples. Their main taboo transgression is touching the dead, and this is what brings them popularity and a special status of sanctity among their lay devotees, who attribute superhuman abilities to them.[22] Their achievements in departure from the bounds of the dominant ethic and aesthetic of this world, and their victory over human nature, give them miraculous abilities, such as communication with spiritual beings and control over malevolent ghosts. The image of Aghori has shamanistic characteristics. Association with the dead, and their creativity and daring, are the sources of these holy men's charismatic influence and their magical abilities.

The Aghori are mainly responsible for the cremation of bodies on pyres and the scattering of their ashes in the water of the holy river. Their lives revolve around postmortem rituals concerning what remains of the body after death; for example, they meditate while sitting on the torso of a corpse, and they wear necklaces of human bones around their necks. Their trademark is the skull. They carry skulls with them and use them as bowls to beg for alms and as dishes from which they eat. What foreigners view as the most appalling of the Aghori rituals is the eating of carrion, and even cannibalism: the symbolic consumption of the flesh of the bodies that they treated. According to rumors that were current in India beginning under British rule as well as hints by the Aghori themselves, they also performed human sacrifice.[23]

Evidently, there is a vast difference between the Aghori and ZAKA, and in the respective cultural and historical contexts in which they appear. Having conceded this, certain similarities between the death priests in India and in Israel are noteworthy. The anthropologist Nurit Stadler was the first to suggest that ZAKA resembles the Aghori, and she presented a few preliminary comparative notes about these two types of religious deathworkers to be elaborated and refined in this subchapter.[24]

Both the Aghori and ZAKA are sacred death specialists that obsessively immerse themselves in the physical remains of the dead. They take responsibility for disposal of corpses, and, in addition, they are preoccupied with the posthumous fate of the soul of the deceased and with the purification of the sites of death in the public space and of the community of mourners. The members of these two exclusive sects devote themselves to demanding deathwork, to a total life career for years. They are satisfied with a life of penury and avoid asking for any recompense beyond the satisfaction offered by their worship.[25] The customs of these two groups of religious virtuosi deviate demonstrably from the hegemonic norms of the surrounding society, whose response is mixed. Some outsiders keep a distance and even condemn them, while many others venerate them.

Both the Aghori and ZAKA violate central taboos of their religion; thence, paradoxically, derives their elevated religious status. The most extreme taboo that they violate is their direct contact with death. Both variants of holy men have the privilege of touching the dead, and this, in turn, contributes to their status as holy men. The Jewish and Hindu death priests are masters who plunge deeply into the lowermost quintessence of pollution, where the height of sanctity resides.

The Aghori and ZAKA are not identical religious phenomena, but they are analogous. In the light of the similarity between them, we will take note of the differences, and, in the light of the differences between them, we will examine their similarity. Here are several stimulating comparative observations.

In their arenas of death—on the steps descending to the vast river in Varanasi or in the municipal vegetable market in Jerusalem—both groups meticulously administer extensive and detailed ritual procedures, with dread that they might deviate from the rules. In both cases they turn the dead into sacrificial victims, ex post factum. Accordingly, they prepare the dead for eternal life or regeneration. The Aghori do this by destruction of the physical body, as, for example, when they smash the dead person's skull to release his soul. ZAKA does this by restoring the physical body, for example, when they join the arms of a corpse to the shoulders, to provide a dwelling for his soul. The highly symbolic deathwork endows those who perform it with extraordinary social capabilities. Thus, admirers approach them for blessings, advice, and mediation. They also have healing powers. Some of them have become famous as miracle workers. In the process, the Hindu death priests protect themselves against various kinds of harm such as disease and old age (and the decomposition of their bodies, as befits saints), and the Jewish ones against terrorist attacks as well.[26]

In their contact with corpses, the Aghori and ZAKA move in the chaotic space between life and death, between pollution and purity, between sin and sanctity, between flesh and spirit, between social marginality and contempt and centrality and high status. Both groups of death priests focus their worship on the fateful immediate aftermath of death, more precisely, on the short but perilous interval between physiological and sociological death. The Aghori and ZAKA are liminal phenomena, performing ritual rites of passage. Both groups of death priests indulge in contact with social extremes. They are inspired and achieve religious excellence by challenging the ethos regarded as decent in their societies and testing the boundaries of correct religion.

The Aghori and ZAKA belong to cultures obsessed with purity that is defended by severe ritual prohibitions. Behind the intense ritualism of the two groups lies deep interest in the social order, which is jeopardized as a result of death, and with the aim of amending it and bringing it to perfection. In the culture of both groups there is an implicit assumption that the state of the body or corpse is parallel with the state of the collective. By manipulating the body immediately after death, the faithful of both religions seek to transform the chaos into a new order. However, contrasting religious ideas guide this project of restoration, the return to what had been before. Hence, they strive for this religious goal in opposite ways. According to the monistic religion of the Aghori, the contrasts prevalent in our society do not exist in deep reality, and common fundamental categorizations—the distinction between good and evil, beautiful and ugly, living and dead, and pure and polluted—are an illusion from which one must free oneself. The Hindu death specialists claim that the pristine state of the cosmos is not binary and hierarchical. Rather there is total harmony, including that between high and low castes. Aghori ritualism seeks to reestablish this ideal situation. ZAKA ritualism also seeks to move time backward, to reinstate the ideal order. However, the perfect situation, for which the Jewish death specialists strive, is one of separation of various categories, distancing and ranking them, after the violent death in the arena erased the boundaries and created an undesirable situation of closeness, unity, equality, and fusion (including that of the Jew and the non-Jew). By embracing death, the Aghori seek to attain the primordial state that preceded the spread of differentiation in the world, whereas ZAKA's embracing of death is intended to re-create the world that existed before the terrorist attack, which blurred important lines of differentiation.

The Aghori death ritual attempts to dissolve the basic hierarchical subunits of Indian society into a timeless and undifferentiated mythical universe, while ZAKA death ritual attempts to re-establish, sharpen, and solidify the elemental and antagonistic sub-units of the Middle East and restore their original, paramount value. In the former case, cosmic holistic eternity is sought after by destroying intra-social divisions. In the latter case, by reconstructing international and religious divisions, the ZAKA volunteers seek to restore the pre-attack regional demarcation.

The Aghori seek the elimination or complete dissolution of the physical body by burning it and scattering the ashes on the water, whereas ZAKA makes every effort to preserve the remains by gathering them, reassembling them, and burying them. Both types of priests try to attain the ante-mortem state by their respective postmortem rituals. The deathwork of the Hindu and Jewish virtuosi is intended to undo the negative effect of death, in a way, to nullify death itself.

*

The Aghori death priests rub their faces and bodies with the ashes of the cremated dead. Some of the ZAKA death priests stain their clothing with the blood of the dismembered dead. These are two parallel ways of displaying intimate attachment to death. In a seminal study of the Aghori, they are called necrophagous.[27] Could ZAKA also be called necrophagous? Feeding on corpses is an extreme form of erasing the boundary between the living person and the corpse by his side.[28] Some of the Hindu death priests, as well as the Jewish, strive for maximal proximity with the corpses and body parts that they treat. They demonstrate this closeness, and they derive their social status from it.[29] I heard senior Haredi volunteers make fun of one of their number, who preferred to gather spilled guts in the arena of terrorism with a pair of trowels, which he held in both hands and pressed together, rather than grasping the dead flesh with his bare hands.[30] As mentioned above, the veteran members of the organization are nostalgic about the time when they worked with bare hands, before they were required to wear rubber gloves for fear of contamination. Then they touched pollution and sanctity with nothing intervening.

## Bonifying Death

It has been argued that not every death is bad. Some deaths are particularly bad, and, by contrast, there are even good deaths.[31] Usually the death of an innocent child is regarded as worse than that of a senile old person; the death of a legendary freedom fighter in an epic battle is better than death in an ordinary road accident, which is just a statistic. Evaluation of death indicates the ability of a culture to relate death to a narrative that will help to accept it, to overcome it, and even to capitalize on it. This depends not only on interpretation concerning the presumed purpose and outcome of the death but also on a sense of control over the contingencies of death, the sharpness of its boundaries, and its finality.

Sociology and anthropology have long since noted the existence of good death, which occurs in the right time and place, for example, when the deceased and the people around him felt that he had exhausted his life and fulfilled his mission in the world, or when he was at home, surrounded by beloved relatives. A good death takes place after spiritual and ritual—sometimes even physical—preparation on the part of the deceased and those around him.[32] Among the conventional characteristics of anticipated death, which was properly prepared, are that it should come after a person's confession to God, after saying farewell to his children and friends, after he has signed his testament, after fasting and ablution. Above all, a good death is one that has a convincing reason and proper justification. The scope of possibilities ranges between death that puts an end to the suffering brought on by terminal illness, to death that is intended to save the lives of many others. A good death can be represented symbolically as a confirmation of the victory of life by the promise of regeneration.

All death has anomic potential and threatens the social order. For that reason, death specialists emerge who manage the various aspects of deathwork in a manner that enables the continued effective functioning of the collective and the individuals who compose it. Religious cultures have their own ideal death. Well-known examples of these can be found in the ancient Egyptian and Tibetan books of the dead. In medieval and Early Modern European Christian culture, for example, there was a literary genre known as "the art of dying" (*ars moriendi*).[33] Judaism has a concept called *menuḥa nekhona* (proper repose). A good Jewish death is conditioned on *sha'at ratson* (a propitious hour), when the gates of heaven open to receive the repentance of a person who merits forgiveness by God. This, however, is not sufficient. It is important to conduct the death according to a meticulous ceremony, which alone can assure the healing of the dead person's soul. Slight deviation from the prescribed procedure is liable to cause the soul's rejection by the upper world. A good death is accepted with joy. Ecclesiastes says, "The day of death is better than the day of birth." (Incidentally, one of the volunteers suggested this biblical verse as ZAKA's motto.) Specific cases of good death are much discussed within ZAKA, such as the death of a *tsadik* whose soul departed while he was wearing a prayer shawl and *tefillin*, reciting psalms. The organization's rabbis told me about a man who thought of his death as so good that in his will he called for hiring a band to play at his funeral.[34] In contrast, some rabbis particularly wanted to have a bad death, to atone for sins they committed during their lives.[35]

The death of victims of terrorism is the categorical opposite of a good death, and death by suicide terrorism is particularly bad. The young healthy woman who walked through a city square on the way to nurse her infant and was caught by the explosion died at the wrong time and place, without any mental, ritual, or administrative preparation of her own or of others. Mainly it is difficult to find an acceptable justification for her death or to attribute a motive or purpose to it. Had it depended on her, she would almost certainly have struggled to stay alive. She left her loved ones and the community in pain, without meaning or hope. It is difficult to reframe and present death from terrorism as positive, and thus it is an emblematic example of how it is not good to die.[36]

ZAKA possess clear indices for determining the value of every sort of death. Many of these depend on the condition of the corpse. According to the Haredi volunteers' scale, the more a body is mutilated and scattered, the worse is the death. In such cases it is impossible to bury the body properly in a manner that will honor it and obey rabbinical law. Because the death of the victims of terrorism is so bad, from the moment of the explosion until the limbs are located, reassembled, and buried, demons can enter them. The most severe danger in the arenas of suicide terrorism, in which bodies are ripped open and inner organs spill out, is when there is contact between Jewish limbs and those of the Palestinian attacker.

In contrast to the death of the victim of suicide terrorism, the attacker's death, that of the human bomb, is particularly good, according to most of the criteria listed above. The suicide terrorist sanctified himself before his mission, and his sanctity increased with the explosion and the mass murder. Not only did he seek his own death and attain it by himself, but his community also regarded his death as something beneficial and exalted. With his death, he achieved for himself and for his collective everything that he could not have achieved in his lifetime. The Palestinian terrorist's death is that of a *shahid*, who sought to join his holy brethren in heaven. It is believed that his body will not rot but will glow and emit the fragrance of perfume. In some of the testaments of those about to set out on suicide attacks, they boast about their imminent death and contrast it with ordinary death, like death from a disease, which they see as contemptible. They especially presented their death at their own hands, while killing the Jewish enemy, as far better than death at the hands of Israelis.

The arena of suicide terrorism confronts the absolute best death for one side with the very worst death for the other; the desired and praised death of the Palestinian attacker depends upon and joins with the humiliating and threatening death of the Israeli victim. ZAKA intervenes in the arena with the aim of retroactively correcting the death of the victims and thus restoring some symmetry among those who die in a suicide explosion.

The bad death from terrorism is a fait accompli, and all that remains is to try and make it better ex post factum. The relatives of the deceased who co-operate with the leaders of the communities to which the deceased belong join in this effort.[37] However, the mission of retroactively ameliorating the imprint of the death by terrorism is the primary expertise, main responsibility, and purpose of most of the efforts of the priests of death.[38] For them this is a religious project, which I define as "bonifying death." This process is partially reminiscent of what is known in the history of Christianity as beatification, the papal declaration that certain people who have died, sometimes generations after their death, are saints, who have received supreme grace and been accepted into heaven.

The bonification of a bad death consists of two parts or stages. The first is perceptual, interpretative, and the second is material, ritual. First, for the death to be thought of as good, voluntarity and agency must be attributed to the victims. Their death must be taken as if they sought it or prepared themselves for it. Hence, there is no possibility of understanding the death as random. Moreover, one must see the death of the victims as if it served a goal regarded as exalted by the mourners, and the consequences of the death must be seen as desired and blessed. Marking the positive implications of the death for the society emphasizes its altruistic and noble nature.

This aspect of bonification is a type of rationalization, an intellectual or theological project. When imagination fails to explain death by terrorism as a result of the victim's wishes, naturally this outcome is attributed to God's will. Death is presented as part of a divine plan. Among the causes for attributing death by terrorism to God's will are to warn the public that they must correct their corrupt ways and to test the people and select between the righteous and the wicked. Frequently it is asserted that God's intentions are hidden, but their a priori justification automatically makes death in terrorism a good death, behind which there was a worthy intention from the start. This situation implies what can be called the paradox of prepared unpreparedness.[39] The victim only apparently did not realize he was going to meet his death; in fact, he had inner awareness in the depths of his faith, that God had decreed his time to die and determined the circumstances of his death in advance.

The second component in the bonification of a bad death in terrorism is the ritual component that completes the process. This component is not satisfied with shaping consciousness but adds the skilled handiwork prescribed by a detailed scenario. This is a physical project revolving around the axis of the victim's remains. Death in terrorism is a particularly bad death because it does not leave behind it a corpse that can be treated, or because it entails the mutilation of the body and the loss of its human form. Hence, bonification requires repair of a corpse or its reconstruction. ZAKA does this by collecting the blood and scraps of bones, gathering the limbs and joining them together to reassemble the body, restoring it to its earlier pre-explosion state.

When the Aghori priests must cope with death that went out of control and was unprepared, and which also damaged the body, as in the case of the death of lepers, they wish to restore the situation to its former state by manipulating the body in the arena of death. They view this as such a bad death that the soul fled from the body and in its place a malevolent ghost took it over. In this state of disharmony, it is impossible to return the dead person to the gods. To replace the blemished body, the Hindu death experts build an effigy of rice. Instead of the body, which was made to disappear by cremation and scattering the ashes, they construct a symbolic replacement in the form of a dummy, in imitation of the human form. This manikin is burned with full control, according to the ritual rules: the dead person is made to die again, in timely fashion, in the right place, according to the procedure dictated by the mythical canon. Then the soul is freed as it should be and rises to heaven to mollify the gods. Thus, they separate the gross, concrete body and the spiritual body, and between medical death and social, ceremonial death. The Aghori ritual of treating the victim of a bad death—for example, a casualty of cancer or accident—is intended to attain a dual repair: repair of the randomness of death and repair of bodily mutilation. By means of yogic procedures connected to the body on the verge of death, and by building an effigy to replace the body immediately after the death, they attain a feeling of control over the circumstances of the time and place of the death, and they also make it possible to imagine the body as if it were intact. Thus, the Aghori reenact the mythological sacrifice. In both the Hindu case, by means of an effigy that restores the body, and in the Jewish case, by reassembling the mutilated limbs of the body, instead of the original brutal and arbitrary death, which violated the cosmic order, they create a different, correct death, and a perfect victim is produced, to restore order.

The ZAKA postmortem ritual is similar in structure and function to the Aghori postmortem ritual. Both bonify death. The bonification of death by terrorism seeks to counteract the capriciousness of this bad death and present it as fulfilling a mission. It turns passive and random death into something active, valuable, and exalted because of its contribution to society. In parallel to the construction of an effigy in the arena of death on the banks of the Ganges, in the arena of bad death in the streets of Jerusalem, they also create a correction or replacement for the body that disappeared or was mutilated. The Hindu effigy is analogous to the reassembled Jewish corpse, which fulfills the aspiration to produce a perfect body. To attain a perfect body, the ZAKA volunteers sometimes go to great lengths, such as joining the arm of one victim to the armless corpse of another victim. In the folklore of the Haredi volunteers, it is widely claimed that, following the horrific suicide attack in the Sbarro restaurant, the volunteers put together the bodies of children with limbs taken from members of the family who were killed with them (August 2001). In the National Institute of Forensic Medicine it is whispered that, for ZAKA, putting a body back together is tantamount to making it Jewish. The volunteers perform a reparation for the bodies by a kind of retroactive conversion, for example by erasing the tattoo of a cross or posthumous circumcision.

Reassembling a body makes it possible to identify it, locating the dead person's personal information, and this is a condition for its burial. The finality of death can only be determined after its bonification, and it is not possible to part forever from the deceased until the death is definitively decreed. The finality of death is conditional on assembling all the scraps, joining them together, and removing them from the arena. Only then does the deceased conclude his social presence in the world. Then one may begin to mourn. Only then is the resurrection of the dead possible. Until the body is whole, regeneration is impossible. The promise of resurrection contributes to the ability of the agonizing individuals and the collective afflicted by anomie to overcome the crisis of death and continue functioning. Coping with death depends on accepting its finality, which, paradoxically, is the key to faith in the continuation of life in the future. The intact body means, as it were, that there was no death. Absolute, final death is good death, which, in turn, is a victory over death.

The ultimate bonification of a bad death is turning it into a sacrifice. The combination of the above-mentioned two components of the bonification of a bad death can be a springboard for turning the victims of terrorism into sacrifices. Death as a sacrifice is an exceptionally good death. Treating death by terrorism as if it were sacrificial is the essence of ZAKA's project of bonifying death.

A sacrificial animal (let alone a human) must not be blemished. Moreover, the offering of sacrifices must follow the rules of the ritual. Then it will fulfill its role as a sacrifice: to atone, to redeem, and to contribute to the well-being of the community. Making the victims sacrificial transforms the Israelis who died in terrorist attacks into agents of atonement, redemption, and revenge.[40] The dismantling and reconstruction of the body are sacrificial actions. The recomposing of the body as a sacrifice is like resurrecting it.

Before ZAKA joined the scene of Middle Eastern terrorism at the beginning of the Intifada, the sacrificial victims in the arenas of death represented only one side of the conflict, that of the Palestinian human bombs, the *shahids*, holy in their own eyes and in those of their dispatchers. The Haredi volunteers make the Israelis whose bodies they treat into sacrificial victims, if not of their own volition before the explosion, but at least, according to the Jewish believers, after the explosion. By its nature, suicide terrorism creates victims on both sides. Thus, there is a kind of equalization and mixture of victimhood. At the sites of terrorist attacks in Jerusalem during the last decade of the past century and the first decade of this one, the sides became equal, partners and competitors in the sacrificial domain.uyr

# 8

# The Spell of Tearing the Body Apart

## The Magic of Piecing the Body Together

### Relics

During the escalation of the armed confrontation between Israel and the Palestinian resistance organizations in the southern Gaza Strip, an IDF armored personell carrier was hit by an anti-tank rocket, and a large explosive charge that was stored in it exploded (Philadelphi Route, 2004). The bodies of the five soldiers who were on board were shattered and their parts were scattered all around, over a great distance. The commanders of the army, backed by rabbis, instructed the soldiers in the unit that had been struck to examine the area of the attack closely, and to collect the remains of their comrades. This Sisyphean and dangerous task was defined as holy. This is how it looked: a broad front of dozens of soldiers, helmets on their heads and rifles strapped to their shoulders, advanced on all fours, shoulder to shoulder, inch by inch. Their gaze was focused downward as they dug with bare hands, delicately sifting the desert sand between their fingers, combing handful after handful, to locate scraps of flesh and fragments of bone, while exposed to enemy fire.

Hair-raising pictures of this event were featured on the news. Not a single viewer was indifferent, and the scene is engraved deeply in Israeli collective memory. A fierce public discussion was not long in coming. The voices critical of risking lives for the sake of the dead, condemning what was labeled "disproportionate" concern for bodies and burial, were overwhelmed by a flood of patriotism tinged with religious phrases.[1] Types of violent death and the state of corpses became the talk of the day.[2] A senior Israeli journalist defined this phenomenon as a symptom of ZAKA Syndrome.[3]

Israeli life offers many illustrations of the prevalence of the idea of the sanctity of dead body parts. The influence of ZAKA's conception of death on the national ethos has also affected the state's relations with the nations of the region. A decided example of this can be found in what is called the Sea

*The Cult of Dismembered Limbs*. Gideon Aran, Oxford University Press. © Oxford University Press 2023.
DOI: 10.1093/oso/9780197689141.003.0008

Commando Disaster (September 1997). A failed IDF mission in southern Lebanon ended with a sizable number of casualties, and their evacuation was complicated because one soldier's body was not found. His body was pulverized and could not be located in the commotion of the battle in the darkness, so its parts fell into the hands of the enemy. Israel made diplomatic and military efforts to recover the remains, and its rival exploited this to advance its interests. The physical remains of the victims of Middle Eastern violence have become players in the regional conflict and have taken on strategic value. In his first public address after the Israeli incursion into Lebanon in 2006, Hizballah leader, Sheikh Nasrallah declared that his organization had in its possession pieces of the bodies of Israeli soldiers. As the subsequent responses proved, he had taken accurate aim at Israeli sensitivities. The Israeli press called it the "Organ Speech." It was accompanied by televised images of severed limbs.

Several times Israel has been pressured into releasing hundreds of Palestinian and Lebanese terrorists in return for the remains of its soldiers.[4] A new kind of culture of trade in dead body parts has taken over the politics of the Middle Eastern conflict.[5] Israel's national and international agenda reverberates with ZAKA's discourse about human remains.

In response to questions regarding the source of Israeli sensitivity to the matter of dead body parts, the ZAKA rabbis point to the organization's prehistory, taking credit for renewal of the Jewish idea of the sanctity of human remains. This stood out when the scandal broke regarding the burial of the sea commando victims. The body parts of a few fallen soldiers were misplaced in others' graves. ZAKA joined the outcry that arose among the public.[6] These incidents are rooted in the Israeli instinct of concern for the sanctity of severed limbs, which ZAKA was the first to arouse, and the Intifada has led to the spread of this concern, so that in the present generation it has gained unprecedented centrality. The scene of the soldiers desperately looking for the scattered remains of their comrades on the battlefield is surely connected to the scene of elderly Haredim who are spontaneously drawn to the sites of explosions in town centers, sneaking past police barriers, and devoting themselves to the collection of scraps of the victims' bodies in market baskets.

*

Dead bodies may have a vitality of their own, exerting political and religious influence.[7] This also applies to parts and fragments of bodies. Ancient and recent history offers us examples of severed limbs with greater posthumous potency than healthy limbs. Many such examples relate to the cult of the martyrs of a nation, tribe, or class. For example, the literature discusses instances in Latin America, such as that of the populist autocrat Juan Perón, whose body, imbued with sanctity, was removed from the grave by his admirers, who cut off his arms to preserve them and to make them into objects of devotion.[8] In the United States, the Confederate general Stonewall Jackson's left arm was severed and buried separately from the rest of his body. That grave became a focus of southern patriotic sentiment and a pilgrimage site.[9] The literature speaks of cases in post-Soviet Eastern Europe where people who were buried years earlier were reinterred and received new life, yoked to nation-building projects.[10] The dead are often called upon in times of crisis. The manipulation of severed limbs arouses powerful emotions and serves to arouse the masses. The phenomenon is carried to absurd lengths with the charismatic effect and agitating capacity even of artificial limbs taken from people who died in admired circumstances, such as the wooden leg of the Mexican general Antonio López de Santa Anna, or the prosthetic arm of Joseph Trumpeldor, the Zionist pioneer.[11]

The origins of such political phenomena can be traced to a shared cultural descent from an essentially religious legacy developed in the early Middle Ages, that is, the Christian cult of the saints.[12] The bodies and limbs of those faithful to the Church were endowed with sanctity after their death, often a long time afterward, based on the image retroactively applied to their lives, sometimes on the basis of the narrative composed to describe their death. The entire body, as well as its parts—leg, heart, eye, even toenail, or lock of hair—was regarded as holy, as were intimate artifacts close to the body such as glasses or a shoelace. There is an element of fetishism in this cult of relics.[13] Every part of the body symbolized the entire body (*pars pro toto*), and sometimes its value competed with the value of the whole that it symbolized. The inanimate object was the basis for the cult of that saint and an intermediary between the faithful and God, providing social integration for the community in hard times, economic stability, and a feeling of security. The dead body parts retain vitality, and they were permeated by mystery and endowed with magical power to effect miracles. These physical remains of the bodies of saints promised new life, resurrection.

The cult of relics is widespread among religious cultures, including Hinduism, Buddhism, and Islam.[14] There is extensive scholarly literature on relics in Christianity.[15] When relics are discovered, as it were, they are preserved and cultivated, and an entire ritual takes shape around them, in honor of the dead holy person, to whom the dead body part or object is attributed. Relics were concentrations of sanctity with beneficial influence, protecting the community and its surroundings.[16] Relics were often buried beneath the altar of a church, which became a pilgrimage site. Sometimes relics (e.g., bone of a saint) were smashed to bits, to increase the number of beneficiaries from its marvelous qualities, such as curing the sick. Competition developed among groups for monopoly over relics, markets for relics arose, and sometimes they were even robbed (*furta sacra*).[17] Striking phenomena connected with the cult of relics appear to this day.[18]

ZAKA's ritual of mutilated body parts at the scene of terrorism partakes of the cult of relics. The attitude of the Haredi volunteers to the drops of blood, the fragments of bone, and even to the scraps of clothing of the Jewish martyrs during the Intifada are analogous in part to the medieval Christian cult of relics. ZAKA locates the remains of bodies, declares them to be holy, and performs an elaborate ceremony around them, endowing them with magical powers. They treat a severed hand, a finger, a tooth found in the arena in that way, as well as bloodstained ritual fringes. In one case, ZAKA volunteers dug under the cover of darkness to remove corpses from their graves, seized pieces of bodies (claimed to be mistakenly buried with the wrong corpse), and brought them to their proper place, for the sake of repentance and redemption, similar to what Christian believers had done more than a thousand years earlier.

There is a parallel and apparently also reciprocal inspiration between ZAKA's cult of relics and those of Israel's adversaries in the Middle East, the Sunni Hamas in Gaza and the Shiite Hizballah in Lebanon, for whom bodily remains also play important religious and political roles. In the organizational culture of the armed resistance to the Israeli occupation, the concrete images of mutilated bodies, rivers of blood, and severed limbs have a prominent place. Special sanctity and a dual, miraculous potential are attributed to them: they kill the enemy and bring the national-religious victory, and they assure the resurrection of the dead, first, to the human bombs themselves. In posters pasted up in the streets of the West Bank, the bodies of *shahids* are portrayed from whose spilled guts young warriors spring, eager to sacrifice themselves to liberate the homeland. In the videos, laden with images of Paradise, severed arms and legs float and become flowering trees, waiting to be rejoined with their owner. In murals in Palestinian refugee camps, an arm severed from its body is seen, plunging a knife into a Zionist heart. The Palestinian Islamic Jihad movement distributed a leaflet stating, "We have no life without the death of Shahids. . . . From the parts of their bodies they create our praise, our history, and our future."[19]

In the death zone of the Middle Eastern conflict one even finds a variation on the medieval theft of relics. The IDF buries the remains of suicide terrorists in a secret cemetery in a remote desert area because it is feared that the place might become a pilgrimage site for Palestinians, and an Islamic saint cult might develop. There are signs that residents of the West Bank have located this cemetery, broken through the barbed-wire fence that surrounds it, and tried to steal the limbs of *shahids*.[20] In Hamas discourse during the Intifada, extensive use was made of the word *ashllah* ("pieces," in Arabic) to describe the severed limbs or remains of a body. *Ashllah el taaher* are the pure body parts, which have exalted national and religious value, that is, relics.[21]

One may infer from the testaments recorded before they left on their missions during the Intifada that the Palestinian suicide terrorists were fully aware that their bodies would be blown to bits and scattered over the arena. Moreover, they predicted the mingling of their own body parts and those of their Jewish victims. As if there were a fatal efficacy of the relics of both sides, they are drawn to each other with murderous purpose, as shown by phrases typical of the terrorists' testaments: "I hope that the shredded limbs of my body would be shrapnel, tearing the Zionists to pieces, knocking on the doors of heaven with the skulls of the Zionists" or "How beautiful for the splinters of my bones to be the response that blows up the enemy."[22]

## Walking Dead

Life is not separated from death by a sharp and permanent boundary. Behind this claim, which has long been accepted in the study of death in the social sciences, there are two interconnected truisms. First, the transition from life to death extends over various periods of time, and it might include intermediate stages, some of which are liminal and contain inner tension. The process can also be bi-directional. In addition to the movement from life to death, there can be movement back from death to life. Second, we must distinguish between different kinds of death, mainly between physical and social death. The latter generally has a ritual expression. Social scientists agree that there need be no synchronization between physical and social death. Indeed, death is possible while one is still alive, as is life after death. This sociological-anthropological perspective can provide several further insights for research into the phenomena of ZAKA and the arena of terrorism.[23]

Social death occurs when a person ceases to maintain relationships with his or her surroundings and to play a role in the life of his or her community or in private life within it. Even a person who has died biologically is alive so long as he is perceived as an active agent or a significant subject by others, and there is communication between him and them, and acknowledgment of mutual influence, even if only symbolically or in the imagination. Sometimes social death can precede physical death. A famous example of this is in the Dogon tribe, which holds funerals for living people, making them sever all contact with members of their group and wander far away, and if, by chance, they do approach, they remain without family or property, even without a name, until their physical death. A familiar example from the modern West is found in hospitals, where hopelessly comatose patients are kept, as if they were merely bodies, inanimate, and in any event their presence is ignored. Sometimes social death comes long after physical death, as in the Hindu practices in Varanasi, where long rites are held near the body, and a person is declared dead only after the Aghori priests smash his skull and wait for the departure of his soul. In our society we know of the phenomenon of bereaved parents who refuse to part with their dead children and visit their graves to speak with them. Only after the parents have died can the community part with their children. The division between physical and social death and the examples presented above demonstrate the human effort to control the cruel capriciousness of death.

A person whose social death precedes his physical death is regarded as dead in life, or living dead, like a prisoner who has been condemned to death and awaits execution. A person whose social death is preceded by his physical death is regarded as alive in death until the funeral. Sometimes the disciples of a venerated religious leader refuse to acknowledge his death and continue to ask him questions, and his answers—for example in their dreams or in words from heaven that they hear—guide them in their lives.[24] From a social standpoint the living, at least some of them, never die. Corpses can thus maintain a presence, sometimes a strong one, in society and culture. They may kick, converse, be managed, and manage affairs. Specifically, corpses can have meaningful relationships with, among others, those who treat them and with other (dead) bodies.

The Palestinian suicide terrorist is both dead in life and alive in death. Before the attack, from the moment he puts on the explosive vest and crosses the border from the West Bank to Israel, until the explosion, he is dead in life. After the attack—from the moment of the explosion until his body is recovered, reassembled, and identified—he is alive in death. The liminal stage between life and death is framed by two systems of ceremonies: recording of the martyr's testimony, purifying his body, and prayer inaugurate the liminal stage; announcement of the martyr's name by the resistance organizations, the erection of a mourning shed at his parents' house, and the broadcasting of his testament on television conclude it.

The human bomb's career as alive in death was short, as was his career as a living dead man, since the ZAKA volunteers cooperated with the experts in forensic medicine and intelligence agents in the effort to deal with the terrorist's body and identify him as quickly as possible, both to separate him from the bodies of his victims and to get onto the trail of his dispatchers.

The arena of suicide terrorism is characterized by confusion of the boundaries of time and by a complex dialectic of the relations between before and after. As a result, death becomes a vague and flexible matter, susceptible to manipulation. For example, the testament of the martyr and attacker is like a death sentence and at the same time a promise of eternal life. These testaments were recorded in secret, before the mission, and then broadcast publicly after it. The suicide predicts his future and dictates it. However, he does not speak in the future tense but rather in the present and the past about the outcome of his terrorist attack. He converses with his parents while alongside his fellow *shahids* in the company of the angels of Paradise. In confident tones and concrete terms he speaks as if he had already crossed the border between Palestine and Israel, and beyond the line between life and death, truly in the bus (or the market or restaurant) at the moment of the explosion, in the moments immediately after it, and finally in the infinite years in the happy, upper worlds. The Palestinian viewers of the video do not know whether he is addressing them from here or from "out there," from this world or from the world to come. Perhaps he himself would find it hard to determine from where he speaks and to whom. Interviews with suicide terrorists who failed in their mission and were captured show that as part of the preparation they viewed their own testament time after time. This was a kind of personal pep talk in a closed circuit, during which the human bomb undergoes the transition from one time frame to another, from the present to the time entirely beyond the horizon. From this moment until the explosion, he lives beyond time. This timeless status continues after the explosion as well since the *shahid* gains eternal life. Thus, the martyr receives absolute immunity from any injury. This is a kind of liminal state, a moratorium that confers a feeling of power and total freedom, which he had not previously enjoyed, and which will end soon. This is a paradoxically prolonged but short moment, the greatest in his miserable life.

In the consciousness of his community, the suicide terrorist lives on after his death as well. Occasionally it is claimed that he lives *only* after his death, because his life was not a life. From the moment he parts from his dispatchers with a hug, and mainly after he has penetrated the site of the planned attack, he is dead while alive in a multitude of ways. The human equivalent of the confusion of times that characterizes suicide terrorism is the hybrid creature called "the walking dead," both in Hebrew (*met mithalekh*, in the language of the IDF) and in Arabic (*almiat al ayiesh*, in the language used in sermons in mosques).[25] As we shall see soon, "the walking dead" is a term applicable not only to the attacker but also to his victims.

Immortality also derives from improved documentary technology, as shown by the recorded testaments. Suicide terrorism, which confounds before and after and blurs the distinction between life and death, fits in with advanced modernity. When we view a photoshopped image of the suicide terrorist holding his own severed head in his hands, are we seeing reality or a fantasy, the past, the present, or the future, a living person or a dead one? With the photograph, at the moment of his social death, the terrorist mimics his physical death. He traces the moment of the explosion and what will come after it in detail. He even imagines the way that the ZAKA volunteers will hold his head.[26]

The arena offers many examples of blurring the distinction between past and present, and the mixture of life and death: following the suicide attack on the restaurant Maxim (October 2003, twenty-one victims), the Palestinian Islamic Jihad circulated a photograph of the arena immediately after the event, which was described as the wedding of "the bride of Haifa," the woman terrorist Hanadi Jaradat. The picture shows ruins and body fragments, alongside the severed head of the attacker, without wounds or deformation. It is wrapped in a clean veil in a manner emphasizing both her attractive vitality and her puritan morals. A second look confirms suspicion that the photo was doctored and modified. Another example is provided by the terrorist who blew himself up near a group of Israelis, but, because of a technical failure, the explosive charge was only partially activated, and he was not mortally wounded. When he regained consciousness in an Israeli hospital, he found himself in the presence of doctors and then interrogators of the secret service, who had trouble convincing him that he was not in the promised Garden of Eden. Furthermore, during the Intifada, children in the Gaza Strip used to announce their own death, mainly with graffiti, although they had not been recruited by any organization for a suicide mission. At that time, processions were organized in the cities, with young people dressed in shrouds from head to foot, like heavenly spirits.

According to Palestinian interpretations, the suicide terrorist is thought of as dead long before recording his testament and donning the explosive vest, since he is discriminated against and humiliated by the Israelis, who trample his basic rights and self-definition and deny him freedom and the minimal conditions of life. This explains his desire to commit suicide, which is merely the physical death that will redeem him from social death. The explosion will put an end to his condition as dead in life and finally give him a full death, which is tantamount to a full life. At the same time, his status as dead in life, which he assumed from the moment he committed himself to the suicide attack, is a source of satisfaction to the terrorist and a reason to boast. He defines himself as someone who has already died and thus adopts a new, rewarding identity. The title that potential suicide terrorists obtain and bear with pride is that of a living martyr (*shahid al hayi*). A terrorist sent by Hamas, Sa'id Khoutri from Kalkilia, who killed himself along with twenty-one Israeli youths in the Dolphinarium Club in Tel Aviv, concluded his testament, which he recorded before leaving for the attack, a "living *shahid*" (June 2001).

The imminent death promised to the suicide terrorist gives him the pleasures of the world to come while he is still alive. In this world he is already a martyr who relishes freedom and other privileges promised to saints after their death. Death that precedes death gives him new, pungent vitality. The operational demands of his mission make it impossible for the candidate for self-immolation to share his honored status as dead in life, and the secret is kept even from his family. However, in the time between recording the testament and the attack, his life is intense and especially meaningful. Paradoxically, he is imbued with a form of optimism. But the satisfactions offered by the state of living-dead are difficult to maintain, and the terrorist wishes to avoid putting off the end. According to the testimony of dispatchers, the suicide terrorists often press them to hasten departure on the mission.

The identity of the living dead is laden with the tension of contradictions typical of this hybrid type in various cultures. Thus, while the suicide terrorist is vulnerable and particularly fragile, he simultaneously possesses magical powers to overcome every obstacle. He is extremely dangerous and yet he has the potential to do good and redeem himself. The living dead on the Palestinian side is both a cursed creature captive to a tragic fate, and a blessed being, with full control over his death, who sees it as the fulfillment of his destiny.

In the perceptive fictional movie *Paradise Now*, two Palestinian friends set out on a suicide mission. One of them blows himself up in a bus in the heart of Israel, and the other gets fouled up, hesitates, and finally returns to the West Bank. During the Intifada there were cases like that, such as that of Arin Sha'ibat, a human bomb who, with her partner in the mission, reached the target, a pedestrian mall in an Israeli city, and, as she alleged, "when she was about to press the activation button, she saw a baby and changed her mind" (May 2002). The career of the living dead does not always end in an explosion. A fair number of suicide terrorists failed to accomplish their missions, either because of some technical operational failure, or because of fear and twinges of conscience. Sometimes terrorists retreated without completing their assignment and returned to their community, or they were captured by Israeli security agents and imprisoned for many years. These are two variations on an illuminating test case: a suicide terrorist who retracted and returned from death to life. However, this life was not life in the full sense of the word. Back home, denounced or ostracized, he becomes living-dead once again, still breathing but doomed as far as his environment is concerned.

Terrorists who did not blow themselves up and managed to return to Palestinian territory found it impossible to be reabsorbed in their communities. Not only were they held in contempt, but they were also suspected of collaboration with the enemy. Efforts were made to send them out immediately on another mission, to repent for their guilt and shame, and to avoid the risk of exposing the secrets of their dispatchers. Sooner or later, they were located by the ISA and arrested. The Palestinian suicide terrorist who sets out on his murderous mission in Israel is like someone who is already dead, and from then on, he is forbidden, so to speak, to return to his home alive. Even if, ultimately, he did not die physically, he cannot extricate himself from the state of social death.

In the arena it is possible to experience several deaths. With the explosion, the suicide terrorist dies physically; before that he has died socially; after it, when his body is located and his name is publicized, he dies socially again. The arena is not the boundary between life and death but a field of play between them. The dynamic of entry and departure from the status of living dead does not characterize only the attacker but also his victims. From the moment that the Palestinian suicide terrorist boards the Israeli bus, all the passengers become potential victims, and they are living dead without knowing it. Those who stay on the bus are condemned to death, and those who reach their destination and get off before the explosion, return to life.[27]

*

With the explosion the dead in life become alive in death. Both the Palestinian attacker and the Israeli victims die physically but are regarded in their respective communities as still alive or as not yet having died completely, that is, socially. This is expressed clearly in the attitude of ZAKA to the corpses lying in the arena. A Jewish dead body feels, thinks, and communicates.[28] Veteran members of the organization speak of bodies that expressed insult or anger in response to improper treatment. In such cases the volunteers apologized to them and asked forgiveness. At the arena of an attack in the southern city of Beersheba, a volunteer was asked to be more delicate, as, so his friends claimed, the corpse indicated that it felt pain. Some volunteers say that the dead thanked them for their treatment.[29]

As with the terrorist, the fate of his adversaries, who will die with him and because of him, is sealed upon entry into the arena, to become dead in life, but, unlike the terrorist, they are denied control over the time and circumstances of their death. Therefore, after the fact, an effort is made to restore the control that was denied them. ZAKA leads this effort. Immediately after the explosion, before the bodies in the arena have been identified, they are already regarded as sanctifying the name of God. That is, they are represented as if, in their lives, they had gone to their deaths with awareness and intention. This interpretation of the Haredi volunteers enables the Israeli public to view the Jewish victims of the attack as if they had sacrificed themselves, just the way the Palestinian public sees its representative, the attacker. Both the Palestinian and Israeli public regard those who died for them in the arena, as having chosen their fate with a sense of mission, and as having been chosen by God to fulfill a national and religious task.

*

The dead in life, like the living in death, are charismatic beings, highly symbolic and potent. In many cases, they are more consequential than people who are still entirely alive or who have absolutely died. This is a glorious chapter in the career both of the attacker and of his victims, as living and dead people.[30] Both the phases of dead in life and living in death are temporary and liminal, playing an important social role, but they are confusing, sensitive, and difficult to bear. Society wants to put an end to them, to strip away one of their dissonant components and to restore them to the stable and continuous state that preceded them, or that which will succeed them. The end of the first intermediary state comes with the explosion. The end of the second intermediary state comes when ZAKA has finished its work at the arena, the purpose being the finalization of the process of dying. Only the collection of the limbs of the stricken victim, the reassembly of their bodies, and their burial makes their death unequivocal, making it possible to part from the dead, and, consequently, to hope for their resurrection. Parting and the hope for resurrection are the conditions for overcoming the death that caused chaos, threatened the well-being of the dead person's relatives, and caused the community to malfunction.

In his research in a tribal society in Borneo, Robert Hertz, the father of the sociology and anthropology of death, found that the basis for the local treatment of the dead lay in belief in the parallel between the state of the body and that of the spirits.[31] As long as the body was formless and repugnant in its looks, the spirits knew no rest. In such a state, the dead person could not be accepted in the world of the dead, and he was forced to remain on the margins of human society, where he was liable to harm his surroundings. Only manipulation of the body, bringing it to a condition more tolerable to the living—a kind of beautification—would pacify the spirits and make it possible for the dead to depart completely from our world. In that way, the malign influence of the corpse is removed from the world of the living, and equilibrium is created between it and the world of the dead. In the arena of terrorism in Israel social death is also conditional on manipulation of the corpses. The Haredi death priests, the ZAKA volunteers, control the process. In the classical case studied by Hertz, parting from the dead and the grief of the living depend on ceremonies involving elimination of blood and flesh, and by the removal of all signs of vitality from the earth, in order to dispel the threat cast by the dead upon the living, and to be rid of their oppressive grip on our world. In the case of the Jewish victims in the Intifada, the departure and mourning depend on a ceremony giving the dead acceptable form in the opposite way: gathering up the blood and flesh and burying them. In the Borneo case, the body must be destroyed, and in the Jewish case it must be refabricated. In both the celebrations of death described here, whether they depend upon the disintegration of the body or on its reassembly, this world is purified of every trace of the dead person in order to guarantee eternal life for him in the world to come.[32]

To be alive or to be thought of as alive, a body is necessary. From analysis of ZAKA a less obvious insight emerges: to be dead as well, or to be regarded as dead, a body is needed. While a person has no body, he is neither alive nor dead, at least not socially dead. Hence, the victims of terrorism need a body that can be buried and mourned. If there is no body, or if the body is mutilated, dispersed, and formless, its parts must be collected, reconstructed, and given human form. This is what ZAKA does in the arena. By re-creating the bodies of the victims that were mutilated in the explosion, ZAKA makes it possible to imagine their rebirth, which helps the denial of their death.[33]

## Everyman: Short-Term Sainthood

Amid the wave of Palestinian suicide terrorism throughout Israel, bus number 830 left Tel Aviv for Tiberias. Halfway there, near Megiddo junction, a commercial vehicle, which had been stolen a few months earlier, and whose license plates had been switched, clung to the back of the bus. It was loaded with dozens of kilograms of explosives and driven by Hamze Samudi, an eighteen-year-old from Jenin, sent by the PIJ. When the two vehicles touched each other, an explosion took place, throwing the bus into the air. After it flipped over twice, it was broken to pieces, and completely burned. Many of the passengers were killed, and the others were seriously wounded (June 2002). At the site of the attack, where ZAKA volunteers worked for many hours, and later in the National Institute of Forensic Medicine , sixteen dead people were identified. Another corpse was so mangled that it was impossible to identify it. The mystery of the victim's identity grew deeper, because after the attack, no one from a worried family contacted the police, asking for the missing person. A month later, with no sign of a solution, the remains were buried in an anonymous grave by a team of Haredi gravediggers in the Ashkelon cemetery, in the fenced lot reserved for non-Jews, lest the Jewish dead might be defiled.

A gifted filmmaker was drawn to the enigma of the anonymous victim's identity and took it upon himself to solve it, with the full cooperation of a team of police investigators. The result was presented in a fascinating documentary called *Number 17*, which is both a detective suspense drama and a nuanced representation of Israeli society at the time of the Intifada.[34]

In the resolute efforts to discover the identity of the seventeenth victim, it was thought that he might have been a foreign worker from China, an illegal Palestinian worker from the West Bank, a fugitive from justice, or a homeless man. The police investigators, accompanied by the director, collected testimony from dozens of people, especially from the surviving passengers, most of whom were wounded and still in shock, and they employed an artist who made several alternative sketches on the basis of various descriptions. After seven months of feverish searching, a clue was found when a taxi driver identified someone he knew in a sketch. After that, the search proceeded rapidly until the mystery was solved. The seventeenth victim was Eliahu Timsit, a man of thirty-two from Sderot in the south. The body of the suicide terrorism victim was removed from its temporary grave and re-interred among Jews.

Timsit did not stand out in any way, and this was what made it hard to locate him. In fact, he had been rather unfortunate in life as well as death. He lived in a dusty, remote town, in a lower-middle-class neighborhood, in a meager apartment with his sick mother, without friends or a profession, drifting between part-time jobs. Half a year after splitting up with his girlfriend, still unemployed and depressed, he took a tent and went to seclude himself on the shore of the Sea of Galilee for an unspecified time.[35]

Indeed, when all the missing information about the seventeenth victim was gathered, it turned out that he came from nowhere. Immediately afterward, with the solution of the puzzle and the completion of the film, he returned to the place whence he came, lost again in oblivion.[36] In the interval between his life and his final burial, when he lacked a body and an identity, then and only then was he in the center of interest, gaining fame and enveloped by magic.

Some parallels between the ups and downs in the career of victim number seventeen can be found in the fate of other victims of suicide terrorism, while their remains were being treated by ZAKA and then in the national Institute of Forensic Medicine. The death specialists swoop down on the remains of the corpse and do not pause in their intense work for hours. From the moment they have reassembled the mutilated body and exhausted all the information about the victim and the circumstances of his death, he is transferred to a refrigerator, and he no longer has much value, except, again as in the past, to his relatives, if he has any. The excellent movie dedicated to victim number seventeen was intended to commemorate him, but it erased his memory.

Many Israeli victims of terrorism, like the Palestinian who killed them, may be characterized as having low or mediocre value on the hierarchy of political power, economic resources, social status, and cultural capital of their own or of their families. They do not usually stand out in their talent or charismatic personality, in their religious and patriotic commitment, or prior involvement in the Middle Eastern conflict.[37] Most of the victims of suicide terrorism, including the human bomb, are marginal and anonymous. Both the attacker and the objects of his attack are *everyman*. Before and after the interval which begins at the moment of their entry into the arena of terrorism and ends when they are removed from it, they are unnoticed, swallowed up in the crowd.

The terrorist attack redeemed the dead from oblivion, at least for a few hours, for a day or two. Earlier, I indicated the reasons for erasing the victims of terrorism from Israeli collective memory.[38] But what is their status in ZAKA's organizational memory and in the personal memory of the volunteers? The latter remembered in detail the sights and activity in the arena of terrorism, but they found it hard to remember the identity of the victims, with certain exceptions, usually neighbors or persons known to them. Even after years they described exactly how the mutilated limbs of a certain body looked, while they had not the slightest idea about the victim's life story.[39] The Haredi volunteers lose interest in the victims of terrorism in the blink of an eye. All the attention and personal and organizational resources of the ZAKA men are given over to the dead while they are still in the arena. However, immediately after they have been located, numbered, and bagged, they are abandoned to the responsibility of the families and the community bureaucracy. Except for certain instances, the ZAKA volunteers do not make time to attend the funerals of the victims of terrorism.

Mourning begins only after burial, or, more precisely, national mourning becomes private mourning, the sole particular interest of the dead person's relatives and friends. Until there is a corpse, or while the corpse is not whole or identified, there is no certainty of the finality of death, and it is impossible to bury the dead person or mourn for him, to part from him forever. ZAKA's deathwork is a process of liberating the living from those who died by terrorism, a way of breaking the spell of a particularly horrible death, of being reconciled with that death, and a return to functioning routine. The tragic history of recent generations offers several examples from all over the world of the aftermath of brutal mass murders, in which, lacking clearly identifiable bodies, there is no certainty about the death, and, as a result, the grief work is delayed, and obstacles pile up on the path of return to normal life. There is a telling equivalence between ZAKA's work in the arenas of explosions in Jerusalem and the exposure of the graves of victims of terrorism whose bodies were mutilated and hidden, and the efforts to identify skeletons in rural areas in southern Sri Lanka in the 1990s.[40]

For a limited period, the victims and the human bomb represent the Israeli or Palestinian collective, respectively, while, before and after it, they represented only themselves. When those who have died from terrorism lie in the arena, and their bodies are mutilated and scattered, they are not known by name, but by the presumed national-religious category to which they belong.[41] The explosion deprives them of their individual identity. Burial restores it. In the intermediate stage, they are in the category of "Jews" or "non-Jews" while they are being treated by ZAKA, and they have no specific biography or body. They are symbolic types. Then they belong to the public, and as such positions and desires can be attributed to them, irrespective of their understanding of themselves while they were alive, including the assumption that they chose to die of their own free will, as if they wanted to sanctify the Name of God from the start. Between their accidental entry into what was immediately to become an arena of horror and their burial, mourning, and departure, a transitional space extends between full life and absolute death. This is the liminal stage, when the corpses are laden with emblematic qualities, and they are endowed with mesmerizing charisma and super-powers, as well as taboo and danger. This combination of contradictions characterizes the sacred.

The input of ZAKA's deathwork, presented earlier as beautifying the death of the victims, moves the victims from a profane to a saintly status, but within a short time the victims will return to the realm of the profane, where they were situated before the explosion. Only during the short time around the explosion, at most until the victims' names are made public to allow their burial—only then do the victims remain sacrificial.

Underlying the idea of sacrifice is the connection between destroying the body, erasing every sign of individual uniqueness, and holiness. Just as the violation of the victim's flesh and tearing of his limbs is sanctifying, so too, the assembly of the victim's body parts restores his body and identity and returns him to the category of the profane. The victim is holy so long as he does not have a (whole) body or a name. The sanctity of the corpse is limited to the time that it is defective.[42] The imperfect state of the corpse creates the peculiar effect, which makes it impossible to be free of it. The magic of the severed limbs is dissipated at the end of the deathwork. Terrorism involves short-term sanctity, which is paradoxical: gathering and reassembling the body parts for the purpose of restoring the wholeness of the body is intended to sanctify it, but the final result of the deathwork in the arena of terrorism is the removal of sanctity from the victim's corpse. Completion of the process of sanctifying the dead leads to its contradiction. In various religions, especially in classical Christianity, the career of the martyr may begin with his burial, and sometimes several generations after it. On both the Israeli and Palestinian sides of the scene of suicide terrorism, burial puts an end to the martyr's career.

The sanctification of the victims of terrorism by ZAKA is probable in cases when the bodies are accompanied by signs that connect them to a clear Jewish identity, meaning, in the volunteers' view, Orthodox Judaism. The sanctity of corpses wearing ritual fringes, with a yarmulka or a *tefillin* bag next to them, was self-evident to ZAKA, and they were regarded as if they had leaped into a fire clinging to a Torah scroll, like their ancestors during the Crusades. However, many of those killed by terrorism were entirely secular, and their sanctity was not a simple matter. Some rabbis were apprehensive lest the retroactive sanctification of secular Jews might legitimize the denial of Torah and the commandments. However, retroactive sanctification exempted them from the problematic issue of treating many of the non-religious victims. The problem was particularly difficult in cases like the terrorist attack on the Dolphinarium Club, where twenty-one young people were killed while they were partying on Sabbath eve, with wild dancing and revealing clothing, smoking and drinking alcohol. Moreover, many of them belonged to families of immigrants from the former USSR, whose Judaism was suspect, according to halakha (July 2001). Nevertheless, after their death ZAKA made them into kosher Jews and made them religious despite themselves. The Muslim religious leaders who supported the suicide terrorism of Hamas faced a similar perplexity: they had to praise as *shahids* those who had openly violated Sharia law, such as drug addicts.

A Palestinian youth from a crowded refugee camp, who became a human bomb, and his Israeli victim—an old women, a new immigrant from Uzbekistan, who lived in a deprived area of Jerusalem—were both disadvantaged, and after their death they both were left without the recognition that they had received during the short hour of grace immediately following the explosion. The dynamic of sanctification on the Palestinian side is like that on the Israeli side. During their lives, the suicide terrorists usually did not have a potential for sanctity that could be developed and retained over time. On the eve of their death and immediately afterward, they were sanctified, but in a short time they were forgotten, and their sanctity faded away. The gallery of Palestinian saints does not contain the human bombs, but their dispatchers. The brief and transitory sanctity of the victims of suicide terrorism as well as of the perpetrators derives to a great extent from the same reason: none of them was made of the material of which saints are made. In both cases, despite their extraordinary deaths, they did not possess, in their lifetimes, the qualities that would make them worthy of commemoration after their deaths or of an exalted religious and national status.

Against this gray background, an isolated few were exceptions, thus proving the rule. These were people who could have been regarded as saintly while still alive, and when they died as they did, it was expected to present them as martyrs. One of these was the woman terrorist Hanadi Jaradat (Maxim restaurant, October 2003). She was smart and beautiful, patriotic and religious, and filled with the spirit of revenge because both her brother and her fiancé had been killed.[43] The Israeli parallel is Dr. David Appelbaum, who was killed in the attack on Café Hillel in Jerusalem (September 2003). Among the seven Israelis who were killed at his side at that incident and the hundreds of Israelis who were killed in the two waves of Palestinian suicide terrorism, he is almost the only one whose name is remembered by the public, whose picture, life story, and circumstances of death are widely known and prominently commemorated. Indeed, his life contains the materials that make for a good human, national, and religious story. Jaradat and Appelbaum are almost the only individuals connected directly to suicide terrorism who are still regarded in their respective communities as saints.

Dr. Appelbaum was a devoutly religious and a profound Zionist, talented and generous, from a big and well-established family, involved, respected, and influential in Jerusalem. He was the admired director of the emergency room in a major hospital, to which the casualties of terrorism were brought during the two Intifadas. Shortly before his death he had returned from New York, where he gave a lecture on emergency medicine, based on his experience in treating the victims of terrorism. He had met his beloved daughter on the last evening before her wedding. After her death, her wedding gown was contributed to the holy site at the Tomb of Rachel in the outskirts of Bethlehem.[44] Her father, whose body was fused to hers, is known to this day in ZAKA as a lifesaving angel.

## The Momentary Emancipation of the Body

While acknowledging the fashionable trend in the social sciences—which, indeed, is not absent from the present volume—to examine death as socially constructed and to see the body as a cultural and political site, need we remind ourselves that death is primarily a physiological fact, and that it has, first, bodily significance?[45] The sites of death of every kind are permeated by physicality. The body is particularly present in cases of violent death. The arena of terrorism is as corporeal as can be. The explosion smashes the body into little pieces and scatters the limbs, its boundaries are penetrated, and it is mingled with other bodies. In this situation, the body bursts into the center of consciousness, but not before undergoing deconstruction. Precisely then, when it is no longer self-evident, the body becomes conspicuous. The deathworkers who deal with the victims of terrorism are ipso facto experts in the body. The practices of the Haredi volunteers, in accordance with their world of imagination and rhetoric, are marked by the body. The arenas where ZAKA is active are overcome by the body, to the point where they contain almost nothing but bodies. In places where bodies can be changed beyond recognition, become formless, and, in fact, vanish, the body acquires totality. The ecstatic attack on the body estranges it. That which is most familiar becomes unfamiliar. The result of suicide terrorism is dismemberment, disfigurement, and dissolution of the body. ZAKA's project of re-composing the corpse implies re-corporealizing it.

Suicide terrorism and dealing with its results are distinctly embodied practices. They are practices in which there is bodily contact, a kind of intimacy.[46] ZAKA's symbolic counterterrorism, no less than suicide terrorism, is a message inscribed in the body.[47] In suicide terrorism the body is not only the target of the attack, nor does it merely wield a weapon; it is the weapon itself.[48] The suicide terrorist's body, which is both object and subject, acts on the bodies of others and on itself. It is both the attacker and one of its victims. ZAKA's deathwork, which deals with the results of suicide terrorism, demonstrates the corporeal dimension of this violent phenomenon. The body of the human bomb and those of the Israelis who happened to be confined with him in a bus or a café, are blown to bits and disintegrate at the same time. Shortly afterward, both receive their whole bodies again: the Palestinian attacker's body is pieced together after his death when Hamas broadcasts his testament, recorded before the mission, and creates the illusion that makes his pre-mortem past into the present. In the case of the Jewish victims, the unbearable situation of "a corpse without a body" is ended by means of the Haredi volunteers' ritual. The disfigurement of the body is what makes for the horror that permeates the arena of terrorism.[49] ZAKA restores the form of the body, thus defusing the horror of the arena in an effort to counteract the harm inflicted by terrorism.[50]

A terrorist attack throws the body to center stage, while it is exposed and open, suddenly free of all the restrictions of social control, to which it is generally subject while alive, before the explosion, and after its death, when it has been dealt with by the deathworkers. Normally bodies, including dead bodies, are regimented, supervised, and concealed.[51] This is not so in the arena. Here, for a short, wild moment, control of the boundaries of the body is lost, along with the boundaries between bodies. The body represents nature, the undomesticated, irrational world. Over against it stands culture, which seeks to restrain it, if not to hide it. Culture does this by distancing the body from other bodies, by dressing it, by cleansing its skin of wounds, sealing openings, regulating its position and movements. In the arena of terrorism, the body is denuded in both the actual and metaphorical sense. It is flesh, a signifier of lustful urges, the locus of sex, promiscuity.[52] The terrorist attack frees the body from the ethics of discipline that prevails in Western civilization in general, and especially in the puritan Haredi sub-culture.[53] In minimal time the ZAKA teams fall upon the untamed bodies and subdue them. They separate corpses that are fused together with the ones lying next to them, close wounds and orifices, cover stripped flesh, straightening and shaping it. Only after the bare emancipated body is recovered from nature and returned to the control of culture, ascetic religiosity, can it be buried and mourned, can it be parted from, and order can be restored in the world. Without a corpse, coping with death is infinitely harder.[54] The relatives of the victims of terrorism wanted to see the corpses of their loved ones, as though to be certain that their death was final, before they returned to the routines of life.[55] After the Haredi volunteers did their essential job in giving the corpse a human look, they monopolized the difficult task of displaying the corpse to the victim's relatives.

Those who entered the arena to cover and curb the body found it surprisingly stimulating. While devoted to restoring the form of the corpses, the Haredi volunteers could not avoid being captivated by the allure of the disfigured bodies. Their fascination with the flesh that permeates the arena is mingled with animated discourse on the spiritual essence hidden behind it. In the spirit of popular Kabballah, the ZAKA rabbis maintain that the condition of the corpse points to the state of the deceased's soul, and, in turn, the state of the soul radiates upon the state of the corpse.[56] The socially intolerable attraction of the deathworkers to the mangled flesh is translated into acceptable expressions about the noble qualities of the dead. This moralistic sublimation is displayed in meticulous descriptions of severed limbs as indices of an individual's traits.

The volunteers say that "the bodies speak," testifying to the character of the deceased. For example, the hands of a dead person whose fists are open are interpreted in the arena as stating, "I have a clean conscience, and I have nothing to hide." Sometimes the condition of a corpse is like a confession of a negative personality trait. An eye wide open is the basis for assuming that the deceased was avaricious. Once, when the volunteers treated the bodies of a couple, they concluded from the condition of the corpses that the husband was wicked, and the wife was saintly. A veteran volunteer told me that throughout his career with ZAKA, he was motivated by the uncontrollable desire to find at last a body untouched by rodents or maggots, a sign of supreme sanctity. In the arenas of suicide terrorism, the deathworkers rush to separate the bodies of the victims from that of the attacker, according to the kind of wounds on their bodies and the tearing of their limbs. Then the Haredi volunteers search the bodies of the victims to find some sign proving their Jewishness and according them the status of saints.

## Rebirth, Torah Scrolls, and the Body of the Nation

Just as the condition of a corpse testifies to a person's past, it also determines and proclaims the deceased's future in the world to come. The similarity between ZAKA's view on this matter and that of the Church regarding the bodies of martyrs is striking.[57] Just as Christian believers found to their surprise upon dissecting the body of an eighteenth-century saint that his heart was preserved almost as new, since it was purified by the fire of divine grace, thus, led by their rabbis, the Haredi volunteers are moved when they discover the *luz* bone (the bone from which, according to rabbinic tradition, the body will be restored when the dead are esurrectted),[58] preserved intact in the bodies of victims of terrorism. Some sources call this bone "the Jewish bone."[59] In the Kabballah it is written that this bone will rise like dough with yeast until a whole body is produced, ready to receive the soul. The learned among the ZAKA men only disagree as to identifying the bone, on the basis of their belief in various exegetical schools.[60] On the volunteers' map of the body, inspired by medieval mystical literature, there is a hierarchy among the organs, even when they are dismembered.[61] The differential religious value of the various body parts has consequences for the practices of the ZAKA deathwork at the arena of terrorism.[62]

Recovering and reassembling the corpse is seen as the key to regeneration, which is not solely spiritual, but also corporeal.[63] In the three Abrahamic religions, the resurrection of the dead involves the restoration of the physical body as an important component of the self. The continuity of the body is a central motive in the worship of saints, as, for example in Christianity from the third to the fourteenth centuries.[64] The dead will rise to life with a body, but how will the risen body look if it was disfigured in death? Did the eschatological belief that the intervention of divine providence would bring about the resurrection of saints include the promise that their resurrected body would be perfect? How fateful, then, was the task of the faithful who prepared the disfigured body of the martyrs for burial? It was widely thought that "Satanic" force, in various guises—the pagans in antiquity, the Jews in medieval Europe, and Hamas in the present Middle East—conspired to mutilate the saints' bodies to make their burial difficult and to prevent their resurrection. In the Judeo-Christian tradition it is commonly assumed that there is a connection between the state of a person's corpse and the state of his body in the world to come. Theological discussions took place in the Church regarding the need to restore the bodies of martyrs, which were hacked to pieces in torture by the enemies of Christ, in order to guarantee their resurrection.[65] In the Jewish tradition there is explicit reference, in the Talmud and in Midrash, to the question of the relation between the state of a body when it is buried and its state when it will rise from its grave.[66] Some rabbis in the organization related to the appearance of the corpses when the messiah comes, to rationalize the great attention paid to the gathering and assembling of body parts in the arena. (This is another motive in the ultra-Orthodox opposition to autopsies.) Various statements by the Haredi volunteers allude to their fear of the possibility that on the day of redemption, the bodies of the dead will not be intact, as befits those who sanctified the Name of God.

*

To better understand ZAKA's treatment of the corpses of the victims of terrorism, we must see it in the context of the traditional Jewish attitude to the body.[67] It is commonly held that Orthodox, especially ultra-Orthodox

Judaism is characterized by alienation and to a large degree rejection of the human body and of bodily matters.[68] Nonetheless, there are quite a few indications that those who are thought to be the heirs of traditional Judaism today are disproportionately concerned with illnesses and wounds that injure the body (so much so that a leading researcher of Haredi society defined it as infected by "health hysteria"),[69] and they are intolerant of deformed bodies. One may speak of a Jewish obsession with the wholeness of the body. The Torah lists kinds of handicapped or blemished people who are prohibited from performing central ritual acts (the blind, the lame, the humpbacked, someone with a cataract, someone with a broken arm or leg, and more). Priests whose bodies were deformed were forbidden to offer sacrifices or even approach the altar, and they were segregated from the public (Leviticus 21). Other passages in the Bible also emphasize the integrity of the body.[70] For example, excessive attention is paid to the disease often mistakenly identified as leprosy, which disfigures the skin and challenges the boundaries of the body. It is seen as punishment from heaven and received ritual significance connected with the laws of purity and impurity, and it required distancing the afflicted person from the camp.[71] Another example is the taboo against disfiguring the body for ornamental reasons, such as the prohibition against tattoos, or to express emotions, such as the prohibition against scratching the face as a sign of mourning.[72] The rabbis of the Talmud continued to be interested in the body and the connection between its integrity and holy worship. To this day Orthodox rabbis argue as to whether a handicapped person may be called to the Torah in the synagogue.

A thought-provoking thesis is proposed regarding the connection between the ideal of the integrity of the Jewish body and research results showing that the attitude toward handicapped people in Israel is less accepting than in other Western countries.[73] Recent studies have produced further findings consistent with that claim. For example, in-utero tests to reduce the chances of giving birth to a handicapped child are relatively frequent among Israeli Jews in Israel.[74] Hence, it is understandable that religious Jews should seek to minimize disfigurements of corpses. For them the body of a dead person is like that of a living person, created in the image of God. A ZAKA volunteer described his deathwork at the site of a terrorist attack as removing "any trace of the public shaming of the image of God, when it is lying ravaged" in the arena.

Orthodox Judaism believes that the Jewish body bears the imprint of the divine name. Hence it is a sacred vessel, like a parchment scroll with a biblical verse written on it. When such a scroll is damaged, it is invalid, and there is a meticulous halakhic procedure to deal with it, ending in its burial. The ZAKA volunteers refer to the complete parallel between the body of a Jew and a Torah scroll.[75] Not only does the body, in the physical sense, reflect the divine corpus, but it can also influence the divinity, as the rabbis of the organization who are familiar with Jewish mystical literature point out.[76] They find identity between the body and the Torah in the details as well. Thus, the human body contains 613 parts, just as there are 613 commandments in the Torah. There are 248 organs corresponding with the positive commandments and 365 organs corresponding with the negative commandments. Every part of the body is parallel to an element in the Torah, to a certain commandment.[77] Joining a severed limb to a body is comparable to performing an additional commandment, and it has supreme religious significance. In ZAKA they quote the sacred texts, saying that one must give full honor to every tiny part of a dead body, just as one must treat the tiniest flaw in a Torah scroll, since a single erroneous letter invalidates the entire scroll. Just as there is no essential difference between a single page of a Torah that has been torn and an entire scroll that has been damaged, so, too, there is no difference between a piece of flesh the size of an olive and an entire corpse.[78]

*

The zeal of the ZAKA volunteers in gathering and assembling the mutilated bodies in the arena must be seen in the context of another ideal body as well. This zeal is rooted not only in the traditional Jewish religion's obsession for the integrity of the body but also in the corresponding obsession in modern Jewish nationalism, Zionism. This claim raises questions first because ZAKA is an organic part of the radical wing of the Haredi community, known for its opposition to Zionism, and also because Zionism proposed an ideal of a new Jewish body, defined as the opposite of the old Jewish body of the Diaspora, regarded as flawed by the pioneers in the Land of Israel.[79] Regarding the former issue, as has been pointed out several times in this book, while ZAKA is deeply rooted in the anti-Zionist religious subculture, Zionism also attracts and influences it. In dialectical fashion, the Haredi volunteers adopted several typical traits of their Zionist rivals, resulting in, among other things, a growing congruence of their body images.

The Haredi and Zionist bodily ideals are the opposite of one another, yet they both value the integrity of the body. Despite differences in nuance, the two outlooks complement one another. Consequently, there are two strata—the religious and the national—in ZAKA's refusal to tolerate the dismembered body.

Throughout this book, we have made use of Mary Douglas' insight, which has become fundamental in discussion of the body in the social sciences: the fact that the body and its boundaries possess basic reality, which is so important ontologically, makes the body and its boundaries an effective symbol, an icon, of the collective and its boundaries. Between the personal body of the individual and the political body of a collective—a nation, a religion, a race—there is natural comparability, mirroring, and mutual influence.[80] When the boundaries of a group are pressed, especially when its territorial integrity is challenged, there arises an anxious fixation regarding the integrity of the physical bodies of the members of the group. Concomitantly, violation of the physical boundaries of the individual members of the group is perceived as impairing the maintenance of the group's intact geopolitical boundaries. A society uses the body—or the corpse—to police its boundaries.[81] [-82]Penetration of the body or of the corpse and the spoiling of its form arouses those who devote themselves to the purity and distinctiveness of the community, and they immediately commit themselves to repairing the damage caused to the body and to the community. In response to terrorism, the priests of death come as emissaries of the stricken public, to bring together the limbs and restore the form of the body, and thus to cure the double-layered trauma.

Like religion, nationalism is also embodied. The embodiment of nations is a universal phenomenon, as demonstrated in the image of the nation in Western countries, which is tested during an armed conflict with another country.[82] National collectivities inscribe their ethos onto the bodies of their citizens. Renewed Jewish ethno-nationalism—the realization of the Zionist vision in Israel—under the conditions of the Middle Eastern conflict, is a particularly conspicuous case. Central to the Zionist project was the goal of creating a new Jew, a Sabra, recognizable first by his body. Lack of tolerance for the old, faulty Jewish body, and the desire for a perfect body, are characteristics of Zionism, and they contained more than a hint of implicit eugenics.[83] Here is yet another explanation of the behavior of the Haredi volunteers in the arena, who, over the years, acquired components of the Zionist obsession with the body. In earlier research, corroboration of Douglas' thesis was found in the rhetoric accompanying the treatment by the National Institute of Forensic Medicine of the bodies of IDF soldiers who were killed in battle and sanctified.[84] We follow in its wake by applying the model of metaphoric parallelism and the reciprocity between the boundaries of the physical body and those of the collective body to the unique practice of ZAKA's treatment of the bodies of the victims of terrorism. Terrorism, even more than war, brings out the body of the nation.[85] During the blood-soaked years of the Intifada, a sense of Israeli nationalism was felt, and even strengthened, through the bodies of the victims of terrorism. By manipulating the corpses left after the explosions, the ZAKA priests of death played a key role in sharpening Jewish national identity.

## Carnal Jews: Slaughter and Priesthood

Jews regard themselves as descended from Ancient Israel as it is reflected in the Hebrew Bible. The source of Judaism is the religion depicted in the canonic text, that of a small Near Eastern tribal society centered around sacrificial cult in the principal temple, administered by a caste of priests. Sacrifice is a bodily act, and the most important object offered in sacrifice is a body (of an animal or of a human). The physical aspect of pristine Hebrew worship is mainly expressed in what is known as the priestly stratum of the Pentateuch.[86] Because of their attachment to the Bible, the Jews have reappropriated the term the "People of the Book" as a means of self-identification, but, as others have already noted, this is a paradox, in that this holy book revolves to a great degree around corporality. The central canon of the Jews is permeated by flesh and blood rituals. Thus, it is possible to regard the Jews as a people of the body.[87] Haredi ZAKA is heir to this fleshly much more than bookish legacy.

The destruction of the Temple in Jerusalem in the first century CE initiated the period of rabbinical Judaism, which lasted for about seventeen hundred years until the dawn of the Modern Age. Judaism adapted itself to the absence of the Temple as well as the lack of its own territorial sovereignty. The place of the priests was taken by the Sages and the rabbis, and prayer and the study of texts replaced sacrifice. However, contrary to the image of this transformed Judaism, as if it had undergone total disembodiment, it still maintained a strong presence of the body. The spiritualization that characterizes rabbinic Judaism was partial. In parallel to it, there developed several symbolic substitutes for sacrifice (such as the *kaparot* ceremony), and especially a wealth of norms was preserved and expanded regarding the body (e.g., sexual relations). An elaborate halakhic corpus was consolidated around the body. In traditional Judaism the body was treated as an object laden with symbolism and as a prominent focus of ritual. Thus, the body remained potent, fascinating, but also threatening.

The Jewish body gathered inherent tensions into itself, masked by excessive legalism and ritualism. The main tension relates to the conception of the body as the image of God, whose integrity must be maintained, requiring sensitivity to the danger of violating its boundaries. Yet, in practice, this ideal is often violated: bodies secrete urine and sweat, sometimes stink, and might become ill, injured, and handicapped. That which applies to the evocative and explosive potential of the living body evidently applies even more so to the corpse.

With the modernization of European Judaism, which was bound up with the Haskalah (Jewish Enlightenment), secularization, religious reform, and migration westward, most Jews made an effort toward disembodiment of the cultural tradition. This was a project originating in apologetics, which became an internalized psychological position. With the aspiration to integrate into progressive surroundings, the Jews sought to rid themselves of their associations not only with mysticism and magic, but also with the great interest in corporality that nourished their negative image as benighted and repulsive, even in their own eyes. Norms that were liable to be interpreted as disproportionate concern for the body (e.g., menstrual purity) were concealed or denied, facilitating adaptation to a world dominated by discourse that claimed to be rational and which was subject to anti-ritualistic Christian influences. Trends toward the spiritualization of Judaism, which emphasized its intellectual, ethical, and political dimensions, at the expense of its behavioral dimensions, became urgent with the rise of antisemitism fixated on Jewish corporality, which it found despicable. Jews were accused of possessing disgusting physical characteristics, such as noses that were too long and the smell of garlic, and at the same time, verbal skills, fantasy, and intelligence were attributed to them, underlaid by no body, or, at best, only a sickly, weak, and distorted body. In response to the corporeal curses leveled at them, the Jews enthusiastically collaborated with the forces that presented them as the People of the Book.[88]

Since dominant currents in Judaism relegated flesh and blood to the subterranean, latent reservoir of Jewish culture, the body and its attractive power had to be rediscovered. With modernization, two unprecedented phenomena appeared on the Jewish horizon, both corporeal. They are opposites of each other, but they equally restore Judaism to the body and the body to Judaism. The first is Jewish nationalism with territorial and political orientation: Zionism. The second, the militant antithesis of the former, is Jewish ultra-Orthodoxy, Haredi traditionalism. ZAKA's investment in the Jewish body shows signs of the influence of these two worlds.

Despite the mutual antipathy between Haredim and Zionists, there are fertile points of contact between them, and unexpected hybrids combining their attitude to the body have emerged. One of these is the Temple movement. This is a coalition of organizations that share the aspiration to build the Third Temple and renew the sacrificial ritual.[89] Some of these groups are politically extreme and demand the imposition of Israeli sovereignty on the entire biblical Promised Land and full control over Jerusalem and the Temple Mount, while other groups focus on pietist observance and messianic belief. The latter range along a continuum between a Haredi-nationalist majority (*hardal*) and a Haredi minority that opposes the state (a clique in Belz Hasidism, for example).[90] These groups act openly and clandestinely, sometimes violently.[91] The dream of renewing the Temple and the sacrifices has been central in rabbinical Judaism for almost two thousand years, as expressed in traditional prayers and ceremonies, but, in the light of unprecedented geopolitical developments, mainly the establishment of powerful Jewish sovereignty over the Land of Israel, for the first time there is an expectation of fulfilling the dream in one's lifetime, and concrete steps to do so have been taken. However, the initiatives to rebuild the Temple and renew sacrifices entails a provocation against the policies of the State of Israel and against the rulings of most rabbinical authorities, which prohibit ascent to the Temple Mount with severe sanctions, for various halakhic reasons, including fear of defiling the location of the innermost holiest section of the Temple by believers infected with the impurity of the dead.[92]

Among the cult-related projects carried out by the Temple faithful are secret infiltration through the lines of the Israeli police and the Muslim Waqf to the Temple Mount for the purpose of prayer, the training of priests to fulfill the duties of the Temple service, the sewing of priestly garments, casting an altar, designing a basin for the washing of hands and feet, producing fire pans and other vessels for the sacrificial service, based on the detailed description in the Bible, and practicing slaughter as outlined in the Talmud. The peak of these activities was the semi-secret rehearsal of the Paschal sacrifice exactly as it was performed in First and Second Temple times. In a ceremony held near the Western Wall, bearded priests, barefoot, in white cloaks woven specially, with tall turbans on their heads, broad sashes around their hips, and knives and torches in their hands, lit a fire on the altar, chopped up the body of the lamb, seared its meat, and poured its blood into the golden bowl, to the sounding of trumpets and the plucking of harps. In the end, certain parts of the sacrifice were eaten by the participants.

Such activities arouse criticism in Israel. In addition to political reservations (antagonizing local Arabs) and moral issues (the cruel killing of animals), there was also theological opposition (regression from the rational and humanistic religiosity to paganism) and aesthetic misgivings. Critics of the latter sort say things like "Imagine in central Jerusalem of the twenty-first century, sights, sounds, and smells of a gigantic slaughterhouse, the lowing of cows, groaning as they perish, puddles of blood, black smoke from burning fat billowing up, stench, filth, and crowding." Such expressions of distaste, which combine disagreement in principle with disgust and derision, are voiced not only by secular Jews but also by neo-Orthodox.

While the critics regarded the Temple faithful as primitive lunatics who want to practice a grotesque and irrelevant ritual, the faithful themselves betray deep longing for pristine, carnal Judaism, for the tangible religious certainty of flesh and blood.[93] Because it is corporeal, the sacrificial ritual is seen as promising a sounder and more authentic religious experience than that which is represented by textual and refined worship and by the sublimated and ostensibly emasculated rites of the Orthodoxy and ultra-Orthodoxy of recent generations. It is claimed that only a sacrificial rite "is a total [religious] experience that shakes and motivates the soul."[94]

The criticism leveled against those who advocate renewal of sacrifices is almost identical to the criticism leveled against the Haredi volunteers who manage the arenas of unnatural death. The similarity is not necessarily on the ideological level, but mainly in the psychological attitude toward these two phenomena. Both critiques employ the same phrases, which express revulsion from the gory side that connects the two: "shocking," "revolting," "nauseating," and the like. The reservations focus on the attraction to the sights and smells of mutilated and burned bodies that characterizes the activists of both organizations. Disgust and aversion to direct contact and processing of flesh and blood, which are identified with the holy work of both the Temple faithful and of ZAKA volunteers, underlie the opposition of various publics to the two organizations. In the background of the condemnation of the religiosity of the Temple faithful and of ZAKA as regressive and sick lies the modern conception of Judaism, which can perhaps be defined as Protestant Judaism. A pious acquaintance defined these two phenomena, which he opposes to an equal extent, with the same biblical term, which expresses sarcastic disgust: *shiquts* (abomination).

The Temple faithful and ZAKA are provocative manifestations of the awakening of corporeal Judaism. A similar sentiment lies behind them both: yearning for powerful religious experience, primal, genuine, and "true," as the believers define it, corporeal and hence erotic, which comes from the ritualistic manipulation of a dismembered body. The Temple faithful and ZAKA are two revivalist initiatives in contemporary Judaism that rebel against the conventions of the normative religion and place the bare body in center stage, the Judaism of sacrifices, of severed limbs, of spilled guts, and bodily excrescences. The practices of deathwork in the arena of terrorism has effects like those of sacrificing a lamb on the altar of the ancient Temple. In both cases excitement is generated with which no other religious ritual can compete. Present-day Western people have distanced themselves from physical rituals, and especially from flesh and blood, which were part of the lives of biblical people. Proximity to flesh and blood stimulates the instincts of the ultra-activist deathworkers, just as it stimulates the instincts of the slaughterer offering a sacrifice. Among the Temple faithful this is a declared political and religious agenda. Among the ZAKA activists, it is a quite unreflective reaction but not denied.

The disorientation that afflicts religion because of the upheavals of advanced modernity, and the desperate efforts of true believers to find a place for themselves in an unfamiliar world, are also connected to their perplexity regarding the nature of the body and their attitude to it. Whereas broad strata in the West, religious and secular, are alienated from the naked crude body, the Temple faithful and the ZAKA volunteers celebrate it. They explore the option of focusing on the body as a creative vehicle for attaining an authentic religious alternative in radically altered circumstances. A material variant of Judaism is represented here, one that yearns to worship God sensually, with touch and smell. With their craving for direct contact with flesh and blood the believers seek direct contact with the divine presence. As in the act of coitus between lovers, the intimacy of corporeal contact can be comparable to the intimacy of contact with the Shekhina, an emanation of the godhead.[95]

*

In a social meeting with Haredi volunteers whom I befriended, one of them said to me, "The site of a terrorist attack is like a sacrificial altar, and we, the ZAKA cadres, are like priests in the Temple." Another replied, with more than half a smile, "If it weren't for ZAKA, many of us would have become *shokhtim* [ritual slaughterers], who kill animals according to the rules of halakha."

## The Bacchae Effect

Today religious violence is identified with the attacks of radical Islamic movements that employ suicide terrorism. Against the background of the murderous initiatives of Al-Qaeda, ISIS, and their offshoots that take place daily in Syria, Iraq, Afghanistan, and Africa, there is a tendency to forget that until a little more than thirty years ago, the exemplars of contemporary religious violence were Jewish Israelis[96] and North American Protestant millenarians such as the Branch Davidians (Waco, Texas, 1993) and Christian Identity associate Timothy McVeigh (Oklahoma City, 1995). The trend in Judeo-Christian religious violence began with the murder-suicides in Jonestown (1978), which was, until 9/11, the most murderous event of our generation. A charismatic minister, Jim Jones, established a new church named People's Temple, a kind of authoritarian counter-society in the spirit of Christian-Communist ideals. He preached racial equality and social justice, but against the background of accusations of economic exploitation and sexual abuse, after running afoul of the law, his church was forced to move from Indiana to California, and from there to a distant and isolated site in Guyana. In the heart of a South American jungle, they established a farm, which suffered from material scarcity and was run autonomously, enforcing a totalitarian regime. A tour of inspection by a congressman from San Francisco deteriorated into an armed confrontation and the murder of the head of the expedition and his escorts. The members of the church felt threatened and responded to incitement by their leader with mass hysteria. Jones led an emotional religious ceremony that lasted all through the night, during which he urged the ecstatic believers to kill themselves. In the audiotape of the last forty minutes of the fatal "White Night" sermon he says, "If we can't live in peace, then let's die in peace [applause]."[97] Masses of his followers drank poison, which had been prepared in advance, after making their spouses and children drink it, while others had poison injected in their veins, and a few, including Jones, were shot to death, for a total of 918 victims, including 260 babies and small children.[98]

The tragedy of Jonestown stands out in the recent history of the West both in its dimensions and in its enigmatic nature regarding its motivations. Among the many academic efforts to solve the mystery, I found the work of Jonathan Smith particularly engaging.[99] He argues that Jones was obsessed by the idea of overcoming human distinctions, mainly those between white and black people. A core value that guided Jonestown was the aspiration to establish a Utopia on earth, which would provide maximal closeness and sameness between races and classes. Smith sees the principle of obliterating differences as a Dionysian pattern, as presented in antiquity by Euripides (and later discovered and interpreted by Nietzsche and used by René Girard).[100] To advance understanding of Jonestown, Smith adopts the model of the Greek tragedy *The Bacchae*. The play is analyzed as a paradigmatic example of religious violence of the Dionysian type, as analogous to the case of Jonestown and a source of insight into it. In *The Bacchae* the distance and boundary between peace and tranquility and violent conflict and cruel terror is shortened and blurred, as is that between man and god and man and beast, as well as that between man and woman, adult and child. Dionysus blurs and destroys all identities, and he is hostile to all definitions and separations, even between nature and culture, between reality and illusion, between joy and grief, between one person and another, between body and body. Similarly, in Jonestown white and black people were meant to be one. Smith describes the catastrophe of the final night in the People's Temple as a desperate effort of exodus from an earthly paradise that was lost, and its conversion into an alternative, heavenly paradise, where they will finally succeed in eliminating all differences without interference. The believers were promised that by killing themselves they would find the absolute equalizer, especially what would be the leveler between the races. They did not know that sometimes in postmortem situations, the differences between people are preserved and even emphasized.

Smith found confirmation of his thesis in Jones' rhetoric. He offers an ingenious reading of the text of the sermon that drove an entire community to its death, but he completely ignores the extraordinary sight of this unique death. Had he looked carefully at the photographs of Jonestown, which were taken during the first hours after the deaths, he could have found hints of what happened in the last hours before the deaths, and thus to propose different conjectures about the circumstances and consequences of the deaths. The photographs of the arena of death show that the hundreds of corpses remained entirely intact and fully dressed, just as they had been in life. Most of them appear to have lain down on their backs by themselves. Some of them placed pillows under their heads, others held hands with their dear ones or hugged them, and their children were laid carefully at their side. One has the impression that they are merely sleeping. Nothing does more to demonstrate the model discipline with which the killing was done than the view from a helicopter over the lawns of the compound. The victims stood in line to receive poison or to be injected, and they lie in orderly rows. Each individual is separated from his fellow and easily identifiable. A black person remains black, a white person is still white. The unequal reality is not erased; it is frozen. The binary categories were not dissolved. Rather, they were perpetuated. Boundaries were not crossed but concretized. There is no sign of the presumed, wild Dionysiac frenzy at the arena.

Smith illustrates the totality of the killing by pointing out that the members of the People's Temple also killed their pet dogs. He found symbolism in the shared fate of humans and animals. However, most likely those responsible for dealing with the aftermath of the mass killing regarded what looked like dogs in the arena just as dogs, especially since they were distinct from their owners, at whose side they lay. Similarly, the distinction between male and female bodies in the arena was clear, and, of course, again, that between blacks and whites. There was no deformation and no interchangeability. I could not help thinking of the contrast between the scene at Jonestown and the arenas of terrorism in Jerusalem.[101] There, too, dogs died. But what made a strong impression on the witnesses of the aftermath of the aggressive Middle Eastern act was the fact that the flesh, bones, and blood of the dead dogs mingled with the human remains. The ZAKA volunteers emphasized on several occasions that they found it difficult to distinguish between the remains of people and of animals, just as they found it difficult to differentiate between the bodies of the various victims. Smith missed out on a critical aspect of the arena of violent death when he wrote, "[T]o have discussed *The Bacchae* is to some degree to have discussed Jonestown." Nevertheless, Smith's error called my attention to this fertile twenty-five-hundred-year-old model.[102]

Below I suggest that to have discussed *The Bacchae* is to some degree to have discussed Palestinian suicide terrorism in Israel. I only made this digression to the arena of death at Jonestown because in an important sense for the argument in the present book, the latter is the diametrical opposite of the arena of death in *The Bacchae*, which, in significant details, does recall the arena of death caused by Hamas, with which ZAKA must cope. In the buses and restaurants of Jerusalem during the Intifada, far more than in Jonestown, we find a distinct expression of the Dionysian effect.

*

In Euripides' *Bacchae*, the god Dionysus (Bacchus) plays a central role. He figures in Greek mythology not only as exemplifying ambiguity, not to say inner contradictions, but as embodying the effort to blunt familiar concepts and forms, to mix basic categories, to do away with binary oppositions. He is the god of duality and transgression. Therefore, he is a constant threat against the existing order. Dionysus is the god of the theater, who wears masks and undergoes many metamorphoses. He may appear as a human, as a god, or as a monster. He is generous and protective or cruel and furious. He offers sublime spiritual inspiration but also sows destruction and horror. He is usually impulsive and emotional, breaking the bonds of the rational, but sometimes he is reasonable and pursues his plots with cunning. He enjoys unbridled freedom but imposes tyrannical discipline. He has an inebriating effect on people, and he infects society with the epidemic of enthusiasm, joy, creativity, and fertility—but he subjects it to his wishes and murderous caprices. He strikes his surroundings with madness, but the madness is divine. Dionysus arouses his followers both to drunken banquets and to hunt people down. In both ways, he overturns the identity of individuals, eliminates their uniqueness, and causes them to change their consciousness and, as it were, to leave their bodies behind in ecstasy, to merge with others and become a single fluid and energetic human mass. In antiquity an orgiastic cult surrounded Dionysus. It is in the nature of the bacchanal that it implants elements of a primordial paradise within horror, before any categorization or distinction between good and evil, and it contains much nakedness and bodily contact.

To summarize the plot of *The Bacchae*, Dionysius, disguised as a woman, arrives in the city of Thebes, which does not recognize him, for the purpose of proving his divinity. The local women follow him, and he infects them with mania. They go out to the mountains with him for a wild festival and a sacrifice. Pentheus, the young king, is curious about the nature of this strange cult and determined to suppress it. Despite his advisors' effort to persuade him to abandon his quarrel, he arrogantly refuses to back down from his original intention. At this point, a reversal occurs. Pentheus changes from ruler to ruled and begins to behave like a reflection of Dionysius. The god toys with the king and tempts him to disguise himself as a woman and join the Maenads, the mythic raving females who worship Dionysius. In a surge of holy rage, they dismember wild animals with their bare hands, and with enormous power, given to them by the god, they throw plundered human organs to the winds. The murderous women are led by Agave, Pentheus' mother, who, in her fury, has severed the head of a lion. Only after she has become sober does she realize that she erred in identifying the victim: the head in her hands, which she intended to offer as a sacrifice to the gods, belonged to none other than her beloved son. Pentheus had changed from predator to prey, and Agave, from being a ruthless hunter became a bereaved mother. Then she mourns her son and, with the help of others, tries to arrange and reassemble her son's severed remains, which were scattered in the mountains, among the rocks, and to create him anew.

Leaving aside the moral of the play, its dramaturgic merit, its contribution to understanding the human soul and the dynamics of religion, and its validity as a reflection of ancient cults and historical events, as much has been written about all these topics, I will merely refer to central scenes in the tragedy, which show remarkable similarity to aspects of suicide terrorism discussed here. These are archetypical human situations, which I propose as a heuristic key for a deeper reading of the phenomenon of religious violence, which is at the focus of our interest.

*

"Wrenched away arm at the shoulder . . . foot still warm in its shoe . . . cut off hand . . . ribs clawed clean of flesh . . .ripped bleeding body torn limb from limb." These words are taken from a fictional depiction of the arena of gruesome death in the mountains near Thebes, a work of genius written in 405 BCE. As we have seen, the reports of observers at the horrifying arena of mayhem in the streets and markets of Jerusalem more than two thousand years later are nearly identical. This is how the arena of terrorism looks as a result of the holy madness of the female followers of Dionysus, and of the young men from the West Bank and Gaza, followers of Hamas.

There are other theatrical and mythological Bacchic motifs which are characteristic of Palestinian suicide terrorism in Israel. In addition to the ecstatic and murderous nature of holy rage, the product of incitement by religious authorities, and the element of ripping the body to pieces, until it no longer looks like a body, we must point out the difficulty of identifying everything and differentiating one thing from another. Specifically, it is difficult to locate the attacker, because of his disguise and mingling with the crowd of his intended victims. This applies to Dionysius, and, to some degree, to

Pentheus, as well as to the human bomb, making it difficult to draw a clear line between attacker and victim, because the attacker makes himself his own victim, like the other victims. Note the fate of Agave and Pentheus, and, like them, of the human bomb.

Dionysius is the god of wine and of blood. In Chapter 1 I presented testimony of the ZAKA volunteers from the arena of suicide terrorism after the attack on the Park Hotel (March 2002). They reported the strong impression made on them by the sight (and odor) of the wine of the Passover Seder, which was spilled and mixed with the blood of the thirty victims who died and the 160 wounded. You might say that Dionysus is the impresario and dispatcher of suicide terrorism, and, in a way, the Bacchae, especially Agave, like Pentheus, are his agents, human bombs, who are both attackers and victims. In the end, Agave and her old father are parallel with ZAKA, gathering up the body parts and severed limbs and trying to reassemble them. Here are passages from the tragedy that describe the arena immediately after the terrorist attack, in which Pentheus' body is torn to pieces by his mother, Agave:

> *Witness*: They played ball with scraps of his flesh.
> The pitiful remains lie scattered,
> one piece among the sharp rocks, others
> lying lost among the leaves in the depths of the forest.
> (*Enter Cadmus [Agave's father] followed by attendants who bear*
>    *upon a bier the dismembered body of Pentheus*).
> *Cadmus*: This was Pentheus
> whose body, after long and weary searching
> I painfully assembled from Cithaeron's glens
> where it lay, scattered in shreds, dismembered
> throughout the forest, no two pieces
> in a single place. . . .
>
> *Cadmus*: And whose head do you hold in your hands?
> *Agave*: A lion's head—or so the [Bacchae] told me.
> *Cadmus*: Look more closely still. Study it carefully.
> *Agave*: No O gods . . . Pentheus' head—I hold. . . .
>
> *Agave*: Is his body entire?
> *Cadmus*: All but the head. The rest is mutilated
> horribly.

> (*Agave lifts up one of Pentheus' limbs and asks for help of*
> *Cadmus in piecing the body together. She mourns each piece*
> *separately before replacing it on the bier*).
> *Agave*: Come, Father. We must restore his head
> to this unhappy boy. As best as we can, we shall make
> him whole again.
> —O dearest, dearest face!
> Pretty boyish mouth! Now with this veil
> I shroud your head, gathering with loving care
> these mangled bloody limbs, this flesh I brought
> to birth.

What a precise perception of the terror, its motives, dynamics, and the natural attempt to counteract its gruesome outcomes! When we read the immortal ancient tragedy in modern Israel, Euripides' mythical characters shed their Greek robes and put on the yarmulkas, beards, and earlocks of the Haredi volunteers.

### *Sparagmos*

*The Bacchae* draws inspiration from distinct ritual and myth. It is based on the ancient Greek rite of ripping apart a living being—either an animal or a human—which is called *sparagmos*, an integral part of the bacchanal orgy. *The Bacchae* is a dramatic literary expression of *sparagmos*, an allusion to a particularly violent practice of pagan priestly worship. It is possible that suicide terrorism contains a deep stratum of that practice of ritual murder. Instigated by Dionysus and led by Agave, the Maenads inadvertently subject Pentheus to *sparagmos*; that is, they kill him with their bare hands in a manner resembling a sacrificial ceremony. We may conjecture that the human bomb is a Maenad-like Dionysian celebrant, a practitioner of *sparagmos*, an enthusiastic executioner.

The Haredi volunteers position themselves at the hub of suicide terrorism attacks, and there, too, they are drawn into the whirlpool of *sparagmos*. Unaware, they are drawn into the eroticism of horrific death, and they plunge into the aesthetics of the mutilated body. The ecstasy that prevails in the arena also seizes the ZAKA activists. Strangely, they change from being responders to the orgy of blood to participants. Tearing the body asunder—eliminating opposites and breaking through boundaries—hypnotizes the ultra-Orthodox Jews just as it does their Palestinian adversaries. Those who came to restore order are captivated by the charm of destroying order. Those who deal with the corpses are an integral part of the scene of Middle Eastern terrorism.

*

One finds direct and indirect references to *sparagmos* in several ancient mythologies. It is a central theme in two well-known mythical plots in which the hero's life ends with his dismemberment. The severed limbs, the remains of his body, have a life cycle of their own and powers they can exert upon living people. Merely the head of Medusa can kill enemies experienced in battle, and her offspring burst from her neck. In this case, the beheaded body is the source of horror, which, the more it is frightening and repugnant, the more it is mesmerizing. This is also true of Orpheus. Toward the end of his adventurous life, he gets lost and by mistake encounters a Dionysian ceremony in full swing. The Maenads attack him, and in their ecstasy, they tear his body to shreds. His head is thrown into the river and proves to be a variation of a relic, developing magical potency.

*Sparagmos*-like elements appear in more than one ancient Greek tragedy, which have become classics of Western civilization, such as *Antigone*, by Sophocles.[103] Another example is Euripides' *Medea*. The ritual dismembering of bodies is also part of Judeo-Christian mythology. Thus, in a foundational event in the sacred history of the Jewish people, the source of mutual obligation between the Jews and God, there is the "covenant of the pieces" (Genesis 15). The Hebrew Bible mentions other cases in which rending the body has symbolic meaning, as in the concubine on the hill (Judges 19–21). These paradigmatic cases relate to the ultimate sacrifice, human sacrifice, which is an ancient, ritualized murder. If the killing by dismemberment is accomplished according to outlines laid out in a holy text, then it is not burdened by guilt, nor does it invite moral condemnation. Rather its execution is elevating. Sacrificing mollifies the god, soothes his rage against human sins, and promises results such as halting a plague or ending a drought. Sacrifice is a cruel but meritorious murder. This apparent inner contradiction is shown clearly in the myths that associate dismemberment with regeneration. Here death has nullified itself, as it were, by increasing the dead person's chances of returning to the world of the living.

Much has been written about the connection between death and regeneration.[104] In the mythologies and rituals of agrarian societies, the connection between the end of life and new life is seen in terms of the cycle of withering and renewal in the natural cycle of the seasons. There is also reference to the specific case of death involving dismemberment and the scattering of body parts. In what may seem paradoxical, in traditional Greek, Egyptian, and Hindu cultures, violent death of this kind is supposed to increase fertility and the chances of resurrection. The dismemberment and scattering of the parts are compared to sowing seeds, which will produce a rich harvest.[105] Beneficial magical powers are attributed to the severed limbs, a kind of relic, and the more they fill the area, the more the results will be positive. Sometimes the dismemberment and scattering are compared to the process of giving birth.[106] What is birth if not tearing the body and removing a severed member? There are historical examples of the dismembering of a body and the scattering of its parts being presented as a key not only to fertilizing an area but also to its sanctification. Thus, temples have been erected on sites where severed limbs have been found. Holy places have been found decorated with friezes of piles of severed arms, legs, heads, and sex organs. In the iconography of the Ancient Near East, death priests officiated in cults of mutilated bodies. The victims did not die in battle but in ritual acts that imitate the deeds of the local god. Dismembering a body and scattering its parts can be seen not only as initiating the transformation of man and nature but also as a reenactment of the act of creation.[107] In ancient Mesopotamia and Rome acts of violent murder play a decisive cosmogenic role: they precede and condition the creation of a new universe. For example, chaos is overcome, and a new order is created by cutting up the body of the Assyrian goddess Tiamat and scattering her blood.[108] An element of creativity is found in ritualized brutal killing.[109]

However, in many cases other than those discussed above, death involving dismemberment of the body and the scattering of the limbs is related to severing the chain of eternal return, whose links are death and regeneration.[110] In other words, it can also be seen as an especially bad death, the result or cause of nullifying the possibility of resurrection. Only murder that produces a mutilated and scattered body will cause final death.[111] The Spanish conquistadores who suppressed the Inca rebellions in the sixteenth century cut their bodies up into little pieces that were scattered far afield, to guarantee ultimate destruction, after which not even mythical thinking offers a potential for revival.[112] Dismembering the body makes it impotent.[113] Compare it to castration. Cutting up the body and scattering its parts makes burial difficult, and without completing the procedure of dealing with the dead, it has no chance of resurrection.

## Counter-mythology

The mythological realm of the Ancient Near East also offers a motif opposite to that of the dismemberment of the body and the dispersal of its parts. This is the myth recounting the effort to locate and gather the dismembered body parts and reassemble them as a new body. These two contradictory motifs mostly appear as two phases of a single developing plot. They follow one another and complement each other.

The best example is the famous legend of Isis and Osiris, taken from ancient Egyptian mythology. This canonical narrative is employed here as another model contributing to understanding suicide terrorism. It also has elements that are variations on the Dionysian theme, but in this plot the center of gravity passes from dismemberment to reassembly. Thus, while the analogy of *The Bacchae* has heuristic value mainly for the project of the human bomb, the analogy of the myth of Isis and Osiris has heuristic value mainly for the project of the ZAKA volunteers.[114]

Synopsis: Osiris, the god of the dead and the underworld in the Pharaonic pantheon, was the primeval king of Egypt.[115] He married his sister, Isis, the goddess of nature and magic. Together they provide the world with culture, thanks to which order and plenty prevail in Egypt. The envy of their brother, Seth, is aroused, and with treacherous plots he murders Osiris, with the aim of succeeding him as king. To make certain of Osiris' death and to prevent his resurrection, he chops up Osiris' body and scatters the parts widely. Following this clear act of *sparagmos* committed by Seth, Isis, the wife and sister of Osiris, mourns for him and sets out on a long journey to find his remains. After many adventures, she locates and collects the severed limbs of Osiris. Now she can reassemble his body, and when this is done, she breathes the spirit of life into his nostrils. Osiris' mutilated body becomes a living being again.[116]

Seth and Isis, the protagonists of the plot, play opposite roles. Seth dismembers and scatters the body parts, and Isis puts them back together. The drama brings together the initiator and responder; one occupies an important place in the other's world. They share the same ritual of blood.

A central activist in the Jerusalem branch of ZAKA confided in me that recently, in the middle of the night, he went to the cemetery by himself. With his bare hands he dug in the still soft soil of a one- or two-day-old grave. In the hole that he dug, he buried some severed fingers, and covered them up again. A few hours earlier he had "rescued" them from a pile of mutilated body parts that was left on the side of a pathological operating theater in the National Institute of Forensic Medicine, which were going to be disposed of according to the accepted administrative procedures. An inner voice filled him with the conviction that they were the fingers of a victim of terrorism, whose family hurriedly buried him, although the reassembly of his body was incomplete.

There have been similar cases in which the Haredi volunteers failed in their determined efforts to associate severed limbs to the body to which they had belonged before the explosion. Usually this became clear after the fact, following posthumous DNA tests. When a part of a body remained separated from it, even a small part, even if the body was already buried, the Haredi activists did not rest easy until they had joined them together and filled the gap. ZAKA volunteers were obsessed with reattaching severed limbs and restoring the integrity of bodies. Their insistence on restoring the state of the dead to what it was in the moment before the explosion was also expressed in their care to dress the corpses in their torn clothes. This was the case especially when the items of clothing showed that the deceased had been an Orthodox Jew. They carefully wrapped the bleeding head of an orthodox Jewish woman in her scarf, which had been blown off her head to the other end of the site of the attack.

ZAKA activists proudly claim to be experts in putting pieces together, whereas the forensic medical experts are contemptuous of their abilities, which are based on gut feelings and simple logic. The head of the ZAKA team in Tel Aviv told me that several hours after they finished clearing the mutilated bodies away from the arena of the attack, on a nearby roof he found a piece of an ear, and he immediately knew to which of the twenty victims it belonged (Beit Lid, January 1995). He acted according to "special signs" that he would not reveal. When a genetic test confirmed his claim, he boasted of heavenly inspiration.

Joining the parts together and constructing a whole body raises associations with the esoteric legend of the Golem, which has been current among traditional Jews since the late Middle Ages. In the folklore of religious mystery, we learn of the efforts made by the Kabbalistic sages of every generation to make the image of a man out of clay and breathe life into it by occult means—usually by placing a note with the explicit name of God written on it in the effigy's mouth. The most famous story about a Golem is connected to the sixteenth-century Rabbi Judah Loew of Prague.

Man is made in God's image, and only God has the ability and the right to create people. Construction of the Golem is like a provocation against heaven. In the Haredi community I have heard one or two isolated, hesitant voices suggest that ZAKA's rituals in the arena of terrorism remind them of the legend of the Golem. These words were spoken in condemnation, but they also showed a degree of wonder and admiration. The response of a rabbi among the ZAKA activists was modest dismissal, embarrassment, and perhaps a smidgen of pride. About ten years later, I told him that I had read a book that paraphrased the story of the Golem and inserted it in the contemporary Middle East. Against the background of the daily religious violence in Iraq, the book was called *Frankenstein in Baghdad*.[117] It is a science drama combining material taken from the tragic situation of the early 2000s, laden with mass fatality, with human compassion. The central protagonist is a super-hero composed of the body parts of victims of terrorism, which were collected at arenas after explosions. The man made up of these limbs sets out on a mission of bloody revenge, but with every act of murder that he commits, one of his limbs falls away. Thus, he must commit more murders to supply himself with replacement parts. The surrealistic cycle of horror continues to spin.

## Two Universal Archetypes

The dismembering of bodies and scattering of the limbs is a basic instinct and a recurring theme in rites and mythologies of various cultures, as is the gathering and reassembling of the body parts. This inborn urge to reassemble the dismembered body is not only a reaction, an antithesis, but also a mental and cultural element that stands on its own, a fundamental thought pattern and a paradigmatic act grounded in autonomous logic. In the arena of Palestinian terrorism in Israel a macabre encounter takes place between two symbolic embodied practices, each of which reverberates with universal archetypes.[118] The archetype of tearing the body apart and that of piecing it back together, with all the tension between them, are parallel to each other

and complementary.[119] The reciprocity that characterizes the connection between these two manifestations of deep structure is not only the product of
the specific conjunction of their occurrence in time and place, unique to the
Intifada. It is also the product of the dialectics of two impulses, two driving
forces, that flow in the social and religious imagination.

# 9
# Pious Counterterrorism

## Blood Touches Blood

At one of the arenas of violent death that I witnessed toward the end of the Intifada, while the ZAKA team was bending over a mutilated body, the volunteers learned from exchanging words with police officers that the victim, a young Jewish woman, had a child who was being raised by his Muslim Arab father. The Haredi activists immediately began what they defined as a rescue mission: locating the child of mixed parentage in a nearby Palestinian village, removing him from there in a complex operation involving risk and the use of force, to make sure the child (who was Jewish according to halakha) received a Jewish education. This mission appeared no less sacred and urgent to them than burying the victim of aggression in a respectful way according to halakha. Even before the body was evacuated, when it was still warm, the volunteers called up their counterparts in the Yad Leaḥim organization to coordinate the details of their joint religious mission. They considered sending disguised Arabic-speaking associates to infiltrate the hostile environment and kidnap the child late at night.

Yad La'aḥim (in Hebrew, "a hand to brethren"), known also as "save fellow Jews," is a Haredi organization dedicated to preventing Jewish assimilation among the gentiles. It concentrates on severing relations between Jews and Arabs, usually intimacy between Israeli Jewish girls and Muslim Palestinians from both sides of the Green Line. With no less enthusiasm, the organization attacks Christian institutions located in Israel, especially those suspected of missionary activity, like the Jehovah's Witnesses, or those who, despite their Christian nature, insist on presenting themselves as Jews, such as the Messianic Jews. The organization's activists do not conceal their mission, explicitly stated as preserving the purity of the Jewish race and the purity of the Holy Land. They focus their efforts on every instance that appears to them as a threat to the boundary between Jews, even secular Jews, and other religious and ethnic groups. This organization overlaps the Lahava movement, whose leaders previously belonged to Kakh, the political party founded by

*The Cult of Dismembered Limbs.* Gideon Aran, Oxford University Press. © Oxford University Press 2023.
DOI: 10.1093/oso/9780197689141.003.0009

Rabbi Kahane, who, when he was a member of the Knesset, proposed a law forbidding marriage and sexual relations between Jews and non-Jews and imposing heavy penalties on those who violated it (1984–1988). In parallel with extensive propaganda and provocative demonstrations, Yad Leaḥim acts clandestinely, frequently inflicting property damage and personal injury. They are proud of their success in locating "kosher daughters of Israel" married to Arabs and living with them in their villages, persuading them to return to Jewish society with their children, and, if necessary, also using deception, bribery, and physical force to do so. They also go out at night in vigilante groups patrolling mixed neighborhoods and breaking into places of entertainment to prevent contact between Jews and Arabs.

There is mutual sympathy and cooperation between the Yad Le'aḥim volunteers and ZAKA volunteers. Haredi activists reject the label "racism" but admit that ZAKA is fitting into the project of assuring the purity of Jewish blood. The ZAKA rabbis supported their colleagues among the Hebron settlers who libeled the head of a yeshiva, attacking him physically as well, for giving halakhic permission to an Israeli Jewish couple to accept a contribution of semen from a gentile for fertility treatment (May 2010).

*

The arena of suicide terrorism is a stage for the crossing and erasing of boundaries. Fundamental and sensitive borders are crossed in dramatic fashion: first, the borders of body, those between one body and another, including the boundaries between the body of the aggressor and that of his victim, between the Palestinian Muslim body and the Israeli Jewish body. Jewish Orthodoxy regards this as a challenge to Judaism, and ZAKA is dispatched to meet this challenge. A strong metonymic expression of the erasure of boundaries is the mingling of blood, the puddles into which the blood of the victims flows. At the arena of suicide terrorism, the blood of the human bomb mixes with that of his target community. ZAKA takes responsibility for separating them anew.

The biblical expression "blood touches blood" (Hosea 4:2) originally described a violent, immoral society where one murder followed or caused another. Later the rabbis of the Talmud glossed it slightly differently, in the context of the destruction of the First Temple in Jerusalem (586 BCE). They interpreted the original Hebrew phrase to mean the mingling of the blood of victims of a mass murderer (the Babylonian general who slaughtered the Jews of ancient Judea). In modern times, the phrase has taken on extended meanings and has been used to express the dense continuity and solidarity that link generations of Jews slaughtered by anti-Jewish gentiles, from the second-century Rabbi Akiva, through the medieval Inquisition and Early Modern pogroms, to the recent Holocaust, and down to the victims of the contemporary Intifada. Currently ZAKA rabbis proposed an even bolder interpretation. They bitterly employ this charged expression to refer to the mixing of the Palestinian terrorist's blood with that of his Jewish victims.

Blood is a fraught element of religious and ethno-national imagination and practice. And blood is, of course, an important ceremonial element in inter-communal, inter-ethnic, and inter-religious conflicts. A case in point is the blood libel—the infamous accusation that, prior to the Passover festival, Jews sacrifice Christian children and use their blood to prepare *matsot* (the unleavened bread eaten on the holiday).[1]

In the present-day Middle East, blood is also an axis of a tribal ritual at the site of suicide terrorism. It is a core cultic element for the Palestinian human bomb[2] and, in parallel and complementary fashion, a focus of ZAKA's cult in the wake of the attack. Blood plays a central role in ZAKA's myth and ethos. At the site, ZAKA volunteers devote a large part of their time and effort to blood. They cut out blood-soaked upholstery, scrape spattered blood from the walls of upper stories, and cut off branches of trees to which drops of blood have adhered. All these bloody items are meticulously collected and taken for burial according to detailed prescribed norms.

ZAKA is strict about separating different kinds of blood and, more so, the blood of different kinds of people. They are especially stringent about the mixed blood of the attacker and his victims. They are permitted to wash away the blood of the Palestinian terrorist, but they are required to estimate the precise proportion of his blood within the total amount of blood at the site. The purpose of this estimation is to apply the halakhic principle of "voided in the sixtieth part" (*batel be'shishim*): if the blood of the Jewish victims makes up more than a sixtieth of the total amount of blood, then all the mixed blood must be brought for burial, even if the presence of the impure blood of the Palestinian attacker remains of troublesome concern.

ZAKA's preoccupation with separating the different kinds of blood is grounded in the universal association between blood and boundaries in human societies. Blood challenges territorial boundaries and boundaries between civilizations, collectivities, and individuals. Particularly intriguing is the ambiguous status of blood with respect to the boundary between the body and its surroundings. When we bleed, it is hard for us to decide whether our blood is an integral part of our body or something external and separate. This ambiguity has made blood a fascinating, confusing, and particularly terrifying presence in many cultures. Blood creates and marks boundaries but also crosses and blurs boundaries. Border conflicts often involve blood-shed, which tends in turn to intensify and perpetuate them.[3] However, blood is spilled not just in combat but also in peace. Covenants are often sealed in blood. The circumcision ceremony, which involves cutting the body and drawing blood, marks, in Jewish tradition, the covenant between God and His Chosen People. Ancient covenants often involved the cutting of flesh—indeed the Hebrew verb that designates concluding an agreement or alliance is *krita*, from the root that means "to cut." The effect of a covenant is to erase the boundary between previously hostile parties and make them one. This ceremony of unification is constructed on a foundation of separation.

In tribal society, like among children, drawing and mixing the blood of different bodies is a compelling expression of brotherhood. This mixing of blood is a classic symbol of obliterating boundaries between parties, and as-similation of one into the other. When people fighting together on the same side are injured or die, and their blood mingles, they are said to be united by blood, the strongest possible bond among persons or groups. While the expunging of boundaries by mixing blood in these circumstances is highly positive, in other circumstances, it is extremely negative. In clashes where the blood of attacker and victim, or of sworn enemies, mixes, this creates a threat to classification and natural order.

The mixing of blood, which can reinforce a sense of unity and identifica-tion, can also elicit fear of the kind of chaos against which taboos are meant to protect. The opposite of the blood covenant is the desecration of blood. Throughout history human beings have regarded the blending of blood as pollution, an abomination. This metaphor of the mixture of blood as contam-ination of the collective organism is a familiar trope in racist societies that seek to maintain distinctions and hierarchies between classes, ethnicities, or peoples. Some notorious regimes prohibited intermarriage and miscegena-tion to prevent the mixture of blood.[4]

Suicide terrorism also creates a fear of pollution via the actual mixing of blood. The terrorist's blood can seep into the bloodstream of the injured through their open wounds. It has not been unusual to find splinters of Palestinian bone deep in the flesh of Israelis injured in an attack. For this reason, the terrorist's blood is thoroughly tested for HIV and hepatitis; to avoid risk, the injured are inoculated against the latter.

ZAKA activists see the mixture of blood as the fruit of a Palestinian scheme, intended at assimilation into Israeliness, a plot to contaminate Judaism. Interviews with Haredi volunteers during the Intifada show that the threat of suicide terrorism is not grasped solely in terms of the physical danger to life but also in terms of the danger of ethno-national contamination. They compare suicide terrorism, which entails imitation and disguise, to chemical and biological warfare. They portray the Hamas bombers as an insidious virus unidentified by the body's immune system.[5] The blood-mixing strategy attributed in ZAKA's imagination to anti-Israeli terrorists is reminiscent of the way Nazi propaganda depicted Jews as conspiring to dilute the Aryan blood of the master race with their Semitic blood.

At the arena of suicide terrorism, there are other manifestations of the erasure of boundaries between the Palestinian aggressor and his Israeli victims, which are mingled into a single mass. I refer mainly to the severed parts of the many bodies, which are thrown in every direction, scattered and mixed together by the force of the explosion, the burning of the bodies and their fusing together because of the heat of the blast. As a result, it is difficult to determine the identity of the dead and to distinguish among them. After the explosion, the suicide terrorist is hard to find, as it is before the explosion when he conceals his Palestinian identity and disguises himself as an Israeli. From the moment the suicide terrorist crossed the border, he looks and acts like his target community. By means of mimicry and disguise, he approaches and penetrates his target. The accomplishment of his murderous mission is founded on his success in assimilating among his intended victims.

Under occupation, two strategies of resistance, liberation, and self-expression are available to the subject people. The first is, of course, violent rebellion against the conquerors. The second is imitation and assimilation into the dominant culture—essentially, passing.[6] The Palestinian human bomb who blows himself up in an Israeli crowd simultaneously performs the two responses of the subjugated, both of which threaten the conqueror. In the shared death of the terrorist and his victims there is both aggression and integration. A conditional relationship is formed between the two components of suicide terrorism: assimilation makes the violent act possible, and the violent act results in assimilation.

A kernel of opposition is inherent in the blurring of differences and mingling. The human bomb is both an expression of the confrontational struggle and an effective substitute for that struggle. The suicide terrorism event that took place at the hitchhiking station just outside Ashkelon

(February 1996) illustrates this phenomenon. When the survivors of the attack were interviewed, it turned out that "the human bomb looked just like another local Jewish guy." They kept asking themselves how they had failed to recognize him as different or strange, even though he stood for some time with a group of alert Israelis.

The amalgamation of the Palestinian human bomb with Israelis happens not just postmortem, when his blood mixes with that of his victims, but beforehand, when the terrorist sets out to commit the attack. The terrorist infiltrator's success in masquerading as an Israeli Jew and blending in with his future victims makes the attack particularly subversive even before it has taken place. Then, when the human bomb explodes, his body penetrates those of his Israeli victims, thus doubling the subversive effect. In treating the bodies that remained at the site of the Ashkelon attack, the chief of the local ZAKA squad said that it was impossible to separate out "the Israeli tissue." The impersonator-assimilator was not identified prior to the explosion and was identified and distinguished after the explosion only with great difficulty.

## Pigs

Suicide terrorism differs fundamentally from other types of terrorism in that it is built on the premise of fusion. The human bomb is mixed in several ways. His identity is hyphenated, as discussed later, first, in that he is Arab-Jew and both aggressor and victim. By disguising himself as an Israeli before his death, and by merging his body with Israeli bodies after his death, the suicide terrorist transforms himself from an Other who confirms and reifies a separate Israeli identity into a blend challenging the very foundation of the Israeli claim to be a distinct, self-evident collective. The absolute otherness of the Palestinian human bomb is not what threatens Israelis but rather the blurring of this otherness by the human bomb's ability to appear very much like his victims and mix with them. The mingling of the occupied with the occupiers and the former's imitation of the latter erodes the binary opposition between them.[7]

At the final stage before the attack and at the stage immediately after it, the subversive effect of suicide terrorism is founded on merging. In the arena of the explosion, actual physical bonding takes place. The human bomb and his dispatchers are highly cognizant of the effect of this bonding while they are envisaging the operation. They have a concrete image of the direct contact that is about to take place between the bodies of the attacker and his victims. This image is idealized, although it is also repulsive and frightening. The projection of fusion is present in the discourse of Hamas, mainly in the recorded testaments declaimed just before going out on the fateful mission. For example, Rim Riashi, a mother of two from Gaza, the first woman sent by Hamas to blow herself up (Erez border crossing, January 2004): less than an hour after she died, along with her four Israeli victims, she was eulogized on Palestinian television by Hamas's leader, Sheikh Yassin, who said, "For years she dreamed of becoming a martyr in the service of Islam, and her final wish was to have her organs scatter in every direction attached to fragments of Jewish bodies."[8]

Through suicide terrorism, the Palestinian human bomb clings to the Jews and kills them at the same time: he clings to them, thus he is enabled to effectively kill them, and he kills them, which allows him to blend and become one with them. Neither one of these two objectives could be achieved by a living Palestinian. Both may be achieved through voluntary death. The instigators of suicide terrorism push the human bombs into this connection, and the latter set out enthusiastically. However, at the same time this connection repulses them. They are fascinated by it, yearn for it, but at the same time are repelled by it.

As with the ZAKA volunteers, the activists and leaders of the Palestinian resistance movements, mainly the devout Muslims among them, regard the vision of the mingling of blood and the melting together of mutilating of bodies as disgusting and threatening for the very same reasons. On both sides they see the potential for pollution in contact of the holy body, living or dead (that of their own side, the attacker or the victims, respectively), with an impure body (of the other side). Ironically, the posthumous contamination, which the spiritual leaders of ZAKA see as a horrible dimension of suicide terrorism, is precisely one of the reasons why the spiritual leaders of Hamas have reservations about the use of suicide terrorism, despite the overwhelming support for it both within their movement and their community. Awareness of the mixing of blood and flesh, which moved Haredi rabbis in Jerusalem to endanger their status by permitting their followers to join the organization and go out to the arena, is exactly what moved sheikhs in the West Bank and Gaza to risk their status and oppose the policy of suicide terrorism, which was so popular in Palestinian public opinion.

The Palestinians regard the human bomb as a saint, and his Israeli victims are explicitly called "pigs" (and sometimes apes), so that contact with their flesh and blood is polluting. These negative ritual consequences of suicide terrorism were brought up before the Palestinian Muslim authorities and threatened to deny its religious validity. However, some Muslim sages issued a Fatwa canceling the ritual prohibition in favor of continued suicide terrorism. This macabre issue concerning the perils of contact between mutilated body parts reached an unsettling peak when some ZAKA activists, agitated by frustrated experts on the fringes of the Israeli defense establishment, proposed burying the remains of suicide terrorists with pigs, claiming that spreading rumors to that effect would deter future suicide terrorists.

## It's All about Classification

The post-explosion dead body of the human bomb, like his pre-explosion living body, exhibits hybridity that cancels oppositions and confuses classifications so vital for organizing humans' inner and outer worlds. The dissolution of the distinction between fundamental categories troubles the Haredi volunteers.

As ultra-Orthodox Jews, ZAKA activists have inherited a religious tradition of obsessive concern with boundaries, classifications, and binary oppositions. This rich tradition is centered on laws of pollution and purity based on the principle of splitting, distancing, and putting things in their proper place. Many chapters of the Pentateuch and one of the six Orders of the Mishna are devoted to it. Note the detailed discussion of the question of the forbidden mixture of various components, such as *shatnez*, cloth made of wool and linen, dealt with in an entire tractate of the Talmud, whose name, *Kilayim* (crossbreeds, mixtures), is indicative of its content.

Religious cultures can be characterized by their relative tolerance for ambiguity, duality, and intermediate situations, and according to the strictness of their distinction. Orthodox Judaism is unique in its absolute rejection of things deriving from blurred boundaries, and in the centrality it attributes to either/or logic and exclusivity. For example, see the rabbinical discussion of the Sabbath (in a tractate entitled *Eruvin* [Boundaries]), which emphasizes the precise and absolute limits of the holy day. Those who abide by halakha know that at the week these lines are written (early May), the Sabbath begins (in Jerusalem) at exactly 19:12 on Friday evening and ends at exactly 20:21 the following day. At the conclusion of the Sabbath a special ceremony is held, called Havdala, meaning "separation," during which benedictions are recited relating to three levels of division: between holy and profane, between light and darkness, and between Jews and gentiles.[9]

Jewish lack of tolerance for hybridity is demonstrated with respect to what is permitted and forbidden to eat, the laws of *kashrut*. Dairy and meat foods are strictly separated, requiring separate vessels and utensils and a delay between eating dairy foods after meat. Similarly, there is a taboo against eating animals whose classification is unclear, such as the eel, which looks like a fish, lives in water, and has fins, but lack scales, and the pig, which has a cleft foot but does not chew its cud. Pork is the definitive taboo. Pork eating is associated with gentiles, from whom one must keep a distance, both physical and symbolic. There is a severe prohibition against contact between the body of a Jew, whose sanctity is signaled by circumcision, and that of an uncircumcised gentile. While alive, they may not have sexual contact, and, after death, they may not be buried on the same side of the cemetery wall.

*

The body of a human being, living or dead, is a "natural symbol" for the collective.[10] The body's boundaries are analogous to the boundaries of the group, and perforation of the body menaces the political and cultural boundaries that define tribal, religious, and ethno-national identity. Mary Douglas' much-cited observations are useful in understanding the arena and ZAKA's deathwork there. According to this metaphoric parallelism, a threat to the boundaries of the collective can produce a tendency toward intense preoccupation with the boundaries of the body, and insults to the boundaries of the body are perceived as challenges to the boundaries of the collective. Hence the compulsive concern with the integrity of the body, and the sharp reactions against any attempt to violate this integrity.[11]

Human beings aspire to maintain order in their life, an order constructed and preserved by dividing experience into categories and by ensuring that the boundaries between them remain distinct. The elimination of these boundaries creates a state of impurity, to which taboos apply. The desire to restore lost order is concealed behind the effort to reestablish the classification, which is perceived as a rite of purification. Society is regarded as a body and the body is a mirror of society. The symbolic correspondence between the human and social bodies produces a magical link between them. Manipulation of the body's boundaries, by violating or rehabilitating them, is charged with ritual meaning that can be interpreted either as an attack on society or as protection of it. Suicide terrorism violates the foundations of the social system. The Palestinian who blows up the bodies of his victims undermines the very foundation of the Israeli order. When ZAKA mobilizes to care for the bodies of the victims, it also acts to restore the violated order.

By distancing a limb lying near a body that is of an obviously different skin color, by bagging body parts along with the pool of blood that lay beside them, the volunteers seek to repair the violation of the body's integrity and to reinstate the boundaries between different bodies.

In this labor to reestablish boundaries, the ZAKA volunteers restore the victims' lost identities. An explosion that cuts a body into many pieces or fuses different bodies together robs victims of their individuality. The bus passengers and pizza eaters—as well as the human bomb—all of whom had names and individual traits before the explosion, receive them again after ZAKA volunteers have completed their work.

The ZAKA volunteers devote tremendous effort to reestablishing the religious or ethno-national boundary between Jew and non-Jew. This distinction receives operational and symbolic expression in their procedures. Each body has a bag of its own, and during sorting and identification, the bags are laid side by side in a row. When the ZAKA volunteers suspect that the body parts they have collected did not belong to a Jew, they place them separately, at a distance from the row of presumably Jewish bodies. At times, the religious or national identity of a terrorism victim may be determined only at a later stage, in the forensic laboratory, but ZAKA volunteers have developed confidence in their ability to make such distinctions on site.[12] Some of them have developed folk methods for determining difference, in addition to circumcision.[13] One rabbi insisted, for example, that "a Palestinian's ear is more convoluted."

Distinguishing between the two categories in the arena of suicide terrorism is often based on a first impression of the corpse's appearance. The volunteers determine the ethnic and religious identity of the dead in the arena according to their style of dress, the color of their skin, details of their anatomies, and the "look of their faces." In cases of doubt, they do not hesitate to examine a dead man's penis.[14] When the ZAKA volunteers locate non-Jews among the victims, they immediately report this to their colleagues. Among the non-Jews who were caught at the arena and became victims of terrorism were foreign workers, tourists, exchange students, and clergymen. When Arabs are found among the dead, this is announced on the communications network with the euphemistic police code (B.M. for a minority person). Bodies identified as non-Jewish are laid down separately at a distance from the bodies of the Jewish victims, and they are wrapped in conspicuously different body bags. From then on, the treatment of the two types of corpses is differential. This is distinguished using ritual practices applicable only to the Jewish dead, who are the first to be buried. The others remain in the Institute's refrigerators for some time, until they are returned to their families or buried without ceremony.

The first and strictest separation is that between the Palestinian terrorist and his Jewish victims. Only afterward do they begin separating the victims from one another. A distinction is made between religious and secular Jews (in many cases there are clear indications of this, such as ritual fringes, a *kippah*, the type of beard), and especially between the Jewish dead and gentiles of various kinds. Those who are identified as Muslim or Arab dead at the arena of terrorism are treated with suspicion, and sometimes clear signs of disgust and hatred, and this is mainly because of the possibility that they might have been involved in the attack, and because they are identified with Israel's violent enemies. However, a few ZAKA volunteers, often the better educated and more sophisticated among them, display a more negative attitude toward the Christian dead. They explain this by saying that Christianity is basically pagan, and between Judaism and Christianity there is not only deeper theological rivalry but also a blood reckoning over a longer range of history than with Islam.

## Ultra-Orthodox Border Policing

In the short time before the explosion and a short time after it, the suicide terrorist cannot be located. Before the explosion, while he is a living person among the living, he has mingled indistinguishably with those who soon will be killed by him, and after the explosion, when he is a dead man among the dead, his body and theirs are mingled. There is close contact in both the antemortem and the postmortem situations, a mixture and exchange between the human bomb and his target group. As a result, important distinctions break down.

The human bomb undermines the self-confidence of the target community and erodes its identity by neutralizing the other side's ability to distinguish between friend and foe, between us and them, which is so crucial in situations of confrontation between groups. Both in the stage when he passes as an Israeli on his way to the explosion site and while infiltrating it, and also in the stage when he is lying dead and mutilated among dead and mangled Israelis, the suicide terrorist makes it very difficult for the Jews to separate themselves from him and, in general, to distinguish themselves from all gentiles, and, more specifically and crucially, from Palestinians.

The Israeli response to the human bomb's two-phase subversive assimilation is detection and segregation. The Israelis endeavor to uncover his identity before he reaches his target—preferably before he sets out on his mission, to prevent the attack. Even if prevention has failed, detection and separation still apply. Prior to the attack the mission is the responsibility of the state's security forces; afterward, it is assigned to the delegates of ultra-Orthodoxy.

The volunteers at the site labor to identify and remove the body parts of the Palestinian terrorist, in order to help the ISA catch his handlers and collaborators as quickly as possible and to analyze the patterns of his act, which can help prevent future bombings. But ZAKA's interest in the terrorist is not confined to these instrumental priorities. Beyond the tactical emergency requirements and their own genuine curiosity about the terrorist, they toil to separate the human bomb from his victims for ritual reasons, and with great stringency.

Once the volunteers have finished their work, they are left with two vexing questions: Could it be that any remains of the Jewish victims were not located and identified, so that they could be brought for proper burial? And equally important, could it be that unidentified pieces of the suicide terrorist made their way into the Jewish bags, stuck together with Jewish pieces and thus polluting them? Israel pursues the human bomb while he is alive, with the aim of averting his attack. And then Israel pursues him after his death, to curtail the damage done by the attack. Yet Israel is also pursued by the human bomb after his death. The nation's emissaries, ZAKA volunteers are haunted by the residue of the human bomb.

Standing guard against the effect of suicide terrorism, which threatens Israeliness by penetrating and subverting it from within, in addition to killing Israelis, is a chain of sentinels at the borders, who locate and defuse (deconstruct) Palestinians who infiltrate Israel under disguise. ZAKA is one link in that chain. The border crossers who look like Israelis—alive or dead—are Palestinian/Jew hybrids, owners of what seems to be mixed or unidentified identity. They pollute Israel with hybridity or fusion. ZAKA deploys against them to purify the land by sorting and again separating the Hebrew and Arab essences, and in so doing it restores order.

Every ethno-national or religious group has border specialists whom it dispatches to protect it against infiltrators and defilers. Those who themselves live on the border, the liminal types, are the most sensitive to its crossing. Because very often they themselves are hybrids, they can discern and deal with other hybrids that might contaminate the group. A good example is Israel's Border Guard (*magav*), the branch of the police force that has the task of patrolling the borders and separating Israelis and Palestinians at roadblocks, or in mixed cities. The Border Guard personnel consists disproportionately of volunteers from the local Druze community, as well as recruits whose families emigrated from Ethiopia and the former Soviet Union. All three of these groups are Israelis whose national and religious identity is borderline and consequently distrustful. The Druze, unlike other Arabs, shoulder the full burdens of Israeli citizenship, including military service, yet, because they are Arabic-speaking and non-Jews, they are not part of the state's hegemonic community; the Jewish status of many immigrants from Ethiopia and the former Soviet Union (and their offspring) is undecided, and many are not recognized as Jews by the official rabbinate and, therefore, by Israeli law. Haredim, too, are liminal and hybrids, with just one foot in Israeli identity. The representatives of the above four sectors of the population are therefore suitable for defending Israeli society against intruding imposters with questionable identity. Those who live on the internal borders are natural candidates for guarding the external border. Police checkpoints at the Green Line dividing Israel from the West Bank are manned by Druze who are said to "distinguish between a Jew and an Arab from a kilometer distance."[15]

ZAKA has been entrusted with this "Orientalist" project of binary distinction that creates Otherness, to define its own identity. Just like the warriors of the Border Guard, ZAKA's Haredi volunteers supervise the border game, while at the same time they are active players with a vested interest in it. As they guard the borders and engage in the work of purification, ZAKA's Haredim (like the Border Guard's Druze) are sensitive to the fragility of the borders and are experts on the question of hybridity. They thus become increasingly aware of their own liminal hybrid status. Furthermore, they purify themselves by becoming more Israeli and in so doing (again, like the Druze in the Border Guard) they upgrade their status on the scale of Israeliness.

ZAKA fights to purify the site of a suicide attack from the hybridity that prevails there, yet it is itself a hybrid difficult to digest, a confusing entity like the human bomb whose body the volunteers tend to. ZAKA's hybridity is primarily found in the bond between its reactionary anti-Zionist roots and its dedication to a project that is comitted to national statism. The nature of ZAKA volunteers as hybrids is also connected to their own marginality within the Haredi world, and the marginality of Haredim within Israeli society. ZAKA is an organic part of the Haredi community, but is also engaged in the modern, civil, patriotic environment, and the Haredi community has both an Israeli and an a-Israeli or even contra-Israeli identity.

Hybrids are thus ranged on both sides of the Middle Eastern divide. At the suicide terrorism site contact is initiated between the hybrid human bomb and the hybrid ZAKA volunteer. The arena of the bombing is thus a mixed space that brings together the Israeli occupier with the subjugated Palestinian, while each is represented by an inconsistent but creative figure, a symbolic—hence potent yet volatile—type.

*

Confrontation with the human bomb takes place in two stages. The first, preceding the explosion, is the effort to prevent the explosion. It ends if the terrorist manages to yank the fuse. The security forces are responsible for confronting him during this stage. In the second stage, beginning with the explosion and ending after the evacuation of the site, the identification of the bodies, and their preparation for burial, the responsibility lies with the Haredi volunteers (along with the National Institute of Forensic Medicine). The work of the ISA before the attack and that of ZAKA thereafter are parallel and continuous. In the pre-attack stage, the ISA agents seek to locate the human bomb to thwart the attack. In the post-attack stage, ZAKA volunteers seek to locate the human bomb to minimize the symbolic impact of the attack. In both stages the goal is to reveal the attacker's identity, to counteract intermingling and assimilation.

The human bomb's opposite number before his death is the ISA agent or the *magav* enlisted man; afterward it is the ZAKA volunteer. Both reestablish boundaries. By mixing blood, the attacker erases or denies identities. ZAKA works to restore the identities of the dead. Giving the victims back their identities as Jews and as individuals makes it possible to honor and bury them in accordance with Jewish tradition. Restoring an identity to the Palestinian attacker makes it possible to separate him from the rest of the dead. By establishing his identity, ZAKA ends the state of ambiguity and blending that is the surreptitious foundation of suicide terrorism.

Uncovering a hidden identity or distilling a single identity from a mixed one—deconstructing hybrids—is an act of purification.[16] ZAKA is an extension of the purification system implemented by the State of Israel in a number of areas. Along with the security forces, governmental agencies, and informal, cultural mechanisms, ZAKA stands at the forefront of the Israeli battle to preserve boundaries. Reestablishment of boundaries—purification—is the response to the subversive impact of suicide terrorism.

The Israeli effort to retain and settle the disputed Territories beyond the Green Line is based on the principle of identification and purification. ZAKA's practice of sorting and separating belongs to the sorting and separating practices used by the governmental authorities, primarily the military, who administer the Arab-populated areas under Israeli control. Just as these agencies seek to keep Israelis and Palestinians apart through space management (e.g., separate roads and separate lines at roadblocks), time management (e.g., a different schedule for prayer services for Jews and Muslims at the Tomb of the Patriarchs), and population management (e.g., separate legal and transportation systems), so ZAKA does it through managing death at the site of suicide attacks.

The Haredi volunteers themselves use the term "purification" to describe their acts of location, classification, and separation of flesh and blood at a site of terrorism. ZAKA's mission at Israel's religious and national front line, its assignment to a project of Jewish purification, is based on identification. Indeed, the name ZAKA is an acronym for the Hebrew words *zihui korbanot ason*, meaning "identification of disaster victims."

ZAKA's mission can be defined essentially as the detection and elimination of impurity. According to Mary Douglas' classical model, the defiled are things and beings that are not in their proper places and lie outside accepted categories.[17] This is pollution regarded by Jewish tradition as abomination. The Jewish response is to return everything to its proper place and to reestablish the lines of separation.

Over time, after ZAKA improved its methods, the volunteers were supplied with two types of plastic bags. White bags with blue writing were used for Jewish victims, and standard, unmarked dark bags were used for the body of the human bomb. The rabbis of the organization ruled that placing the abominable body of the suicide terrorist in a white bag was a sacrilege. In a terror attack in Jerusalem, in which a Jew was killed by police fire, he was mistakenly identified as a terrorist and his body was placed in a black bag. As soon as the error was discovered, the Jew was wrapped again in a pure and purifying bag.

# Epilogue: Headhunting, Smiles, and Human Sacrifice

Saint Denis, the first bishop of Paris, was a Christian martyr of the third century who was executed by decapitation by order of the Roman emperor. According to church hagiography, after being beheaded on Montmartre, Saint Denis bent over, picked up his head, placed it under his arm, and walked preaching to the believers for ten kilometers, until he fell over and perished. This famous legend and its depiction in basilica sculptures come to mind when looking at any one of the several variations of a photograph from the testament of a Palestinian suicide terrorist, taken on his eve of departure on his violent mission and broadcast after his remains were gathered and identified by ZAKA.[1] The picture shows the living terrorist's upper body against a wallpaper background displaying the Dome of the Rock in Jerusalem, his hands holding a tray, and on it his severed head.[2] The head was obviously photographed separately, from a
slightly different angle, cut off at the neck and photoshopped onto the earlier picture. Drops of blood were also photoshopped onto the picture, flowing from the slash in the neck.

The human bomb's severed head, offered by its owner to the Palestinian community that sent him on his suicide mission, is a gesture of self-sacrifice in the strict sense of the word. Posing for the picture in preparation for the attack, the terrorist looks forward to the outcome of the attack, contemplating himself after the explosion, his alienated expression scorning his own death, but also mourning for himself. He appears as though he were the hunter of his own head, flaunting his heroism. With the image of his severed head, the terrorist also addresses his Israeli viewers, telling both rival sides that he is in control, entirely conscious of the consequences of his deed, a self-aware sacrifice. He presents his head—living or dead—as a chilling gift for his victims, and first and foremost to those first-responders who will soon be handling his severed head: ZAKA.

This photograph is an expression of the Palestinian martyr's two-layered status, as victim and as sacrifice. The human bomb is the victim of his own aggression (and, from his point of view, a victim of Israeli aggression), while, at the same time, he is a sacrificial offering, someone who voluntarily raises himself above his egotistical instincts for the sake of a cause more exalted than his personal, physical needs. Self-sacrifice is a retroactive legitimation of massacre, providing immunity against the accusation of inhuman murderousness.

During the Intifada, the terrorist organizations and the Palestinian public showed great interest in the fate of the human bomb's head after the attack. Like other Middle Eastern natives, they were aware of the combined effect of the laws of ballistics and human anatomy: the heavy head is severed from the weak neck bones, propelled far from the center of the explosion, and lands whole, almost unscathed by the blast and hardly bloodstained. Unlike the shattered chest and abdomen and the severed arms and legs, the head retains its look from before the violent death. The Palestinians interpreted the preservation of the head as a sign of divine grace for the deceased. Ironically, the mythological father of the human bombs, "The Engineer" Yahya Ayyash—who was responsible for the death of at least seventy Israelis in suicide attacks—was killed by an explosive charge that the ISA planted in his cell phone, pulverizing his head and leaving his body intact. In a poster glued to the walls in Gaza, Ayyash was depicted as headless, a blank space over his shoulders and a Koran and crossed pair of assault rifles, firing bullets, above. Without a head, he still walked, sowed destruction on his surroundings, and trampled the bodies of Israelis under his bare feet.[3] In other posters the separation of the head from the body is shown in an opposite way: we see the head of the suicide terrorist without a body. Nevertheless, the head, standing by itself, has life and prospects. Its future and its end lie before it.

A similar motive in the Palestinian imagination related to the attacks of *shahids* is their facelessness. In wall paintings from the time of the Intifada, also from Gaza, the head of the suicide terrorist is seen without facial features: no eyes, nose, mouth, cheeks, or chin. The lack of a face and of any human expression corresponds to the custom of Gazans participating in support rallies for suicide terrorism to wrap their heads in masks, thus concealing their identity. In contrast, the photographs of suicide attack arenas published by the Palestinians give a different expression to their obsession with the severed head. In place of representing the suicide terrorist's body, since it is virtually non-existent or entirely mutilated, they seek to show the severed head in its intact glory. This is especially the case with female human bombs, such as Hanadi Jaradat, sent by the PIJ and responsible for the death of dozens of Israelis in the Maxim restaurant in Haifa. In the organization's PR, a photograph of the arena of the attack was given a central place, with the victims' blood and body tissue covering the floor and clinging to the shattered furniture. Under one of the tables in the corner of the dining room lay Jaradat's severed head. In the original, uncensored photograph, taken by the Israeli police, her hair was disheveled and her face twisted. In the Palestinian version, a passport photograph of the terrorist was substituted, her face intact and clean, her eyes made up, her smiling lips red with lipstick. Along similar lines, the Hamas Internet site published a close-up picture of the severed head of the woman suicide terrorist Zinab Abu-Salem after it had rolled to the edge of the arena. The picture does not betray any hint of the extremely violent death Abu-Salem had experienced. A poem of praise in honor of Zinab, which appeared as a caption beneath the picture of her severed head, emphasized that her veil remained undamaged, proof of her glorious holy purity.[4]

On the other side of the Palestinian-Israeli divide, the heads of suicide bombers also attracted much interest. For ZAKA, as for Hamas, the severed head is a focus of the celebration of death. This is expressed dramatically in the Haredi volunteers' rite at the site of the suicide attack after the explosion. Upon entering the arena, immediately after completing the mission of saving the lives of the wounded, the volunteers turn to the task of isolating the bomber's body and, even at the price of slightly delaying the treatment of the Jewish victims, locating the severed head. A macabre race spontaneously develops, often against the rules and regulations—who will be the first volunteer who manages to pick the head up? A veteran member of the organization used the word *shtufen*, meaning "jostling" in Yiddish, to describe this wild competition. The word *shtufen* usually refers to the way Hasidim push and pull to try to get a piece of the food that their rebbe throws during the *tish* ceremony. Shoving each other with determination, employing ruses and elbows, they often emerge bruised and scratched from this holy pursuit. A Hasid who manages to seize and swallow a piece of chicken or challah that the rebbe has nibbled on is thought to absorb some closeness to sanctity. Could a similar form of sanctity be the object of the ZAKA volunteers' jostling for the severed head of the Palestinian suicide bomber?

The human bomb is both absent and present at the scene of the attack. With the explosion the bomber vanishes, leaving the victims in the center of interest and activity. But the human bomb's disappearance from the arena attracts attention and effort. When he entered the arena and lingered there until the explosion, his presence was unnoticed. After the explosion, his absence is very conspicuous. In the early stages of the attack, he had no presence in the arena, because he was disguised as an Israeli and had mingled with the Israelis, and in the later stages of the attack, he has no presence mainly because he has no body. The remains of the human bomb preoccupy both the security forces and the ZAKA volunteers. The urgency surrounding the head derives from its importance for intelligence and operations (so that it can be identified by photography and DNA, and to allow a certain count of the number of victims). Uncovering his identity enables the launching of a manhunt to capture his handlers. But above all, the suicide bomber's head is of symbolic importance.

The Haredi volunteers are eager to find the head, though locating it is not always a simple task. Sometimes the head is found far away in an unexpected place. The site where the head lies—according to ZAKA lore, once it was on the balcony of a building across the way—also becomes a focus of sanctity. At a certain stage in ZAKA's activity, there are two centers of gravity in the arena of the explosion, two hearts of carnage, two hearts of irresistible charm. For a short time, the volunteers are torn between the desire to touch the bodies of the Jewish victims and the desire to touch the human bomb's head.

Any dismembered part of a human body arouses dread and revulsion; more than any other, this is true of a severed head—not the skull, but the human head that breathed, spoke, and looked until a moment ago. A head without a body is the epitome of horror.[5] Nevertheless, or possibly for just that reason, ZAKA finds special merit in the severed head. Hence, direct contact with the suicide terrorist's severed head is an honor reserved for the aristocracy of the organization, and such contact advances the status of a member. Some volunteers are reluctant to touch the head, while for others this contact is the high point of their career in the organization. One man told me that if he were required to deal with the head of the terrorist, he would put on a double pair of rubber gloves, while another told me that he felt special pleasure in dealing with the head directly, without any gloves at all. More than once they passed the head from hand to hand so that as many volunteers as possible could have the presumed privilege of touching it.

There is a disproportion between the number of instances in which the detached head of a terrorist was thrown far from the rest of his body and the centrality of this topic in the discourse of the ZAKA volunteers and the excitement it arouses. In discussion with me, the volunteers steered the conversation so that the severed head would be mentioned quite often. In discreet conversations among themselves, they discuss alternatives to holding the head by the hair. They argue as to whether the yarmulka that the terrorist had pinned to his head to disguise himself as a Jew remained in place. In a newspaper interview, a central activist joked, saying that for them, "to clear your head" (*litpos rosh*) didn't refer to stepping aside for a moment of calm repose.[6] A veteran volunteer showed me a selfie with him holding a severed head. Others exchange pictures of terrorists' heads among themselves.[7]

Contact with the severed head violates a taboo, an exciting and challenging prohibition. It is regarded as a difficult test that demands virtuosity. Contact of this kind is identified with righteousness in ZAKA. Some of the ZAKA members, who are regarded as saintly, are said to have treated the heads of terrorists in various arenas of terrorism. The prestige associated with the volunteers' contact with severed heads and their tendency to exaggerate the number of heads with which they have dealt is such that one cannot avoid comparing it to the phenomenon of headhunting, as discussed in the anthropological literature.[8] I find thought-provoking similarities between those who held the severed heads of their enemies in ancient civilizations, in tribal societies, and in recent wars, and those who do so in the Middle Eastern terrorism arena, the ZAKA activists. Among the themes common to historical cases of headhunting and the practices of the Haredi volunteers in the Intifada bombing sites are the head as a trophy, a proof of victory, and a display of manhood. In these two analogous cases of ritualized violence, holding the head can express dominance over the soul of one's enemies, immunization against them, and acquisition of their courage and prowess.[9]

Quite often the head of the Palestinian attacker that arouses a great deal of attention is subject to various manipulations, and it is displayed prominently. The suicide terrorist's head remains uncovered in the arena for some time; activists crowd around it until it is examined officially and documented; they hold it by the hair and raise it with the face forward. They parade with it the length and breadth of the site with rooster-like pride, seemingly unaware of the gaze of the onlookers. Even those who are not highly esteemed among the volunteers seek to approach the head, touch it, and experience holding it before it is sent to the Forensic Institute.

The volunteers frequently have themselves photographed with the severed head in various poses. This can be seen as a response to the photographed pose of the Palestinian terrorist with his own head before being sent out on his suicide mission. Before the explosion, the human bomb held his head, and after the attack, the ZAKA volunteer holds it. Both seek to overcome the dread of death by grasping the head, each in his own way, and to affirm life. ZAKA is the last, closing a circle, taking revenge, felt to be correcting an injustice and making retribution.

The Palestinian terrorist, who offers his severed head on a platter, is probably not aware that he is precisely imitating the New Testament scene of Salome, the vengeful Herodian princess, who places the head of John the Baptist on a platter, a gesture represented countless times in paintings and statues.[10] It is equally doubtful that the Haredi volunteer is aware that by holding the severed head of the terrorist by the hair he is reiterating a prevalent motive in the folklore and art of various cultures and periods. Illustrations can be noted from the biblical iconography (David holding the head of Goliath)[11] to the iconography of the French Revolution (the executioner holding the head of Robespierre after he was guillotined).[12] The severed head excites the imagination of our civilization and appears time and again in its myths.[13] Nothing could be more relevant to the present discussion than the head of Medusa, whose gaze remains formidable even after it is severed. After she was hunted down and decapitated, the Medusa's head continues to interact intensively with its surroundings, and its attractive but petrifying potency does not fade away.

Let us relate the fatal exchange of gazes that characterizes the arena of suicide terrorism, before and after death, to the ancient Greek legend of Medusa. In brief: Athena transformed Medusa's lovely hair into serpents and made her face so terrible to behold that anyone who gazed directly upon her would turn to stone. To fulfill a rash oath, Perseus was sent to bring back her head. He was provided with a mirror shield and warned that if he looked directly at her he would die. He accomplished the impossible mission of beheading the monster while looking at her reflection in his mirrored shield, thus avoiding her lethal gaze. Thereafter he used her severed head, which retained its power, to put his enemies to death.

The Medusa's gaze has been widely discussed in the humanities as a representation of dread and cruel death.[14] It is described as terror incarnate.[15] The Medusa's gaze is repulsive and terrifying, but it is also captivating. It is difficult to resist the temptation to look at the Medusa's head and to try to overcome her gaze. The fascination of the monster's head did not cease after it was severed. Indeed, it might have increased. The magnetic attraction of the ZAKA volunteers to the severed head of the terrorist is similar.

The volunteer's victory procession, holding the severed head of the suicide terrorist by the hair, ends with the ceremony of placing it in a sack in preparation for removal of the body parts from the arena. However, it turns out that the ritual of parting from the head has not yet been exhausted. The thought occurs to the observer that, if they could, some of the ZAKA volunteers would attach the heads to their belts and carry them wherever they went, like tribal headhunters, who display their valor in that way, and like the Hindu death priests, the Aghori, whose magical abilities derive from their attachment to the skulls of those whose death they handled.[16] The Haredi volunteers are drawn as though hypnotized to the head in the sack. They stop their work of searching and scrubbing to approach it again and again, to peek at it, to touch it—just one more glimpse of the head, one more photograph with it, one more touch of its cheek, between a slap and a caress.

The director of ZAKA's Ashdod branch confessed that, after wrapping up the operation following a suicide bombing at his city's port (March 2004), he felt "compelled" to satisfy his "need" to look at the polluted but mesmerizing head of the suicide bomber, packed up in its bag and relegated to the edge of the site, set apart as objects that are taboo and holy.[17]

A vexing question that naturally cannot be answered definitively relates to the dynamics of the arena of suicide terrorism during the short and fateful interval before the explosion. What is the nature of the reciprocal relations between the attacker and those who are at the site and who will immediately become his victims? We can only speculate.

Between the Palestinian attacker, or his severed head, and the Israelis whom he killed or their representatives in the arena, two rounds of face-to-face proximity took place. In the first round, during the last moment before the explosion, the victims were an object of the all-knowing, devious, but also tense and nervous gaze of the terrorist. In the second round, in the moments after the explosion, the terrorist's head was the object of the ZAKA volunteers' gaze. However, it could be that before the explosion the attacker was also an object—his face might have expressed horror at his imminent demise, of which he was well aware.[18] After the explosion, the terrorist's head is also a subject. Despite his death, he remains an agent with impact on his surroundings, responding to their thoughts and emotions.

It is said that "neither the sun nor death can be looked at with a steady eye."[19] By contrast, ZAKA volunteers cannot avert their gaze from the terrorist's severed head. They look at it, while they are convinced that it is looking at them. Finding the head is a compensation for the absence of a body, an object upon which it is possible to focus all their anger and hatred. The disappearance of the terrorist's body frustrates their desire for revenge. What will the volunteers concentrate their pain and fury on? With no body to curse, to kick, they desperately seek everything whole that remains of the terrorist. Once a Haredi volunteer told me, "It's hard to get angry at a foot or a scrap of shoulder." One can be angry at a head with a face. They attribute evil to the suicide terrorist, and they find the essence of it in the head, a concretization of that evil. Grasping the head is daring, provocative contact with evil. It overcomes evil, but it is also fascinated by it, addicted to it.

The head arouses a strong feeling in the ZAKA activists, a combination of fear and antipathy, but these are mingled with genuine curiosity. The volunteers wonder who the suicide terrorist was, and they seek the answer in the head that is before them. They try to decipher the expression frozen on the face by the explosion. During the years of the Intifada, a consensus emerged among those present in the arena that the severed head "has its eye on them," and it always has a smile.

According to witnesses of attacks, which nourished urban legends that became undisputed facts in the advertising of the Palestinian organizations and gained a foothold in Israeli public opinion too, the suicide terrorist smiles at the moment when he sets off the charge on his body. An injured survivor of the Dolphinarium suicide attack reported that he clearly remembers the human bomb's smile (Tel Aviv, June 2001, twenty-one casualties).[20] Once an Israeli border policeman killed a man who was approaching him "because something in his behavior aroused his suspicion." Indeed, an explosive charge was found on the man's body. In his testimony, the suspicious policeman said, "He came toward me, put his hand in his pocket, and smiled. I immediately realized he was a suicide terrorist."

Those present in the arena in the aftermath of the explosion insist that the smile does not leave the terrorist's face even after his death. According to ZAKA's interpretation, it is a wicked smile showing the suicide terrorist's satisfaction at his success in fooling the Israelis and claiming many victims among them. It shows, supposedly, no less satisfaction because he killed himself and thus prevented the Israelis from punishing him. They attribute brazenness and Schadenfreude to him. Many of the men I interviewed claimed that the head, lying in the arena, did not cease expressing sarcastic mockery. They take it as especially humiliating hubris.

Communication takes place between the severed head and those who look at it or hold it. The volunteers try to make it speak, and it, as it were, teases them. They are convinced that it addresses them, and they miss no opportunity to answer it. In the arena of the explosion insults are exchanged. This weird dialogue is generally aggressive but sometimes a smidgen of humor sneaks in. I have been shown photographs of ZAKA volunteers sticking out their tongues at the head of a terrorist.[21] When caught in the act, the volunteers justify their attitude by claiming that Palestinian suicide bombing ridicules them, and they wish to show who gets the last laugh. It is as if they said, "The severed head stuck its tongue out at us, and we're only responding in kind." Remarkably, in Ancient Greek art, the severed head of Medusa appears as an apotropaic symbol with magical powers. Usually it inspires dread and deters those who might do one harm, but sometimes it laughs at them with mockery and contempt. In the façade of the Temple of Artemis on the Island of Corfu, a relief of Medusa appears, dating from the sixth century BCE. She is smiling from ear to ear and sticking out her tongue at the viewer.[22]

The ZAKA volunteers make all kinds of derisive faces at the terrorist's head, but some of them surprise their Haredi colleagues with gestures of respect for the human bomb. The suicide terrorist's head impresses them. Moreover, contact with the head creates, paradoxically, a certain attenuation of the horror. Lacking a body, only the head can represent the person behind the figure of the terrorist. The head is the only part of the terrorist's body whose form is familiar and can be recognized as human. Thus, it humanizes the terrorist and brings an element of empathy into the brutal relationship between the opposing sides of the conflict. In the bewildering anonymity prevailing in the arena, the severed head reveals a particular individual the volunteers cannot overlook.

The terrorist's head is holy to the Palestinians, and, strangely, it is also invested in holiness by the Jews who deal with it. The main remains of the attacker's body became a sacrifice offered to God by his victims.

*

In the arena of Middle Eastern suicide terrorism two parallel sacrificial rites take place: one is Palestinian-Muslim, and the other is Israeli-Jewish. The two rites allude to each other, and they inadvertently cooperate. The tragic scene is a ritual co-production, neither intended nor acknowledged. While both sides believe they sacrifice themselves, it may be argued that they also sacrifice their counterpart. We have adduced some evidence regarding the Palestinian conception of the suicide terrorist as offering the Israeli casualties on the altar of the regional conflict.[23] Below is evidence of a different sort, complementary and entirely unexpected: the conception of the arena of suicide terrorism as a Jewish sacrificial ceremony in which the Haredi volunteers are the priests, while the offering, whose blood has been shed, is the suicide terrorist or parts of his body. Thus, the attacker is not only a victim, but also a sacrifice from the view of the Palestinians and plausibly also from that of the Jews. In the Jewish canon there are precedents for offering the enemies of Israel as a sacrifice.[24]

The conception of the Palestinian human bomb as a sacrifice of the Jews in Israel is demonstrated by the following event, depicted in a photograph in my possession and confirmed by several interviews.[25]

During the Al Aqsa Intifada, toward the end of ZAKA's "holy service" at the site of a suicide attack, several ZAKA activists headed for the depths of the arena, far from the public eye, and took the severed limb of a body (which they determined categorically was that of the human bomb). They picked up a large piece of a man's bleeding leg, raised it above their heads, and swung it around three times. While doing so they recited the following verses, which, like every Haredi, they know by heart: "This is my substitute, this is my contribution, this is my atonement, this . . . will go to death, and I will go to a good long life and peace."

No mistake can be made in identifying this phrase: it is recited during the ceremony known in Jewish tradition as *kaparot* (atonements), which to this day is performed on the eve of Yom Kippur by the ultra-Orthodox. It is assumed that this is an attenuated version of biblical sacrifice, or of the ancient Israelite scapegoat ceremony, another way of asking forgiveness for sins by placing the guilt on another body. Nowadays the offering swung in the air for atonement is a live rooster, which is then slaughtered.[26]

Obviously in the scene described above there was a certain stratum of gallows humor to relieve the tension that had accumulated during ZAKA's work, and, of course, this is an expression of the volunteers' contempt for the Palestinians, and anger in response to the massacre. There could also be another, deeper level, an authentic sign that points to repressed remnants of the desire to deal with blood and flesh, perhaps also attraction to human sacrifice. While critics described this as a manifestation of mental pathology, observers close to the participants in the event suggest that it shows a true need for expiation.[27]

ZAKA volunteers report that while they are still in the arena of terrorism, and especially when some of the casualties are children, they are very disturbed by the issue of blame: Who is responsible for the terrible killing? When the head of the suicide terrorist is found, they place the blame on him. Despite a certain consolation they find in this, they are unable to free themselves from the feeling that their own sins also have a part in causing the tragedy. The question of guilt and its connection to the complex of sin and atonement continue to trouble them.

Indeed, the exegetical space is open, and several layers of interpretation are available for this rite, some charged with internal tension.[28] Often a ritual, like a dream, may have unconscious significance, which develops into something different from apparently reasonable interpretations. The power of a ritual draws upon these contradictory meanings.[29]

I suggest that the *kaparot* ceremony performed by ZAKA may be interpreted as a usurpation of the expiation potential inherent in the body of the suicide terrorist.[30] If ZAKA volunteers believe that the blood of the rooster assures atonement, then they probably believe that human blood would be even more effective, since it is closer to the thing itself. They creatively ask why should someone have died so brutally in vain? It is better to exploit the privilege that he confers for the sake of the atonement they need so badly because of their own sins. The suicide terrorist is a "ready-made" for sacrificial use. Compare the case of Jesus, the ultimate sacrifice. Christians reason that the messiah is so pure that his death was not needed to atone for his sins; hence his death could atone for the multitudes who have faith in him. The suicide terrorist, by contrast, is a champion sinner. However, his spilled blood still could atone for sins, so it is better to use it to atone for our sins rather than his. The death of the Israeli victims of the human bomb, his sacrifice, will atone for their sins, and the atonement that can come from the death of the suicide terrorist can be directed away from the enemies of the Jews for the benefit of the Jews. This is the logic behind the slaughter of an animal as an offering. Because it is merely a beast, the sacrifice cannot atone for its sins, only for ours. It is doubtful that the suicide terrorist was a person with a pure conscience. Those who recruited the suicide terrorists imbued many of them with the tormented feeling that he was a sinner in need of atonement. The mission of the suicide terrorist was meant to assure his own purification from sin as well as purifying the sins of all the Palestinians who stood behind him. Now the Jews have come and deprived him of this atonement and appropriate the redemptive catharsis intended for their nemesis. Confiscation of the suicide terrorist's expiatory power, and its preemption and enlistment in the service of the ZAKA volunteers, punishes the Palestinians metaphysically, as it were, and restores justice to the world. Blood that has been shed always has a core of atonement, and in retribution against the murderers their blood serves the atonement of their victims.

Many of the human bombs believe that their life was religiously and morally deficient, and that in their death they will be purified of these deficiencies. That is, suicide terrorism is a holy mission of sacrifice, which brings atonement for the terrorist and for the community from which and in whose name he set out. However, the ZAKA volunteers came and diverted the expiatory religious potential that was in the severed members of the human bomb's body in the Jewish direction. The Jews took revenge against Islam by usurping the magical power inherent in the dismembered limbs of the suicide terrorist and directing it for the benefit of Israel.

In the arena of suicide terrorism, both sides in the bloody Middle East conflict are sacrificed by themselves or by those who dispatch them, and both sides sacrifice themselves and their enemies. The suicide terrorist sacrifices himself and, with him, those whom he kills. The ZAKA volunteer sanctifies the dead Israelis and makes them into sacrificial offerings, and he may be said to sacrifice—unintentionally sanctifying—the Palestinian suicide terrorist as well.

# Notes

## Preface

1. Gideon Aran, *The Smile of the Human Bomb: New Perspectives on Suicide Terrorism* (Ithaca, NY: Cornell University Press, 2018).
2. For list of Palestinian suicide attacks in Israel during the 1980s through 2008, see https://en.wikipedia.org/wiki/List_of_Palestinian_suicide_attacks.
3. Jonathan Parry, *Death in Banaras* (Cambridge: Cambridge University Press, 1994).
4. Drew Gilpin Faust, *This Republic of Suffering: Death and the American Civil War* (New York: Alfred Knopf, 2008).
5. Ziv Koren. See the documentary film about him: Solo Avital, *More Than One Thousand Words* (Hebrew), 2006.
6. Noam Shalev, *ZAKA: Living with Death*, documentary film (Hebrew), 2004; Tom Aspell, "Israeli Volunteers Face Gruesome Task," NBC News, July 17, 2002; Nitza Gonen, *True Kindness*, documentary film (Hebrew)) 2004Israeli TV).
7. Cf. Parry, *Death*, Introduction.
8. Cf. Frantz Fanon, *Black Skin, White Masks* (London: Pluto Press, 1986), 64.
9. The "Double" suicide attack, Beit Lid Intersection, twenty-two casualties, (January 1995).
10. Compare to the obsessive return of young German artists and filmmakers to the horrors of World War II. Saul Friedlander, *Reflections of Nazism: An Essay on Kitsch and Death* (Bloomington: Indiana University Press, 1993).
11. This last paragraph is taken from my book *The Smile*.

## Chapter 1

1. Cf. Veena Das, ed., *Mirrors of Violence: Communities, Violence and Survivors in South Asia* (Delhi: Oxford University Press, 1990).
2. A phrase used by the Jews upon hearing bad news, mainly in connection with the death of a close relative.
3. David Viztum, *Breaking News: TV Coverage of National Security Events* (Jerusalem: Keter, 2005) (Hebrew); Tamar Liebes, "Television's Disaster Marathons," in *Media Ritual and Identity*, ed. Tamar Liebes and James Curran (New York: Routledge, 1998), 71–86.

4. A Haredi volunteer once told me that the coverall reminded him of a *kitel*, a white cloth garment resembling a shroud, which the groom wears on the day of his wedding, a reminder of the destruction of the Temple.

5. Cf. Marcelo Suarez-Orozco, "Speaking the Unspeakable: Toward a Psycho-social Understanding of Responses to Terror," *Ethos* 18.3 (1990): 353–383.

6. Cf. Anna Powel, Deleuze and Horror Film (Edinburgh: Edinburgh University Press, 2008).

7. Cf. Raya Morag, "Sound, Image, Terror and Memory: Israeli Narrative Cinema in the Age of the Second Intifada (Shorts)," *Israel* 14 (2008): 71–88 (Hebrew).

8. The motive of the impossibility of seeing something one is attracted to, and the transformation of the mode of seeing someone to the mode of seeing someone who is seeing someone, is common in the cinema. Take, for example, a scene of a child witnessing a murder (or his parents having intercourse) through a keyhole. The frustrated audience must guess, visualize, and fantasize about what the child is seeing.

9. A theme developed by Roland Barthes.

10. Compare to various observations in the social sciences on other kinds of disaster, for example, Gary Kreps, "Sociological Inquiry and Disaster Research," *Annual Review of Sociology* 10 (1984): 309–330; Anthony Oliver-Smith and Susanna Hoffman, *The Angry Earth: Disaster in Anthropological Perspective* (London: Routledge 1999); Susanna Hoffman and Anthony Oliver-Smith, eds., *Catastrophe and Culture: The Anthropology of Disaster* (Santa Fe, NM: School of American Research Press 2002).

11. Adriana Kavarero, *Horrorism* (New York: Columbia University Press, 2011), 97, also 104, 121.

12. The term "abjection" refers to crossing the boundary between what is inside and outside of the body. When that boundary is crossed, we become anxious. See Julia Kristeva, *Powers of Horror: An Essay on Abjection* (New York: Columbia University Press, 1982). On the application of this term in research to acts of suicide terrorism performed by Palestinian women, see Joanna Long, "Border Anxiety in Palestine–Israel," *Antipode*, 1 January 2006.

13. In the art world, a grotesque body is associated with "wild exaggeration" and "absolute kitsch," which are utterly unforgivable or hopeless. Before this term was coined, these representations of the body, mingling human and animal attributes, appeared on the gargoyles of medieval cathedrals, intended to keep Satan away.

14. Cf. Talal Asad, *Suicide Bombing* (New York: Columbia University Press, 2007), 70.

15. Cf. Kavarero, *Horrorism*, 47.

16. Gadi Faran, Ami Pedahzur, and Arie Perliger, *Coping with Terrorism in Jerusalem*, #103 (Jerusalem: Jerusalem Institute for Israeli Studes, 2006), 149, 153 (Hebrew).

17. See explanation in Chapter 6.

18. Cf. Michael Taussig, "Transgression," in *Critical Terms in Religious Studies*, ed. Marc Taylor (Chicago: University of Chicago Press 1998), 157–174.

19. Only once a year on the holy Yom Kippur, wearing special dress and after a special prayer.

20. See Chapter 3, in the section "Individual Profiles."

21. In one of the arenas of death that I observed, they removed blood-soaked mattresses and sheets for burial.
22. Leviticus 17:11.
23. One informer told me secretly that he listens to Hasidic music as long as he is close to home, while moving away from the Haredi neighborhood he switches to Western "forbidden" music.
24. For example, Nisan Rubin, *The End of Life: Mortuary Rites according to the Ancient Jewish Sages* (Tel Aviv: Hakibutz Haneuhad, 1996) (Hebrew).
25. One ZAKA activist hinted to me about "sexual arousal" after dealing with a terror event.
26. These are the hours when public transportation, markets, and streets are crowded with pedestrians, and the murderous effect is greatest. A minority of attacks took place at night, mainly in places of entertainment and dance clubs.
27. For example, stillborn fetuses, which the volunteers are summoned to dispose of, especially in home miscarriages in the Haredi community.
28. April 2006.
29. Gideon Aran, "Religiosity and Super Religiosity: Measures of Radical Religion," *Numen* 6.3–2 (2013): 491–411.
30. After the draft of this book had been completed, ZAKA announced the inauguration of a new campaign titled "Silent," in which volunteers make weekly regular visits to old people's homes to make sure they are alive.
31. Tractate Yoma, Chapter 8, Mishna 9.

# Chapter 2

1. Sixteen dead, twenty-five severely wounded. The terrorist, Abd el-Hani Gnaim, age twenty-five, PIJ supporter from Gaza, was sentenced to sixteen life sentences but released in Shalit Deal (October 2011).
2. The connection between the bus event and Hasidic arousal recalls the novella by A. B. Yehoshua, *The Night Trip of Yatir* (1963). A femme fatale in a remote mountain settlement hatches a satanic plot to derail the express train that tears through her village every night without slowing or stopping, causing it to plunge into the deep ravine, so that the catastrophe will awaken the place from its slumber and so that the residents will have the exalted moral experience of evacuating the dead and wounded. The violent action liberates repressed destructive forces and endows people with renewed vitality.
3. See the section "May God Avenge Their Blood" in Chapter 7.
4. The Haredim derive the importance of Moses' act from the end of the Pentateuch, where it is said that God Himself performed his burial.
5. The burial society of the *prushim*, a Haredi faction in Jerusalem.
6. In the throes of the war in Lebanon, I witnessed the initiative of a Haredi rabbi in an army uniform who, without orders or permission, laid down his rifle, took up a spade,

and began to dig proper graves for Syrian commandos whose mutilated bodies were dispersed around us on the battlefield.

7. Cf. the training of Hamas suicide terrorists, who, according to rumor, are forced to spend a night in a grave in Gaza to make death more present.

8. Most of the earlier episodes of Haredi violence were focused on observance of the Sabbath and the conscription of yeshiva students. An exception was the scandal around treatment of the skeletons discovered during excavations near the Tomb of Maimonides in Tiberias, 1956.

9. Because if their honor is preserved, they will merit resurrection.

10. See Michael Feige, "The Broken Bones Vision: Haredim vs. Archeologists in the City of David," in *Israeli Haredim*, ed. Immanuel Sivan and Kimi Kaplan )Jerusalem: Van Leer, 2003(, 56–81 (Hebrew).

11. Professor Yigal Shilo, archaeologist, colleague, and acquaintance.

12. *Skhik tamia* in Aramaic. ZAKA volunteers wanted him to suffer what, according to them, he had done to the dead whose graves he had exposed. The grave curse that they invoked upon him had been directed in the past at Titus, the Roman general, later emperor, the son and heir of Vespasian, who had put down the great Jewish revolt and destroyed the Temple in the first century CE.

13. Yehuda Meshi-Zahav and Zvi Meshi-Zahav, The Slope of the Temple Mount: War Journal, unpublished manuscript, Jerusalem, 1983–1984.

14. Disturbing a grave is permitted in exceptional instances such as removal of a skeleton from abroad for burial in the Land of Israel, or the removal of Jewish bodies from gentile cemeteries, for burial among Jews.

15. Harvey Goldberg, *Jewish Passages: Cycles of Jewish Life* (Berkeley: University of California Press, 2003), 201.

16. The Torah does not explicitly prohibit cremation, though it is hinted at in Genesis 3:19: "thou art dust and unto dust thou shalt return." However, venerable halakhic rulings rejected that option. One may surmise that the extensive discussion of this topic was somewhat influenced by the association of the burning of Jewish bodies with the Nazi action in the extermination camps.

17. Compare to the Aghori Hindi death priests' custom of eating from a bowl made of an empty human skull. Parry, *Death in Banaras*.

18. The present discussion does not relate to the Palestinian aggression against Israeli civilians prior to the conquest of the West Bank and Gaza in 1967 (e.g., 1954–1956, 1964–1967).

19. The Palestinian resistance organizations adopted a new type of terrorism: attacks with mortars and rockets, arson, kidnaping attempts, ramming with cars, and knife attacks. All of these had considerable psychological effect, but the number of victims is negligible.

20. Toward the end of the Intifada, the number of Israeli victims declined to about 6 percent of the peak number in the Intifada (30 dead in 2006, compared to 450 in 2002). Ten years later the number rose slightly (47 dead in 2016), and recently it has declined to the minimum in many years (18 dead in 2017).

21. In 2017, 144 attempts were thwarted.

22. For example, the daily *Haaretz*, 2 January 2006.

23. An attempt to promote an idea like this was made by several not well-known members of the British Parliament.

24. This rich collection, along with the ZAKA archive, was made available to me for examination and served as an important source for my research.

25. Among other things, the ZAKA office in Jerusalem set a price list for contributions: $150 for a dayglo vest; $700 for a first aid kit; $10,000 for an emergency-equipped motorcycle; $190,000 annually for psychotherapy.

26. For example, *NewZaka* 171, 31 March 2011.

27. For example, *NewZaka* 123, 1 January 2009.

28. The inner organ of ZAKA reported a similar instance, which developed into a blunt confrontation between the organization and the Israeli railroad office. The volunteers who took care of the remains of a suicide who threw himself under a train were accused at 4 a.m. of "loitering on the tracks."

29. In various times and places, there is often a fine line or a gray area between terrorist and criminal murder. Sometimes aggression begins as ethno-national violence but ultimately declines into criminal violence, sometimes criminal violence is enlisted in an ethno-national cause, and sometimes the motives—criminal and ethno-national—are mixed from the start.

30. A total of eighteen people received salaries, including the only two women on the organization's staff, a secretary and a bookkeeper.

31. For example, appointing Meshi-Zahav's brother as the head of a department, and his son-in-law as office manager.

32. In that year the debt amounted to 8 million shekels.

33. Field notes, August 2005.

34. In that year ZAKA dealt with 18,368 incidents of lifesaving, locating, and evacuation.

35. In 2007 announced that they had fifteen hundred available volunteers. Other publications claim seven hundred.

36. For example, the Haifa branch, composed mainly of Vizhnitz Hasidim, claim that their volunteer actions began under the aegis of the Civil Guard, administered by the police, somewhat before the Jerusalem branch, following the bus-terrorist attack of April 1994. See also the 770 Branch, composed solely of Habad Hasidim.

37. Mainly the branch in Judea and Samaria, which is composed of religious settlers from the West Bank.

38. See, for example, the smaller branches in the southern part of the country, in Netivot, Ashdod, or Eilat.

39. These include gravediggers, purifiers of corpses, embalmers, coffin builders, cemetery administrators, and others.

40. Faran et al., *Coping with Terrorism*.

41. On a new area of medical specialization, which arose and developed against the background of the expansion of terrorism in general and particularly of Palestinian terrorism during the Intifada, see J. Hiss, M. Freund, U. Motro, and T. Kahana, "The Medicolegal Investigation of the el-Aksa Intifada," *Israel Medical Association Journal* 4 (2002): 549–553.

42. For example, NATAL, the Israel Trauma and Resiliency Center, a volunteer organization established during the Intifada, whose open line was overwhelmed by victims of terrorism, crying out for professional assistance, maintains close contact with ZAKA.

43. The sixth month of the Hebrew calendar.

44. According to the tradition, his burial place is unknown to avoid according him divine status and to prevent his grave from becoming a site of idolatry. As for the identity of the one who buried him, there is a tradition that God himself performed the burial, and another tradition has him burying himself. The Bible states only that he was buried on the far side of the Jordan, a moment before fulfilling his dream of entering the promised land, in punishment for the sin described in Numbers 20.

45. A belief found in various religious traditions, common to which is the idea that the soul of the dead person ascends to the divine world and then is reincarnated in an infant.

46. This date was mainly observed in Jerusalem. In some other cities the burial societies chose another day for their holiday, usually 29 Shevat (but not on the Sabbath).

47. At these celebrations the separation between men and women is suspended, and, along with mystical meditation, there is a market, betting, and the like.

48. The Hasidim say that Zaddiks in particular are affected by the evil impulse, but they overcome it. The absolute response of the Lithuanians is that life is intended for Torah study and performance of the commandments. Therefore, a minute in life is worth more than life in the world to come. Allen Nadler, *The Faith of the Mithnagdim* (Baltimore, MD: Johns Hopkins University Press, 1997), 103–126.

49. "Table" in Yiddish, a festive meal with enthusiastic singing, in which the Rebbe eats at the head of the table, and the Hasidim gather around, listening to words of Torah and blessings and wait for the leftover food that the Rebbe throws to them.

50. In honor of the festivity, a special pamphlet is distributed to the volunteers with a selection of penitential prayers, laws, and customs.

51. Starting at 10 p.m.

52. The tractate of the Mishnah, containing fourteen chapters dealing with death and bereavement, is called euphemistically *semaḥot* (Happy Occasions).

53. Cf. withering and regeneration in both ancient and modern myths.

54. Avriel Bar-Levav, "The Concept of Death in the 'Book of Life' (*Sefer ha-Hayyim*) by Rabbi Shimon Frankfurt" (PhD diss., Hebrew University, 1999), 249

55. On multi-vocality of symbols, see Victor Turner,*Myth, Symbol and Ritual: Revelation and Divination in Ndembu Ritual,* Ithaca: Cornell University Press, 1975.

56. Pirqei Avot, 1:2.

57. BT Shabbat 156b.

58. Psalm 85:10 states, "Mercy and truth are met together."

59. *Pesiqta zutrata* on Exodus 13, item 19.

60. Exodus 11:2.

61. Exodus 13:19.

62. The laws relating to burial developed only in medieval Europe.

63. *Acte Gratuit.* Compare to the Greek *Kedas* and to the Latin.

64. Marcel Mauss, *The Gift: The Form and Reason for Exchange in Archaic Societies* (London: Routledge, 2000).

65. The parallel to giving without expecting a reward as discussed here is organ donation. In the case of ZAKA, this is a gift from the living to the dead, and in the analogous case, conversely, it is the gift of the clinically dead to the living. On organ donation, see Fulton Robert, ed., *Death and Identity* (Bowie, MD: Charles Press, 1976), 18.

# Chapter 3

1. For example, Tzvia Greenfeld, *They Are Afraid,* (Tel Aviv: Yediot, 2005) (Hebrew). The author is a Haredi women who is critical of Haredi society.

2. In any event, I am not professionally qualified to determine the clinical status of the volunteers. Moreover, this would be liable to divert interest from the main point and to undermine the effort to explain this sociological-anthropological phenomenon. Compare to attempts to explain suicide terrorism in psycho-pathological terms. For example, Ariel Merary, *Driven to Death* (New York: Oxford University Press, 2010), chapter 5.

3. This anecdote also appears in a manual issued by the Rabbinic Counsel of ZAKA, titled *The Living Shall Be Concerned* (n.d.).

4. The Haredi world offered many kinds of traditional alternatives to therapy based on science and the modern ethos. See Yehuda Goodman, *The Exile of the Shattered Vessels* (Tel Aviv: Yediot, 2013) (Hebrew).

5. Babylonian Talmud, Kiddushin, 39b.

6. Volunteers' wives report that their husbands often scream during sleep.

7. Z. Solomon and R. Berger, "Coping with the Aftermath of Terror: Resilience of Zaka Body Handlers," *Journal of Aggression, Maltreatment and Trauma* 10.1 (2005). 593-604.

8. This activist introduces himself to strangers with a business card that is entirely black.

9. Mark Schuster, Bradley Stein, et al., "National Survey of Stress Reactions after the September 11 Terrorist Attack," *NEJM* 345.20 (November 2001). 1507-12

10. Sixteen percent were actually exposed to a terrorist incident, 60 percent reported impairment of the feeling of personal security; 58 percent reported feelings of sadness and depression; 50 percent suffered from sleep disorder, tension, and nervousness; 37 percent were disturbed by thoughts, images, and nightmares connected with severe incidents; and 27 percent reported dissociative symptoms and others connected with psychological pressure. As for their ways of coping, the vast majority respond by frequently checking the safety of their loved ones, and by sharing experiences with friends. Many of them listen with great frequency to reports on the situation in the media, and they cope by means of humor, denial, and distraction. A minority uses medication and excessive smoking and drinking. More than half of them find strength in religious faith. See Avi Bleich, Marc Gelkop, and Zahava Solomon, "Exposure to Terrorism, Stress Related Mental Health Symptoms and Coping Behaviour: Israel,"

*JAMA* 290.5 (August 2003). See also Eli Somer and Avi Bleich, *Mental Health in Terror's Shadow: The Israeli Experience* (Tel Aviv: Ramot, 2005). 612-620.

11. Howard Fine, "Evaluating Resilience Factors in the Face of Traumatic Events: A Study of Zaka" (PhD diss., Surrey University, 2004).

12. *Haaretz*, 15 December 2006. Compare this to the 13 percent of the firefighters who were traumatized when they were exposed to the terrorist bombing in Oklahoma City in 1995.

13. *Haaretz,* 31 December 2009.

14. This thesis was mainly advanced by Dr. Roni Berger, a psychologist with the NATAL organization, who treated ZAKA volunteers, in interviews with me toward the end of the Intifada.

15. Zahava Salomon and Roni Berger, "PTS and Repressive Coping with Trauma in ZAKA," *Hevra U'Revakhah*, 28.1 (2008): 59–84 (Hebrew), https://www.researchgate. net/publication/233141695_Coping_with_the_Aftermath_of_Terror-Resilience_of _ZAKA_Body_Handlers.

16. https://www.haaretz.com/1.4758438.

    Jonathan Lis, "Black Humor and Faith Help ZAKA Volunteers Overcome Terror Trauma", *Haaretz* November 17 2004

17. Gideon Aran, "Can Fundamentalism be Funny," in *Fundamentalisms Comprehended*, ed. Martin Marty and Scott Appleby (Chicago: American Academy of Arts and Sciences and University of Chicago Press, 1995), vol. 5, 321–353.

18. Paraphrasing the famous slogan of the NOKIA cell phone company, "Connecting people."

19. Cf. Avriel Bar-Levav, "Games of Death in Jewish Books for the Sick and Dying in the Early Modern Period," *Kabbalah* 5 (2000): 11–33.

20. Gideon Aran, "Striking Home: Ideal-Type of Terrorism," *Terrorism and Political Violence* 27 (March 2017). 987-1004

21. Babylonian Talmud, Baba Batra, 91a.

22. This belief is attributed to Rabbi Haim Yosef David Azulai (1724–1806). Today this practice is used as a spell for success in examinations.

23. According to the halakha, this benediction should be recited within three days of rescue, with a quorum of men, while standing, after being called to the Torah. The volunteers did this, for example, after the suicide attack in Dimona (February 2008), where one of the terrorists remained alive after the explosion, and, had he not been killed by a policeman the moment he raised himself, he might have taken the lives of the security forces, the paramedics, and the ZAKA volunteers.

24. The testament left by Muhammed Atta, the leader of the suicide pilots of the attack on the World Trade Center, indicates a similar concern. Assuming that his body will be handled by "good Muslims," he asks them to wear gloves so as to not touch his genitals. Listening in on ZAKA discourse gives the impression that they are engaged in a mute dialogue with the suicide bomber, a tacit exchange about both machoism and purity.

25. The volunteers' sexual interest in the body was more tolerable because she was killed in an automobile accident and was not a victim of terror. It was reported to ZAKA that she was a citizen of the former USSR.

26. Enlightening comments concerning the motive of sex in ZAKA were offered by my former student Moran Banit.

27. *Kol ha'ir*, March 2002. In an official statement ZAKA apologized and promised that similar episodes would not be repeated.

28. Gideon Aran, Nurit Stadler, and Eyal Ben-Ari, "Body, Violence and Fundamentalism," *Religion* 38.1 (2008). 25-53

29. Haredim are effectively exempted from full military service. In recent years a minority of Haredim have volunteered to serve in the army. Some of them are even combat soldiers, mainly in the framework of special Haredi units, known as the Haredi NAHAL. This unit provides an alternative path for the *shababnikim*.

30. For example, *lotar, pakal, morak*. Note the adoption of military jargon in Lubavitcher Hasidism. Sue Fishkof, *The Rebbe's Army: Inside the World of Chabad* (New York: Schocken Books, 2003).

31. Gideon Aran, "Denial Doesn't Make the Haredi Body Go Away," *Contemporary Jewry* 26 (2006). 75-113

32. For example, Nurit Stadler, "The Military in the Eyes of the Haredim: Dream, Fantasy, and Evil Inclination," *Israeli Sociology* 6.1 (2004) (Hebrew). 69-90

33. This group mainly consists of newly religious people, who are characterized by certain religious peculiarities, such as climbing trees and shouting at the top of their voice after midnight in isolated places.

34. For a roster of events of Haredi violence, see Nachman Ben Yehuda, *Theocratic Democracy* (New York: Oxford University Press, 2019), chapter 5.

35. This sentence must be qualified by noting that in the recent generation the grassroots of the Haredim tend in fact to support right-wing, hawkish policies, and they tend to take violent steps against Arabs.

36. The festival celebrating the completion and re-beginning of the annual cycle of reading of the Torah.

37. Michel Foucault, *Discipline and Punish* (New York: Vintage, 1995).

38. Babylonian Talmud, Shabbat, fol. 156.

39. Cf. Philip Zimbardo, *The Lucifer Effect: Understanding How Good People Turn Evil* (New York: Random House, 2007).

40. For example, Bruno Bettelheim, *The Informed Heart* (1960; New York: Penguin, 1991), chapter 4; Elizabeth Howell, "Ferenczi's Concept of the Identification with the Aggressor," *American Journal of Psychoanalysis* 74.10 (2014): 48–59.

41. See Chapter 5.

42. Limor Darash-Samimian, *Violence, Control, Enjoyment: Issues in the Training of the IDF Duvdevan Unit* (Jerusalem: Shain #10 Working Papers, 2005).

43. Dave Grossman, *On Killing: The Psychological Cost of Learning to Kill in War and Society* (Boston: Little, Brown, 1995); Janice Gibson, "Training People to Inflict Pain: State Terror and Social Learning," *Journal of Humanistic Psychology* 31.2 (1991): 72–87.

44. Aran, *Smile,* chapter 7 and afterword.

45. Cf. Primo Levi, *The Drowned and the Saved* (New York: Vintage, 1988), chapter 2.

46. See, for example, *Regulations of the Burial Society* (Cracow: Alef, 1899).

47. The Ethics of the Fathers in the Mishnah. A Midrash on the verse in the Bible describing Moses, who saw an Egyptian beating a Hebrew, one of his kinsmen. He turned this way and that way and, seeing no one about, he struck down the Egyptian (Exodus 2:12). The literal meaning is that Moses checked to see whether anyone would report him or punish him. According to another interpretation, common in ZAKA, a person is responsible for fulfilling a sacred mission, even if it is difficult and dangerous, when there are no other people around who will go out of their way and take it upon themselves to do so.

48. Nitza Gonen, *True Kindness.* Documentary film, 2004 (Hebrew)

49. With a mixture of admiration and mockery, ZAKA people tell about the Rabbi of Brisk, an archetypical Lithuanian, who never entered a cemetery all his life, not even to visit the graves of his family.

50. That is to say, they are more modest and don't try to impress anyone with heroic deeds.

51. Succah is a temporary shelter or booth used by Orthodox Jews for meals during the originally biblical festival of Tabernacles. The obligation to eat in the *succah* does not apply to anything smaller than an egg.

52. Separation of the upper part of the body, which contains the heart and the brain and is holy and close to heaven, from the lower part of the body, where the potentially impure genitals are located.

53. On another occasion he said it was thirty-four.

54. I heard this from Ehud Olmert, who was the mayor at that time.

55. This is the number of people who were killed in Intifada terrorism by that date.

56. The Ethics of the Fathers, 3:1.

57. A best-selling novel by Haim Beer, *'Et hazamir* (Time of Trimming), about soldiers in the army rabbinate who deal with burial. One of the characters in this novel (apparently the silent one) is based on the author's acquaintance with Rabbi Roje.

58. Yigael Amir murdered Prime Minister Rabin in 2004 after certain rabbis ruled that he was subject to *din rodef,* the law permitting the preemptive killing of an attacker, after he signed the Oslo Agreements, which included the removal of Jewish settlements from the West Bank.

# Chapter 4

1. They quote the Mishnah: "The place where repentants stand is one where the absolutely saintly cannot stand." Berakhot 21–22, 34b.

2. *Shot Maharshadam* (Responsa of Rabbi Samuel de Medina) (Part Ten, sig 100).

3. The Order Zera'im, Tractate Peah, 1:1.

4. Yisrael Eichler, *The Haredi Camp.* (n.d. reference – in Yidish - by haredi informer).

5. Cf. Nurit Stadler's claim that ZAKA is the best example of the transfiguration of piety, in her *Yeshiva Fundamentalism* (New York: New York University Press, 2009), 136.

6. Babylonian Talmud, Hagiga, 5b.

7. Jerusalem Talmud, Pesaḥim 3:7.

8. In developing this argument I was helped by the generous advice and thoughtful publications of Yehuda Goodman. See his *The Exile*.

9. Noteworthy in this context is Sarit Barzilay's Ph.D. dissertation, "The Path to the Secular: Leaving Haredi Society" (Hebrew University, 2001).

10. Victor Turner, "Betwixt and Between," in Turner, *The Forest of Symbols: The Liminal Period in the Rites of Passage* (Ithaca, NY: Cornell University Press, 1967), chapter 4.

11. In the desert the Torah was given to the Israelites.

12. I remember the protagonist of Molière's *Bourgeois gentilhomme*, who was astonished to learn that for many years, every time he asked his servant for his slippers, he was speaking in prose.

13. Personal exchange with Professor Paul Frosh of the Hebrew University Department of Communication and Journalism.

14. Cf. Charles Liebman and Eliezer Don-Yehiyh, *Civil Religion in Israel* (Berkeley: University of California Press, 1983).

15. See Juliana Ochs, *Security and Suspicion: An Ethnography of Everyday Life in Israel* (Philadelphia: University of Pennsylvania Press, 2011), 26.

16. In Gush Emunim they disputed whether the sanctity of the land joins religious and secular Jews together, or whether the land was holy because its settlement united religious and secular Jews. See Gideon Aran, *Kookism* (Jerusalem: Carmel, 2013).

17. For a while, in ZAKA's bi-weekly, a section appeared entitled "Written about Us," with quotations from the press in praise of ZAKA.

18. In 1967 Judea and Samaria were conquered, areas identified with the biblical Land of Israel. In 1973, in the wake of the Yom Kippur War and the crisis in leadership and identity, the movement of repentance, or return to the religion, began. In 1977 the political upheaval brought the right-wing parties to power, along with upgrading the status of the religious parties that became effective in setting the national agenda.

19. For example, George Mosse, *Fallen Soldiers: Reshaping the Memory of the World Wars* (Oxford: Oxford University Press, 1990).

20. For example, Idit Zertal, *The Nation and Death* (Tel Aviv: Dvir, 2002).

21. Alex Weingrod, "Dry Bones," *Anthropology Today* 11.6 (December 1995). 7-12

22. In May 1982. Many Israelis also criticized the waste and inappropriate bombast, and mocked it by holding a counter-ceremony on the hill across the way.

23. Sixty-six percent of Israeli Jews see great importance in holding a religious funeral for themselves and their relatives, according to a poll by the Gutman Center and the Israel Democracy Institute in February 2002.

24. At the height of the Intifada, the most brilliant and insightful satirist in the Hebrew press dubbed Israel, stricken by terror and clinging to the security ethos, the "SHABAK-ZAKA State" (SHABAK = ISA). Doron Rosenblum, "medinat zaka-shabak" *Haaretz*, March 19, 2004.

25. Talia Shay, "Can Our Loved Ones Rest in Peace: Memorialization of the Victims of Hostile Activities," *Anthropological Quarterly* 78.3 (2005): 709–723. See also Yossi Sarid, "Memorial Day for Soldiers, but Not for Citizens," *Haaretz*, June 22, 2007

(Hebrew), or Tom Segev, "The Prime Minister Honored Us with His Absence," *Haaretz*, July 3, 2007 (Hebrew). On the public and judicial status of those who died in terrorist attacks and the struggle to raise their status to that of fallen soldiers, see No'a Kaspin, "Shall We Remember Them All?," a seminar paper in a course on law and ethics given by Professor Alon Harel in the Law School of the Hebrew University, December 31, 2006.

26. The withdrawal of the IDF from southern Lebanon (2000) and from Gaza (2006) shows that guerrilla fighting against a standing army is more effective than terrorism, which strikes at citizens on the home front, which never led to strategic concessions.

# Chapter 5

1. *Lo tashḥit* (you may not destroy). It is also liable to cause *gezel* (theft), which is also forbidden by the Torah.

2. A Torah scroll or any ritual article in which the name of God is written is forbidden for any use if it is damaged. It may not be thrown away or destroyed, but it must be treated carefully, usually given a religious burial.

3. Rabbi Ḥayim Devir, *Zakh venaqi* (Pure and Clean), I. (Jerusalem, n.d. Booklet. Internal circulation only)

4. Many English translations of the Bible, including the King James version, state that he was buried in a city of Gilead, a distortion of the source that misses the point.

5. Breshit Rabba, Parasha 60, n. 3.

6. The topic of death is mainly treated in the Tractate Mo'ed Qatan.

7. Rabbi Avramski.

8. Interview with Rabbi Roje, *NewZaka*, March 2005.

9. *Sefer ḥasidim*, 361. It states there that it is considered dangerous to study certain tractates, and therefore they must be studied in haste. However, one must actually be more diligent in them.

10. Sylvie Anne Goldberg, *Crossing the Jabbok*, Berkeley: University of California Press, 1996. 12.

11. Originally this referred to disinterring an existing grave, and many questions arise from it, such as, for example, whether it is a halakha from the Torah or from the rabbis. Can a grave that has been vacated be used?

12. Regarding the first stages of embryonic development. There is another chapter, still in a draft form, a few pages long about the laws of dealing with aborted fetuses.

13. Rabbi Yechiel Tikochinsky, *Bridge of Life*, 3 vols. (private printing, 1947), (Hebrew). See also the books on the halakhot relating to death consulted by Haredim: Yitsḥaq Adler, *Le'et metso: Dinei haqevura vehametim* , (Lost); Avraham Avidan, *Darkhei ḥesed: Hatsa'at pirqei halakha la'osqim bedemilut ḥesed shel emet*, Jerusalem: A. M. Avidan, (1978); and see Tzvi Rabinowicz, *A Guide to Life: Jewish Laws and Customs of Mourning* (London: Jason Aronson, 1989); Nisan Rubin, *Kets haḥayim: Tiqsei qevura veevel bameqorot ḥazal* (Tel-Aviv, Kibbutz Meuchad, 1996); Moshe Lam, *Darka shel hayahadut bemavet veavlut* (Jerusalem: Urim, 2005). On Jewish practices

related to death, see the anthropological study by Samuel Heilman, *When a Jew Dies* (Berkeley: University of California Press, 2001). On Jewish death, see also Hillel Halkin, *After One Hundred and Twenty: Reflections on Death, Mourning and Afterlife in Jewish Tradition* (Princeton, NJ: Princeton University Press, 2016).

14. For example, Yaacov Ariel, "Gezel hagoy bemilḥama" (Stealing from a Gentile in War) or "Ḥaluqat shalal bemilḥama beyameinu" (Division of Plunder in War in Our Day), in *Teḥumin 23* (Alon Shevut: Tsomet, 2002–2004), 11-17, 22–24.

15. Rabbi Yisrael Rosen, "Yishuv be'irua' pigua'" (Settlement in a Terrrorist Event), *Teḥumin* 23 (2003). 73-88

16. Among the halakhic rulings presented is poisoning the olive orchards in Palestinian villages, which is a basic source of livelihood and the possession of land, regarded as holy, disputed by the two sides—is it permitted or commanded? Another issue discussed there is how to respond to the throwing of stones at Israeli automobiles that go through hostile villages. See also Rabbi Yisrael Ariel, "Ha'intifada ba'halakha" (Jerusalem: Mekhon hamiqdash, n.d.).

17. Meir Hatina, *Martyrdom in Modern Islam* (Cambridge: Cambridge University Press, 2014), 446–429.

18. Jacob Katz, *Shabbes Goy: A Study in Halkhic Flexibility* (Philadelphia, PA: Jewish Publication Society of America, 1989).

19. The former function of the halakhic work *Gesher haḥayim* was described to me in similar terms.

20. Cf. Aviad Kleinberg, *Flesh Made Word: Saints' Stories and the Western Imagination* (Cambridge, MA: Harvard University Press, 2008).

21. On Book Tradition and Life Tradition in contemporary Judaism, see Haym Soloveitchik, "Repture and Reconstruction," *Tradition* 28 (1994). 64-130

22. Eric Hobsbawm and Terrence Ranger, eds., *The Invention of Tradition* (Cambridge: Cambridge University Press, 2012).

23. Avriel Bar-Levav, "Leon Modena and the Invention of Jewish Death Tradition," in *The Lion Shall Roar,* ed. David Malkiel (Jerusalem: Magnes Press, 2003), 83–99; Avriel Bar-Levav, "Ritualization of Jewish Life and Death in the Early Modern Period," *Leo Baeck Institute Yearbook* 37 (2002).69-82

24. Rabbi Aharon Berakhia da Modina, *Ma'avar yaboq*, first printed in Mantua in 1626. See Avriel Bar-Levav, "Rabbi Aharon Berakhia of Modena and Rabbi Naftali Hacohen Katz: The Founding Fathers of Books on the Sick and the Dead," in *Asufot*, vol. 9, ed. Meir Benayahu (1995) 189-234 (Hebrew). In June 2008 the chief rabbi of the IDF forbade the use of DNA testing on the bones of unidentified soldiers, based on a ruling from the seventeenth century in *Ma'avar hayaboq.*

25. Compare to the significant changes over history in the Christian countries of Europe. See Philippe Aries, *The Hour of Our Death* )New York: Vintage, 1981).

26. Avriel Bar-Levav calls the model presented in the books of death, "To die according to the book."

27. Mainly in Leviticus, the parashot of Tazria'-metsora', and Numbers, parashat Ḥuqat.

28. The book of Halakhot, *Gesher haḥayim,* goes into great detail about the impurity arising from a corpse lying in a house. For example, if the body is placed in a room

with doors to other rooms, the impurity spreads to them as well, unless the passageway is narrower than a handsbreadth (8–10 cm.).

29. Men are not required to perform ritual immersion for purification, unlike women after menstruation.

30. To remove evil spirits, according to a kabbalistic tradition.

31. In recent years, in certain religious circles in Israel, interest has grown in the laws of purification in general, with particular attention to the impurity of corpses. These are messianic circles which focus on building the third temple and renewal of sacrifices. See, for example, the 'Ateret Kohanim yeshiva in the Old City of Jerusalem, and even the Haredi Elbaum family.

32. The rabbinate forbids Jewish access to the Temple Mount because the exact place of the Holy of Holies is unknown, and it might become unintentionally polluted by impurity of the dead. It may be assumed that men of priestly lineage, as cautious as they may be, are also affected by the impurity of the dead. Hence, the rabbis decreed that one must strive "not to increase impurity," and even the impurity of the dead has gradations.

33. This saying continues: "and the wicked in their lives are as if they were dead" (Berakhot 18).

34. *Sefer ḥasidim* sig. 533, twelfth century; *Ma'avar yabok* (Sefat emet, chapter 25).

35. The veteran ZAKA activists are proud of the respect they paid to a Greek Orthodox priest who was killed in a suicide terrorism attack, when they learned that in the past he had cooperated with them in the arena of death in an attack near his monastery.

36. The incident of poisoning by products of Remedia caused the death of five infants and severe injury to many others (November 2003).

37. According to *Gesher haḥayim*, having a gentile move a body on the Sabbath is conditional on the agreement of the deceased's relatives.

38. The ZAKA rabbinical council ruled that, in urgent cases, the "how" was more important than the "who."

39. Committed by two terrorists who blew themselves up simultaneously at a distance of ten meters from each other, causing the death of sixteen and injury of eighty.

40. Six people were killed, including two foreign workers from China. The terrorist was a woman, a member of Fatah.

41. Babylonian Talmud, Shabbat 71b.

42. Shim'on Ben Gamliel, Braita, Babylonian Talmud, Shabbat 151b.

43. The suicide attack on the Maxim restaurant in Haifa (October 2003) stands out among them.

44. If there is no alternative except to travel by car, any act that isn't vital must be avoided, even turn signals. When they arrive at the arena, they avoid closing the doors of the car. "Some Arab will be there who can do that for us."

45. To deal with parts of the body of a victim of a Palestinian mortar attack, the ZAKA volunteers arrived on bicycles (May 2008). The use of bicycles is prohibited on the Sabbath, but the rabbis consider it the least of the available evils.

46. They refer to the Bible's concern lest the Israelites who pass through the land of the Philistines on their way to Canaan might see the bodies of the members of the tribe

of Ephraim who died in battle there earlier, and then they would be frightened and return to Egypt. Rabbi Nebenzahl, on these matters, mentions the soldiers of King David, who were petrified when they saw the body of Asahel (2 Samuel 23), *Teḥumin* 22, 2002, p. 109, n. 22.

47. Devir, *Zakh venaqi* I 2004.

48. Allen Dundes, *The Shabbat Elevator and Other Sabbath Subterfuges* (Lanham, MD: Rowman & Littlefield, 2003).

49. Examples of *shinui* on the Sabbath that were mentioned in conversation with ZAKA volunteers: carrying a medical device under one's hat; carrying an object which one is permitted to carry no more than four cubits by putting it down after walking three cubits, over and over again, or passing it from hand to hand every three cubits.

50. Aran, *Kookism.*

51. Samuel Heilman and Menachem Friedman, *The Rebbe: The Life and Afterlife of Menachem Mendel Schneerson* (Princeton, NJ: Princeton University Press, 2010).

52. Avriel Bar-Levav, "Jewish Attitudes towards Death: A Society between Time, Space and Texts," in *Death in Jewish Life: Burial and Mourning Customs among Jews of Europe and Nearby Communities,* ed. Stephan Reif and Avriel Bar-Levav (Berlin: de Gruyter, 2014) 3-15 . The story about King Saul, who consulted the witch of Endor, is the exception that proves the rule.

53. Benjamin Brown, "The Return of Naive Faith," in *'Al haemuna—'iyunim bemusag haemuna vetoldotava bamasoret hayehudit,* ed. Moshe Halbertal et al. (Jeruslaem: Keter, 2005) 403-441 (Hebrew). The following section is based on this article.

54. Based on the prayer recited by soldiers in the IDF before going into battle or on a security mission.

55. On God's preference for Torah, see the rabbinic Midrashim on Jeremiah 16:11, Midrash Raba: "If only they might abandon me and preserve my Torah."

56. On the kabbalistic dimension in Jewish death rites, see Avriel Bar-Levav, "Death and the Blurred Boundaries of Magic," *Kabbalah: Journal for the Study of Jewish Mystical Texts* 7 (2002): 51–64.

57. Kohelet Raba, Section 5.

58. A paraphrase of Jonathan Parry (*Death in Benares,* 1), where he describes the Hindu death experts as no less propagandist than ritualists.

59. According to some rabbis, this custom was condemned when they realized that it was a Christian practice.

60. Rabbi Roje, "Halakha lema'ase" (Halakhic Practice), *NewZaka,* no. 53 (2007).

61. Responsa of the Ḥatam Sofer, 10, sig. 346.

62. On the mystical strata in the depths of the laws and practices of death in Judaism see Goldberg, *Crossing the Jabbok,* 86–92.

63. On the death of Zaddiks and its meaning, see Benyamin Minz, *Sefer hahistalqut* (The Book of Departure) (Tel Aviv: Ktuvim, 1930). See also, on Rabbi Nachman's obsession with death, Mendel Piekaj, *Meḥqarim beḥasidut bratslav* (Studies in Bratslav Hasidism) (Jerusalem: Bialik, 1974), 172–181 (Hebrew).

64. Eli Yasif, *Sipur ha'am ha'ivri* (The Hebrew Folk Tale), (Jerusalem: Bialik, 1994) s.v. "mavet" (death) in the index (Hebrew).

65. *Sefer ḥasidim*, 319–320.

66. A distinction must be drawn between the soul (*neshama*), which returns to its source with death, its home with the Shekhina, and the spirit (*ruaḥ*), which immediately rises to heaven and enters paradise, if it is worthy. Another entity, the *nefesh*, for which there is no distinct term in English, remains in the vicinity of the body for some time, floating above it. The terms *neshama, ruaḥ,* and *nefesh* refer to different concepts, though they are closely related and there is a tendency to confuse them. In this book, I do not make the complicated distinction among them and refer only to the *neshama*. On this distinction, see, for example, Rabbi Tsevi Hirsh Kaidanover, *Sefer qav ha'yashar*, esp. chapter 71. This book, in Hebrew and Yiddish, was a widely circulated ethical work full of references to spirits and ghosts, a link between the medieval *Sefer ḥasidim* and present-day books. See also another influential book, *Shnei luḥot habrit* by Rabbi Yesh'ayahu Horowitz.

67. The Ofakim branch, which was proud until then of being mixed Mizrahi and Ashkenazi.

68. Compare the role of ghosts and spirits in dealing with the results of deadly terrorism in Sri-Lanka (and in Africa). Sasanka Perera, "Spirit Possession and Avenging Ghosts: Stories of Supernatural Activity as Narratives of Terror and Mechanisms of Coping," in *Remaking a World: Violence, Social Suffering and Recovery*, ed. Veena Das et al. (Berkeley: University of California Press, 2001), 157–200.

69. Like the *dybbuk, iḥuz* (possession), and the spirit of pollution, the *sitra aḥra*, etc.

70. See, for instance, the Jewish custom of *Hakafot*: "a practice at the funerals of males in which men circumambulate a grave seven times. According to Jewish mystical belief, the ejaculated sperm that was not meant for recreation (resulting from masturbation, etc.) turned into bodiless demonic beings, never having an inheritance from their father, were attracted to his funeral to claim what was theirs, or to harm him." Goldberg, *Jewish Passages*, 211.

71. On this see the book of halakhot about death, *Gesher haḥayim* (chapter 3, p. 2) and the Babylonian Talmud, Shabbat, 150a. During purification before burial the anus of the corpse is plugged. Sealing of the bodily orifices symbolizes the separation from life.

72. Cf. Yoram Bilu, *Without Bounds* (Detroit, MI: Wayne State University Press, 2017), 127 n45. Also see Edvard Westermack, *Ritual and Belief in Morocco* (London: Macmillen, 1926), 104, 266, 277.

73. It is told that because the Amora Rav, from the city of Sura, treated the dead, his neighborhood was saved from the plague (Ta'anit 21, p. 2).

74. For example, Babylonian Talmud, Brakhot 18a. For a summary of the laws of *shemira* (watching over), see Rabbi Roje, *Zakh venaqi*, I.

75. This appears in the manuscript of the ZAKA book of halakhot, which has not yet been published.

76. *Mishna brura* (siman b. 160 b.)

77. Tractate Horayot, 4, 13, p. 2.

78. According to the Zoharic kabbalah, the sins of a person appear on the faces of living people as well, in glowing and prominent letters, shining and disappearing by turns. Rabbi Isaac Luria, a seventeenth-century mystic, was thus able to "read" people.

79. *Maʿavar yaboq*, 43 89.

80. According to the *hadith*, one is not supposed to wash the martyr's body or wrap it in shrouds. In any case the virgins will wash him in Paradise.

81. For a rabbinical discussion of the purity of the victims of terrorism, see, for example, Lam, *Darka shel hayahadut bemavet ubeʾavlut* (Jerusalem: Urim, 2005) esp. the chapter on extraordinary circumstances, Hebrew).

82. Rabbi Ovadia Yosef, the late chief rabbi of Israel, developed this argument toward the end of the 2000s. A leader of the Sephardic Haredim, he was regarded as the greatest of his generation (*Kol mevaser*, vol. 1, chapter 1).

83. The book is entitled *Hadrat kodesh*, written in 1400 in Regensburg, quoted by Yuval, *Shnei goyim bevitnekh* (Two Nations), 152 (Hebrew), MS Moscow-Ginzburg 482, fol. 25a.

84. The prayer, *Av haraḥamim* (Father of Mercy), was composed during the Crusades and is recited in Ashkenazi synagogues on Sabbath mornings.

85. Very few insist on adding "God will avenge his blood" on the tombstones of soldiers who died. Among the reasons presented to the army for refraining from doing so are the fact that the state, the army, and their comrades, rather than God, will avenge their death. It may also be said that their death was a "good" one, which does not require vengeance.

86. See Yuval, *Two Nations*. Also, personal communication with the author.

87. Yom Tov Assis, Jeremy Cohen, Ora Limor, Aharon Kedar, and Michael Toch, eds., *Facing the Cross: The Persecutions of 1096 in History and Historiography* (Jerusalem: Magnes Press, 2000).

88. Cf. Arthur Droge and James Tabor, *A Noble Death: Suicide and Martyrdom among Christians and Jews in Antiquity* (San Francisco, CA: Harper, 1992); Friedrich Avemarie and Willem Henten, *Martyrdom and Noble Death* (New York: Routledge, 2002); Joyce Salisbury, *The Blood of Martyrs: Unintended Consequences of Ancient Violence* (New York: Routledge, 2004).

89. The suicide of Jews in response to pressure to convert during the persecutions accompanying the Crusades was not only an object of praise but also an object of criticism, both outside and within Judaism. What some people took for heroic faith was seen by others as murder of children and contemptible suicide. See Yuval, *Two Nations*, 75–173. Some authorities regard this behavior by Jews as contrary to Jewish law, arguing that those who are called sanctifiers of the name should be buried beyond the pale. See Hayim Soloveitchik, "Religious Law and Change: The Medieval Ashkenazi Example," *AJS Review* 12 (1987): 205–221.

90. Yisrael Yuval, "The Revenge and the Curse, the Blood and the Libel: From the Behavior of Saints to the Blood Libels," *Zion* 58.1 (1993): 33–90 (Hebrew).

91. The collecting of blood for the purpose of urging God to bring redemption may be compared to the provocation on the part of a radical wing of Habad Hasidism, who

posted signs in the street calling for "Moshiach Now," which is to say that they openly demanded that God should rush redemption.

# Chapter 6

1. Because of the large number of suicide terrorism attacks during the Intifada, an atmosphere of fear and suspicion prevailed in Israel, which was expressed in the wide circulation of instructions on how to identify Palestinian suicide terrorists. See Ochs, *Security*, 85–86.

2. There is a typical body language of ultra-Orthodox Jews. When reading or praying they tend to rhythmically move their head right and left, and their upper body forward and backward. See Gideon Aran, "Denial Does Not Make *the Haredi Body* Go Away: Ethnography of a Disappearing Jewish Phenomenon," *Contemporary Jewry* 26 (2006). 75-113

3. Cf. Israel's Orthodoxy alarm in the face of "provocative" Church initiatives embodied in figures like Brother Daniel (Rufeisen) or Cardinal Lustiger (of Paris), both converts from Judaism who served as active Christian clergy while refusing to deny their original Jewish identity. Their insistence on being considered Jews, not renouncing their commitment to Jewish ideals despite their papal allegiance, was interpreted as a conspiracy to blur the distinction between the two religions, hence "destroy Judaism from within."

4. Babylonian Talmud: Pesaḥim 3b.

5. See Mishnah, Tractate Tamid, chapter 1.

6. For example, Hamas presented the aged Habad Rabbi Schneerson, who, since his death, has been regarded as the messiah by a faction of Lubavitcher Hasidim, as the incarnation of satanic forces. See Anne Marie Oliver and Paul Steinberg, *The Road to Martyrs' Square*, New York: Oxford University Press, 2005. 21.

7. Arie Erlich, "The Eternal Jew," *Bamishpaḥa*, 29 October 2015.

8. See Ben-Yehuda, *Theocratic Democracy*, New York: Oxford University Press, 2010. 116

9. See also the suicide attack in Hotel Park at the Seder—the Passover festive meal.

10. Rashmi Singh, *Hamas and Suicide Terrorism* (London: Routledge, 2012), 109.

11. See, for example, the rich material on martyrs' testaments and placards in Palestinian communities in Gaza and the West Bank (Aran, *The Smile*, 244–255).

12. Every year on March 30, Shahid Week begins at the university.

13. Photographs from the author's archive. The Jewish victims could also be identified as Gush Emunim settlers.

14. In 2014 a poster that became popular appeared in the West Bank, showing a tree with a Haredi Jew hiding behind it, wearing a black hat, with a beard and earlocks. His expression is one of ridiculous panic. In the background, among the branches of the tree, a verse from the Koran appears, calling upon the servants of Allah to kill the Jew hiding behind it.

15. *Haaretz*, 2 November 2005.

16. Aran, *The Smile*.

17. On the depiction and analysis of Haredim and Arab Sunni Muslims as fundamentalists, and on fundamentalism in general, see Martin Marty and Scott Appleby, eds., *Fundamentalisms Observed* (Chicago: University of Chicago Press, 1991), chapters 4, 6. For a description and comparison of both as fundamentalists, see Gabriel Almond, Emmanuel Sivan, and Scott Appleby, *Strong Religion* (Chicago: University of Chicago Press, 2002).

18. Cf. the Modesty Patrols in the Haredi neighborhoods of Jerusalem.

19. Oliver and Steinberg, *Martyrs' Square*, 148.

20. Yehuda Meshi-Zahav, TV interview in *Arutz 2* Night News (2000s, date not found)

21. At that moment one of the insights fundamental to my present study was born.

# Chapter 7

1. This Hasidic term refers to enthusiastic devotion and profound intention, which has the mystical dimension of the effort to cleave to God.

2. This song was sung on another occasion, when the volunteers arrived at the site of an attack on the Sabbath but were not permitted to enter the arena until the sappers finished examining the area. While waiting on the sidelines, they spontaneously burst out in this song.

    According to a rumor, during the 1948 war, after the Jewish Quarter of the Old City fell, the men were taken into captivity, while the women and children were evacuated in a bus, accompanied by Haredim, whose rabbis instructed them to join the trip, even though it was on the Sabbath. On the way they sang, "May the observers of the Sabbath be joyous in your kingdom."

3. One of the Haredi who spoke with me remembered what he experienced on Yom Kippur, about thirty years earlier, on 6 October 1973, when the war broke out. On the one hand, the cries of the worshipers, the sounding of the shofar in synagogues, and, on the other hand, the wailing of sirens, bulletins on the radio, panicked telephone calls, and reserve soldiers rushing to join their units—these sounds clashed and also melded into "a marvelous melody," which increased the total sanctity of the moment infinitely.

4. Cf. Kristeva, *Powers of Horror*.

5. Peter Stallibrass and Allon White, *The Politics and Poetics of Transgression* (London: Methuen 1986); Michael Taussig, "Transgression," .157-174

6. In recent years the orthodox rabbinate have forbidden the especially sensitive matter of men disguising themselves in women's clothing.

7. The attraction to boundaries and crossing them can be seen as a general attribute of Hasidism, and of Bratslav Hasidism in particular. For example, see Yosef Weiss, "The Attractive Force of the Boundary" Chapter 7 in his *Meḥqarim beḥasidut breslav* (Studies in Bratslav Hasidism) (Jerusalem: Bialik, 1974), 96–108 (Hebrew).

8. Cf. Michele Lemont and Virge Molner, "The Study of Boundaries in the Social Sciences," *Annual Review of Sociology* 28 (2002): 167–195. For a fine use of boundary crossing to analyze religious movements, see Yoram Bilu and Zvi Mark, "Saint and

Messiah: Comparative Study of Chabad and Breslaw," *Iyunim Betkumat Israel* 23 (2013): 350–377.

9. Turner, *Forest of Symbols.*

10. Cf. Allen Dundes, *The Shabbat Elevator and Other Sabbath Subterfuges: An Unorthodox Essay on Circumventing Custom and Jewish Character* (Lanham MD: Rowman & Littlefield, 2002).

11. Cf. Asad, *Suicide Bombing,* 85–86; Taussig, "Transgression," 350.

12. For example, Haredim who drive their wives to the maternity ward on the Sabbath are careful not to take off their prayer shawls, which are visible from a distance, as if they were still attending Sabbath prayers.

13. Quotations from a Halakhic ruling by the ZAKA rabbis, which were circulated in a leaflet distributed to the volunteers in 2004.

14. Rabbi Ḥayim Devir, letter in answer to Rabbi Yehoshua' Hershkovitz, 2004. (Personal communication. Hebrew)

15. Cf. Jonas Franken and Orvar Lofgien, eds., *Forces of Habit* (Lund: Lund University Press, 1996).

16. They cite a moral proverb from the Talmud, "If someone commits a sin and repeats it over and over again, it might become [felt] as if permitted."

17. The Haredim attached the pejorative label of "Sabbateanism" to Zionism, including to religious Zionism.

18. *NewZaka* 139, July 2009.

19. January 2010.

20. I was exposed to the Aghori for the first time during a visit to India of several months many years ago. I extended my knowledge of the phenomenon through the anthropological work of Jonathan Parry, mainly in *Death in Banaras.* I am grateful to my colleague Nurit Shtadler who recommended this book.

21. Their legendary father is Kina Ram, believed to be the incarnation of Shiva, who died in the eighteenth century at the age of 150.

22. Cf. Tony Walter, "Modern Death: Taboo or Not Taboo?," *Sociology* 52.2 (1991): 293–310.

23. Some of the extreme practices of the Aghori are rare, and cannibalism has not been observed by any reliable researcher. As for human sacrifice, the literature contains only indirect or old evidence, which is controversial.

24. Nurit Stadler, "Terror, Corpse Symbolism and Taboo Violation: The 'Haredi* Disaster Victim Identification Team in Israel,'" *Man* 12.4 (2006): 837–858.

25. This resonates with the Virtue of True Benevolence. However, the Aghori priests do not live by their proud words: they beg and receive a kind of payment for their work. After all, unlike ZAKA, the Aghori provide a service to patrons.

26. Cf. the Merina women, who dance with corpses to help them overcome fear of death. Maurice Bloch, *Placing the Dead: Tombs, Ancestral Villages and Kinship Organization in Madagascar* (London: Seminar Press, 1971), 168.

27. Jonathan Parry, "Sacrificial Death and the Necrophagous Ascetic," in *Death and the Regeneration of Life,* ed. Maurice Bloch and Jonathan Parry (Cambridge: Cambridge University Press, 1982). 74-110

28. Critics of ZAKA compared the Haredi volunteers to deviants who eat carrion and dig about in graves.

29. Cf. James Frazer, *The Golden Bough*, London: Macmillan, 1911. vol. 9, 377. Native people in North America handle pieces of the flesh of the deceased and even nibble them to prove that they are under heavenly providence.

30. In a personal communication, a colleague suggested that eating huge servings of meat in the banquet of seventh of Adar, after the annual fast for the dead, is a sublimation of eating the flesh of the dead.

31. Bloch and Parry, *Death and the Regeneration*, 1–44; Henry Abramovitch, "Good Death and Bad Death," in *Traumatic and Nontraumatic Loss and Bereavement*, ed. Ruth Malkinson, Simon Rubin, and Eliezer Witztum (New York: Psychosocial Press, 1999), 255–272; Tony Walter, "Historical and Cultural Variants on the Good Death," *British Medical Journal* 327 (2003): 218–220.

32. In *Death with Interruptions*, José Saramago describes a man who receives notice of his death a week in advance, so that he can prepare, but the intervening days prove to be hellish, and he asks to die without warning.

33. For example, Sister Mary O'Connor, *The Art of Dying Well* )New York: Columbia University Press, 1942).

34. Upon his request, an orchestra was invited to his funeral, but, contrary to his instructions, it played mournful music.

35. It is told that Rabbi Yitsḥaq Shar'abi ordered that his burial should be with "humiliation." The gravediggers refused to honor this request, but during the funeral Arab robbers appeared, scattered the mourners, and shoved the rabbi's body into the grave with contempt. Thus, unintentionally, the Zaddik's request was honored. See Reuven Qashani, "Yalqut minhagei petira II," in *Shevet ve'am*, ed. David Siton (Jerusalem: Va'ad 'edat hasefardim, 1973) (Hebrew).

36. See the discussion of "bad death" in the American Civil War in Faust, *This Republic of Suffering*, chapter 1, esp. p. 9.

37. Cf. James Boyden, "The Worst Death Becomes a Good Death: The Passion of Don Rodrigo Calderon," in *The Place of the Dead*, ed. Bruce Gordon and Peter Marshall (Cambridge: Cambridge University Press, 2000) 17-43 .

38. A distinction must be made between the phenomenon described here and the common custom in the United States of mortuary makeup: dressing, making up, cutting the hair, and manicuring the corpse, so that it will look good before the coffin is closed and buried.

39. Faust, *This Republic of Suffering*.

40. This victimhood is effected according to the model of Jesus, who died like a thief in the market, though much later, the Church presented his death as atoning and redeeming all of humanity. On this it has been said, Christ's passion is a midpoint in the transformation of the (dead) body "from decay to splendor." See Manuele Gragnolati, "From Decay to Splendor: Body and Pain in Bonvesin de la Rivera's Book of the Three Scriptures," in *Last Things: Death and the Apocalypse in the Middle Ages*, ed. Carolyn Bynum and Paul Freedman (Philadelphia: University of Pennsylvania Press, 2000), 83–98.

# Chapter 8

1. For example, the popular author Meir Shalev wrote in a daily newspaper, "[W]e have become addicted to graves and bodies." "Yeladim veavot," *Yedi'ot Aḥronot*, 14 May 2004 (Hebrew). On the same day other headlines appeared in the press, such as "The society in Israel has lost its sanity and makes every lifeless scrap of skin a holy relic."

2. Even among several radical rabbis, doubt arose lest this was excessive respect for the dead. For example, Rabbi Yehuda Zoldan, "Taking Risks In Order to Bring IDF Soldiers for Burial" *Teḥumin* No' 25, 2005. 420-425 (Annual review of hakhic issues related to contemporary Israeli politics and society, in Hebrew)

3. Nachum Barnea, "ZAKA Syndrom", *Yediot Aḥronot*, 14 May 2004.

4. Especially memorable is the case of the returning of the body parts of the soldiers Eldad Regev and Ehud Goldwasser (July 2008). The head of the ZAKA rabbinical council took part in identifying the limbs.

5. In response to the cynical extortion on the part of Hamas and Hizballah, Israel also took up the accounting of bodies and body parts. It only returns them to the movements that demand them in return for accepting its demands. This policy arouses criticism within Israel. People called upon the government to cease trading bodies, as has become customary in the Middle East, in "necrophiliac politics" and "the pathology of pinky, nose, and foot." See the editorial in *Haaretz* in response to the "gesture" of transferring the remains of eighty-four bodies of terrorists to the Palestinian Authority ("Stop the Corpse Trade", 7 July 2011).

6. Quite a few Israelis regarded dealing with the subject as disrespect for the dead, and they accused ZAKA of it. For example, see the ironic poem by Rami Ditzani which was dedicated to "The holy ZAKA, risking their lives for a scrap of pinky." He addressed a plea to the Haredi volunteers: "Brothers, enough of this particle theory, leave the pieces alone, give swift repose to the burned bodies. Stop identifying our loved ones with bits of hair on a sack of testicles" ("Brothers! Dig a Mass Grave for Them", *Haaretz*, 7 October 2004).

7. This book treats the victims of violent death from the viewpoint of those who honor them, identify with them, and mourn for them. In parallel, there are studies that relate to the victims of violent death from the attacker's viewpoint, the one who caused their cruel death and acts violently against their remains to express hatred for them and to reinforce victory over them. Whereas this book discusses the ritualization of bodily remains and brings out the tendency to sanctify them, in the parallel studies, the purpose of treatment of the bodily remains is to make them disappear and to deny their existence, and the existence of the violence that produced them. See Jean-Marc Dreyfus and Elisabeth Gessat-Anstett, eds., *Destruction and Human Remains: Disposal and Concealment in Genocide and Mass Violence* )Manchester: Manchester University Press, 2014).

8. Another example is Che Guevara, who was secretly buried, and after some time his body was discovered and reinterred, but not before the story of his life as a hero, sacrificing himself for the revolution, was woven around his bullet-riddled body.

Lyman Johnson, ed., *Death, Dismemberment, and Memory* )Albuquerque: University of New Mexico Press, 2004), esp. chapter 1, "Why Dead Bodies Talk."

9. Adam Aronson, "Stonewall Jackson's Arm Lies Here: What a Memorial for an Amputated Limb Can Teach Our Society about Wounded Veterans," *The Atlantic*, 2 May 2012. Also Jurgen Buchenau, "The Arm and Body of a Revolution," in Johnson, *Death, Dismemberment, and Memory*.179-206

10. Katherine Verdery, *The Political Lives of Dead Bodies: Reburial and Post-socialist Change* (New York: Columbia University Press, 1999).

11. Trumpeldor is one of the pillars of the Zionist pantheon. After he lost his arm in the Russo-Japanese War, he emigrated to Palestine, where he became known as a settler and charismatic leader. He died in the mythic battle to defend settlements in the Galilee (1920). A fierce dispute took place over the right to display his prosthetic arm between the museum at Kfar Gil'adi and the museum at Tel Yosef, in parallel to efforts to appropriate his tradition by two rival political camps (the Labor Movement and the Revisionist Movement). Compare to Johnson, *Death, Dismemberment, and Memory*, 4–6.

12. Peter Brown, *The Cult of the Saints* (Chicago: University of Chicago Press, 1982).

13. Great importance is attributed to an object which becomes an object of erotic desire.

14. For example, the sanctity of places where the footprint of the Prophet Muhammad is seen on the floor. Stupas were built in places where the Buddha's body parts were buried, for it was divided into eight parts after his death. Hinduism has fewer relics because of the practice of cremation.

15. Caroline Bynum, *The Resurrection of the Body in Western Christianity* (New York: Columbia University Press, 1995), 104–109; Rosalind Brooke and Christopher Brooke, *Popular Religion in the Middle Ages* (London: Thames and Hudson, 1984).

16. The potency attributed to bodies and severed limbs is evident in the attitude of religious groups to the relics of their rivals. In sixteenth-century Europe, the Protestants dug up the graves of Catholic saints and burned their remains to purify the earth. The Catholic response was not only to throw the bones of Protestant saints into rivers, but also to tear the flesh of the dead, throw it to the dogs, and perform posthumous castration. See Natalie Z. Davis, "Rites of Violence", *Past & Present,* No' 59, 1973. 33-91.

17. Patrick Geary, *Furta Sacra: Thefts of Relics in the Central Middle Ages* )Princeton, NJ: Princeton University Press, 1998).

18. In 2014, in Abruzzo, a piece of the blood-stained cloak worn by Pope John Paul II, when he was shot in Saint Peter's Square in 1981 was stolen.

19. Distributed 21 March 2001.

20. In Palestinian vernacular the place is called Arqam, from the word for the numbers that mark the graves, since the Israelis did not place names on them, to make it harder to make the dead into saints.

21. In sermons at Hamas mosques, during the Intifada, *ashla al yahud* was also mentioned: the body parts of the Jewish victims (which are like pieces of pork).

22. Singh, *Hamas and Suicide Terrorism*; Zaki Chehab, *Inside Hamas* (New York: Norton, 2007). Compare this to the Iranian youths who, during the Shat-al-Arab war against

Iraq, were sent to break trails in minefields. Before their certain deaths in explosions, they asked to be wrapped in blankets so that their body parts would not be scattered. Christoph Reuter, *My Life Is a Weapon* (Princeton, NJ: Princeton University Press, 2002), 48.

23. A sample of popular sociological works on death: Clark David, ed., *The Sociology of Death* (Oxford: Blackwell, 1993); Seale Clive, *Constructing Death: The Sociology of Death and Bereavement* (Cambridge: Cambridge University Press, 1998); Walter Tony, *The Revival of Death* (London: Routledge,1994; Catherine Exley, "Review of the Sociology of Dying, Death and Bereavement," *Sociology of Health and Illness* 26.1 (2004): 110–122.

24. Cf. Yoram Bilu, *With Us More Than Ever: Making the Absent Rebbe in Messianic Chabad* (Stanford, CA: Stanford University Press, 2020).

25. The inhabitants of the Gaza Strip used this term to describe themselves, in their bitter despair.

26. See the epilogue.

27. This point has been beautifully put by the Noble laureate poet Wisława Szymborska in a poem titled "The Terrorist":

> The bomb will explode in the bar at twenty past one.
> Now it's only sixteen minutes past.
> Some will still have time to enter,
> Some to leave.
> A woman in a yellow jacket, she enters.
> A man in dark glasses, he leaves.
> A girl, she walks by, a green ribbon in her hair.
> Eighteen minutes past.
> The girl's disappeared.
> Was she stupid enough to go in, or wasn't she.
> We shall see when they bring out the bodies.
>
> ...................................
> It's twenty past one.
> Yes, now.
> The bomb, it explodes.

28. Cf. Philipe Aries, *The Hour of Our Death* (Oxford: Oxford University Press, 1991), 353–358.

29. If the dead person did not do so in the arena, he will appear in their dream seven days after the burial and express gratitude for the favor done to him.

30. Cf. Oliver and Steinberg, *The Road to Martyrs' Square*, 118.

31. Robert Hertz, *Death and the Right Hand* (London: Routledge, 1960).

32. Richard Huntington and Peter Metcalf, *Celebrations of Death: The Anthropology of Mortuary Ritual* )Cambridge: Cambridge University Press, 1979).

33. Cf. Annika Jonsson, "Post-mortem Social Death: Exploring the Absence of the Deceased," *Contemporary Social Science* 10.3 (2005) 1-12. .

34. David Ofek, director and producer, *The Seventeenth Victim*, documentary television, Israel, 2003 (Hebrew).

35. Years after the film was screened, it turned out that the victim was a petty criminal who had lived in hiding for many years. His family might not have searched for him, because they assumed he had died in a fight with other criminals.

36. Cf. Raya Morag, "The Living Body and the Corpse: Israeli Documentary Cinema and the Intifada," *Journal of Film and Video* 60.3–4 (2008) 3-24. .

37. Aran, *The Smile*, chapters 2, 3.

38. See Chapter 4.

39. In parallel, in interviews with Palestinians from the West Bank, including community leaders, I repeatedly asked about the details of the life stories of suicide terrorists. Usually my informants couldn't say anything about the terrorists beyond their act of martyrdom, unless they came from where my informants lived. In a long conversation with Sheikh Ahmad Yasin in his cell, the spiritual leader of Hamas was unable to name a single suicide terrorist, including those whom he had eulogized and praised as *shahids* (personal information from the criminologist Dr. Anat Berko).

40. Sasanka Perera, "Spirit Possessions and Avenging Ghosts: Narrative of Terror and Mechanisms of Coping and Remembering," in Das et al., *Remaking a World* 157-200..

41. In other cases, in in response to a threat to the collective body, such as war, there is a tendency to identify it with the individual body. For example, take the massive military rape, bordering on genocide, that was committed against ethnic and religious background in Bosnia-Herzegovina. Maria Olujic, "Embodiment of Terror," *Medical Anthropology Quarterly* 12.1 (1998): 31–50.

42. Cf. the holiness of medieval Christian saints which was often equated with self-denial in the form of harms to the body. This damage to the flesh amounts to self-sacrifice (eucharistic act). See:Bynum, *Resurrection*.

43. Aran, *The Smile*, 53, 145–147, 208–209.

44. Half the gown serves as a curtain in the tomb of the mythological biblical matriarch, to whom barren women come and pray, and the other half is used as a marriage canopy in the weddings frequently celebrated there. The Jewish virgin who went to heaven in a terrorist attack has become a symbol of fertility.

45. For thirty years the thesis of the social construction of the body has been applied to the body, especially in contexts of gender, politics, and violence. A leading figure in research on the political dimension of the body was Foucault. In studies of violence, the body as an analytical category plays a central role, especially in connection with death. For example, see Leen Van Brussel and Nico Carpentier, eds., *The Social Construction of Death: Interdisciplinary Perspectives* )London: Palgrave Macmillan, 2014).

46. Aran, *The Smile*, chapter 1.

47. Cf. Gayatri Chakravorty Spivak, "A Speech after 9/11," *Boundary* 2 (2000): 95.

48. For example, Reuter, *My Life*.

49. Cavarero, *Horrorism*; Asad, *On Suicide Bombing*.

50. On social-cultural approach toward the dead body and particularly in rites concerning mutilated corpses, see Mary Bradbury, *Representations of Death* (London: Routledge, 1999). Also see Lindsay Prior, *The Social Organization of Death* (London: Macmillan,

1989); David Armstrong, *Political Anatomy of the Body* (Cambridge: Cambridge University Press, 1983).

51. Foucault, *Discipline and Punish*; Michel Foucault, *History of Sexuality*, 4 vols. (London: Penguin, 1984).

52. Brian Turner, "The Body in Western Society," in *Religion and the Body*, ed. Sarah Coakley (Cambridge: Cambridge University Press, 1997).

53. Aran, "The Haredi Body."

54. Compare this to the prominent instances of difficulty in dealing with death in the absence of corpses: the Holocaust and 9/11.

55. Tsipi Kahana, Maya Freund, and Yehuda Hiss, "Suicidal Terrorist Bombing in Israel." *Journal of Forensic Sciences* 42(2): 1989 260-4

56. See Sefer Chasidim, sig. 319,331, reference in Avriel Bar-Levav, "The Concept of Death in the 'Book of Life' by Rabbi Shimon Frankfurter" (PhD diss., Hebrew University, 1997), 130.

57. For example, Piero Camporesi, *The Incorruptible Flesh* (Cambridge: Cambridge University Press, 1988); Joice Salisbury, *The Blood of Martyrs* (New York: Routledge, 2004).

58. Bereshit Raba 28:3.

59. In ZAKA it is believed that among the Jews this bone is so hard that it is impossible to grind or burn it, and the effort to smash it will break the hammer and anvil.

60. 1. The neck joint. 2. The tail bone. 3. The bone to which the strap of the head *tefillin* is attached.

61. Against my expectations, I found no sign of the kabbalistic and classical preference for the right side of the body.

62. The conception of man being in the image of God is connected with the anthropomorphic image of God. As Mary Douglas (*Natural Symbols,* New York: Routledge, 1995) comments, the God of Israel has organs of motion and sensation (hand, nose, etc.), but he does not have organs of digestion of excretion, as they are identified with imperfection or impurity .However, these organs are conspicuously present in the arena of terrorism, with which ZAKA copes.

63. Cf. Maurice Bloch and Jonathan Parry, eds., *Death and the Regeneration of Life* (Cambridge: Cambridge University Press, 1982).

64. Bynum and Freedman, *Last Things*.

65. Caroline Bynum, *The Resurrection of the Body in Western Christianity 200-1336,* New York: Columbia University Press, 2017.

66. For example, see Babylonian Talmud, Sanhedrin 90b, Kohelet Raba 1:4.

67. Compare to other religions' conceptions of the body, for example, Coakley, *Religion and the Body*; Meredith McGuire, "Religion and the Body," *Journal for the Scientific Study of Religion* 29 (1990): 283–296; Lawrence Sullivan, "Body Works: Knowledge of the Body in the Study of Religion," *History of Religion* 30 (1990): 86–99.

68. David Biale, *Eros and the Jews* (Berkeley: University of California Press,1997).

69. This does does not refer to preference for sports but to something similar to hypochondria. See Benjamin Brown, *Guide to Haredi Society* (Tel-Aviv: Am Oved, 2017) (Hebrew).

70. Johaness Pederson, *Israel: Its Life and Culture* (London: Oxford University Press, 1926), 263–264, 358–359.

71. Leviticus 13–14.

72. Leviticus 19:28.

73. This thesis was suggested by Meira Weiss in her book appropriately entitled *The Chosen Body* (Stanford, CA: Stanford University Press, 2002).

74. According to another finding from this study, when infants are born with handicaps, they are rejected by their parents far more often than in other countries.

75. Cf. Nisan Rubin, "From Corpse to Corpus: The Body as a Text in Talmudic Literature," in *Self, Soul and Body on Religious Experience*, ed. Albert Baumgarten, Jan Assman, and Guy Stroumsa (Boston: Brill, 1998), 171–183.

76. Cf. Louis Jacobs, "The Body in Jewish Worship," in Coakley, *Religion and the Body*, 71–89.

77. According to Jewish mystics, in the lower Paradise the body is made of the commandments, whereas in the upper Paradise, the body is made of the reasons for the commandments.

78. *Sefer haḥayim*, "Honor to the Dead," p. 65 (Hebrew).

79. Michael Gluzman, *The Zionist Body* (Tel Aviv: Kibutz Me'ukhad, 2007) (Hebrew); Oz Almod, *The Sabra* (Tel Aviv: Am Oved, 1997) (Hebrew); Anita Shapira, *New Jews—Old Jews* (Tel Aviv: Am Oved, 2003) (Hebrew).

80. Douglas, *Natural Symbols*.

81. Douglas, *Purity and Danger* New York: Routledge, 1966

82. George Mosse, *Nationalism and Sexuality in Modern Europe* (Madison: University of Wisconsin Press, 1985); Jonathan Heany, "Embodied Nationalism: Nations, States, Emotions," paper presented at the 14th European Sociological Association Conference, Manchester, UK, 2019.

83. Shani Litman, "How Far Israel Goes to Ensure the Birth of Flawless Children," *Haaretz*, 6 June 2019; Miri Bentwitch, "Is It a New Kind of Eugenics," *Haaretz*, 14 June 2019.

84. Meira Weiss, "The Body of the Nation," *Anthropological Quarterly* 75.1. 2002. 37-62

85. Cf. Olujic, "Embodiment of Terror."

86. This is the most important and extensive stratum of the Bible, including most of Leviticus and many chapters of Genesis and Exodus. Probably from the fifth century BCE.

87. During the last decades of the twentieth century historians and social scientists discovered the body. Influenced by new academic areas such as gender studies and post-structuralism, and in light of the critical writings of Freud and Foucault, they saw the body as the key to understanding mankind and human culture. Religious studies also joined this trend. Until recently, scholars of the Judeo-Christian faithful focused on sacred texts, ideas, and values. Influenced by Protestantism, they mainly studied words, seldom observing the deeds and feelings of believers, what they touch, smell, or swallow, physical matters, the body, the corpse, flesh, and blood. All the latter were regarded as manifestations of popular religion, inferior and hardly authentic. Nevertheless, after a closer look, these things, such as relics,

prove to be the throbbing heart of a religion. Cf. Gregory Schopen, *Bones, Stones, and Buddhist Monks: Collected Papers on the Archaeology Epigraphy and Texts of Monastic Buddhism in India* (Honolulu: University of Hawai Press, 1997). Abundant publications on various aspects of the topic have appeared, including illuminating work on the Christian body. Prominent among them is Bynum, *Resurrection,* and Brown, *Cult of Saints.* Some pioneering books on the Jewish body have also appeared: Sander Gilman, *The Jew's Body* (New York: Routledge, 1991); Biale, *Eros and the Jews;* Howard Eilberg-Schwartz, ed., *People of the Body: Jews and Judaism from an Embodied Perspective* (Albany: State University of New York Press, 1992); Daniel Boyarin, *Carnal Israel: Reading Sex in Talmudic Culture* (Berkeley: University of California Press, 1993); Howard Eilberg-Schwartz, *God's Phallus: And Other Problems for Men and Monotheism* (Boston: Beacon Press, 1994).These scholars sought to correct the conception of Judaism as a spiritual culture by narrowing the spotlight on its corporeal dimensions. However, they ran into a trap: revealing the numerous textual sources dealing with the body—rather than expanding to shed light on physical practices—did not contribute to modifying the traditional, prevalent image of Jews as a People of the Book. On the contrary, it reinforced it. Textual analysis was not a substitute for actual observation of the place of the body in social behavior among the Jews. Cf. Naomi Seidman, "Carnal Knowledge: Sex and Body in Jewish Studies," review essay, *Jewish Social Studies* 1.1 (1994) 115-141 .

88. The first clear formulation of the insight presented in this paragraph must be credited to Eilenberg-Schwartz. His article in the book he edited (*People of the Body*), impressed me, and his influence is evident in the following remarks.

89. On the Temple Mount Movement, see Sarina Chen, *Speedily in Our Days: The Temple Mount Activists and the National Religious Society in Israel* (Sde Boker: Ben Gurion University, 2017) (Hebrew); see also Nadav Shragai, *The Mount of Dispute: The Struggle for the Temple Mount: Jews and Muslims, Religion and Politics since 1967* (Jerusalem: Keter, 1995) (Hebrew); Motti Inbari, *Jewish Fundamentalism and the Temple Mount: Who Will Build the Third Temple?* (Albany: State University of New York Press, 2009).

90. Various generations of the Elbaum family stand out; they insisted on going up to the Temple Mount, provoking a direct confrontation with the Hasidic leadership and threats of excommunication.

91. Aran, "Jewish-Zionist Fundamentalism"; Haggai Segal, *Dear Brothers* (Woodmare, NY: Beit Shamai Publications, 1988).

92. For an example of a halakhic argument on the subject of erecting the Temple and offering sacrifices in the present day, by a rabbi who does not belong to the Conservative majority which rejects this possibility, see Yehiel Tukachinsky, "On the Possibility of Sacrifice in the Present Day," in Tukachinsky, *'Ir haqodesh vehamiqdash*, vol. 4 Part 5 (Jerusalem: No publisher name 1970) (Hebrew).

93. Mira Balberg explains this phenomenon in the Freudian terms of "the return of the repressed." See also her enlightening comments in "Once More, with Feeling: Sacrificial Worship between Rabbinic Literature and Contemporary National-Religious Discourse," *Theory and Criticism* 46 (2016): 13–39 (Hebrew).

94. An Israeli rabbi who was exposed to the Temple faithful who were preparing them-selves for the Paschal sacrifice tried to connect with the sacrificial ritual in our day. He wrote, "The fact that most of us are alienated from Leviticus, is not because it is inappropriate but because we are decadent religious people. We have adapted too well to two thousand years of destruction and become a religion of words and of synagogues where people sit on upholstered chairs. The absence of exciting religi-osity that includes real ceremonies causes boredom. . . . A person feels full of guilt and believes that he deserves punishment for an act that disturbs his conscience. He sees the animal, which he has brought as a sacrifice, as it is slaughtered and placed on the altar to be burned, and he knows that he should have been in its place. He senses that the cruel burning of the animal constitutes a substitute for the punish-ment to which he must sentence himself. This brutal, physical act creates an expe-rience of moral purification." Rabbi Feuerstein, "Leviticus and the Sacrifices: Only For the Spirit," on Ynet, 23 March 2006 (Hebrew).

95. The religious longing of certain Jews to return to the basics of life and of death has a certain analogy with the Christianity of the past generation: a peculiar mix of Catholics who oppose the reforms of Vatican II and evangelicals of the ilk of Jimmy Swaggart. These religious radicals proclaim de-sublimation of the mass and empha-size the flesh and blood of Christ in the Eucharist. See the film by Mel Gibson, *The Passion of the Christ*, and Jimmy Swaggart's song "Look to the Lamb of God."

96. For example, the settler underground on the West Bank, 1984, or Dr. Goldstein in the Cave of the Patriarchs in Hebron, 1994. See Gideon Aran and Ron Hassner, "Jewish Religious Violence: Past and Present," in *Terrorism and Political Violence*, 25(3) 2013. 355-405.

97. Extracts of the transcript were published in *New York Times*, 15 March 1979.

98. On Jonestown, see John Walliss, *Apocalyptic Trajectories: Millenarianism and Violence in the Contemporary World* )Bloomington, IN: Peter Lang, 2004); David Chidester, *Salvation and Suicide: An Interpretation of Jim Jones, the Peoples Temple and Jonestown* (Bloomington: Indiana University Press, 1991); John Hall, *Gone from the Promised Land* (New Brunswick, NJ: Transaction, 1987).

99. Jonathan Smith, "The Devil in Mr. Jones," in Smith, *Imagining Religion* (Chicago: University of Chicago Press, 1982) 102-120.

100. Rene Girard, *Violence and the Sacred* (Baltimore, MD: Johns Hopkins University Press, 1972).

101. There are significant similarities between the Jonestown tragedy and Middle Eastern suicide terrorism. Mainly, they both combine murder with suicide and the attacker with the victim.

102. After writing the present text, I became acquainted with an interesting book, one of whose chapters pointed out the Dionysian-bacchanal element in present-day ter-rorism (I was surprised to find there was no reference to Jonathan Smith's seminal article, under discussion here). As shown below, despite the similarity in our orig-inal argument, we develop the discussion in different directions. Terry Eagleton, *Holy Terror* (Oxford: Oxford University Press, 2005).

103. See *Antigone*, ll. 998ff.

104. For example, Hertz, *Death and the Right Hand*, 79; Bloch and Parry, *Death and the Regeneration of Life*.

105. For example, James Frazer, *The Golden Bough* (London: Macmillan, 1908), vol. 6, 96–103.

106. There is another version, in which Dionysius himself, one of the legendry fathers of the cutting-up-of-bodies legacy, was born from the cutting up of a body. Titans tore his body to bits, but Athena managed to save his heart from them, and from it the seed of a new god grew up. Thus, everyone has a bacchic element.

107. Mircea Eliade, *Patterns of Comparative Religion* (New York: Sheed & Ward, 1958), 346. In Babylonian mythology cutting up the body of Tiamat, the mother of the gods, gives her son, Marduk, the basis for creating heaven and earth. In Greek mythology, the body of Uranus is cut up by the plow of his son, Chronos, during the creation of the world. Cf. the vision of Ezekiel about the dry bones that are garbed in flesh and come alive.

108. For example, Scott Noegel, "Dismemberment, Creation and Ritual: Images of Divine Violence in the Ancient Near East," in *Belief and Bloodshed*, ed. James Wellman (London: Rowman and Littlefield, 2007), chapter 1. 13-27

109. Jonathan Smith employs the idiom "creative murder." See "The Pearl of Great Price," in his *Imagining Religion*.

110. Mircea Eliade, *Cosmos and History: The Myth of the Eternal Return* (New York: Harper, 1959).

111. Compare this to shooting a rival's body after he was clearly killed, which is regarded as illegitimate.

112. Ward Stavig, "Tupac Amaru, the Body Politic and the Embodiment of Hope," in Johnson, *Death, Dismemberment, and Memory*, 133-152.

113. Cf. traditional custom in the tribe of Bayanda, in Frazer, *The Golden Bough*, vol. 8, 271.

114. Compare the use of this analogy made by Ilana Pardes, to describe the biography of the Jewish people: Ilana Pardes, *The Biography of Ancient Israel: National Narratives in the Bible* (Berkeley: University of California Press, 2002).

115. The Greek historian Herodotus long ago stated that Osiris is Dionysius. Like Osiris, he is parallel to the Mesopotamian Tammuz and the Greek Adonis.

116. According to one version, Isis was impregnated by the seed of the dead Osiris.

117. Ahmed Saadawi, *Frankenstein in Baghdad* (New York: Penguin Books, 2013), winner of the International Prize for Arabic Fiction.

118. Carl Jung, *Man and His Symbols* (London: Aldus, 1964); Carl Jung, "Archetypes of the Collective Unconscious," in *Collected Works*, vol. 9 (part 1): *Archetypes and the Collective Unconscious* eds. Gerhard Adler and R.F.C Hull. (Princeton, NJ Princeton University Press, 2014; Ami Ronnberg, ed., *The Book of Symbols: Reflection on Archetypical Images* (Koln: Taschen, 2010).

119. Compare this to the pairs of opposites analyzed by Levi-Strauss in the context of the binary tension that characterizes the mythic cognitive pattern, by means of which people grasp their surroundings: Hot-Cold; Right-Left; Cosmos-Chaos; Live-Dead. We may add Piecing together–Tearing apart.

# Chapter 9


1. Magda Teter, *Blood Libel: On the Trail of an Antisemitic Myth* (Cambridge, MA: Harvard University Press, 2020).

2. Aran, *The Smile*, chapter 7.

3. In writing the preceding paragraph and others in this chapter, I was inspired by the Albanian novelist Ismail Kadare, *Broken April* (Lanham, MD: Rowman & Littlefield, 1990).

4. An embarrassing reminder of such sensitivity to the mixture of blood in Israeli society came when, in 1996, blood donations by Ethiopian new immigrants were discarded by the state official first aid organization. All those involved were aware of the symbolic importance of the act of giving blood and of the explosive potential of the connection between blood transfusion and ethnic integration. The immigrants wanted to mix their blood into the national blood bank and thus be accepted by Israelis. It was not hard to predict how offended they were when their blood was rejected, a rejection couched in medical language that referred to the local African community as suspected carriers of HIV and other infectious agents.

5. In the Yad Le'aḥim organization (Lahava), they compare closeness to Arabs to the danger of virulent bacteria invading a healthy organism.

6. The theme of these opposing strategies appears in the literature on Western colonialism in Asia and Africa.

7. Homi Bhabha, "Of Mimicry and Man: The Ambivalence of Colonial Discourse," *October* 28 (Spring 1984). 125-133

8. Later it came to light that she was having an extra-marital affair with a senior member of Hamas. When word got out, the cuckolded husband and the lascivious leader conspired to send her on a suicide mission to avoid shaming them.

9. In the book of Genesis, the act of creation itself is portrayed as an act of separation. Strict observance of these distinctions thus preserves the natural order established by God. Their violation, through mixture and the blurring of distinctions subverts God's authority and undermines the foundations of the world.

10. Douglas, *Natural Symbols*.

11. Douglas, *Purity and Danger*.

12. CF. Liisa Malkki, *Purity and Exile: Violence, Memory and National Cosmology among the Hutu Refugees in Tanzania* (Chicago: University of Chicago Press, 1995). Also see Karen Kruger, "The Destruction of Faces in Rwanda 1994: Mutilation as Mirror of Racial Ideologies," *L'Europe en Formation*, 1010/3.

13. Mary Douglas has commented on this: "The social body constrains the way the physical body is perceived." She continues, "The physical experience of the body always modified by the social categories through which it is known, sustains a particular view of society." Mary Douglas, ed., *Rules and Meanings: The Anthropology of Everyday Knowledge* (Harmondsworth: Penguin, 1973), 93.

14. ZAKA activists are of course aware that Muslim men are also circumcised.

15. Amos Eilon, *Haaretz*, 1967.

16. Bruno Latour, *We Have Never Been Modern* (Cambridge, MA: Harvard University Press 1993).
17. Douglas, *Purity and Danger*.

# Epilogue: Headhunting, Smiles, and Human Sacrifices

1. Some people claim that one of these photoshopped versions was made by the terrorist's family *after* the suicide attack, on the basis of his picture, taken on the eve of his departure on the mission. See Ariel Merari, *Driven to Death*, New York: Oxford University Press, 2010 95.
2. In another version, the severed head is made smaller and lies on the outstretched palm of the suicide terrorist. See Danny Setton, *Suicide Bombers: Secrets of the Shahid*, documentary film, 1998.
3. See poster #35 in Oliver and Steinberg, *The Martyrs' Square*.
4. The picture and the quotation are taken from the movement's children's we site, no. 38, dated 10 October 2004. It was brought to my attention by the scholar No'a Meridor.
5. Cavarero, *Horrorism*.
6. Nati Tokker, reportage on "Hayim Otmazgin," *Marker Week*, 5 September 2013.
7. Compare this to the confessions of GIs who fought in the Vietnam War about the excitement of holding the severed heads of Vietcong soldiers, and on their custom of exchanging photographs of heads after they came home from the war.
8. For example, Renato Rosaldo, *Ilongot Headhunting, 1883–1974: A Study in Society and History* (Stanford, CA: Stanford University Press, 1980); George Keneth, *Showing Signs of Violence: The Cultural Politics of 20th Century Headhunting Rituals* (Berkeley: University of California Press, 1996); James Weingartner, "Trophies of War: US Troops and the Mutilation of Japanese War Dead 1941–45," *Pacific Historical Review* 61 (1992): 53–67.
9. Cf. Frazer, *The Golden Bough*, vol. 8, 153.
10. For example, Donatello 1423, Caravaggio 1607.
11. For example, Gustave Dore, *The Bible in Pictures* (New York: Dover, 1974). Also note the case of King Saul in Gilboa (1 Samuel 31).
12. Dominique Vivant Denon, *Severed Head of Robespierre*, 1794.
13. For example, think of the many old masterpieces that depict Judith holding the severed head of the Assyrian general Holofernes.
14. Cavavero, *Horrorism*. Medusa's gaze has been discussed mostly by literary scholars, social critics, and psychologists. For example, Marjorie Garber and Nancy Vicker, eds., *The Medusa Reader* (Abingdon: Routledge, 2003).
15. Jane Harrison, *Prolegomena to the Study of Greek Religion* (Princeton, NJ: Princeton University Press, 1991).
16. Cf. Mark Orzech, "Human Skulls in Aghori Spiritual Practice," paper submitted to Anthropology course, Dr. Adam Dunstan, University of North Texas, 4 April 2017; Parry, *Death in Banaras,* chapter 8.
17. A double attack under the joint responsibility of Hamas and Fatah, leaving ten dead.

18. The look of Medusa, so famous for its mesmerizing attraction, is not just inspiring terror but conveys the state of being terrorized as well. This is precisely the way it was ingeniously depicted by the master artists Caravaggio (1596) and Rubens (1618), who portrayed Medusa's face as terribly startled and shocked. The killer knows she is doomed to be killed very soon. Medusa, as an archetype of the human bomb, is terrified no less than terrifying, both aggressor and victim. Medusa's look implies and causes death, but it also gazes upon death.

19. Francois La Rochefoucauld, *"The Moral Maxims and Reflections"*. Paris, 1678. Maxim 26.

20. Vered Lee, "Homeless," *Haaretz*, 3 April 2015.

21. This specific terrorist's bomb exploded before he reached his target—what has come to be called a "work accident" in colloquial Israeli discourse.

22. Brought to my attention by the art historian Professor Rina Talgam in personal communication.

23. Aran, *The Smile*, 203–224.

24. One rabbi called my attention to a biblical chapter which appears to describe the work of the volunteers in the arena of terrorism: purifying the holy earth from the bodies of the enemies of the Israelites who died in their territory, and offering them as a sacrifice to God (*zevakh*). At the end of the passage an almost Bacchanalian orgy is described of drinking the blood of the victim (Ezekiel 39:11–20).

25. While some respondents took pride in this event, others doubted its very existence and denied the authenticity of the photo (a copy of which I have seen in the possession of several ZAKA volunteers). For ethical and aesthetic reasons, and so as not to embarrass the people who were involved, I abbreviate and disguise details.

26. Many contemporary Orthodox redeem this sacrifice by donating money to charity.

27. Cf. Michael Graulich, "Aztec Human Sacrifice as Expiation," *History of Religions* 49.4 (2000). 352-371

28. Cf. Victor Turner, *Forest of Symbols* (Ithaca, NY: Cornell University Press 1970).

29. Various examples in Harvey Goldberg, *Jewish Passages: Cycles of Jewish Life*. Berkeley: University of California Press, 2003. e.g. 83

30. This interpretation was elaborated in collaboration with D.S., a colleague of mine, a genuine Jewish pietist who is convinced that what happens in our world has a metaphysical cause and a purpose, and a religious moral. He is used to thinking in terms of sin and atonement, and he always tends to link them to bloodshed (murder? sacrifice?), while he automatically associates any bloodshed with sin and expiation. In the wake of the suicide attack on bus number 2 in Jerusalem (August 2003, twenty-three dead, almost all of them Haredi, many of them children), he joined a small number of rabbis who called for declaring a day of fasting and for a campaign of penitence.

# Index

*For the benefit of digital users, indexed terms that span two pages (e.g., 52–53) may, on occasion, appear on only one of those pages.*



353